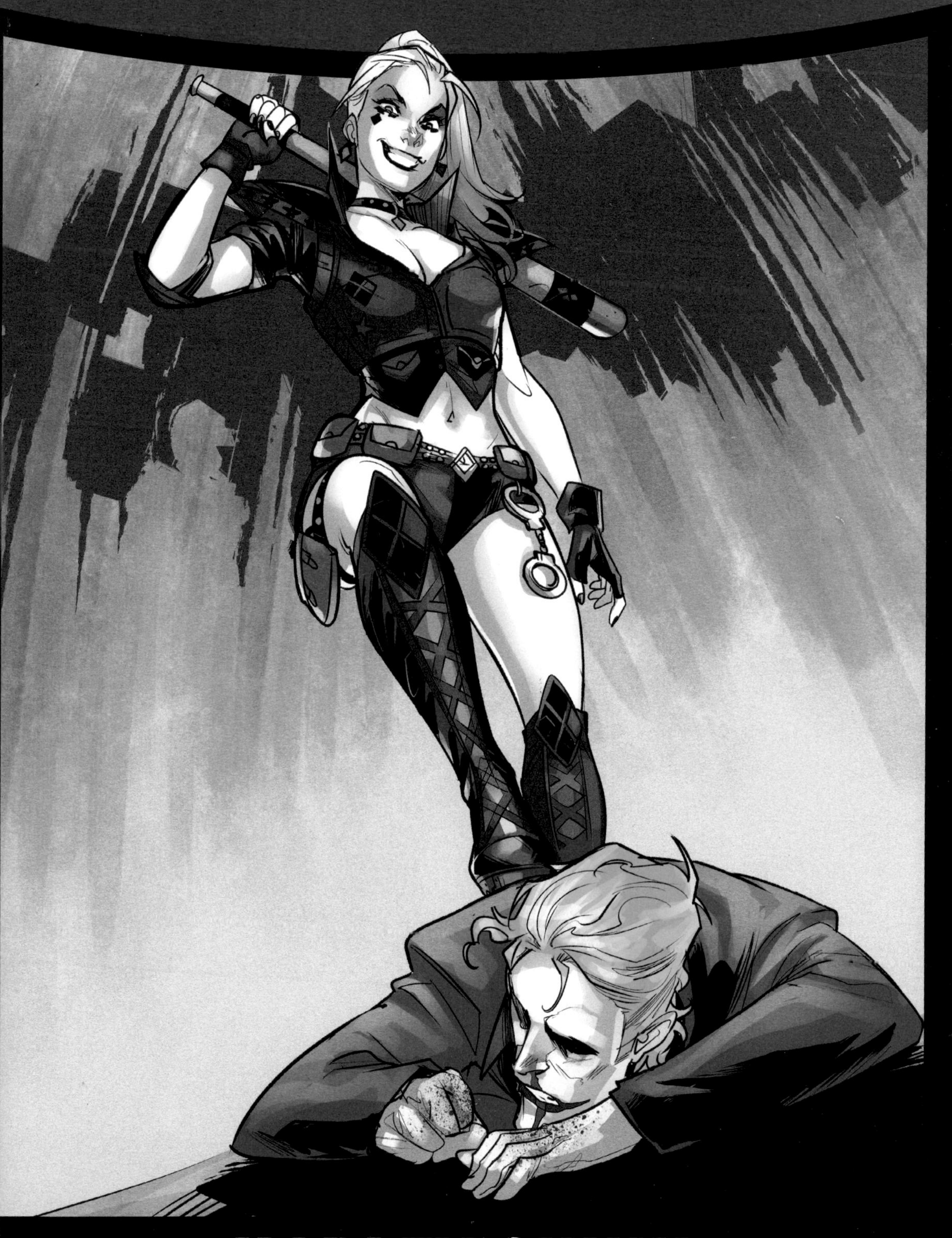

# HARLEY QUINN

## VOL.6 ANGRY BIRD

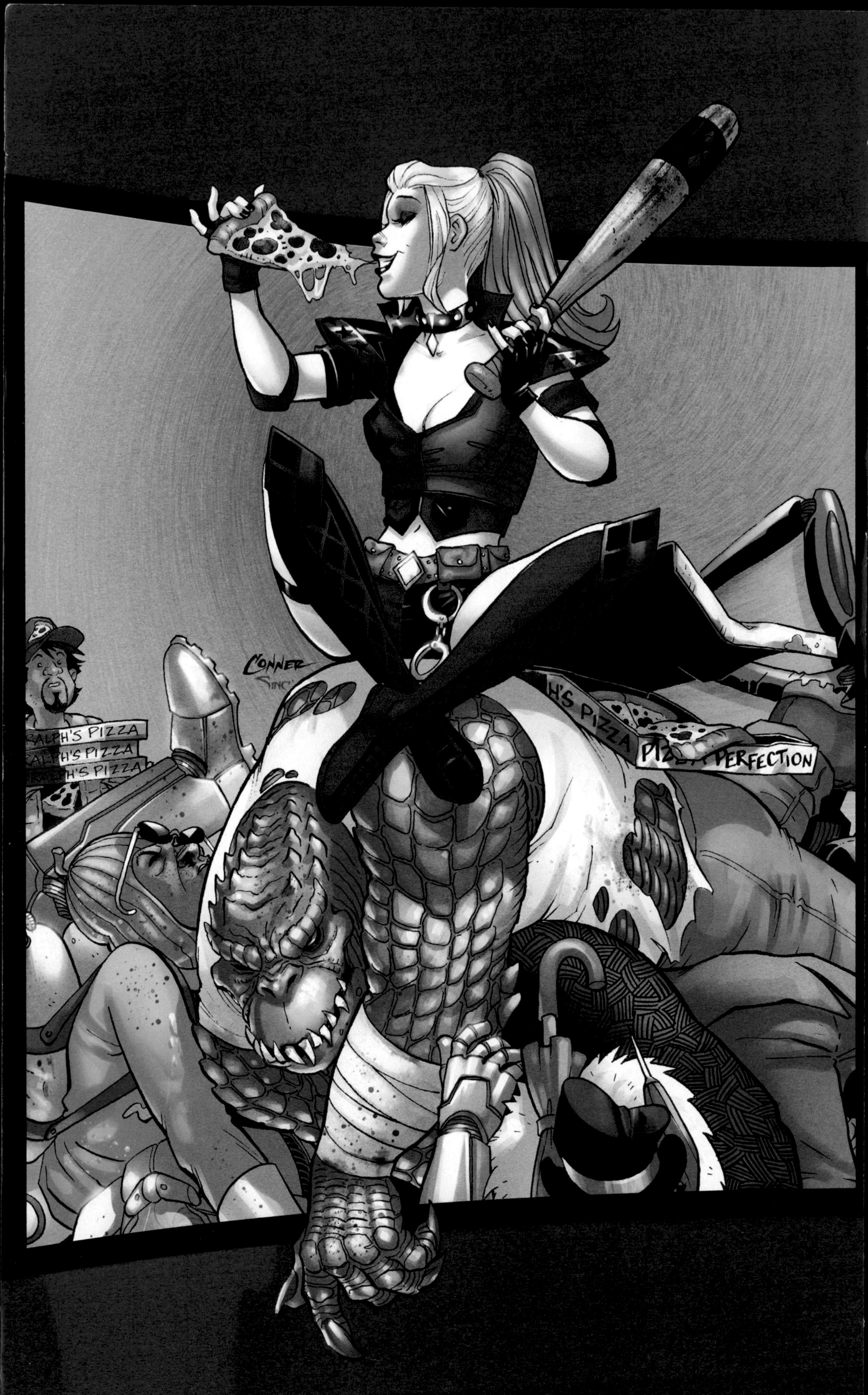
CONNER
RALPH'S PIZZA
ALPH'S PIZZA
ALPH'S PIZZA
H'S PIZZA
PERFECTION

# HARLEY QUINN
## VOL.6 ANGRY BIRD

**FRANK TIERI**
writer

**INAKI MIRANDA** * **MIRKA ANDOLFO**
ELEONORA CARLINI * JOHN TIMMS * MORITAT * MAURICET
artists

**ALEX SINCLAIR**
JEREMIAH SKIPPER * PAUL MOUNTS
colorists

**DAVE SHARPE**
letterer

**AMANDA CONNER** and **PAUL MOUNTS**
collection cover artists

HARLEY QUINN created by **PAUL DINI** and **BRUCE TIMM**

COLD BEER

**CHRIS CONROY** Editor - Original Series * **ANDREW MARINO** **DAVE WIELGOSZ** Assistant Editors - Original Series
**JEB WOODARD** Group Editor - Collected Editions * **ROBIN WILDMAN** Editor - Collected Edition
**STEVE COOK** Design Director - Books * **MONIQUE NARBONETA** Publication Design

**BOB HARRAS** Senior VP - Editor-in-Chief, DC Comics
**PAT McCALLUM** Executive Editor, DC Comics

**DIANE NELSON** President * **DAN DiDIO** Publisher * **JIM LEE** Publisher * **GEOFF JOHNS** President & Chief Creative Officer
**AMIT DESAI** Executive VP - Business & Marketing Strategy, Direct to Consumer & Global Franchise Management
**SAM ADES** Senior VP & General Manager, Digital Services * **BOBBIE CHASE** VP & Executive Editor, Young Reader & Talent Development
**MARK CHIARELLO** Senior VP - Art, Design & Collected Editions * **JOHN CUNNINGHAM** Senior VP - Sales & Trade Marketing
**ANNE DePIES** Senior VP - Business Strategy, Finance & Administration * **DON FALLETTI** VP - Manufacturing Operations
**LAWRENCE GANEM** VP - Editorial Administration & Talent Relations * **ALISON GILL** Senior VP - Manufacturing & Operations
**HANK KANALZ** Senior VP - Editorial Strategy & Administration * **JAY KOGAN** VP - Legal Affairs * **JACK MAHAN** VP - Business Affairs
**NICK J. NAPOLITANO** VP - Manufacturing Administration * **EDDIE SCANNELL** VP - Consumer Marketing
**COURTNEY SIMMONS** Senior VP - Publicity & Communications * **JIM (SKI) SOKOLOWSKI** VP - Comic Book Specialty Sales & Trade Marketing
**NANCY SPEARS** VP - Mass, Book, Digital Sales & Trade Marketing * **MICHELE R. WELLS** VP - Content Strategy

**HARLEY QUINN VOL. 6: ANGRY BIRD**



DC Comics, 2900 West Alameda Ave., Burbank, CA 91505
Printed by LSC Communications, Kendallville, IN, USA. 7/13/18. First Printing.
ISBN: 978-1-4012-8152-6

Library of Congress Cataloging-in-Publication Data is available.

PEFC Certified
Printed on paper from sustainably managed forests, controlled sources
PEFC
PEFC/29-31-337
www.pefc.org

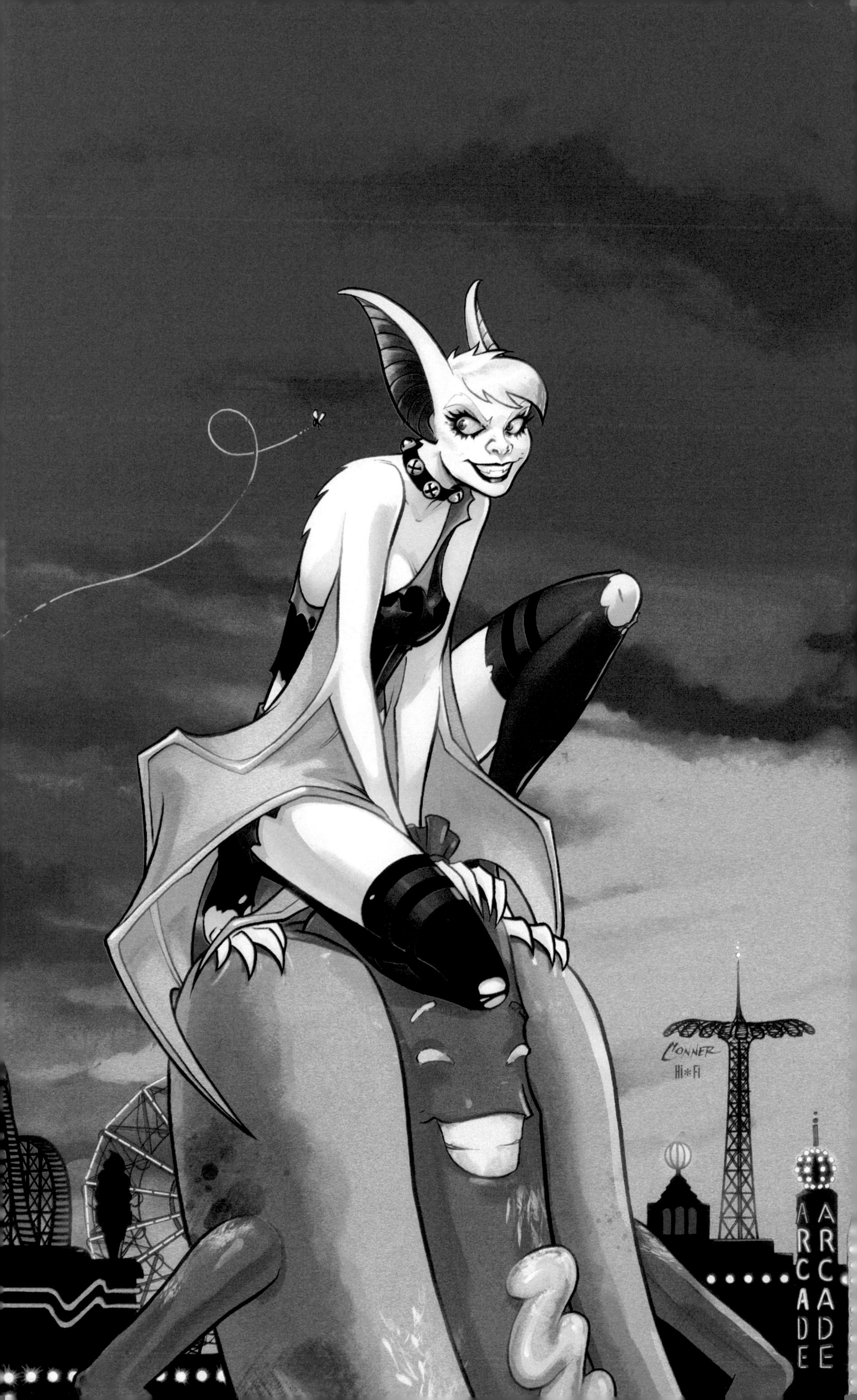
CONNER
Hi*Fi
ARCADE
ARCADE

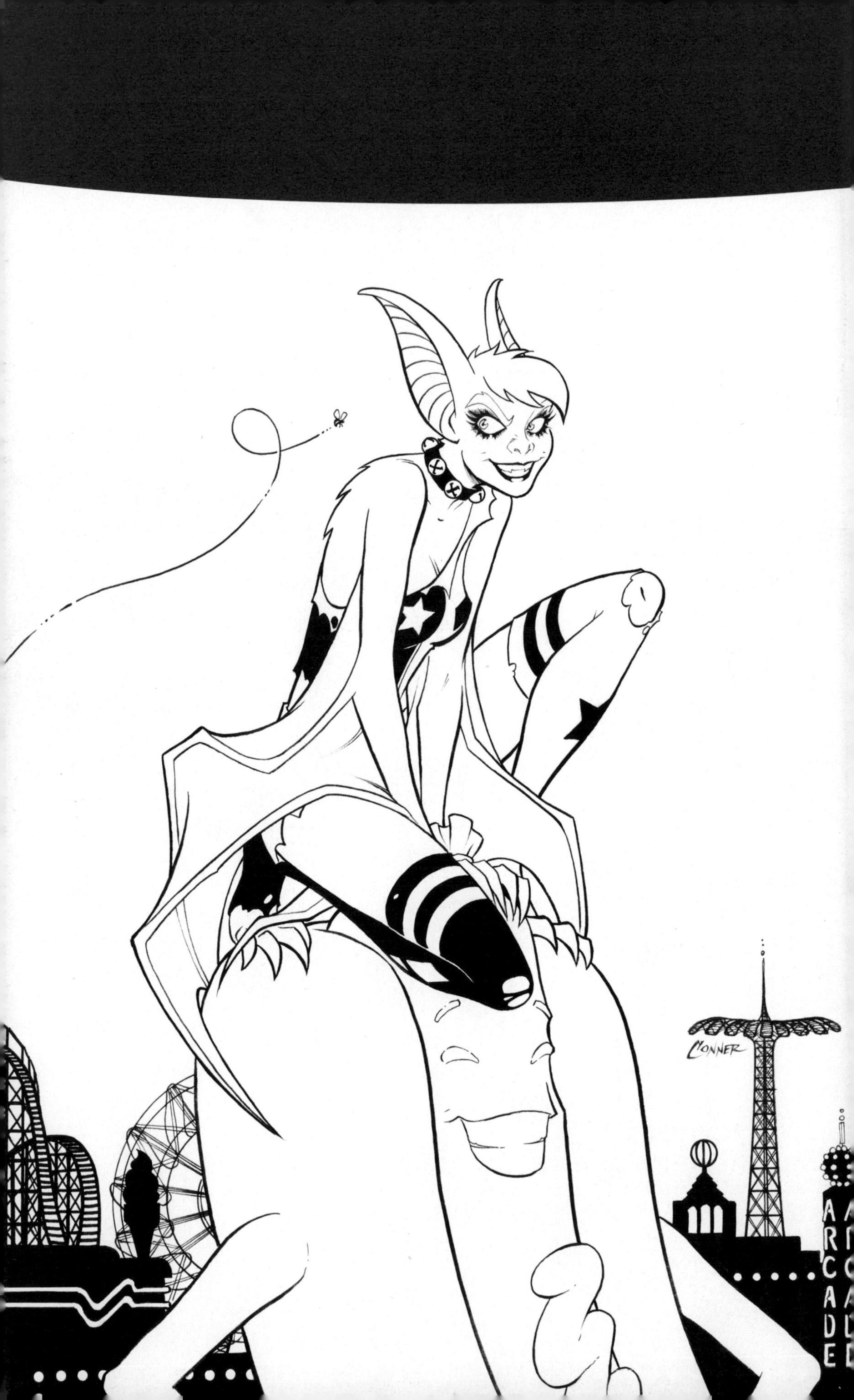
CONNER
ARCADE

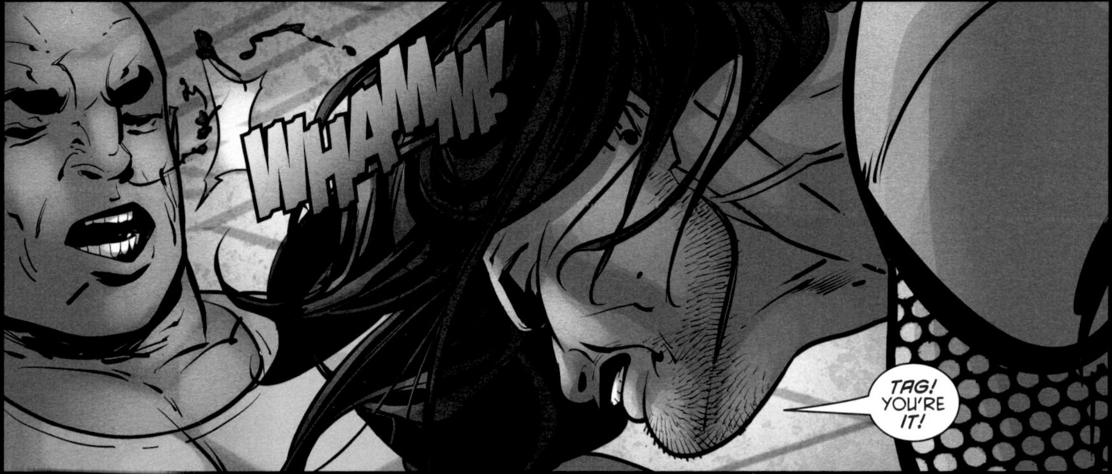
WHAMM!
TAG! YOU'RE IT!

# BATTER UP PART ONE

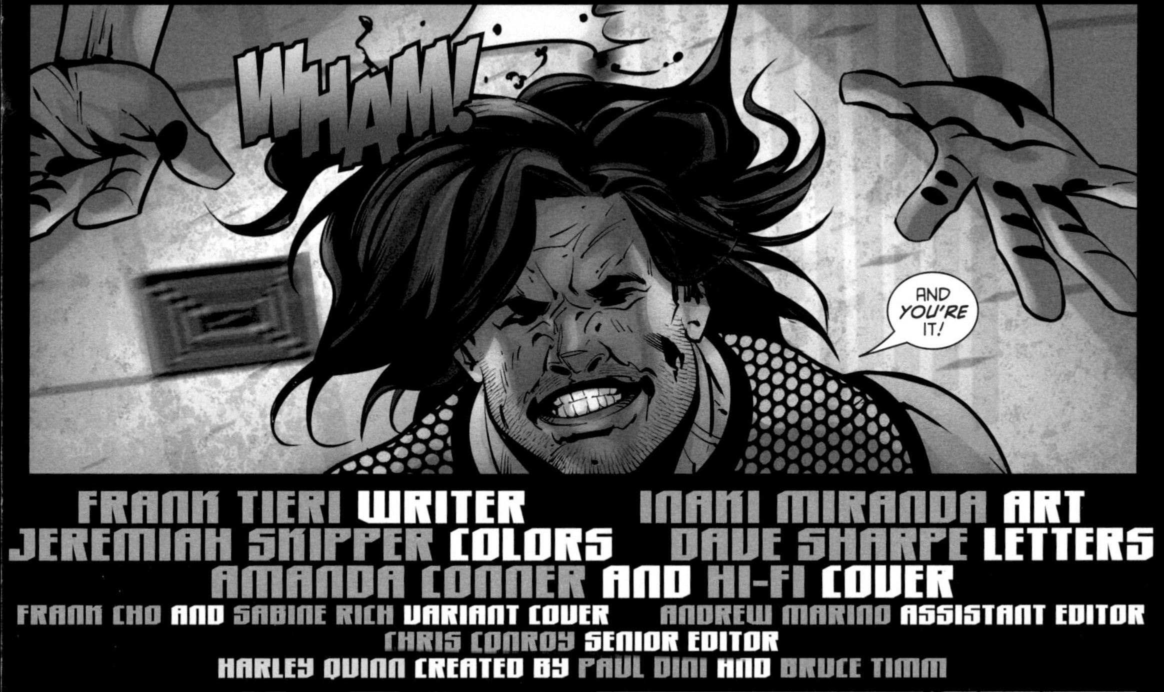
WHAM!
AND YOU'RE IT!

FRANK TIERI WRITER INAKI MIRANDA ART
JEREMIAH SKIPPER COLORS DAVE SHARPE LETTERS
AMANDA CONNER AND HI-FI COVER
FRANK CHO AND SABINE RICH VARIANT COVER ANDREW MARINO ASSISTANT EDITOR
CHRIS CONROY SENIOR EDITOR
HARLEY QUINN CREATED BY PAUL DINI AND BRUCE TIMM

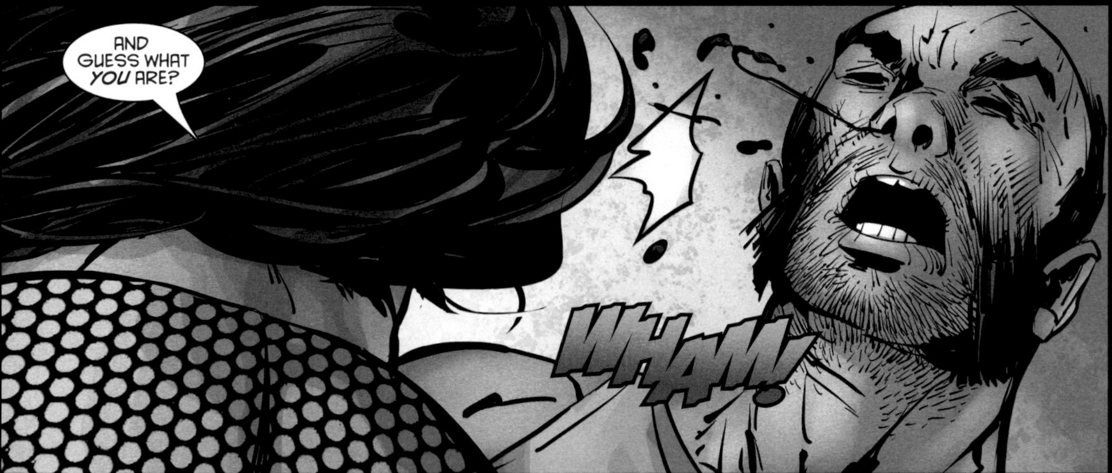
AND GUESS WHAT YOU ARE?
WHAM!

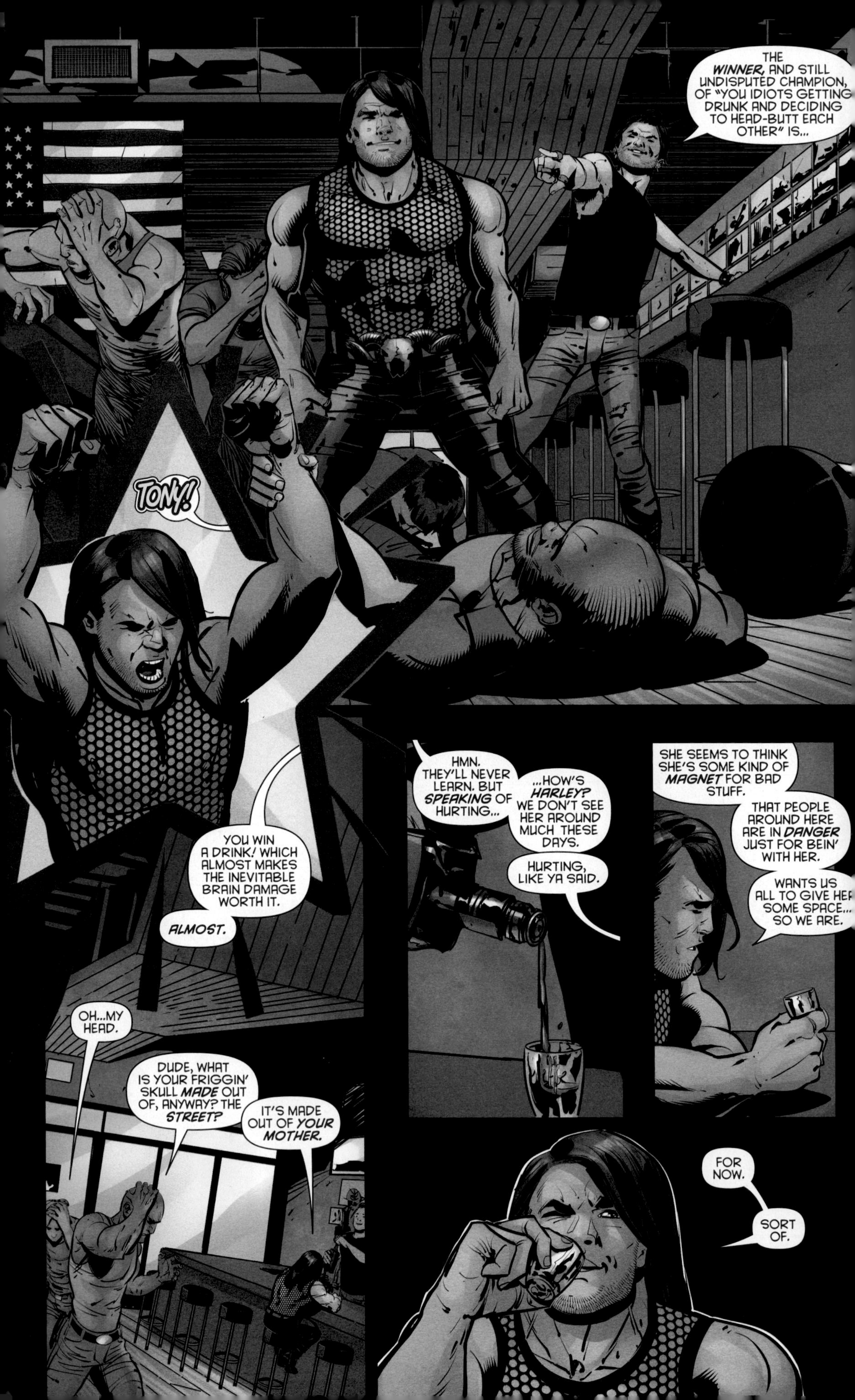
THE WINNER, AND STILL UNDISPUTED CHAMPION, OF "YOU IDIOTS GETTING DRUNK AND DECIDING TO HEAD-BUTT EACH OTHER" IS...
TONY!
YOU WIN A DRINK! WHICH ALMOST MAKES THE INEVITABLE BRAIN DAMAGE WORTH IT.
ALMOST.
OH...MY HEAD.
DUDE, WHAT IS YOUR FRIGGIN' SKULL MADE OUT OF, ANYWAY? THE STREET?
IT'S MADE OUT OF YOUR MOTHER.
HMN. THEY'LL NEVER LEARN. BUT SPEAKING OF HURTING...
...HOW'S HARLEY? WE DON'T SEE HER AROUND MUCH THESE DAYS.
HURTING, LIKE YA SAID.
SHE SEEMS TO THINK SHE'S SOME KIND OF MAGNET FOR BAD STUFF.
THAT PEOPLE AROUND HERE ARE IN DANGER JUST FOR BEIN' WITH HER.
WANTS US ALL TO GIVE HER SOME SPACE... SO WE ARE.
FOR NOW.
SORT OF.

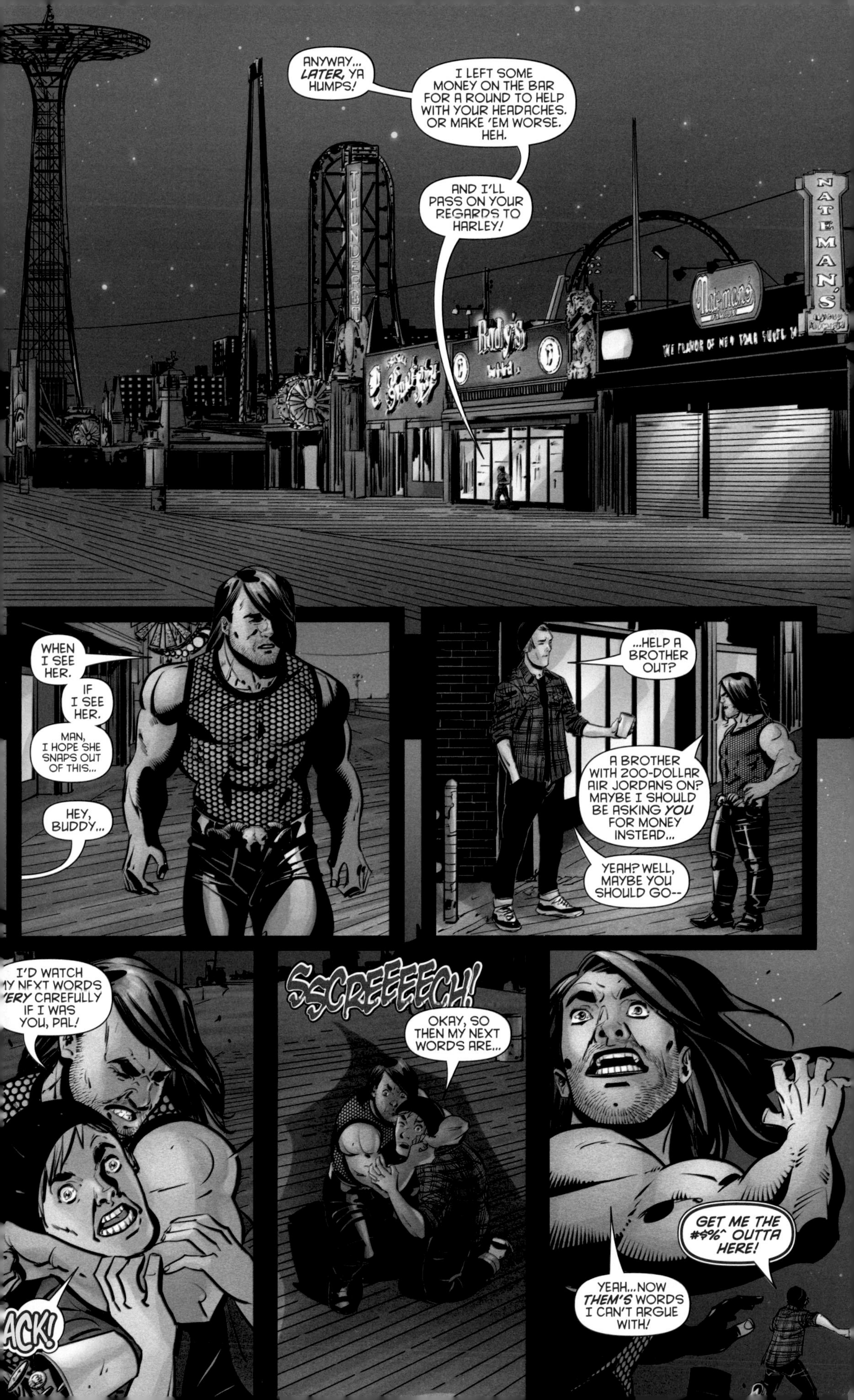
ANYWAY... LATER, YA HUMPS!
I LEFT SOME MONEY ON THE BAR FOR A ROUND TO HELP WITH YOUR HEADACHES. OR MAKE 'EM WORSE. HEH.
AND I'LL PASS ON YOUR REGARDS TO HARLEY!
THUNDERBOLT
NATEMAN'S
WHEN I SEE HER.
IF I SEE HER.
MAN, I HOPE SHE SNAPS OUT OF THIS...
HEY, BUDDY...
...HELP A BROTHER OUT?
A BROTHER WITH 200-DOLLAR AIR JORDANS ON? MAYBE I SHOULD BE ASKING YOU FOR MONEY INSTEAD...
YEAH? WELL, MAYBE YOU SHOULD GO--
I'D WATCH MY NEXT WORDS VERY CAREFULLY IF I WAS YOU, PAL!
ACK!
SSCREEEEECH!
OKAY, SO THEN MY NEXT WORDS ARE...
GET ME THE #$%^ OUTTA HERE!
YEAH...NOW THEM'S WORDS I CAN'T ARGUE WITH!

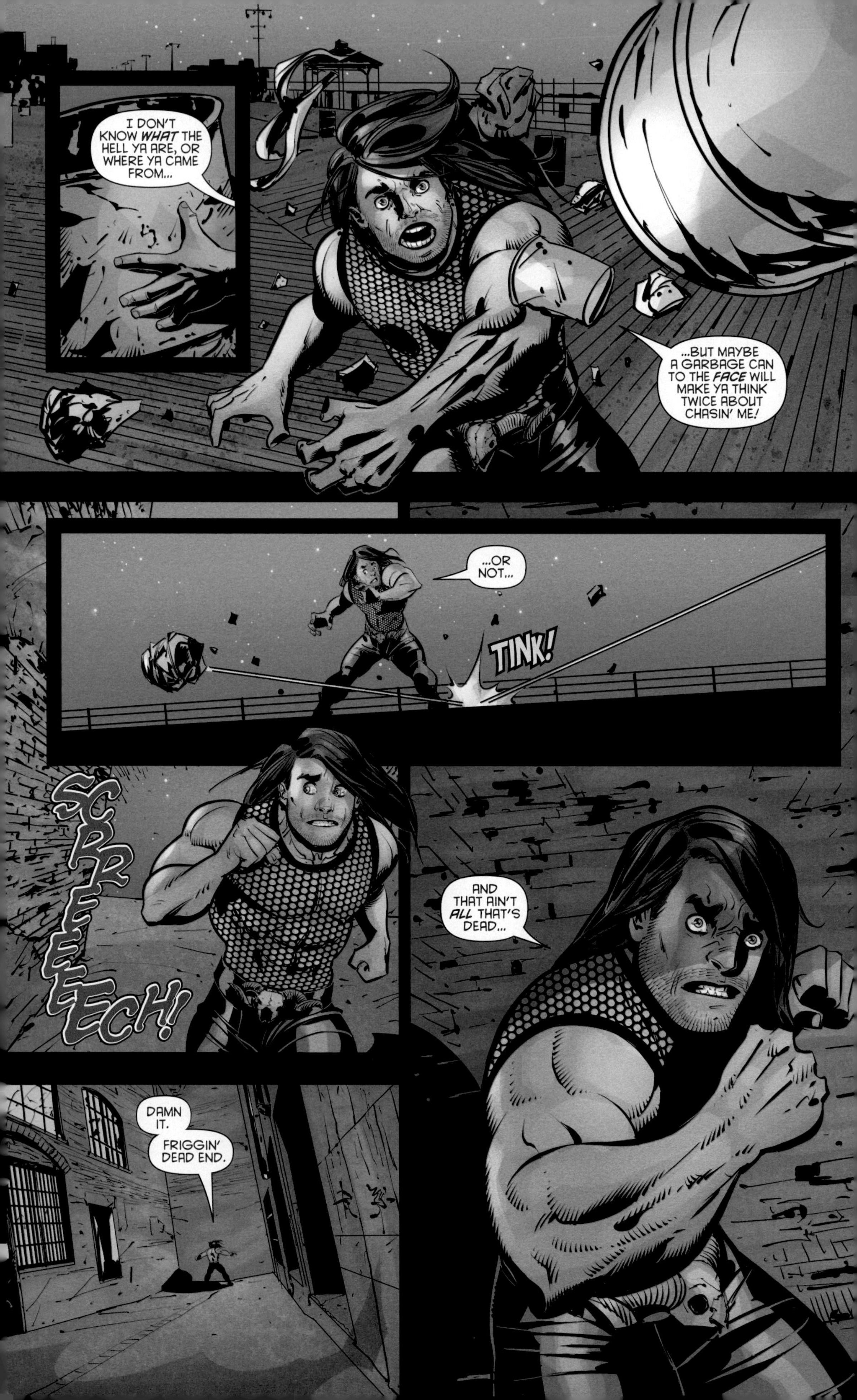
I DON'T KNOW *WHAT* THE HELL YA ARE, OR WHERE YA CAME FROM...
...BUT MAYBE A GARBAGE CAN TO THE *FACE* WILL MAKE YA THINK TWICE ABOUT CHASIN' ME!
...OR NOT...
TINK!
SCREEEEECH!
AND THAT AIN'T *ALL* THAT'S DEAD...
DAMN IT.
FRIGGIN' DEAD END.

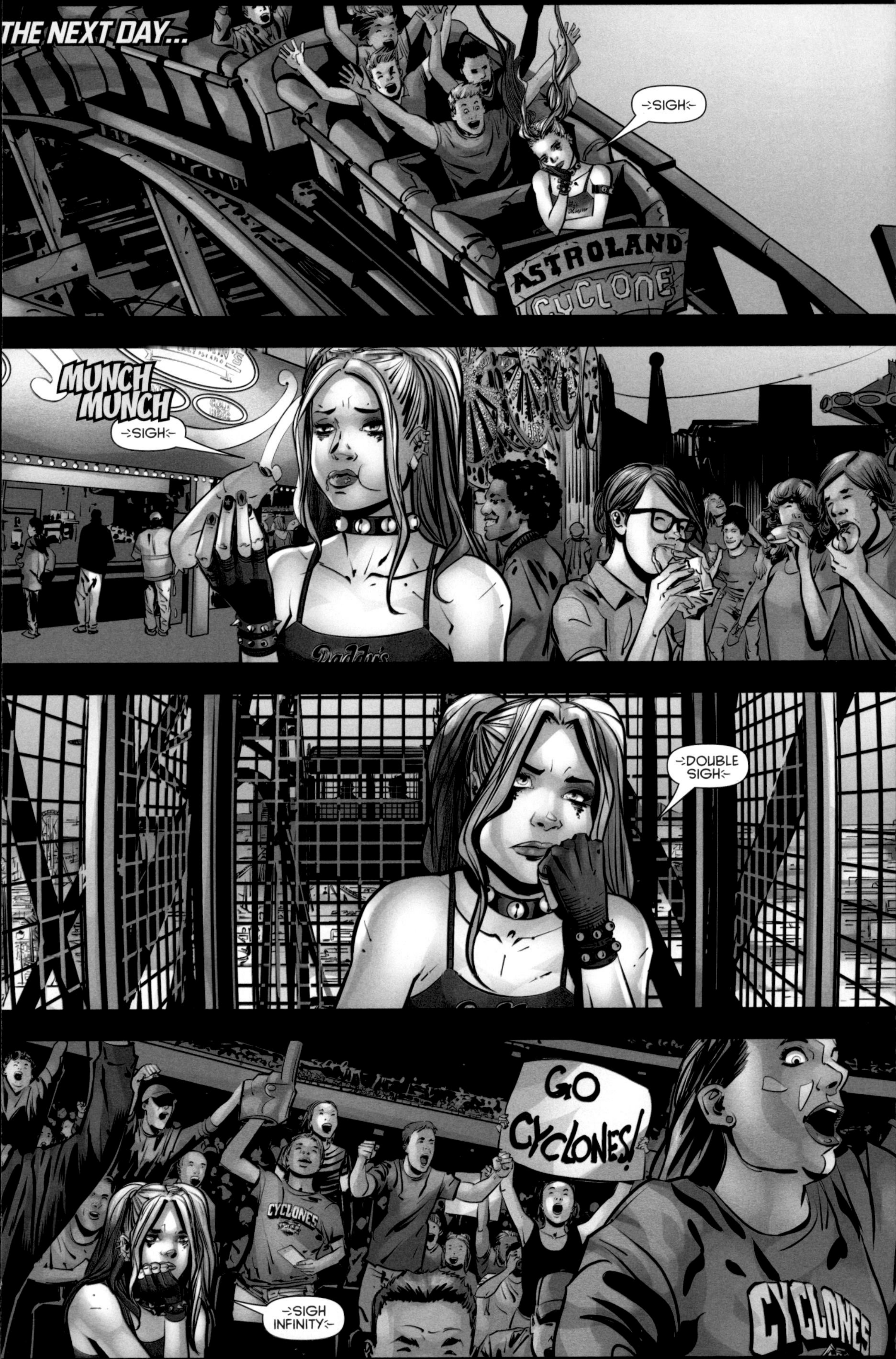
THE NEXT DAY...
SIGH
ASTROLAND CYCLONE
MUNCH MUNCH
SIGH
DOUBLE SIGH
GO CYCLONES!
SIGH INFINITY
CYCLONES
CYCLONES

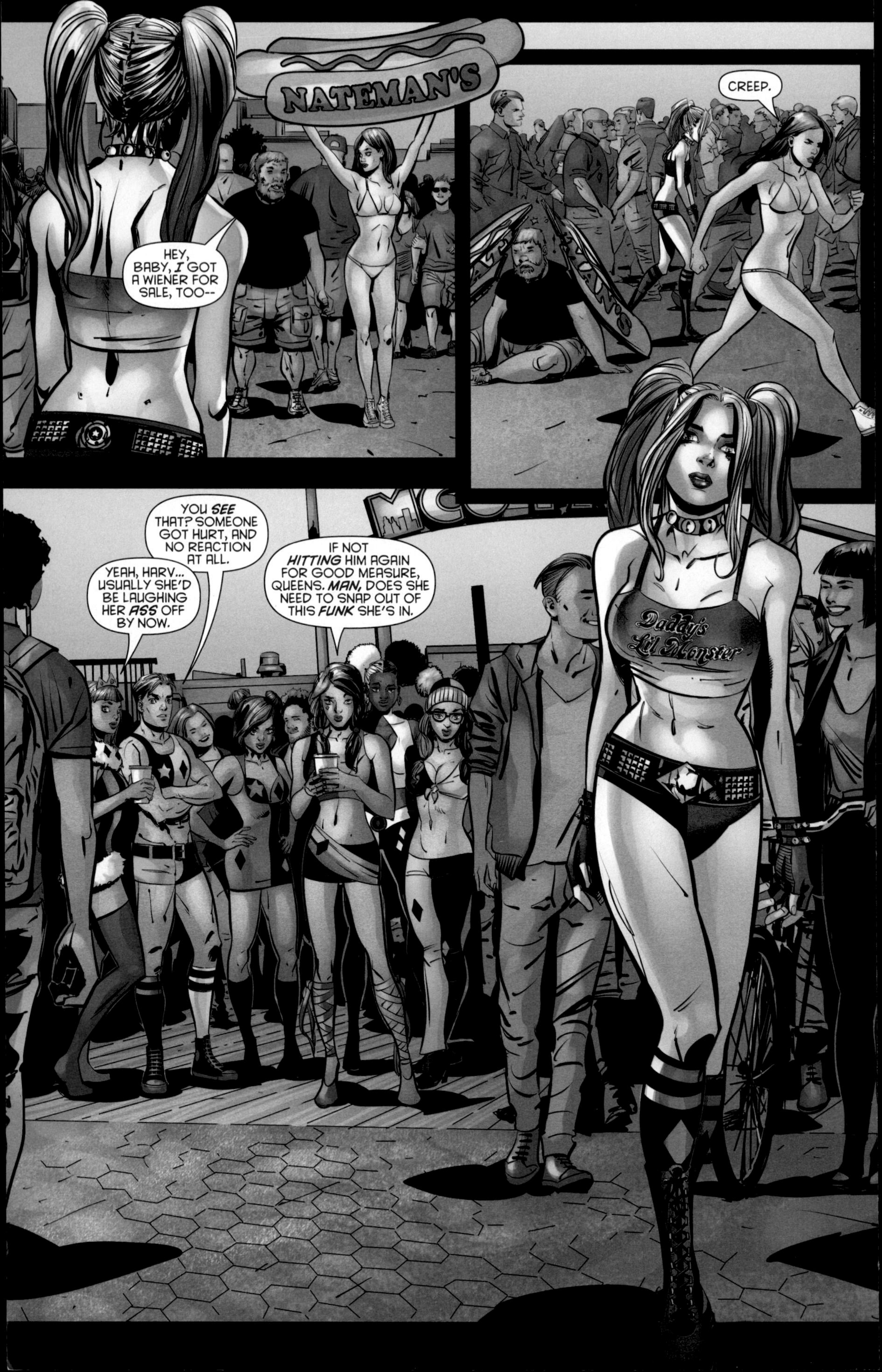
NATEMAN'S
HEY, BABY, I GOT A WIENER FOR SALE, TOO--
CREEP.
YOU SEE THAT? SOMEONE GOT HURT, AND NO REACTION AT ALL.
YEAH, HARV... USUALLY SHE'D BE LAUGHING HER ASS OFF BY NOW.
IF NOT HITTING HIM AGAIN FOR GOOD MEASURE, QUEENS. MAN, DOES SHE NEED TO SNAP OUT OF THIS FUNK SHE'S IN.
Daddy's Lil Monster

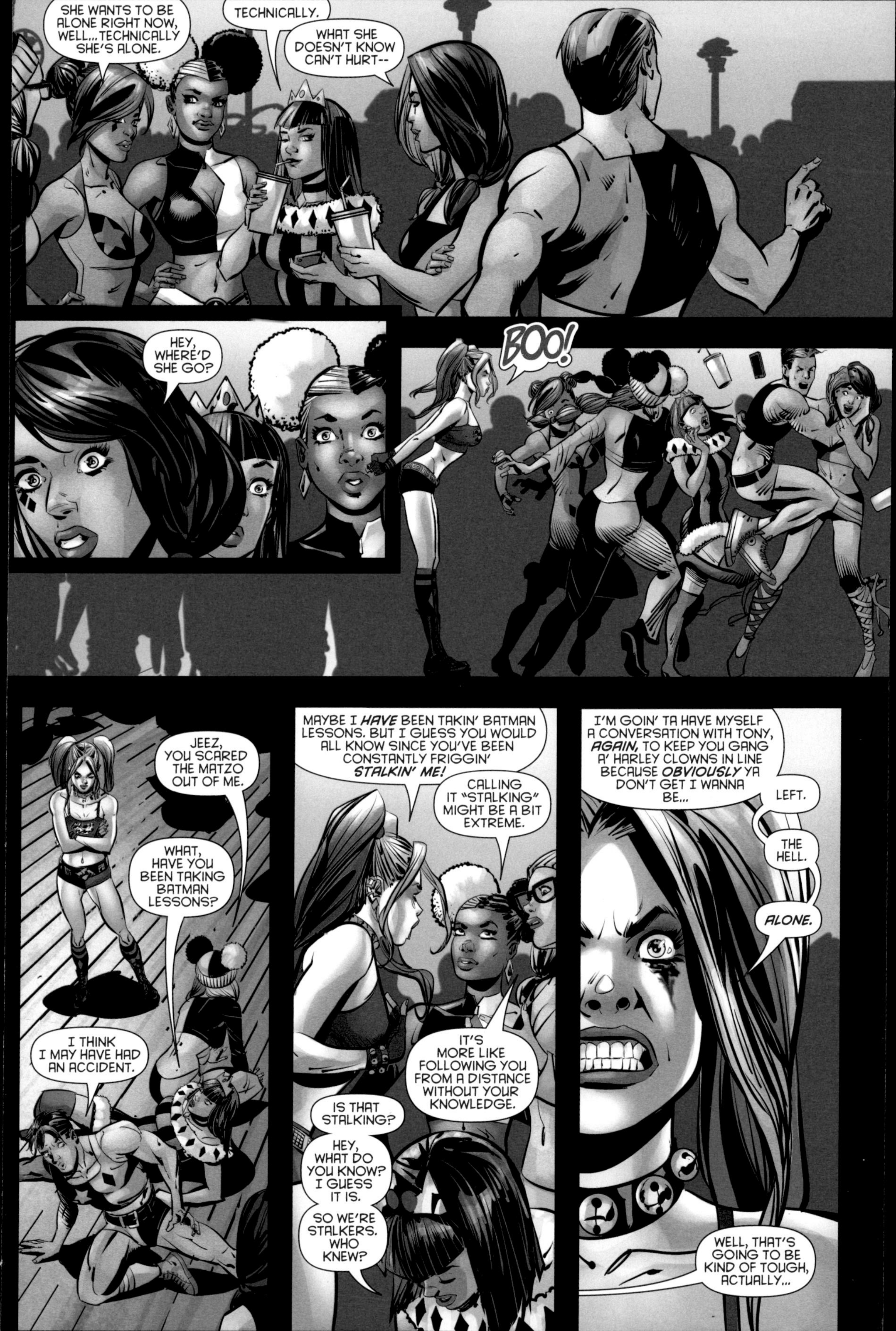
SHE WANTS TO BE ALONE RIGHT NOW, WELL... TECHNICALLY SHE'S ALONE.
TECHNICALLY.
WHAT SHE DOESN'T KNOW CAN'T HURT--
HEY, WHERE'D SHE GO?
BOO!
JEEZ, YOU SCARED THE MATZO OUT OF ME.
WHAT, HAVE YOU BEEN TAKING BATMAN LESSONS?
I THINK I MAY HAVE HAD AN ACCIDENT.
MAYBE I HAVE BEEN TAKIN' BATMAN LESSONS. BUT I GUESS YOU WOULD ALL KNOW SINCE YOU'VE BEEN CONSTANTLY FRIGGIN' STALKIN' ME!
CALLING IT "STALKING" MIGHT BE A BIT EXTREME.
IT'S MORE LIKE FOLLOWING YOU FROM A DISTANCE WITHOUT YOUR KNOWLEDGE.
IS THAT STALKING?
HEY, WHAT DO YOU KNOW? I GUESS IT IS.
SO WE'RE STALKERS. WHO KNEW?
I'M GOIN' TA HAVE MYSELF A CONVERSATION WITH TONY, AGAIN, TO KEEP YOU GANG A' HARLEY CLOWNS IN LINE BECAUSE OBVIOUSLY YA DON'T GET I WANNA BE...
LEFT.
THE HELL.
ALONE.
WELL, THAT'S GOING TO BE KIND OF TOUGH, ACTUALLY...

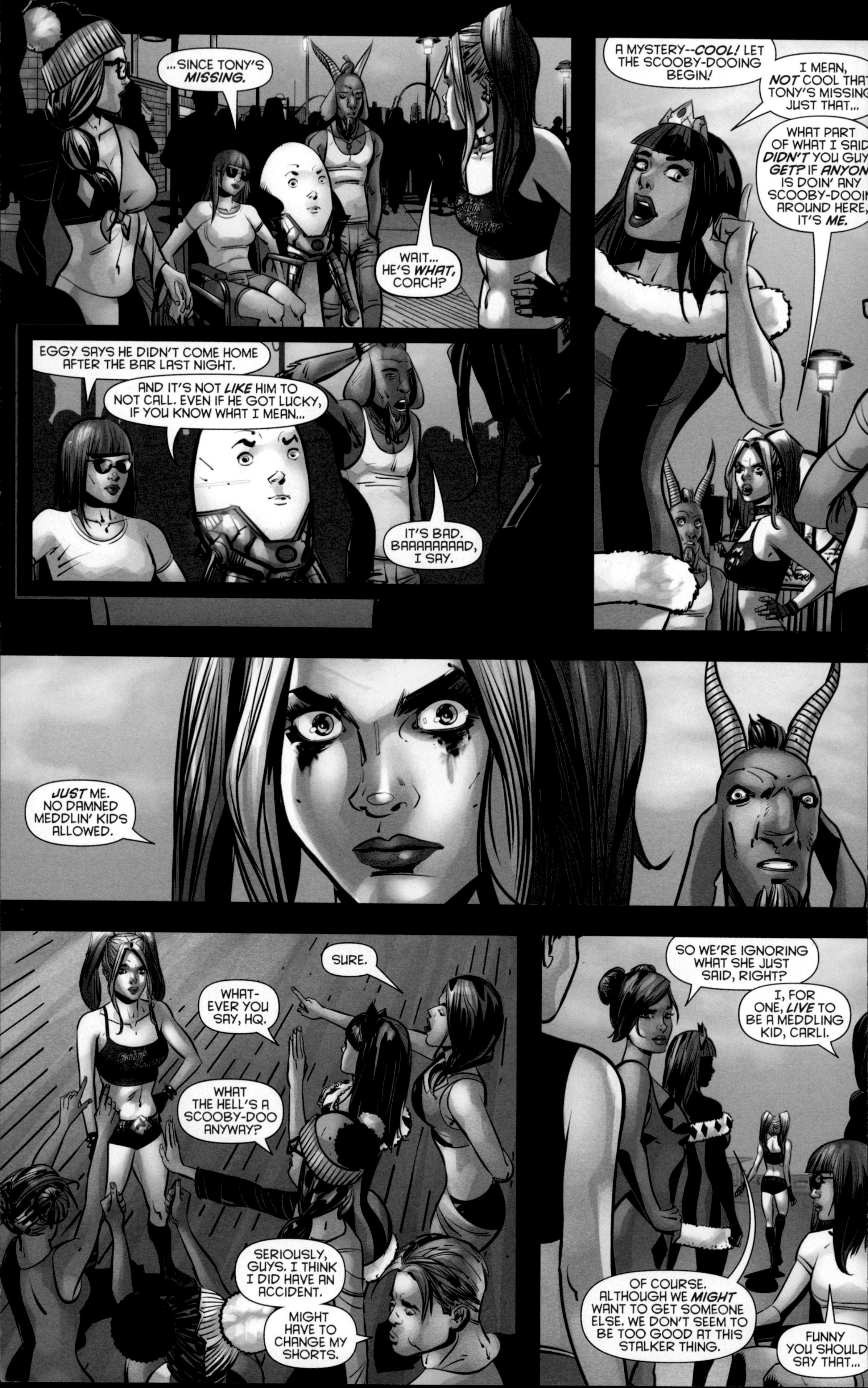
...SINCE TONY'S *MISSING.*
WAIT... HE'S *WHAT,* COACH?
A MYSTERY--*COOL!* LET THE SCOOBY-DOOING BEGIN!
I MEAN, *NOT* COOL THAT TONY'S MISSING JUST THAT...
EGGY SAYS HE DIDN'T COME HOME AFTER THE BAR LAST NIGHT.
AND IT'S NOT *LIKE* HIM TO NOT CALL. EVEN IF HE GOT LUCKY, IF YOU KNOW WHAT I MEAN...
IT'S BAD. BAAAAAAAAD, I SAY.
WHAT PART OF WHAT I SAID *DIDN'T* YOU GUY *GET?* IF *ANYON* IS DOIN' ANY SCOOBY-DOOIN AROUND HERE, IT'S *ME.*
*JUST* ME. NO DAMNED MEDDLIN' KIDS ALLOWED.
SURE.
WHAT-EVER YOU SAY, HQ.
WHAT THE HELL'S A SCOOBY-DOO ANYWAY?
SERIOUSLY, GUYS. I THINK I DID HAVE AN ACCIDENT.
MIGHT HAVE TO CHANGE MY SHORTS.
SO WE'RE IGNORING WHAT SHE JUST SAID, RIGHT?
I, FOR ONE, *LIVE* TO BE A MEDDLING KID, CARLI.
OF COURSE. ALTHOUGH WE *MIGHT* WANT TO GET SOMEONE ELSE. WE DON'T SEEM TO BE TOO GOOD AT THIS STALKER THING.
FUNNY YOU SHOULD SAY THAT...

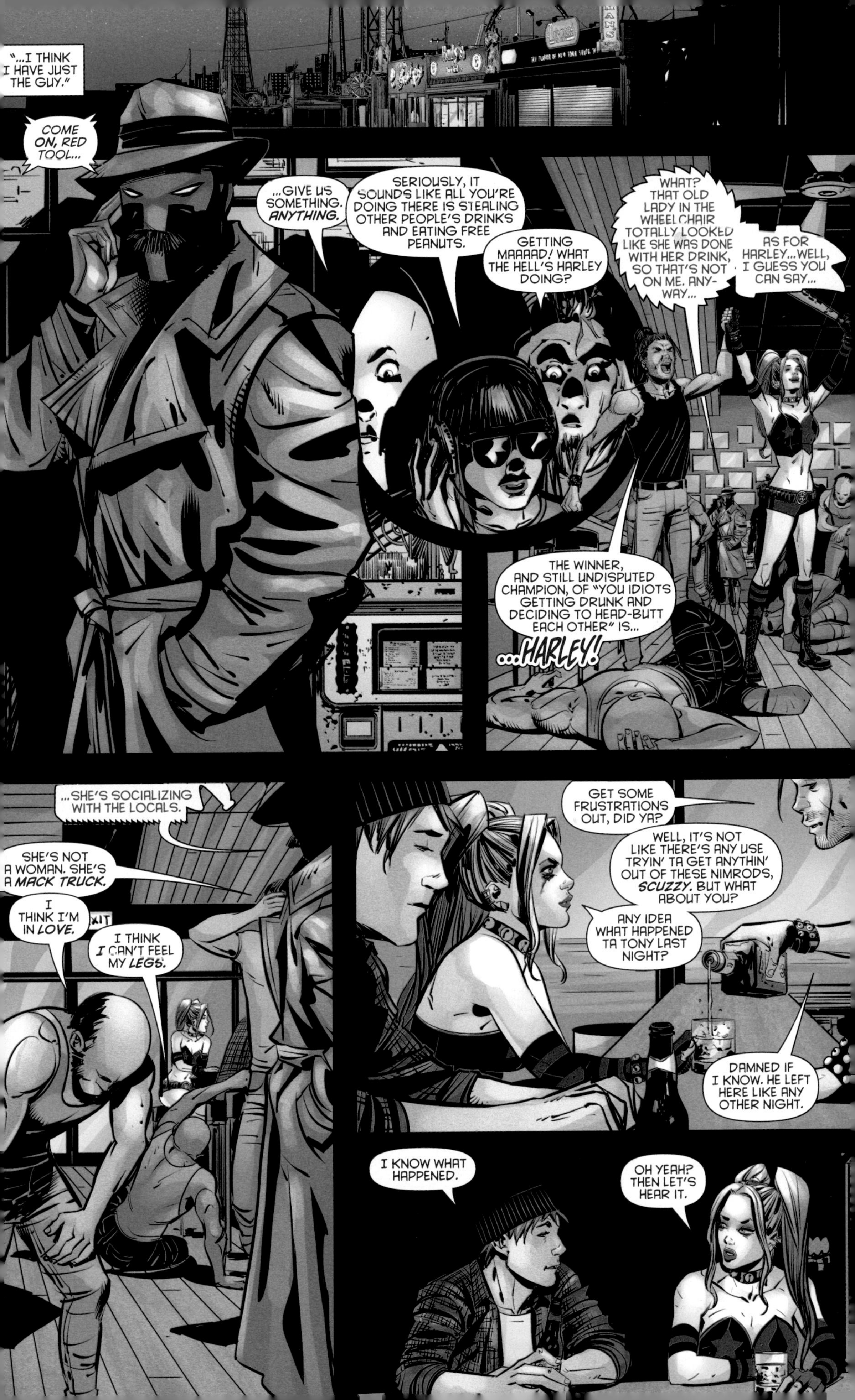
"...I THINK I HAVE JUST THE GUY."
COME ON, RED TOOL...
...GIVE US SOMETHING. ANYTHING.
SERIOUSLY, IT SOUNDS LIKE ALL YOU'RE DOING THERE IS STEALING OTHER PEOPLE'S DRINKS AND EATING FREE PEANUTS.
GETTING MAAAAD! WHAT THE HELL'S HARLEY DOING?
WHAT? THAT OLD LADY IN THE WHEELCHAIR TOTALLY LOOKED LIKE SHE WAS DONE WITH HER DRINK, SO THAT'S NOT ON ME. ANY-WAY...
AS FOR HARLEY...WELL, I GUESS YOU CAN SAY...
THE WINNER, AND STILL UNDISPUTED CHAMPION, OF "YOU IDIOTS GETTING DRUNK AND DECIDING TO HEAD-BUTT EACH OTHER" IS...
...HARLEY!
...SHE'S SOCIALIZING WITH THE LOCALS.
SHE'S NOT A WOMAN. SHE'S A MACK TRUCK.
I THINK I'M IN LOVE.
I THINK I CAN'T FEEL MY LEGS.
GET SOME FRUSTRATIONS OUT, DID YA?
WELL, IT'S NOT LIKE THERE'S ANY USE TRYIN' TA GET ANYTHIN' OUT OF THESE NIMRODS, SCUZZY. BUT WHAT ABOUT YOU?
ANY IDEA WHAT HAPPENED TA TONY LAST NIGHT?
DAMNED IF I KNOW. HE LEFT HERE LIKE ANY OTHER NIGHT.
I KNOW WHAT HAPPENED.
OH YEAH? THEN LET'S HEAR IT.

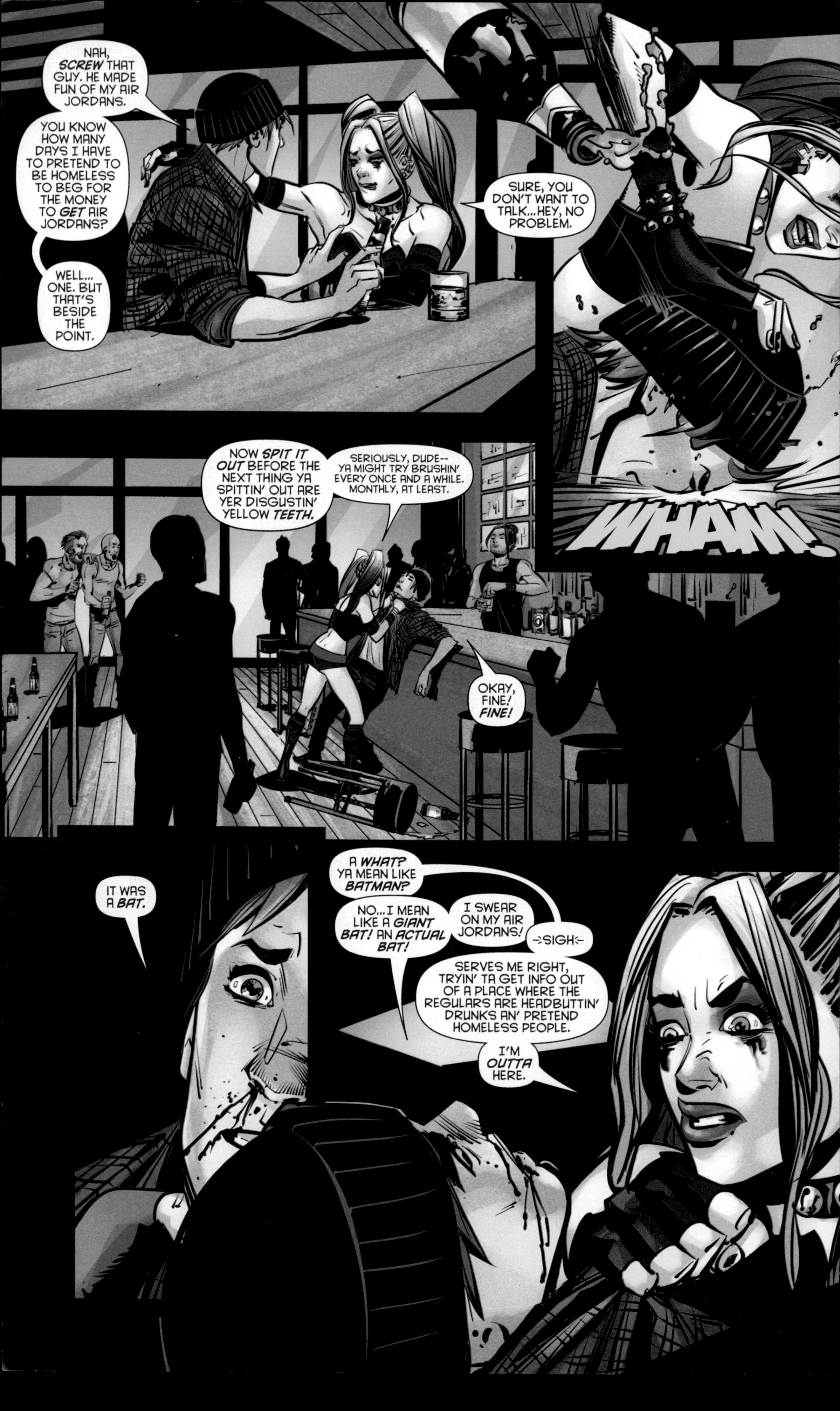
NAH, SCREW THAT GUY. HE MADE FUN OF MY AIR JORDANS.
YOU KNOW HOW MANY DAYS I HAVE TO PRETEND TO BE HOMELESS TO BEG FOR THE MONEY TO GET AIR JORDANS?
WELL... ONE. BUT THAT'S BESIDE THE POINT.
SURE, YOU DON'T WANT TO TALK...HEY, NO PROBLEM.
WHAM!
NOW SPIT IT OUT BEFORE THE NEXT THING YA SPITTIN' OUT ARE YER DISGUSTIN' YELLOW TEETH.
SERIOUSLY, DUDE-- YA MIGHT TRY BRUSHIN' EVERY ONCE AND A WHILE. MONTHLY, AT LEAST.
OKAY, FINE! FINE!
IT WAS A BAT.
A WHAT? YA MEAN LIKE BATMAN?
NO...I MEAN LIKE A GIANT BAT! AN ACTUAL BAT!
I SWEAR ON MY AIR JORDANS!
SIGH
SERVES ME RIGHT, TRYIN' TA GET INFO OUT OF A PLACE WHERE THE REGULARS ARE HEADBUTTIN' DRUNKS AN' PRETEND HOMELESS PEOPLE.
I'M OUTTA HERE.

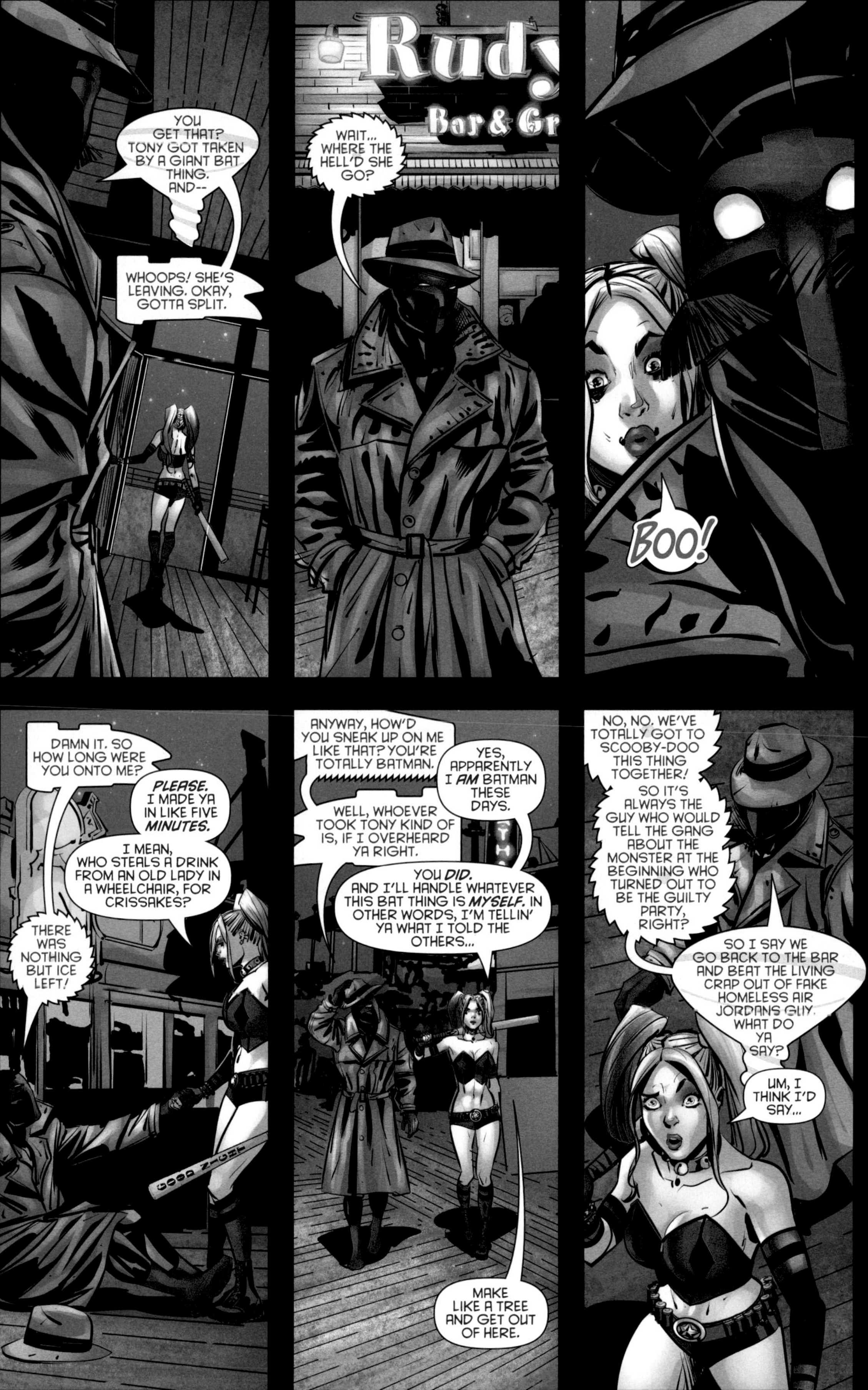
YOU GET THAT? TONY GOT TAKEN BY A GIANT BAT THING. AND--
WHOOPS! SHE'S LEAVING. OKAY, GOTTA SPLIT.
Rudy
Bar & Gr
WAIT... WHERE THE HELL'D SHE GO?
BOO!
DAMN IT. SO HOW LONG WERE YOU ONTO ME?
PLEASE. I MADE YA IN LIKE FIVE MINUTES.
I MEAN, WHO STEALS A DRINK FROM AN OLD LADY IN A WHEELCHAIR, FOR CRISSAKES?
THERE WAS NOTHING BUT ICE LEFT!
GOOD NIGHT
ANYWAY, HOW'D YOU SNEAK UP ON ME LIKE THAT? YOU'RE TOTALLY BATMAN.
YES, APPARENTLY I AM BATMAN THESE DAYS.
WELL, WHOEVER TOOK TONY KIND OF IS, IF I OVERHEARD YA RIGHT.
YOU DID. AND I'LL HANDLE WHATEVER THIS BAT THING IS MYSELF. IN OTHER WORDS, I'M TELLIN' YA WHAT I TOLD THE OTHERS...
MAKE LIKE A TREE AND GET OUT OF HERE.
NO, NO. WE'VE TOTALLY GOT TO SCOOBY-DOO THIS THING TOGETHER!
SO IT'S ALWAYS THE GUY WHO WOULD TELL THE GANG ABOUT THE MONSTER AT THE BEGINNING WHO TURNED OUT TO BE THE GUILTY PARTY, RIGHT?
SO I SAY WE GO BACK TO THE BAR AND BEAT THE LIVING CRAP OUT OF FAKE HOMELESS AIR JORDANS GUY. WHAT DO YA SAY?
UM, I THINK I'D SAY...

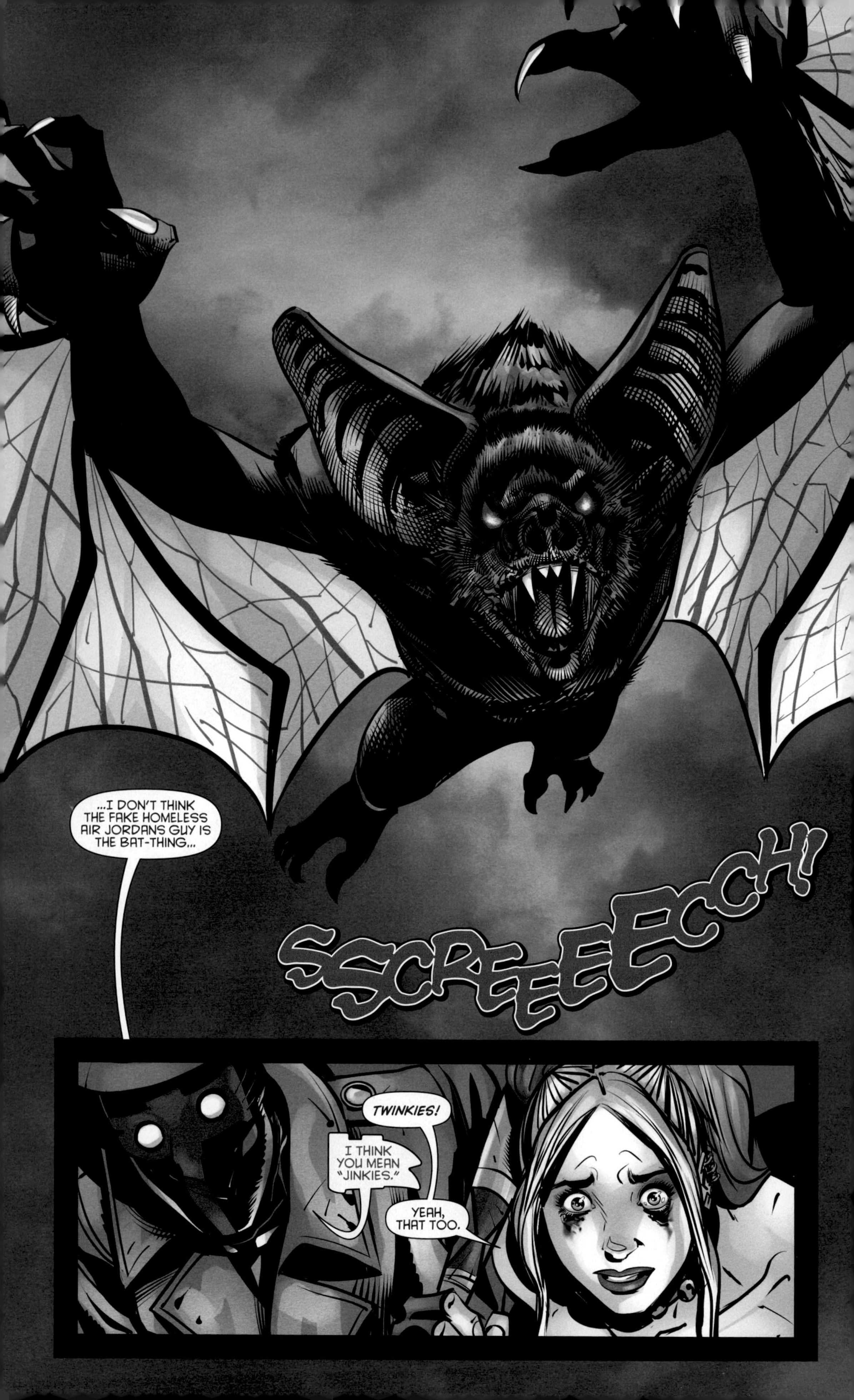
...I DON'T THINK THE FAKE HOMELESS AIR JORDANS GUY IS THE BAT-THING...
SSCREEEEECCCH!
TWINKIES!
I THINK YOU MEAN "JINKIES."
YEAH, THAT TOO.

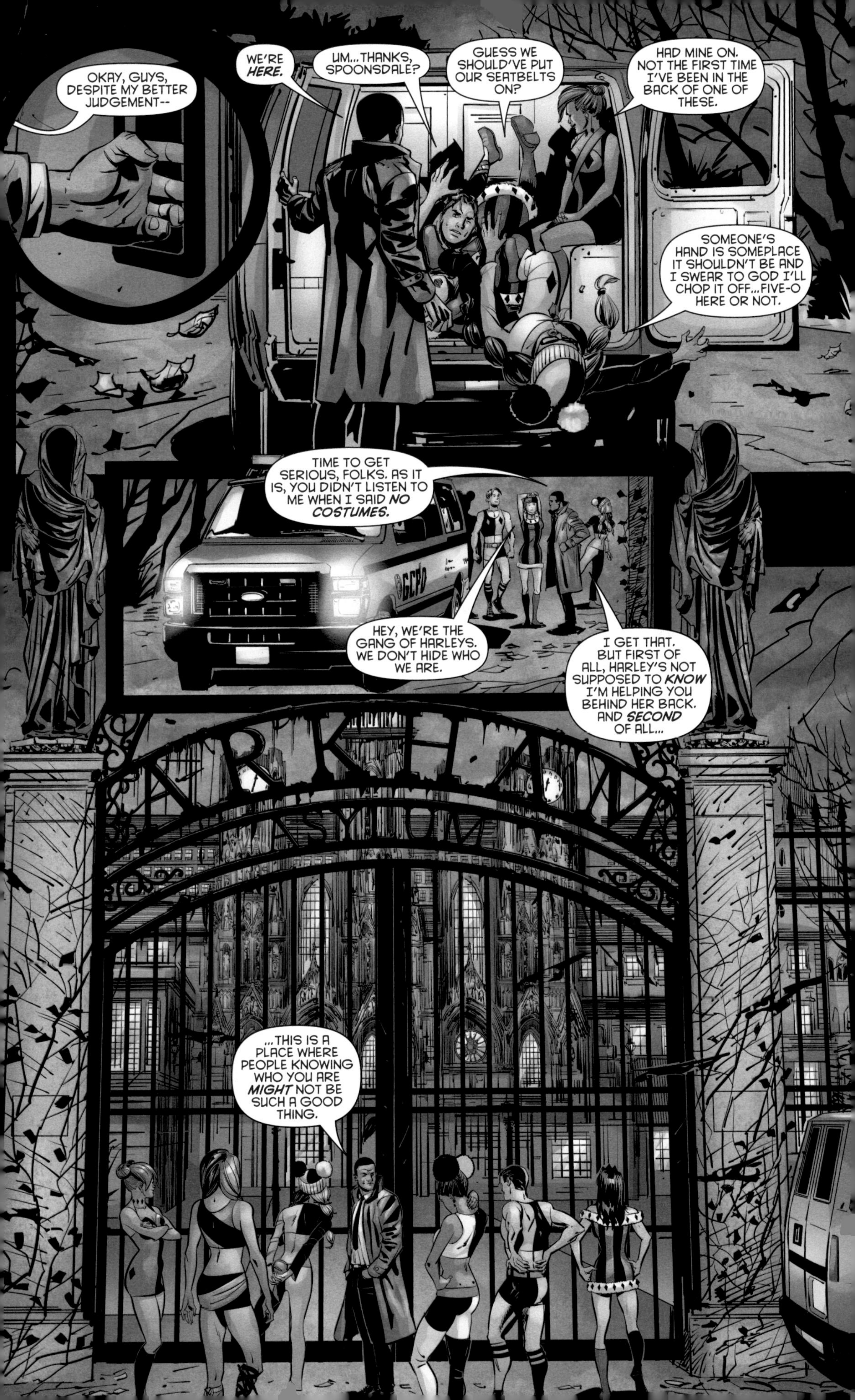
OKAY, GUYS, DESPITE MY BETTER JUDGEMENT--
WE'RE *HERE.*
UM... THANKS, SPOONSDALE?
GUESS WE SHOULD'VE PUT OUR SEATBELTS ON?
HAD MINE ON. NOT THE FIRST TIME I'VE BEEN IN THE BACK OF ONE OF THESE.
SOMEONE'S HAND IS SOMEPLACE IT SHOULDN'T BE AND I SWEAR TO GOD I'LL CHOP IT OFF... FIVE-O HERE OR NOT.
TIME TO GET SERIOUS, FOLKS. AS IT IS, YOU DIDN'T LISTEN TO ME WHEN I SAID *NO COSTUMES.*
GCPD
HEY, WE'RE THE GANG OF HARLEYS. WE DON'T HIDE WHO WE ARE.
I GET THAT. BUT FIRST OF ALL, HARLEY'S NOT SUPPOSED TO *KNOW* I'M HELPING YOU BEHIND HER BACK. AND *SECOND* OF ALL...
ARKHAM ASYLUM
...THIS IS A PLACE WHERE PEOPLE KNOWING WHO YOU ARE *MIGHT* NOT BE SUCH A GOOD THING.

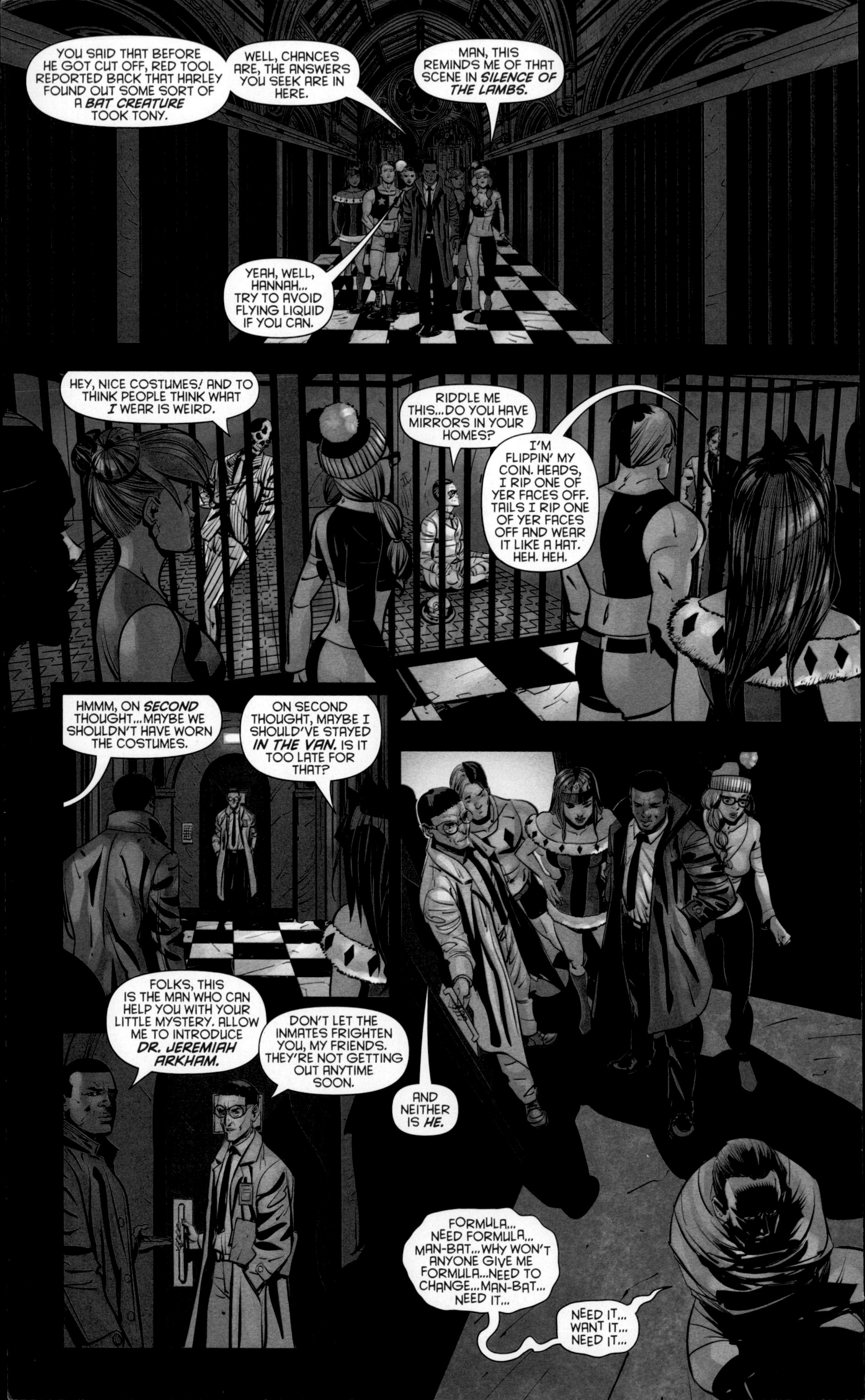
YOU SAID THAT BEFORE HE GOT CUT OFF, RED TOOL REPORTED BACK THAT HARLEY FOUND OUT SOME SORT OF A BAT CREATURE TOOK TONY.
WELL, CHANCES ARE, THE ANSWERS YOU SEEK ARE IN HERE.
MAN, THIS REMINDS ME OF THAT SCENE IN SILENCE OF THE LAMBS.
YEAH, WELL, HANNAH... TRY TO AVOID FLYING LIQUID IF YOU CAN.
HEY, NICE COSTUMES! AND TO THINK PEOPLE THINK WHAT I WEAR IS WEIRD.
RIDDLE ME THIS...DO YOU HAVE MIRRORS IN YOUR HOMES?
I'M FLIPPIN' MY COIN. HEADS, I RIP ONE OF YER FACES OFF. TAILS I RIP ONE OF YER FACES OFF AND WEAR IT LIKE A HAT. HEH. HEH.
HMMM, ON SECOND THOUGHT...MAYBE WE SHOULDN'T HAVE WORN THE COSTUMES.
ON SECOND THOUGHT, MAYBE I SHOULD'VE STAYED IN THE VAN. IS IT TOO LATE FOR THAT?
FOLKS, THIS IS THE MAN WHO CAN HELP YOU WITH YOUR LITTLE MYSTERY. ALLOW ME TO INTRODUCE DR. JEREMIAH ARKHAM.
DON'T LET THE INMATES FRIGHTEN YOU, MY FRIENDS. THEY'RE NOT GETTING OUT ANYTIME SOON.
AND NEITHER IS HE.
FORMULA... NEED FORMULA... MAN-BAT...WHY WON'T ANYONE GIVE ME FORMULA...NEED TO CHANGE...MAN-BAT... NEED IT...
NEED IT... WANT IT... NEED IT...

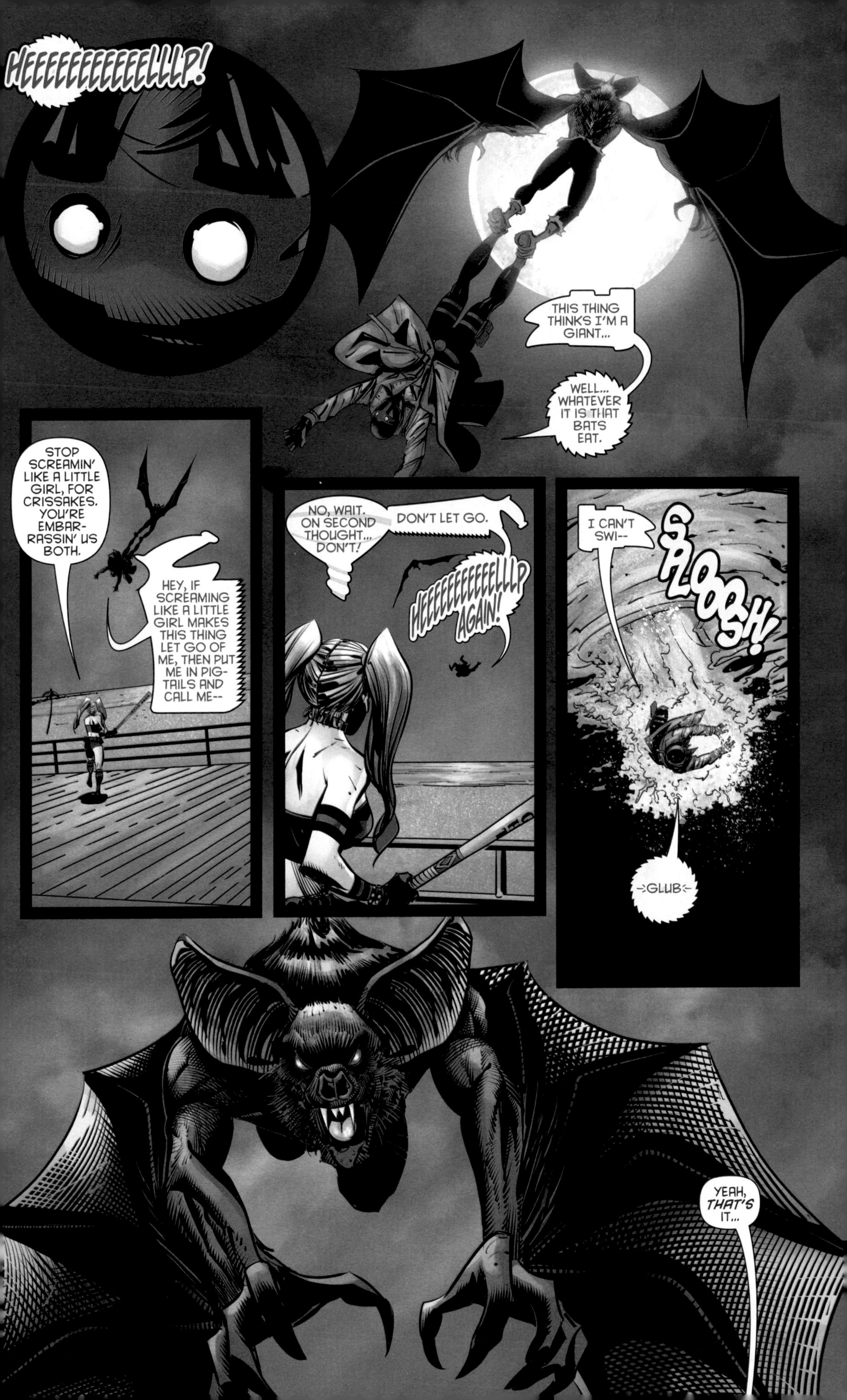
HEEEEEEEEEEEELLLP!
THIS THING THINKS I'M A GIANT...
WELL... WHATEVER IT IS THAT BATS EAT.
STOP SCREAMIN' LIKE A LITTLE GIRL, FOR CRISSAKES. YOU'RE EMBAR-RASSIN' US BOTH.
HEY, IF SCREAMING LIKE A LITTLE GIRL MAKES THIS THING LET GO OF ME, THEN PUT ME IN PIG-TAILS AND CALL ME--
NO, WAIT. ON SECOND THOUGHT... DON'T!
DON'T LET GO.
HEEEEEEEEEEEELLLP AGAIN!
I CAN'T SWI--
SPLOOSH!
GLUB
YEAH, THAT'S IT...

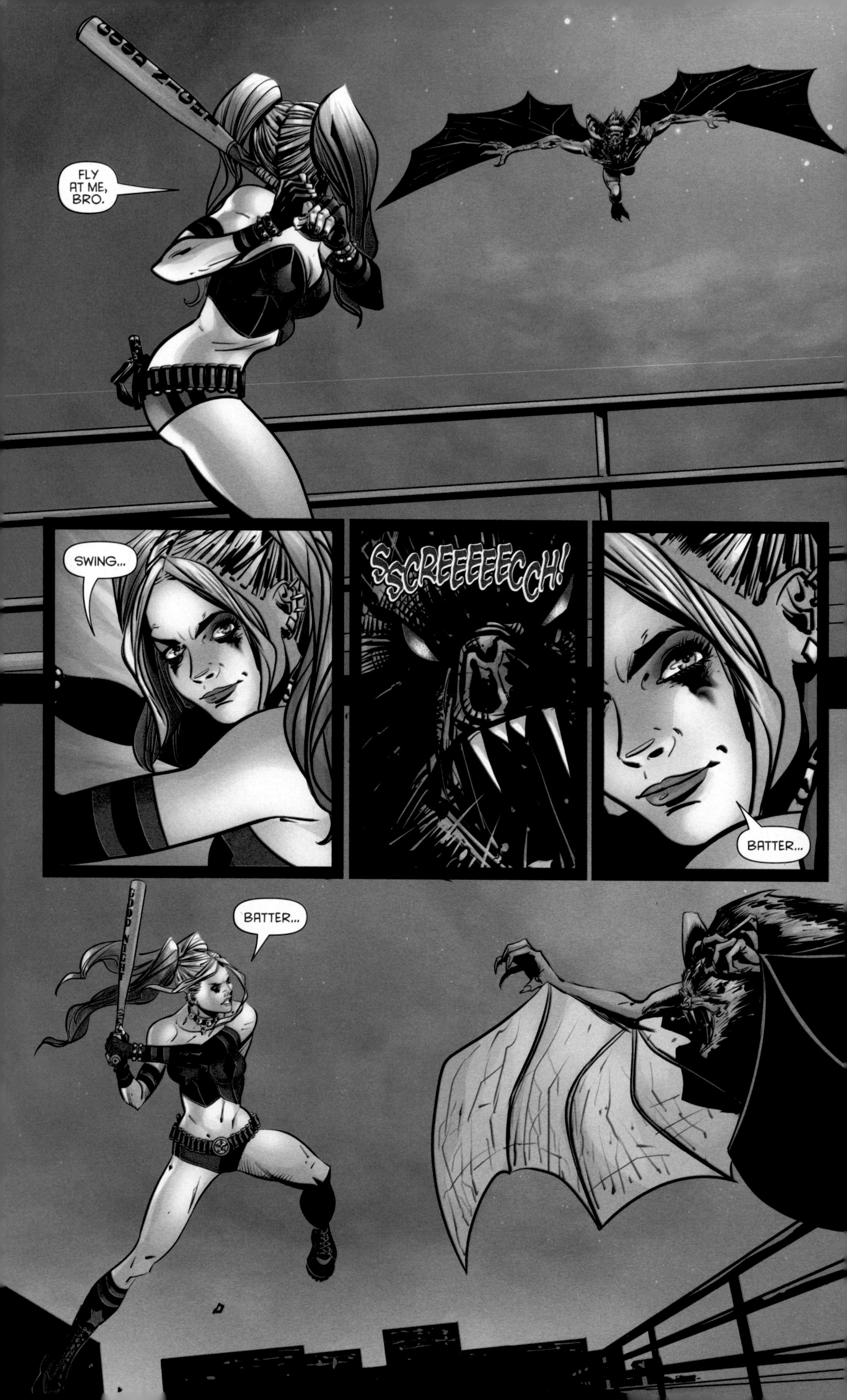
FLY AT ME, BRO.
SWING...
SSCREEEEEECCH!
BATTER...
BATTER...

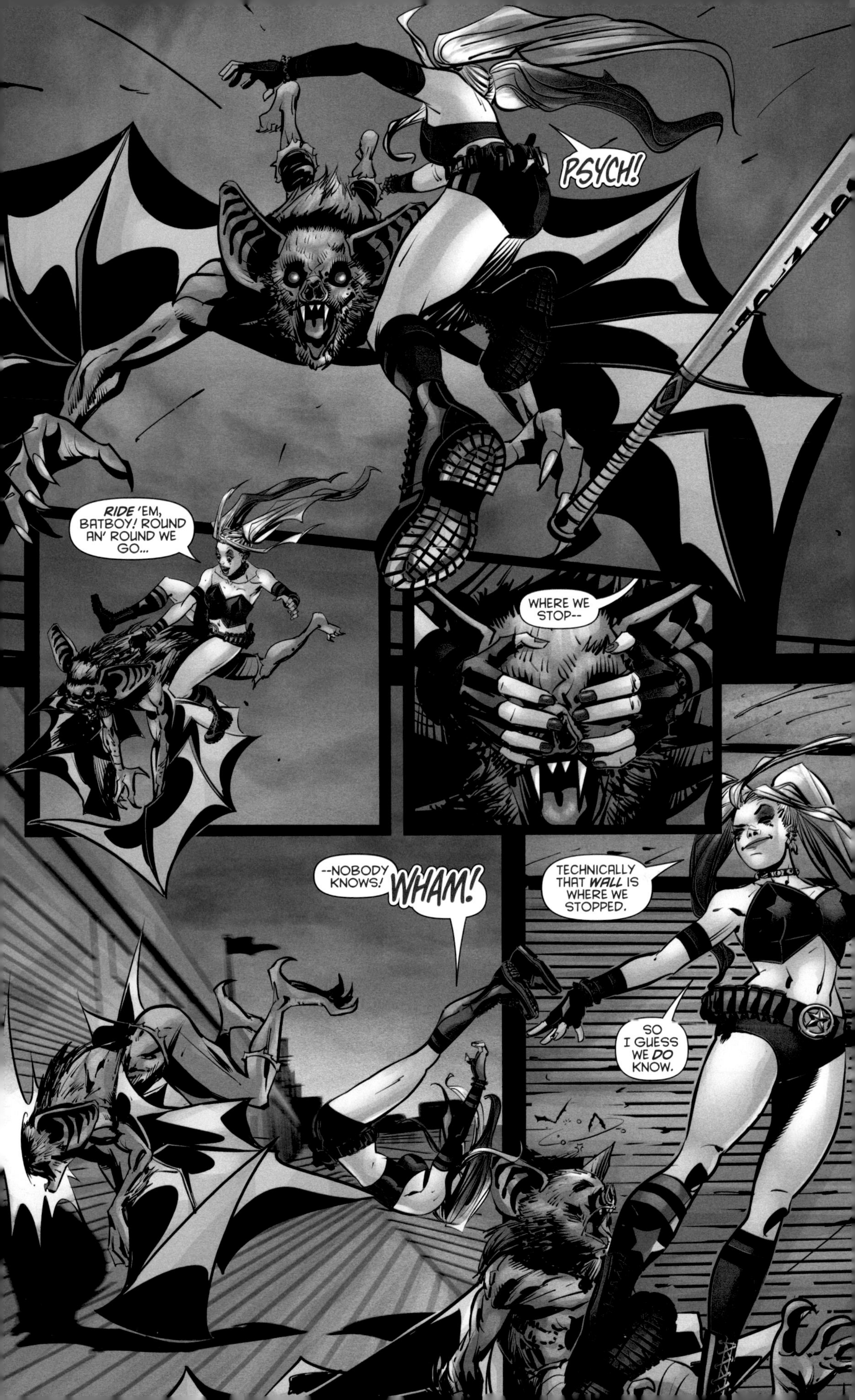
PSYCH!
RIDE 'EM, BATBOY! ROUND AN' ROUND WE GO...
WHERE WE STOP--
--NOBODY KNOWS!
WHAM!
TECHNICALLY THAT WALL IS WHERE WE STOPPED.
SO I GUESS WE DO KNOW.

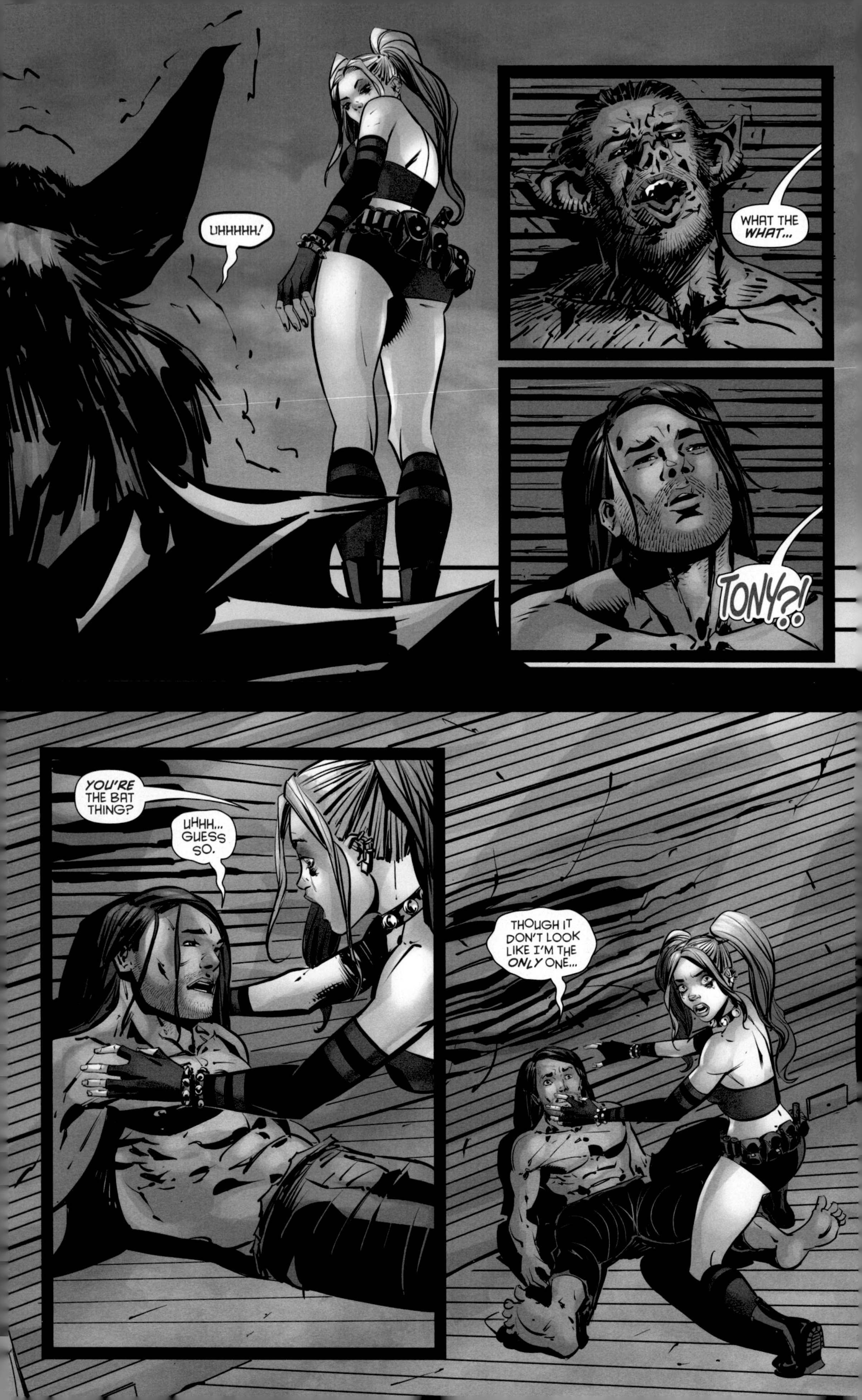
UHHHHH!
WHAT THE WHAT...
TONY?!
YOU'RE THE BAT THING?
UHHH... GUESS SO.
THOUGH IT DON'T LOOK LIKE I'M THE ONLY ONE...

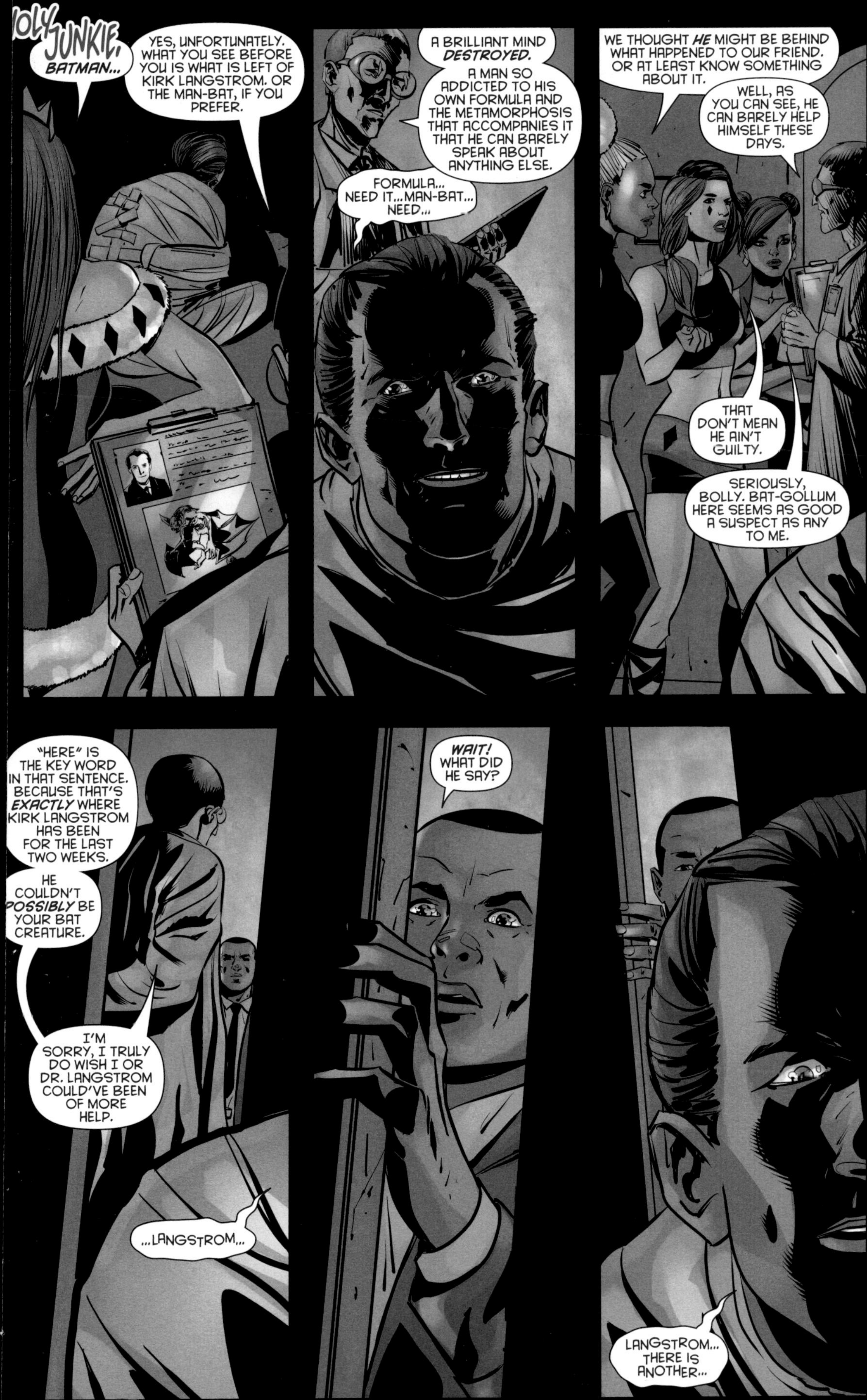
HOLY JUNKIE, BATMAN...
YES, UNFORTUNATELY. WHAT YOU SEE BEFORE YOU IS WHAT IS LEFT OF KIRK LANGSTROM. OR THE MAN-BAT, IF YOU PREFER.
A BRILLIANT MIND DESTROYED.
A MAN SO ADDICTED TO HIS OWN FORMULA AND THE METAMORPHOSIS THAT ACCOMPANIES IT THAT HE CAN BARELY SPEAK ABOUT ANYTHING ELSE.
FORMULA... NEED IT...MAN-BAT... NEED...
WE THOUGHT HE MIGHT BE BEHIND WHAT HAPPENED TO OUR FRIEND. OR AT LEAST KNOW SOMETHING ABOUT IT.
WELL, AS YOU CAN SEE, HE CAN BARELY HELP HIMSELF THESE DAYS.
THAT DON'T MEAN HE AIN'T GUILTY.
SERIOUSLY, BOLLY. BAT-GOLLUM HERE SEEMS AS GOOD A SUSPECT AS ANY TO ME.
"HERE" IS THE KEY WORD IN THAT SENTENCE. BECAUSE THAT'S EXACTLY WHERE KIRK LANGSTROM HAS BEEN FOR THE LAST TWO WEEKS.
HE COULDN'T POSSIBLY BE YOUR BAT CREATURE.
I'M SORRY, I TRULY DO WISH I OR DR. LANGSTROM COULD'VE BEEN OF MORE HELP.
...LANGSTROM...
WAIT! WHAT DID HE SAY?
LANGSTROM... THERE IS ANOTHER...

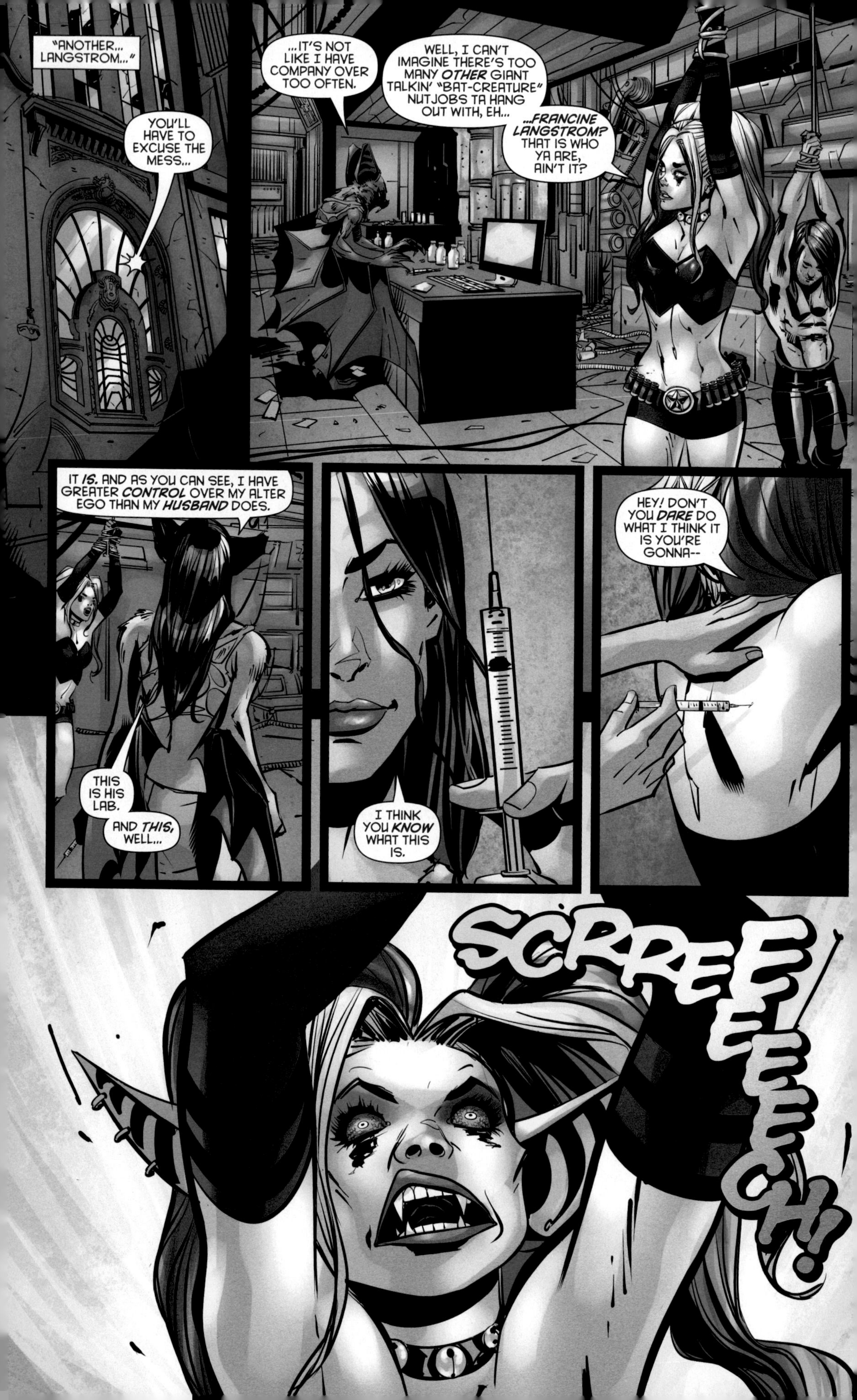
"ANOTHER... LANGSTROM..."
YOU'LL HAVE TO EXCUSE THE MESS...
...IT'S NOT LIKE I HAVE COMPANY OVER TOO OFTEN.
WELL, I CAN'T IMAGINE THERE'S TOO MANY OTHER GIANT TALKIN' "BAT-CREATURE" NUTJOBS TA HANG OUT WITH, EH...
...FRANCINE LANGSTROM? THAT IS WHO YA ARE, AIN'T IT?
IT IS. AND AS YOU CAN SEE, I HAVE GREATER CONTROL OVER MY ALTER EGO THAN MY HUSBAND DOES.
THIS IS HIS LAB.
AND THIS, WELL...
I THINK YOU KNOW WHAT THIS IS.
HEY! DON'T YOU DARE DO WHAT I THINK IT IS YOU'RE GONNA--
SCRREEEEECH!

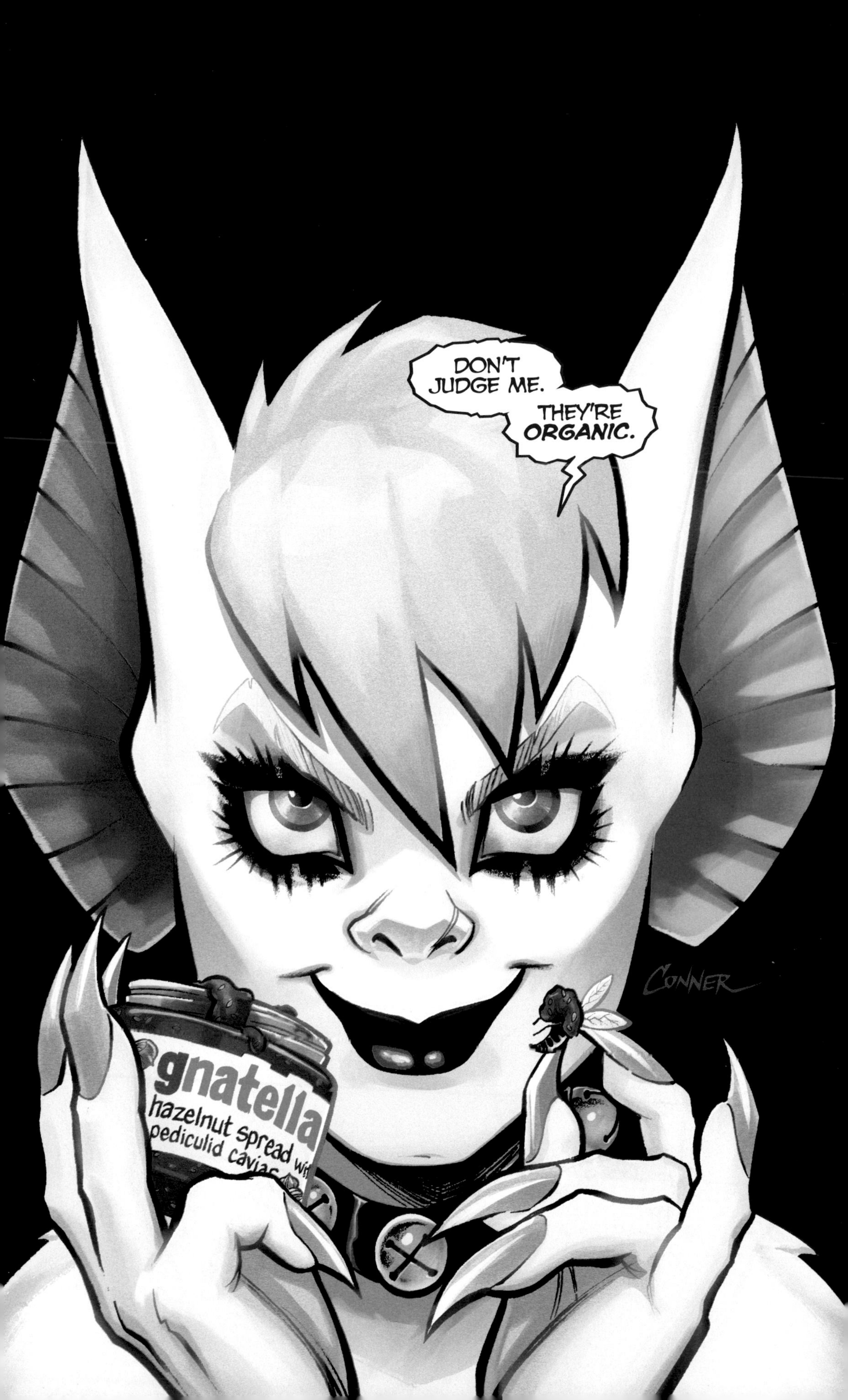
DON'T JUDGE ME.
THEY'RE ORGANIC.
gnatella
hazelnut spread with
pediculid caviar
CONNER

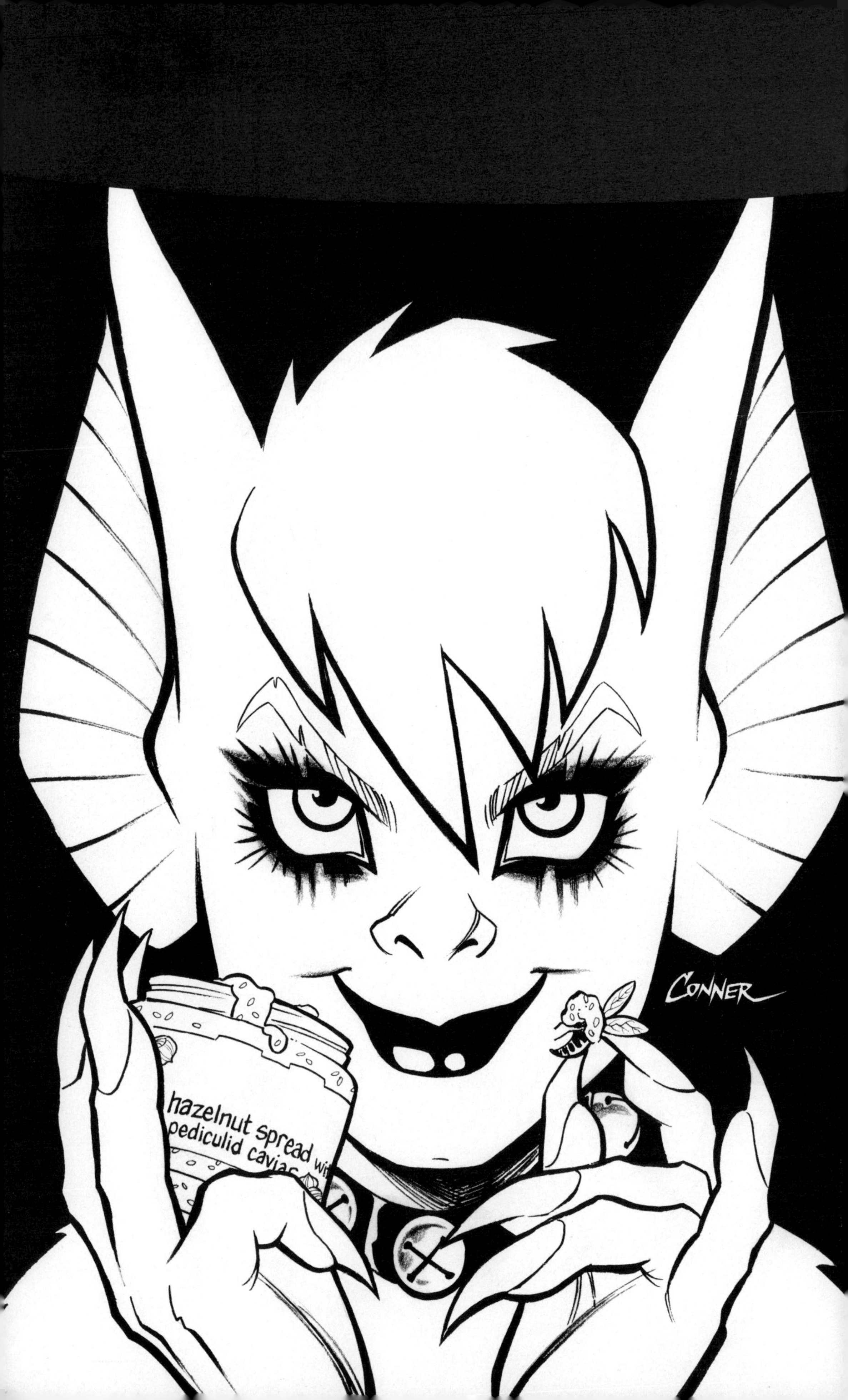
CONNER
hazelnut spread wit
pediculid caviar

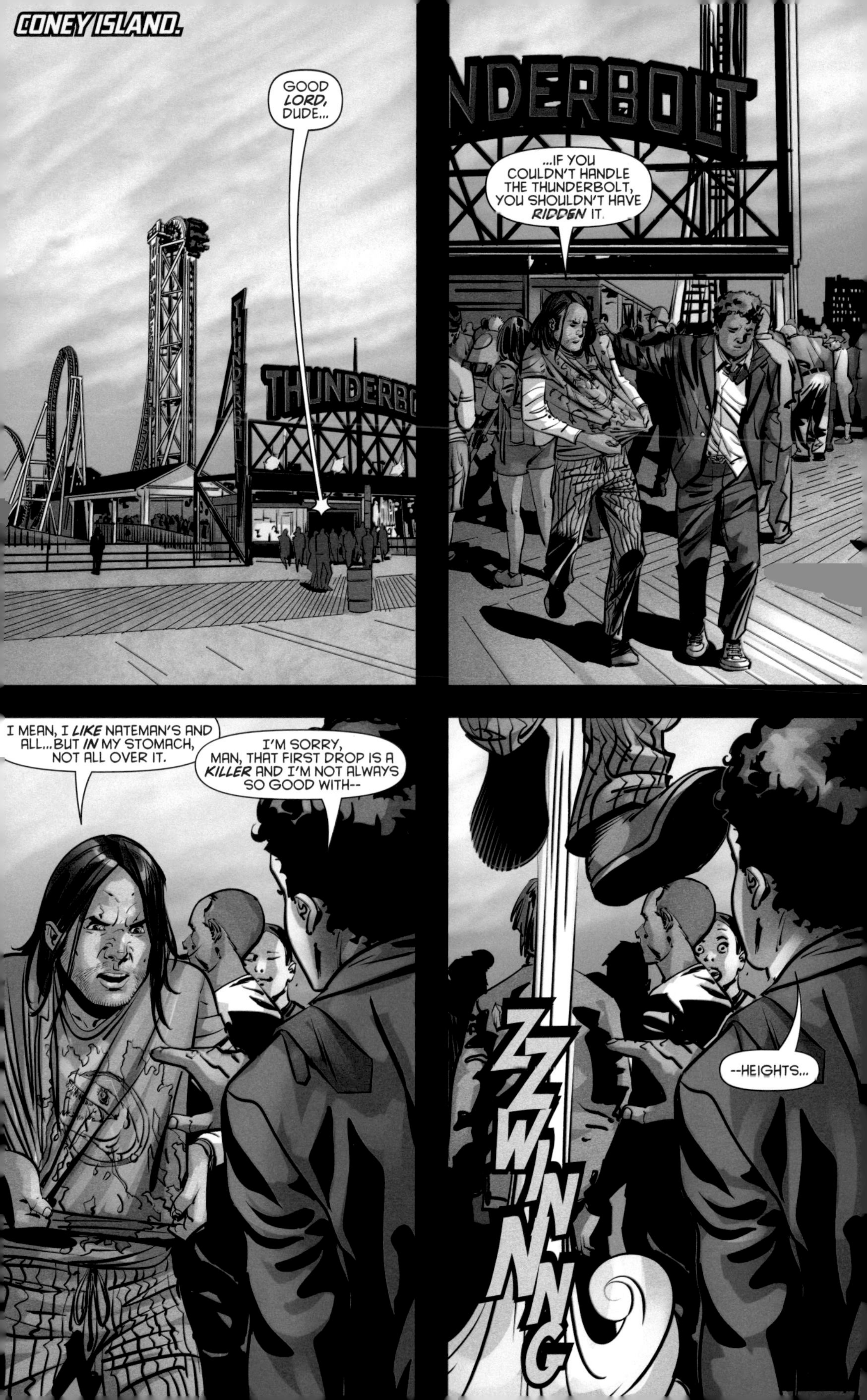
CONEY ISLAND.
GOOD LORD, DUDE...
THUNDERBO
NDERBOLT
...IF YOU COULDN'T HANDLE THE THUNDERBOLT, YOU SHOULDN'T HAVE RIDDEN IT.
I MEAN, I LIKE NATEMAN'S AND ALL...BUT IN MY STOMACH, NOT ALL OVER IT.
I'M SORRY, MAN, THAT FIRST DROP IS A KILLER AND I'M NOT ALWAYS SO GOOD WITH--
ZZWINNNNG
--HEIGHTS...

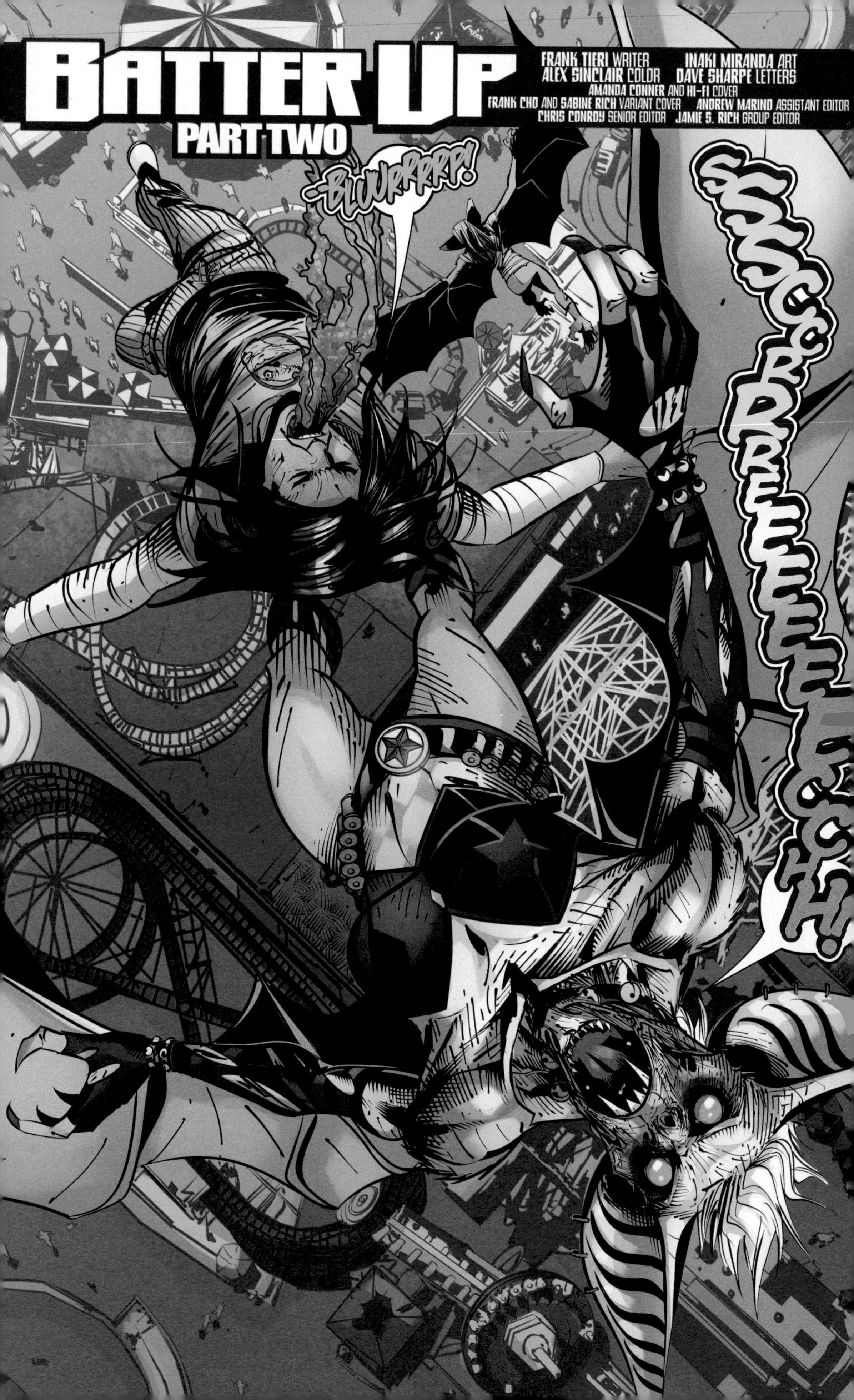
BATTER UP
PART TWO
FRANK TIERI WRITER INAKI MIRANDA ART
ALEX SINCLAIR COLOR DAVE SHARPE LETTERS
AMANDA CONNER AND HI-FI COVER
FRANK CHO AND SABINE RICH VARIANT COVER ANDREW MARINO ASSISTANT EDITOR
CHRIS CONROY SENIOR EDITOR JAMIE S. RICH GROUP EDITOR
-BLUURRRRP!
SSSCCRREEEEEECCH!

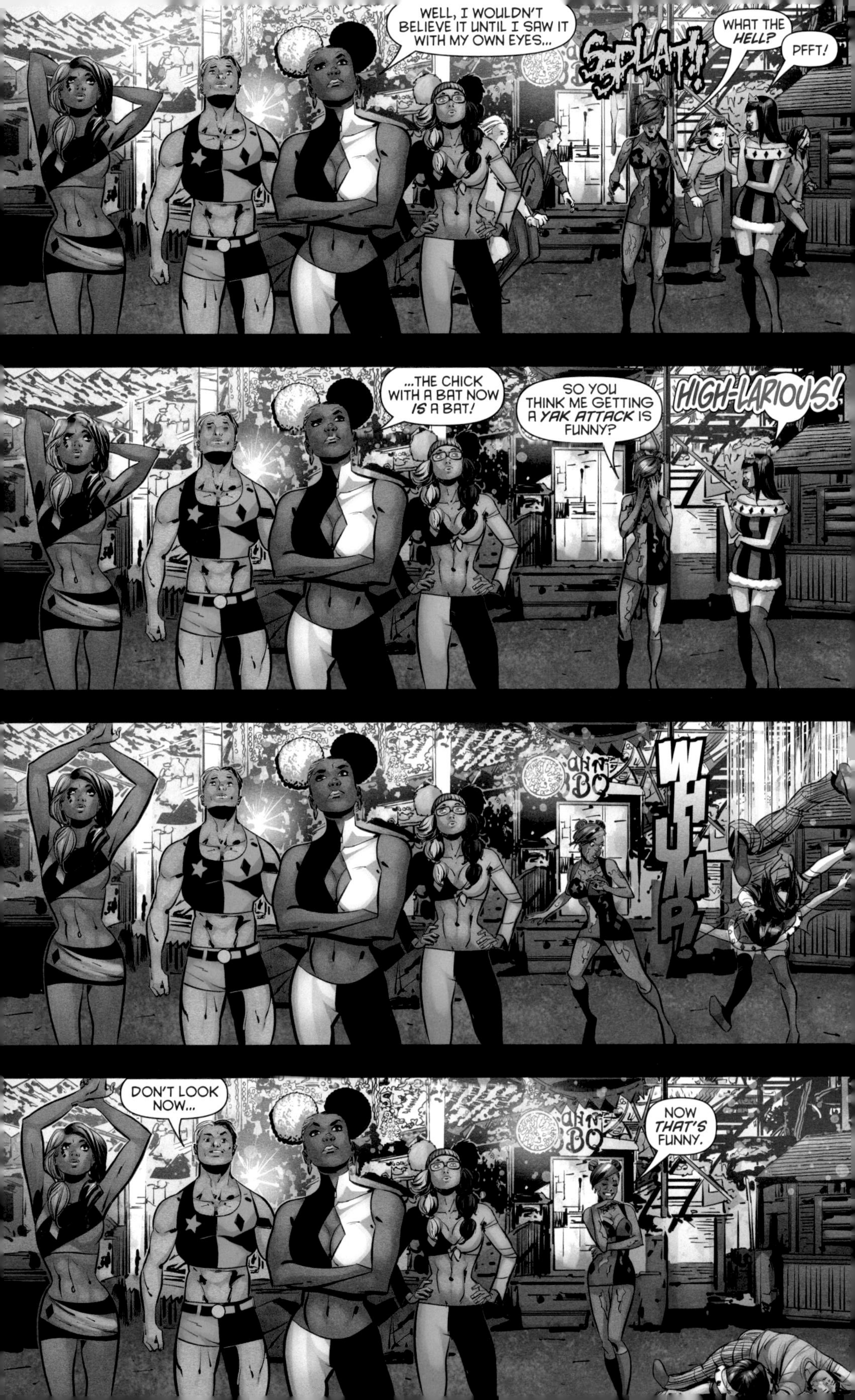
WELL, I WOULDN'T BELIEVE IT UNTIL I SAW IT WITH MY OWN EYES...
SPLAT!
WHAT THE HELL?
PFFT!
...THE CHICK WITH A BAT NOW IS A BAT!
SO YOU THINK ME GETTING A YAK ATTACK IS FUNNY?
HIGH-LARIOUS!
WHUMP!
DON'T LOOK NOW...
NOW THAT'S FUNNY.

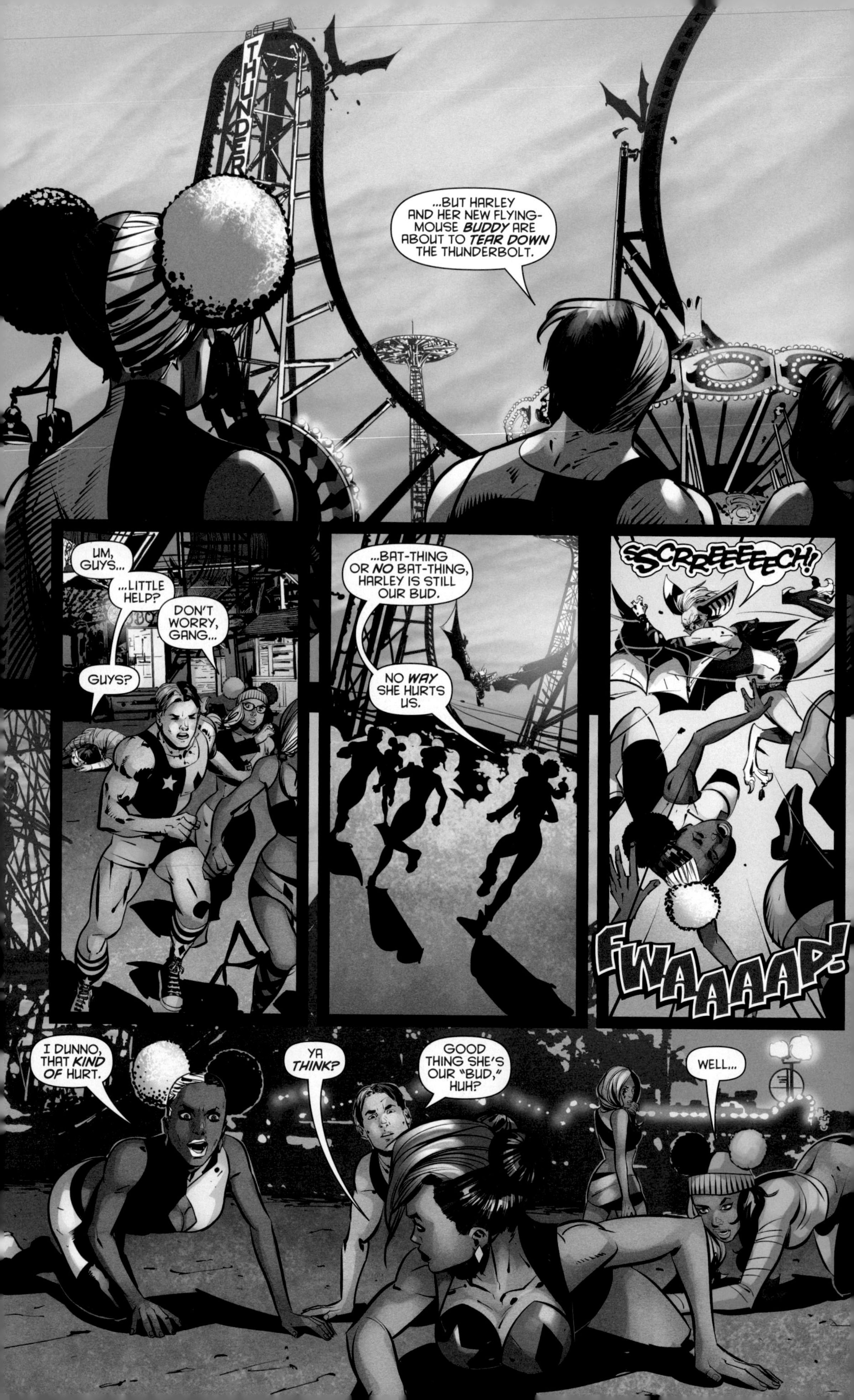
...BUT HARLEY AND HER NEW FLYING-MOUSE BUDDY ARE ABOUT TO TEAR DOWN THE THUNDERBOLT.
UM, GUYS...
...LITTLE HELP?
DON'T WORRY, GANG...
GUYS?
...BAT-THING OR NO BAT-THING, HARLEY IS STILL OUR BUD.
NO WAY SHE HURTS US.
SSCRREEEEEECH!
FWAAAAAP!
I DUNNO, THAT KIND OF HURT.
YA THINK?
GOOD THING SHE'S OUR "BUD," HUH?
WELL...

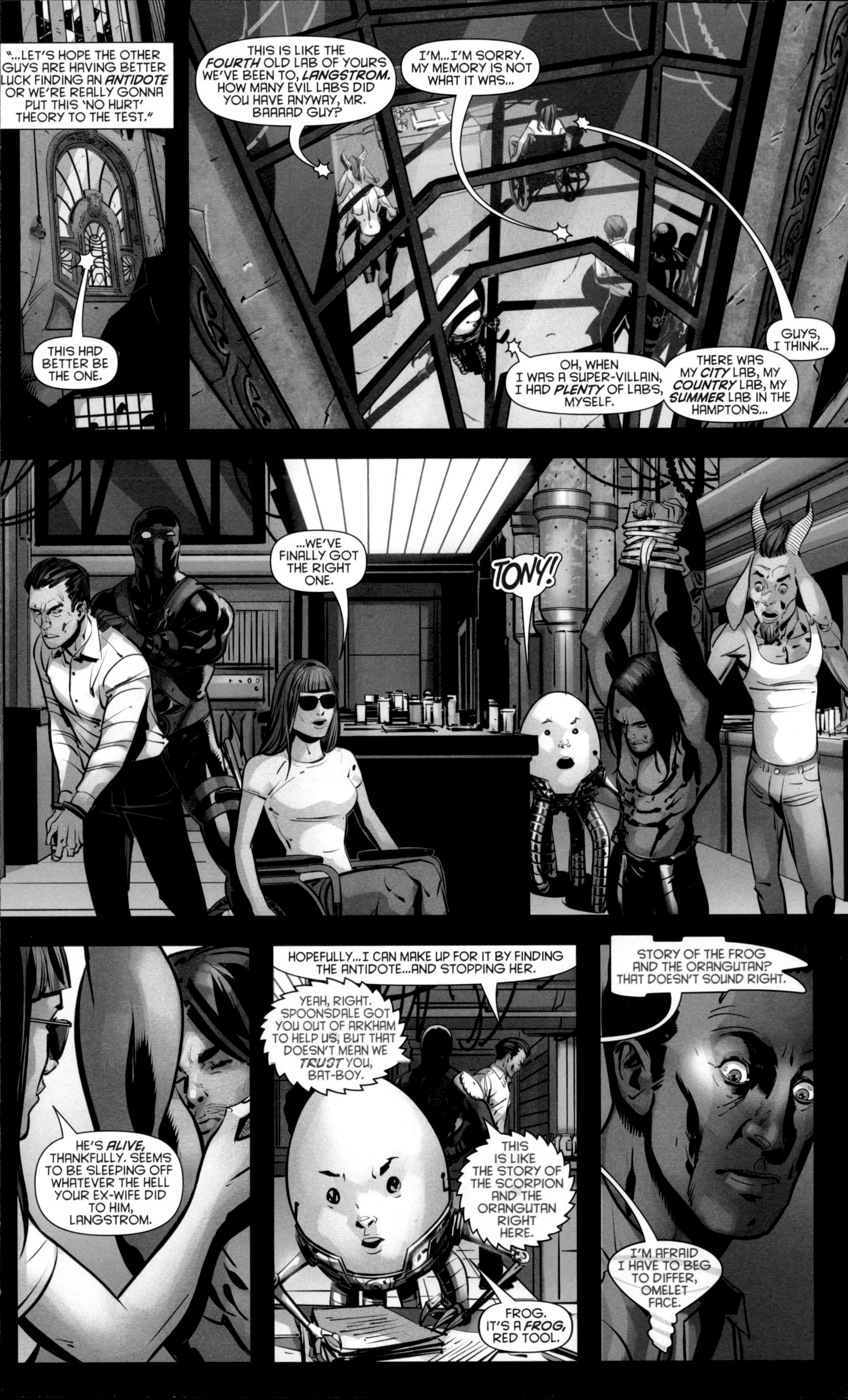
"...LET'S HOPE THE OTHER GUYS ARE HAVING BETTER LUCK FINDING AN ANTIDOTE OR WE'RE REALLY GONNA PUT THIS 'NO HURT' THEORY TO THE TEST."
THIS HAD BETTER BE THE ONE.
THIS IS LIKE THE FOURTH OLD LAB OF YOURS WE'VE BEEN TO, LANGSTROM. HOW MANY EVIL LABS DID YOU HAVE ANYWAY, MR. BAAAAAD GUY?
I'M... I'M SORRY. MY MEMORY IS NOT WHAT IT WAS...
OH, WHEN I WAS A SUPER-VILLAIN, I HAD PLENTY OF LABS, MYSELF.
THERE WAS MY CITY LAB, MY COUNTRY LAB, MY SUMMER LAB IN THE HAMPTONS...
GUYS, I THINK...
...WE'VE FINALLY GOT THE RIGHT ONE.
TONY!
HE'S ALIVE, THANKFULLY. SEEMS TO BE SLEEPING OFF WHATEVER THE HELL YOUR EX-WIFE DID TO HIM, LANGSTROM.
HOPEFULLY...I CAN MAKE UP FOR IT BY FINDING THE ANTIDOTE...AND STOPPING HER.
YEAH, RIGHT. SPOONSDALE GOT YOU OUT OF ARKHAM TO HELP US, BUT THAT DOESN'T MEAN WE TRUST YOU, BAT-BOY.
THIS IS LIKE THE STORY OF THE SCORPION AND THE ORANGUTAN RIGHT HERE.
FROG. IT'S A FROG, RED TOOL.
STORY OF THE FROG AND THE ORANGUTAN? THAT DOESN'T SOUND RIGHT.
I'M AFRAID I HAVE TO BEG TO DIFFER, OMELET FACE.

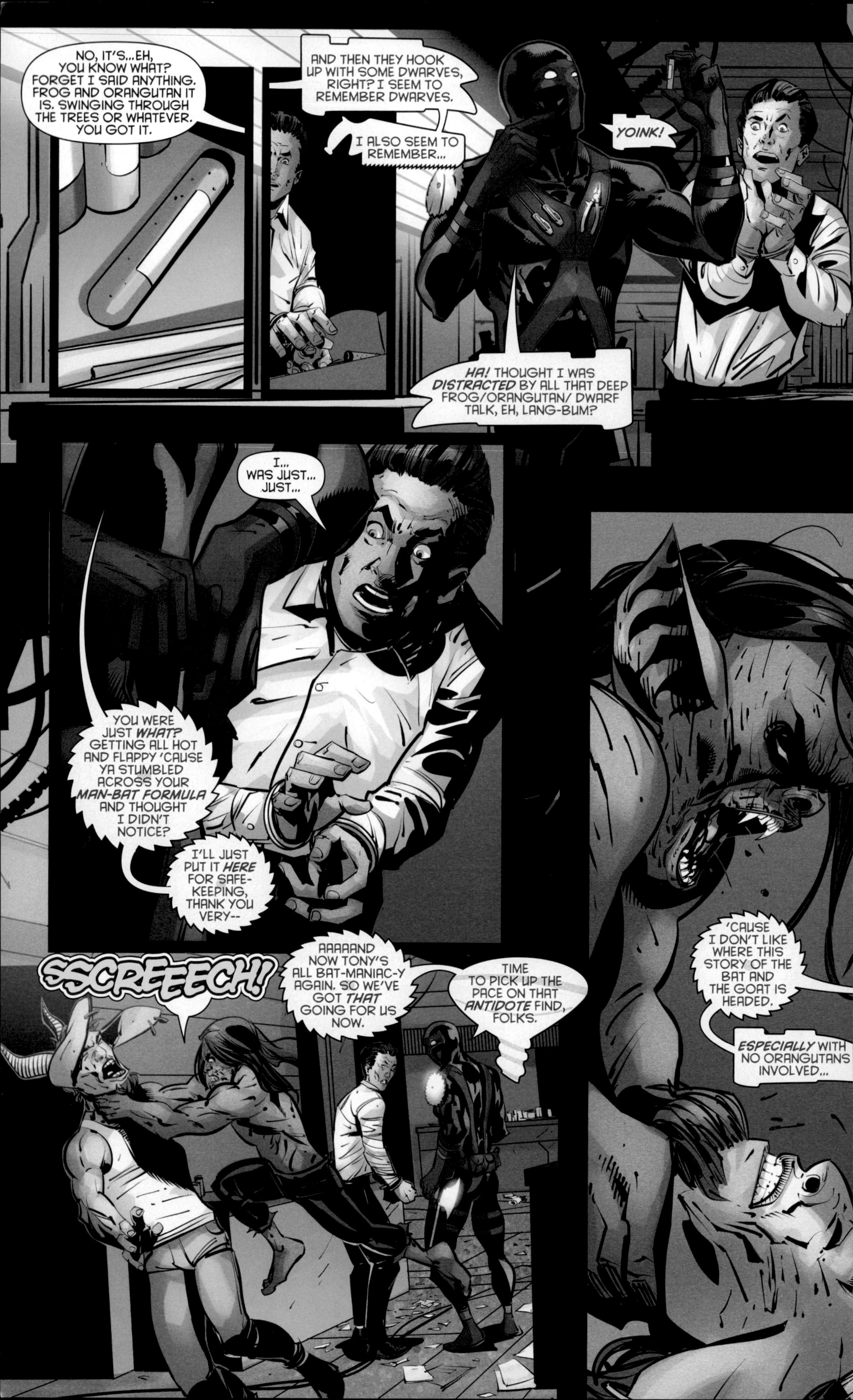
NO, IT'S...EH, YOU KNOW WHAT? FORGET I SAID ANYTHING. FROG AND ORANGUTAN IT IS. SWINGING THROUGH THE TREES OR WHATEVER. YOU GOT IT.
AND THEN THEY HOOK UP WITH SOME DWARVES, RIGHT? I SEEM TO REMEMBER DWARVES.
I ALSO SEEM TO REMEMBER...
YOINK!
HA! THOUGHT I WAS DISTRACTED BY ALL THAT DEEP FROG/ORANGUTAN/ DWARF TALK, EH, LANG-BUM?
I... WAS JUST... JUST...
YOU WERE JUST WHAT? GETTING ALL HOT AND FLAPPY 'CAUSE YA STUMBLED ACROSS YOUR MAN-BAT FORMULA AND THOUGHT I DIDN'T NOTICE?
I'LL JUST PUT IT HERE FOR SAFE-KEEPING, THANK YOU VERY--
'CAUSE I DON'T LIKE WHERE THIS STORY OF THE BAT AND THE GOAT IS HEADED.
ESPECIALLY WITH NO ORANGUTANS INVOLVED...
SSCREEEECH!
AAAAAND NOW TONY'S ALL BAT-MANIAC-Y AGAIN. SO WE'VE GOT THAT GOING FOR US NOW.
TIME TO PICK UP THE PACE ON THAT ANTIDOTE FIND, FOLKS.

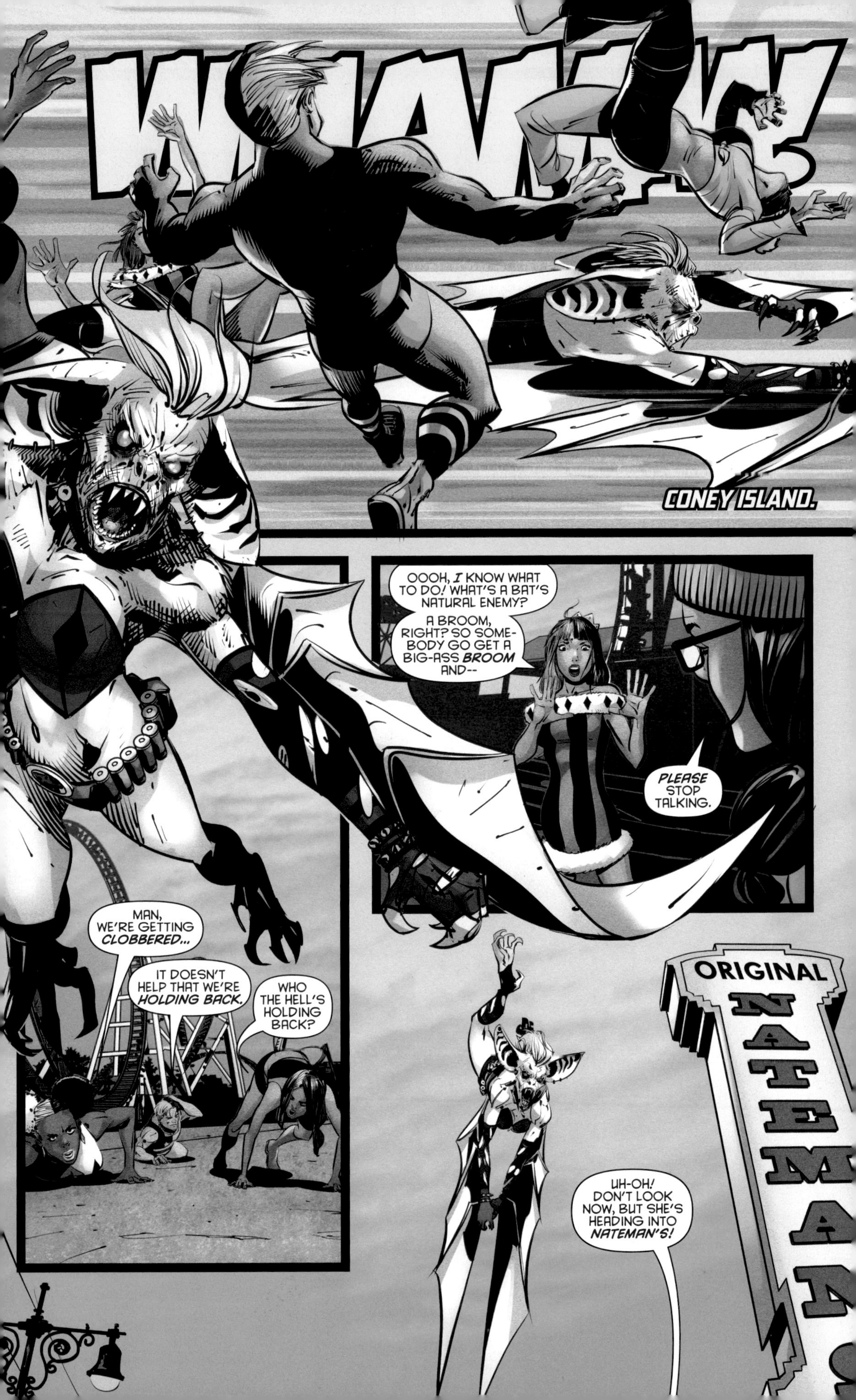
CONEY ISLAND.
OOOH, *I* KNOW WHAT TO DO! WHAT'S A BAT'S NATURAL ENEMY?
A BROOM, RIGHT? SO SOMEBODY GO GET A BIG-ASS *BROOM* AND--
*PLEASE* STOP TALKING.
MAN, WE'RE GETTING *CLOBBERED...*
IT DOESN'T HELP THAT WE'RE *HOLDING BACK.*
WHO THE HELL'S HOLDING BACK?
ORIGINAL
UH-OH! DON'T LOOK NOW, BUT SHE'S HEADING INTO *NATEMAN'S!*

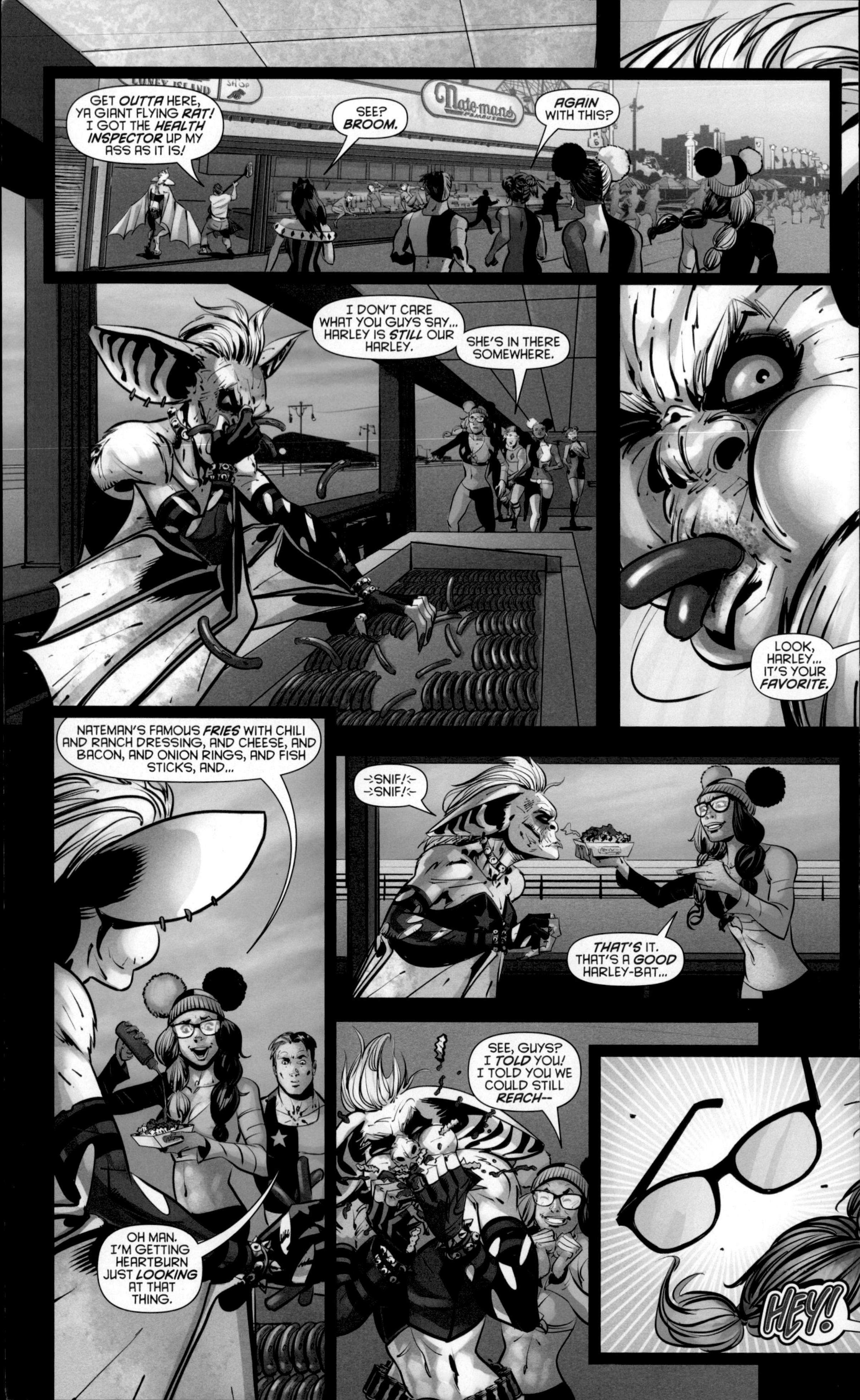
CONEY ISLAND
SHOP
Nate-man's FAMOUS
GET OUTTA HERE, YA GIANT FLYING RAT! I GOT THE HEALTH INSPECTOR UP MY ASS AS IT IS!
SEE? BROOM.
AGAIN WITH THIS?
I DON'T CARE WHAT YOU GUYS SAY... HARLEY IS STILL OUR HARLEY.
SHE'S IN THERE SOMEWHERE.
LOOK, HARLEY... IT'S YOUR FAVORITE.
NATEMAN'S FAMOUS FRIES WITH CHILI AND RANCH DRESSING, AND CHEESE, AND BACON, AND ONION RINGS, AND FISH STICKS, AND...
OH MAN. I'M GETTING HEARTBURN JUST LOOKING AT THAT THING.
-SNIF!-
-SNIF!-
THAT'S IT. THAT'S A GOOD HARLEY-BAT...
SEE, GUYS? I TOLD YOU! I TOLD YOU WE COULD STILL REACH--
HEY!

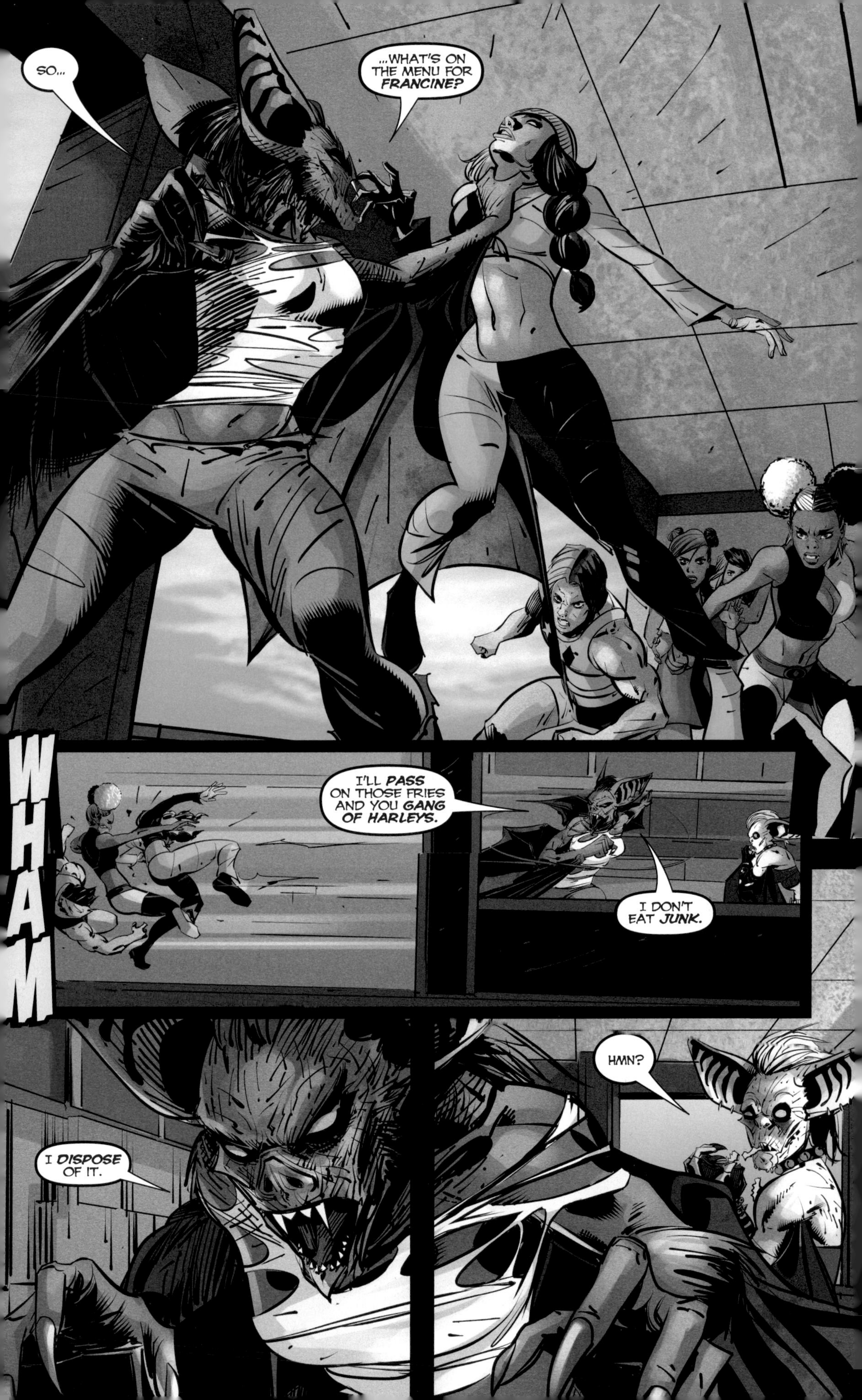
SO...
...WHAT'S ON THE MENU FOR FRANCINE?
WHAM
I'LL PASS ON THOSE FRIES AND YOU GANG OF HARLEYS.
I DON'T EAT JUNK.
I DISPOSE OF IT.
HMN?

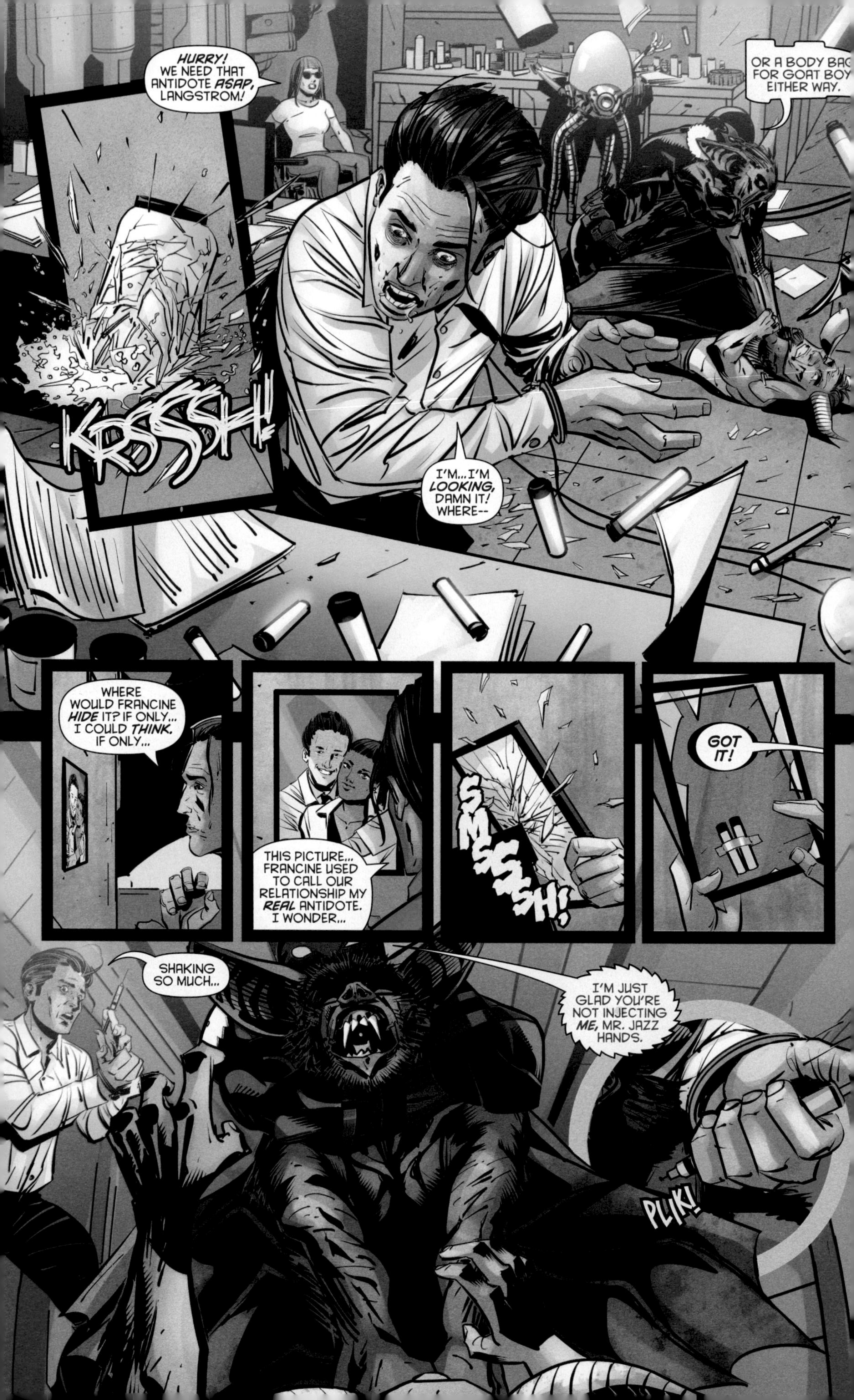
HURRY! WE NEED THAT ANTIDOTE ASAP, LANGSTROM!
OR A BODY BAG FOR GOAT BOY EITHER WAY.
KRSSSH!
I'M...I'M LOOKING, DAMN IT! WHERE--
WHERE WOULD FRANCINE HIDE IT? IF ONLY... I COULD THINK. IF ONLY...
THIS PICTURE... FRANCINE USED TO CALL OUR RELATIONSHIP MY REAL ANTIDOTE. I WONDER...
SMSSSH!
GOT IT!
SHAKING SO MUCH...
I'M JUST GLAD YOU'RE NOT INJECTING ME, MR. JAZZ HANDS.
PLIK!

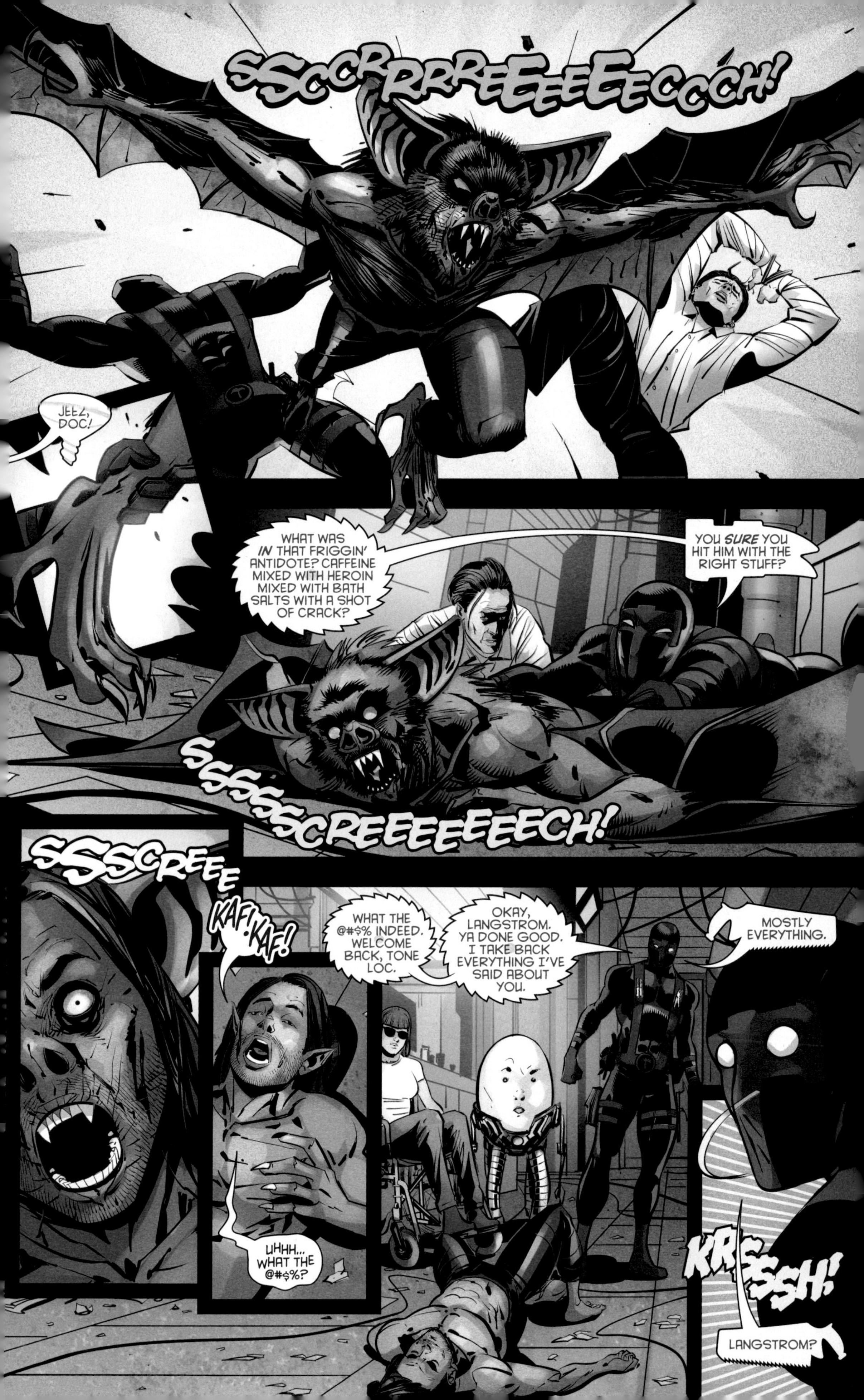
SSCCRRRRREEEEEEECCCCH!
JEEZ, DOC!
WHAT WAS *IN* THAT FRIGGIN' ANTIDOTE? CAFFEINE MIXED WITH HEROIN MIXED WITH BATH SALTS WITH A SHOT OF CRACK?
YOU *SURE* YOU HIT HIM WITH THE RIGHT STUFF?
SSSSSSCREEEEEEEEECH!
SSSCREEEE
KAF! KAF!
UHHH... WHAT THE @#$%?
WHAT THE @#$% INDEED. WELCOME BACK, TONE LOC.
OKAY, LANGSTROM. YA DONE GOOD. I TAKE BACK EVERYTHING I'VE SAID ABOUT YOU.
MOSTLY EVERYTHING.
KRSSSH!
LANGSTROM?

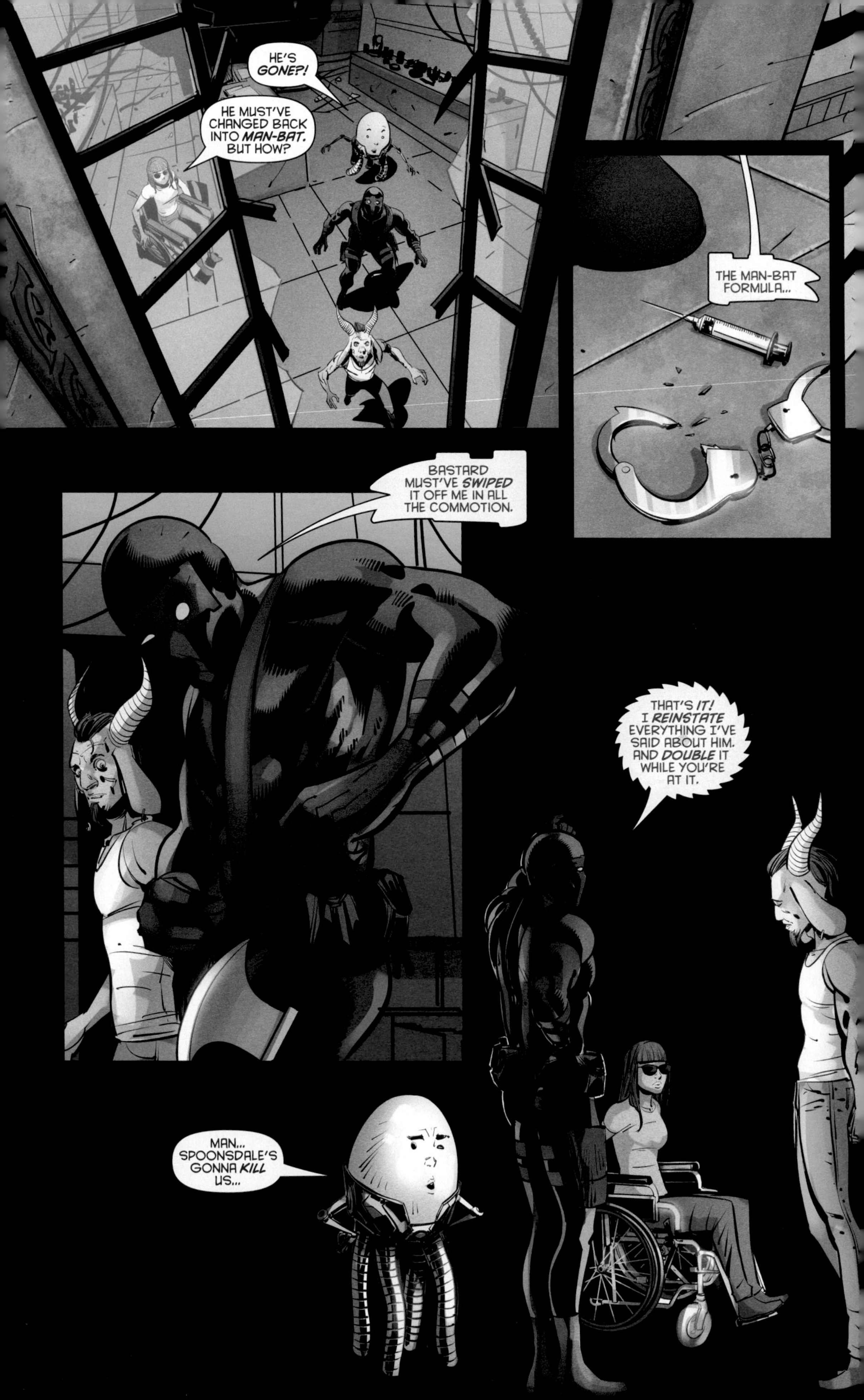

HE'S *GONE?!*
HE MUST'VE CHANGED BACK INTO *MAN-BAT.* BUT HOW?
THE MAN-BAT FORMULA...
BASTARD MUST'VE *SWIPED* IT OFF ME IN ALL THE COMMOTION.
THAT'S *IT!* I *REINSTATE* EVERYTHING I'VE SAID ABOUT HIM. AND *DOUBLE* IT WHILE YOU'RE AT IT.
MAN... SPOONSDALE'S GONNA *KILL* US...

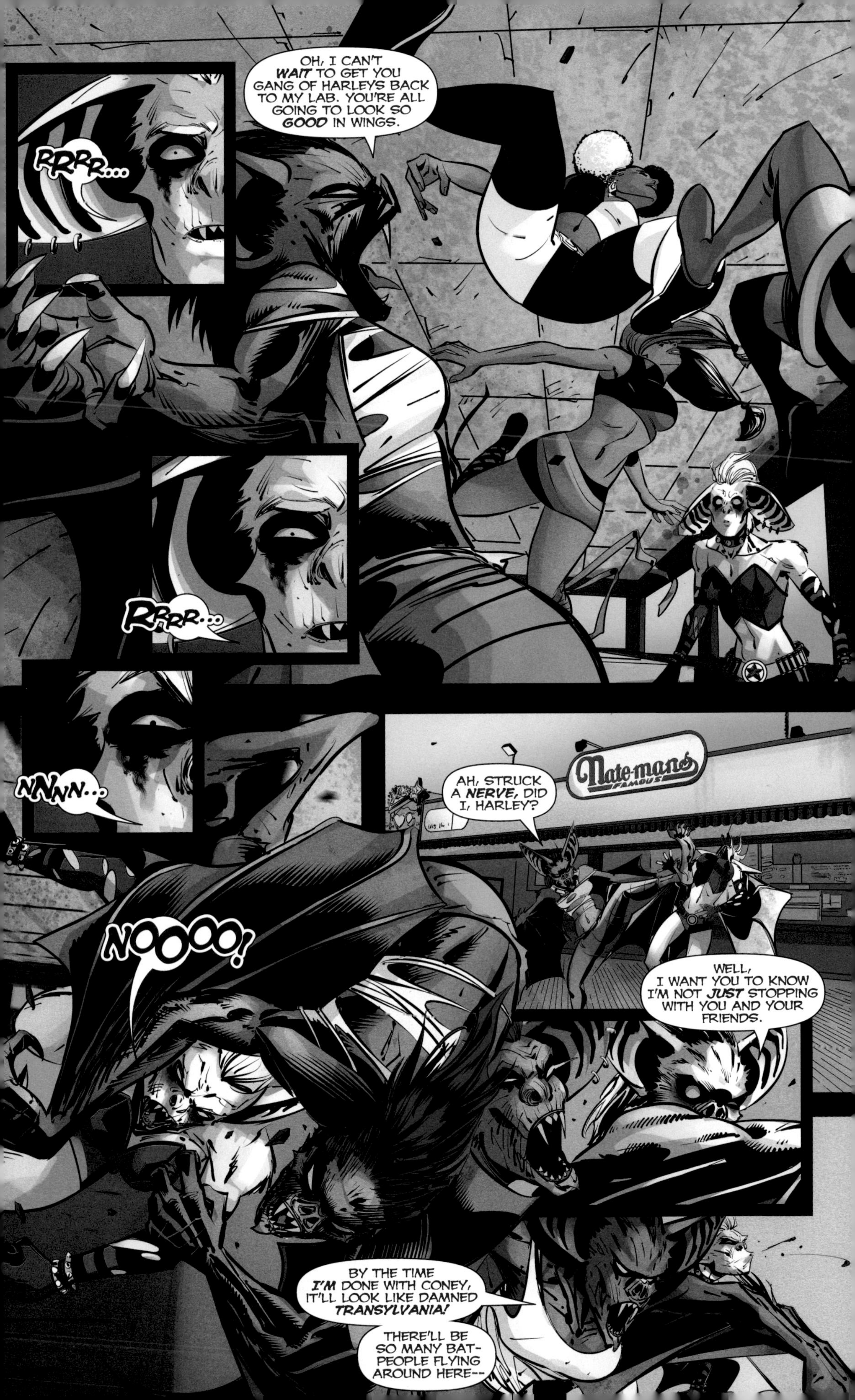
OH, I CAN'T *WAIT* TO GET YOU GANG OF HARLEYS BACK TO MY LAB. YOU'RE ALL GOING TO LOOK SO *GOOD* IN WINGS.
RRRR...
RRRR...
NNNN...
Nate-mans FAMOUS
AH, STRUCK A *NERVE*, DID I, HARLEY?
NOOOO!
WELL, I WANT YOU TO KNOW I'M NOT *JUST* STOPPING WITH YOU AND YOUR FRIENDS.
BY THE TIME *I'M* DONE WITH CONEY, IT'LL LOOK LIKE DAMNED *TRANSYLVANIA!*
THERE'LL BE SO MANY BAT-PEOPLE FLYING AROUND HERE--

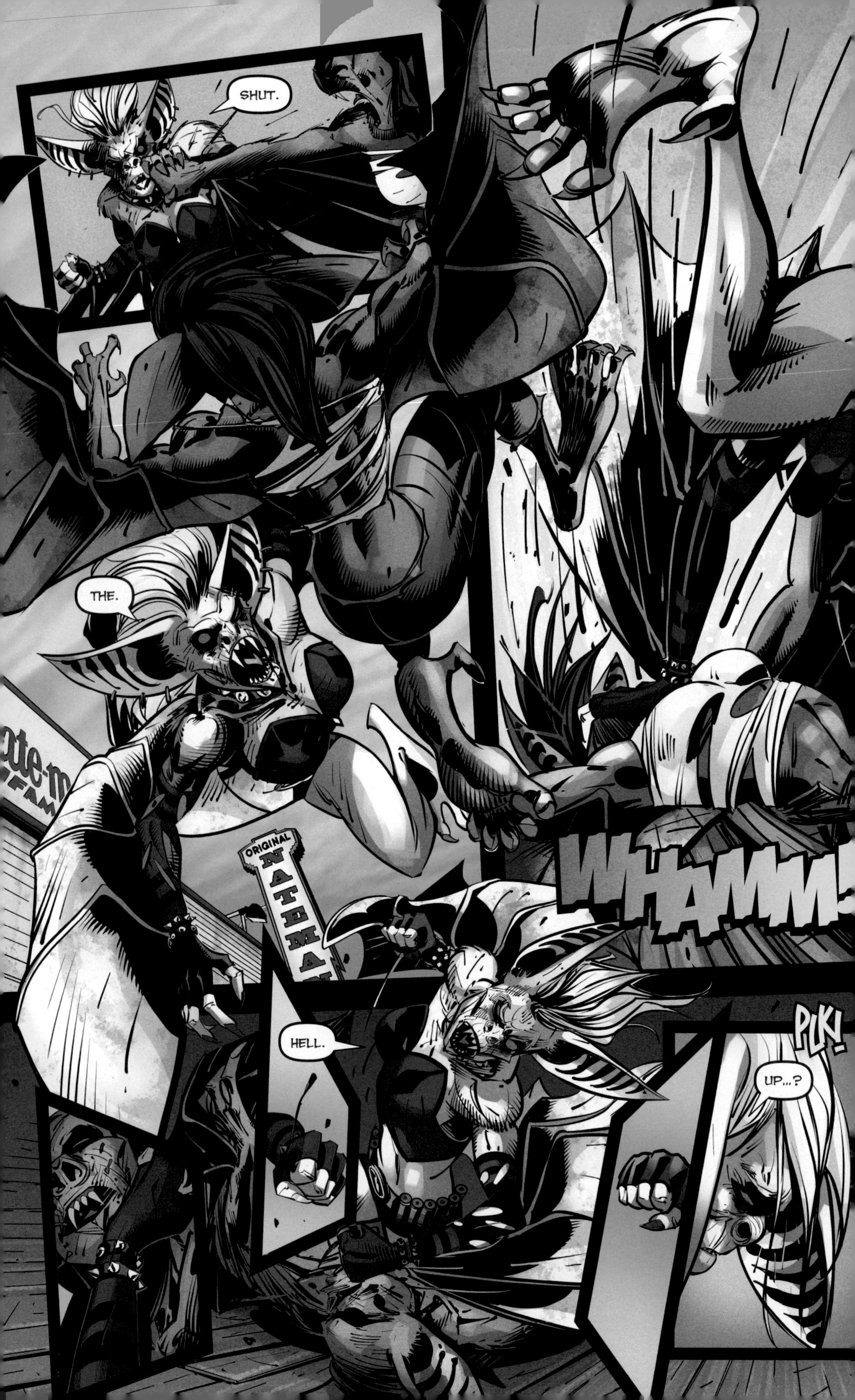
SHUT.
THE.
ORIGINAL
NATEMA
WHAMM!
HELL.
PLK!
UP...?

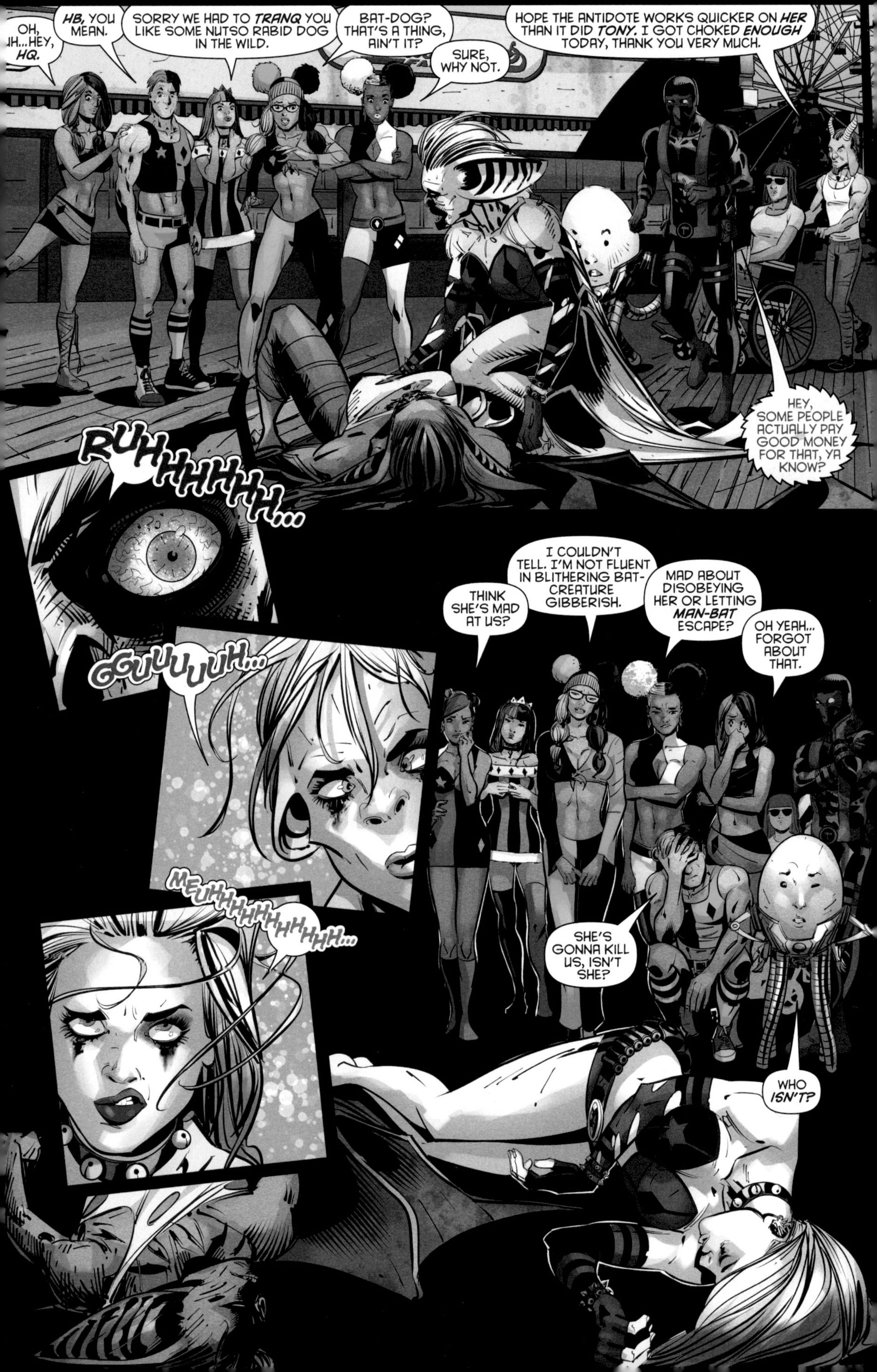

OH, UH...HEY, HQ.
HB, YOU MEAN.
SORRY WE HAD TO TRANQ YOU LIKE SOME NUTSO RABID DOG IN THE WILD.
BAT-DOG? THAT'S A THING, AIN'T IT?
SURE, WHY NOT.
HOPE THE ANTIDOTE WORKS QUICKER ON HER THAN IT DID TONY. I GOT CHOKED ENOUGH TODAY, THANK YOU VERY MUCH.
HEY, SOME PEOPLE ACTUALLY PAY GOOD MONEY FOR THAT, YA KNOW?
RUHHHHHHH...
GGUUUUUUH...
MEUHHHHHHHHHHH...
THINK SHE'S MAD AT US?
I COULDN'T TELL. I'M NOT FLUENT IN BLITHERING BAT-CREATURE GIBBERISH.
MAD ABOUT DISOBEYING HER OR LETTING MAN-BAT ESCAPE?
OH YEAH... FORGOT ABOUT THAT.
SHE'S GONNA KILL US, ISN'T SHE?
WHO ISN'T?

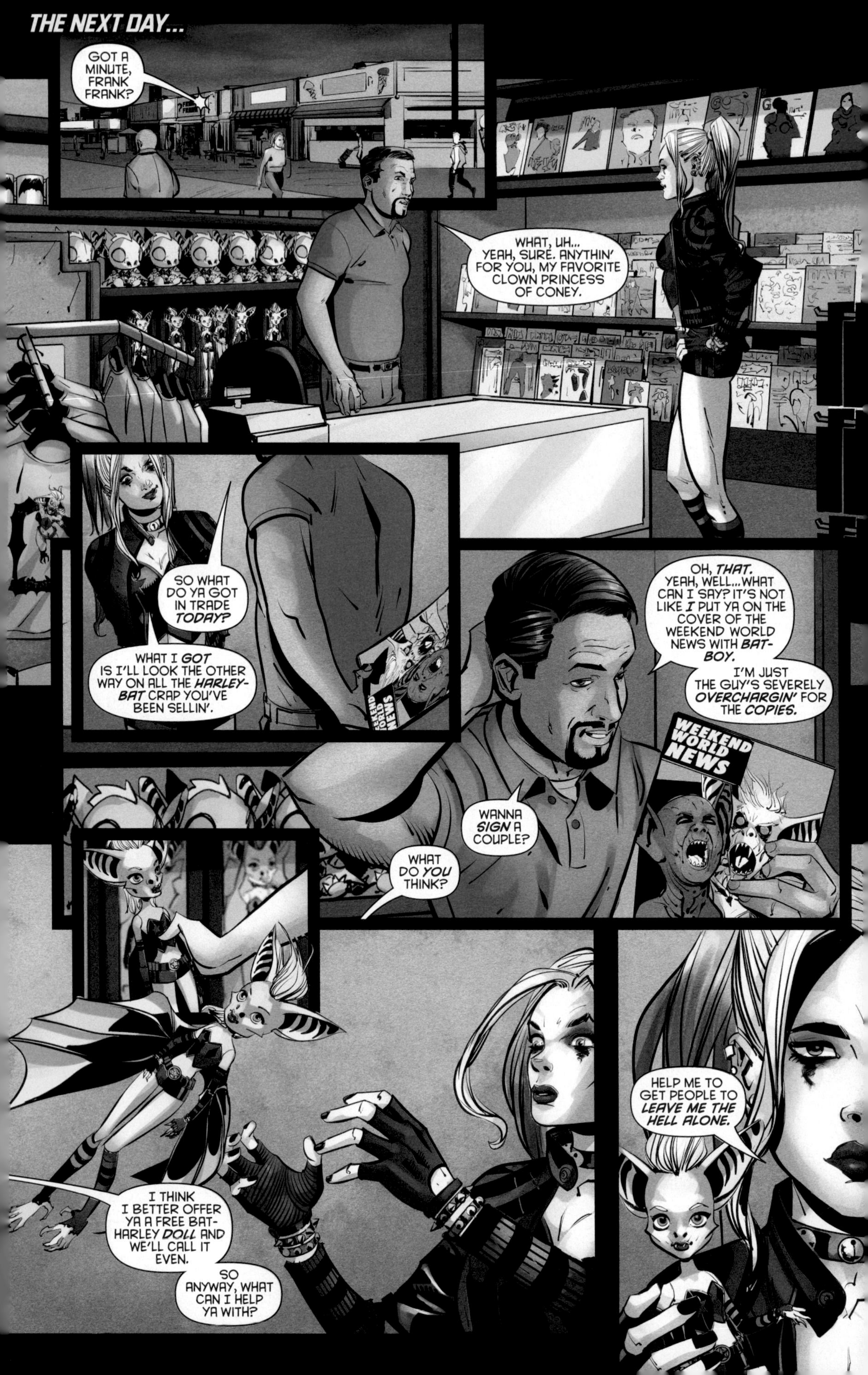
THE NEXT DAY...
GOT A MINUTE, FRANK FRANK?
WHAT, UH... YEAH, SURE. ANYTHIN' FOR YOU, MY FAVORITE CLOWN PRINCESS OF CONEY.
SO WHAT DO YA GOT IN TRADE TODAY?
WHAT I GOT IS I'LL LOOK THE OTHER WAY ON ALL THE HARLEY-BAT CRAP YOU'VE BEEN SELLIN'.
OH, THAT. YEAH, WELL...WHAT CAN I SAY? IT'S NOT LIKE I PUT YA ON THE COVER OF THE WEEKEND WORLD NEWS WITH BAT-BOY.
I'M JUST THE GUY'S SEVERELY OVERCHARGIN' FOR THE COPIES.
WEEKEND WORLD NEWS
WANNA SIGN A COUPLE?
WHAT DO YOU THINK?
I THINK I BETTER OFFER YA A FREE BAT-HARLEY DOLL AND WE'LL CALL IT EVEN.
SO ANYWAY, WHAT CAN I HELP YA WITH?
HELP ME TO GET PEOPLE TO LEAVE ME THE HELL ALONE.

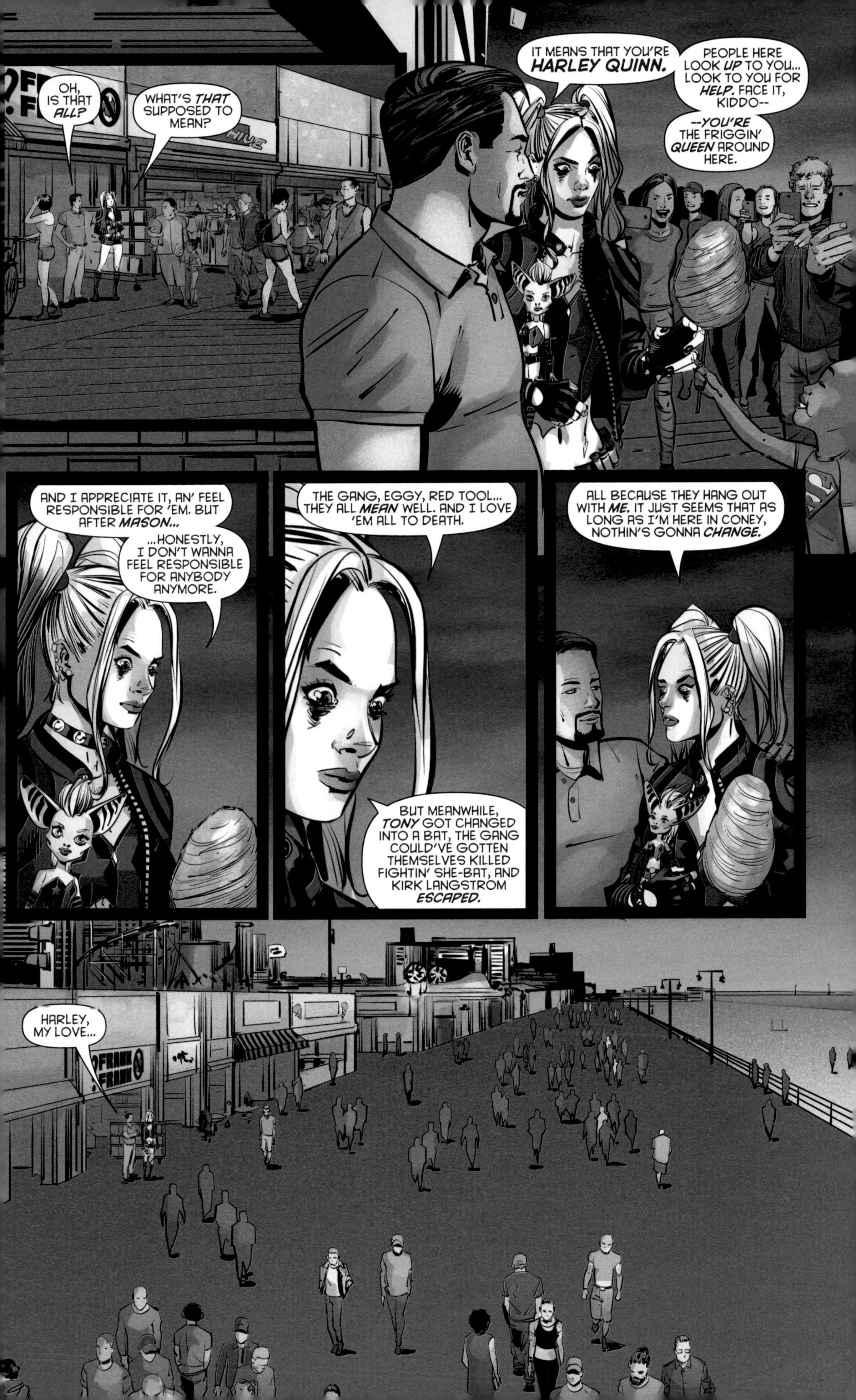

OH, IS THAT ALL?
WHAT'S THAT SUPPOSED TO MEAN?
IT MEANS THAT YOU'RE HARLEY QUINN.
PEOPLE HERE LOOK UP TO YOU... LOOK TO YOU FOR HELP. FACE IT, KIDDO--
--YOU'RE THE FRIGGIN' QUEEN AROUND HERE.
AND I APPRECIATE IT, AN' FEEL RESPONSIBLE FOR 'EM. BUT AFTER MASON...
...HONESTLY, I DON'T WANNA FEEL RESPONSIBLE FOR ANYBODY ANYMORE.
THE GANG, EGGY, RED TOOL... THEY ALL MEAN WELL. AND I LOVE 'EM ALL TO DEATH.
BUT MEANWHILE, TONY GOT CHANGED INTO A BAT, THE GANG COULD'VE GOTTEN THEMSELVES KILLED FIGHTIN' SHE-BAT, AND KIRK LANGSTROM ESCAPED.
ALL BECAUSE THEY HANG OUT WITH ME. IT JUST SEEMS THAT AS LONG AS I'M HERE IN CONEY, NOTHIN'S GONNA CHANGE.
HARLEY, MY LOVE...

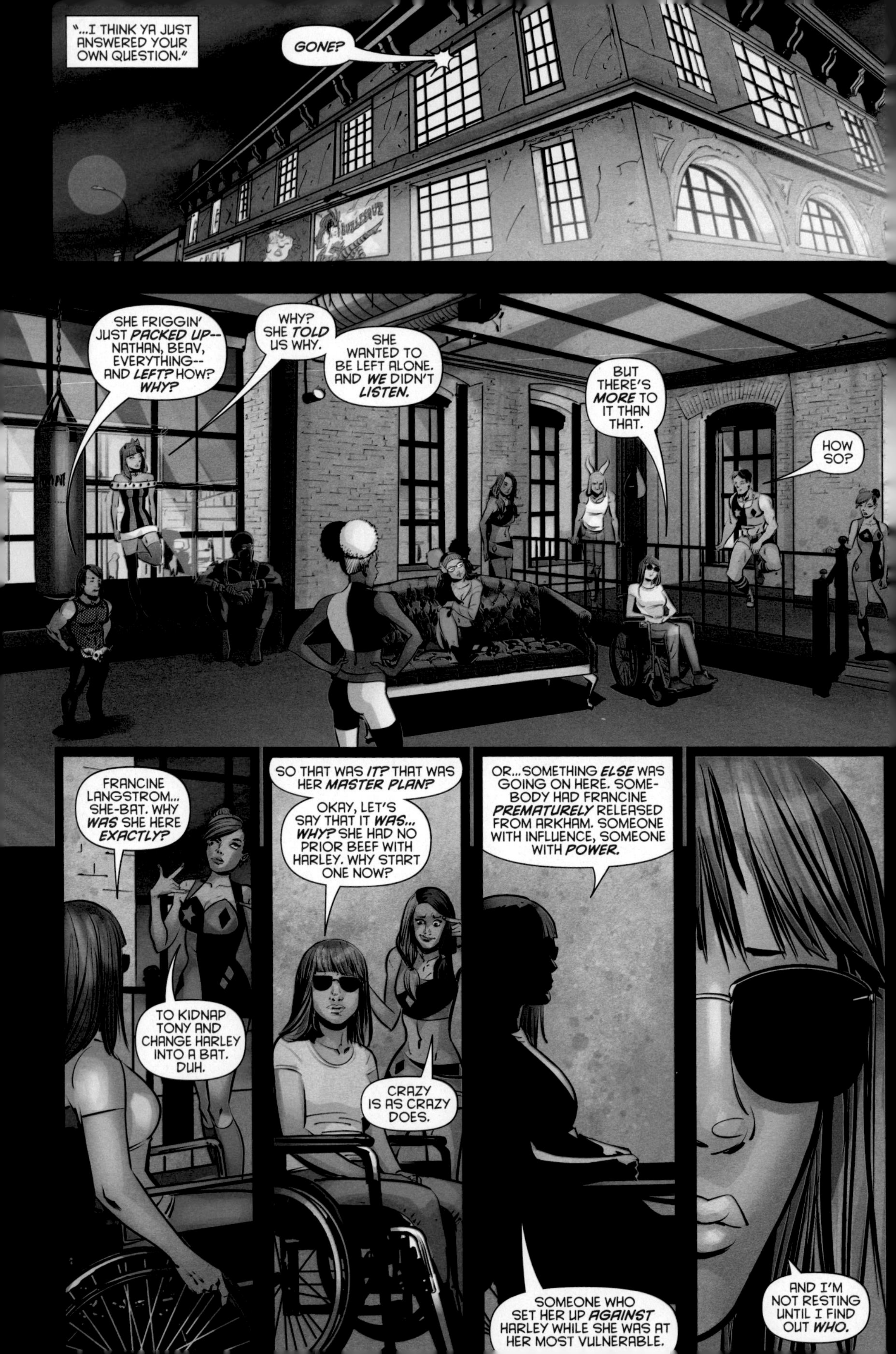
"...I THINK YA JUST ANSWERED YOUR OWN QUESTION."
GONE?
SHE FRIGGIN' JUST PACKED UP-- NATHAN, BEAV, EVERYTHING-- AND LEFT? HOW? WHY?
WHY? SHE TOLD US WHY.
SHE WANTED TO BE LEFT ALONE. AND WE DIDN'T LISTEN.
BUT THERE'S MORE TO IT THAN THAT.
HOW SO?
FRANCINE LANGSTROM... SHE-BAT. WHY WAS SHE HERE EXACTLY?
TO KIDNAP TONY AND CHANGE HARLEY INTO A BAT. DUH.
SO THAT WAS IT? THAT WAS HER MASTER PLAN?
OKAY, LET'S SAY THAT IT WAS... WHY? SHE HAD NO PRIOR BEEF WITH HARLEY. WHY START ONE NOW?
CRAZY IS AS CRAZY DOES.
OR... SOMETHING ELSE WAS GOING ON HERE. SOMEBODY HAD FRANCINE PREMATURELY RELEASED FROM ARKHAM. SOMEONE WITH INFLUENCE, SOMEONE WITH POWER.
SOMEONE WHO SET HER UP AGAINST HARLEY WHILE SHE WAS AT HER MOST VULNERABLE.
AND I'M NOT RESTING UNTIL I FIND OUT WHO.

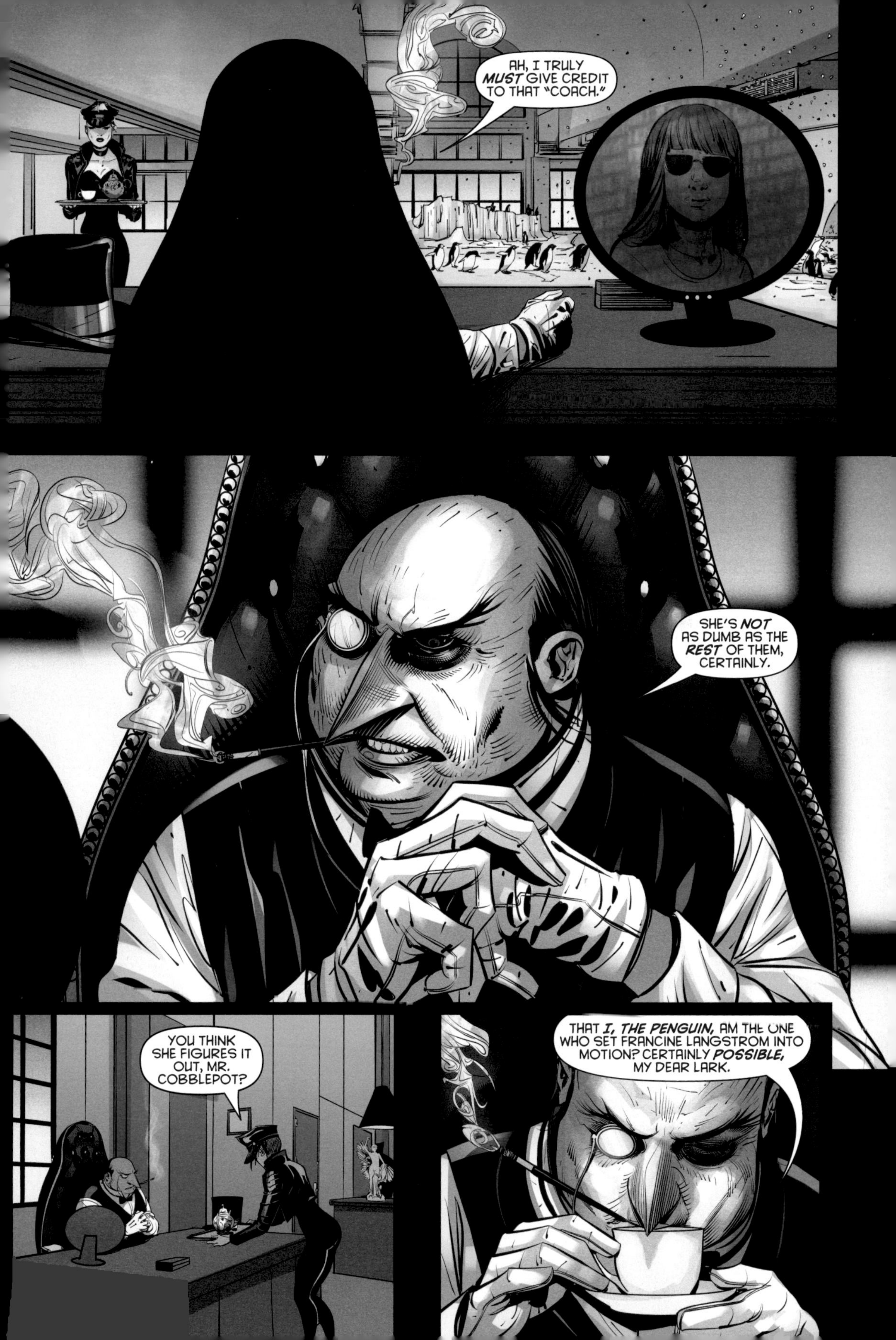
AH, I TRULY MUST GIVE CREDIT TO THAT "COACH."
SHE'S NOT AS DUMB AS THE REST OF THEM, CERTAINLY.
YOU THINK SHE FIGURES IT OUT, MR. COBBLEPOT?
THAT I, THE PENGUIN, AM THE ONE WHO SET FRANCINE LANGSTROM INTO MOTION? CERTAINLY POSSIBLE, MY DEAR LARK.

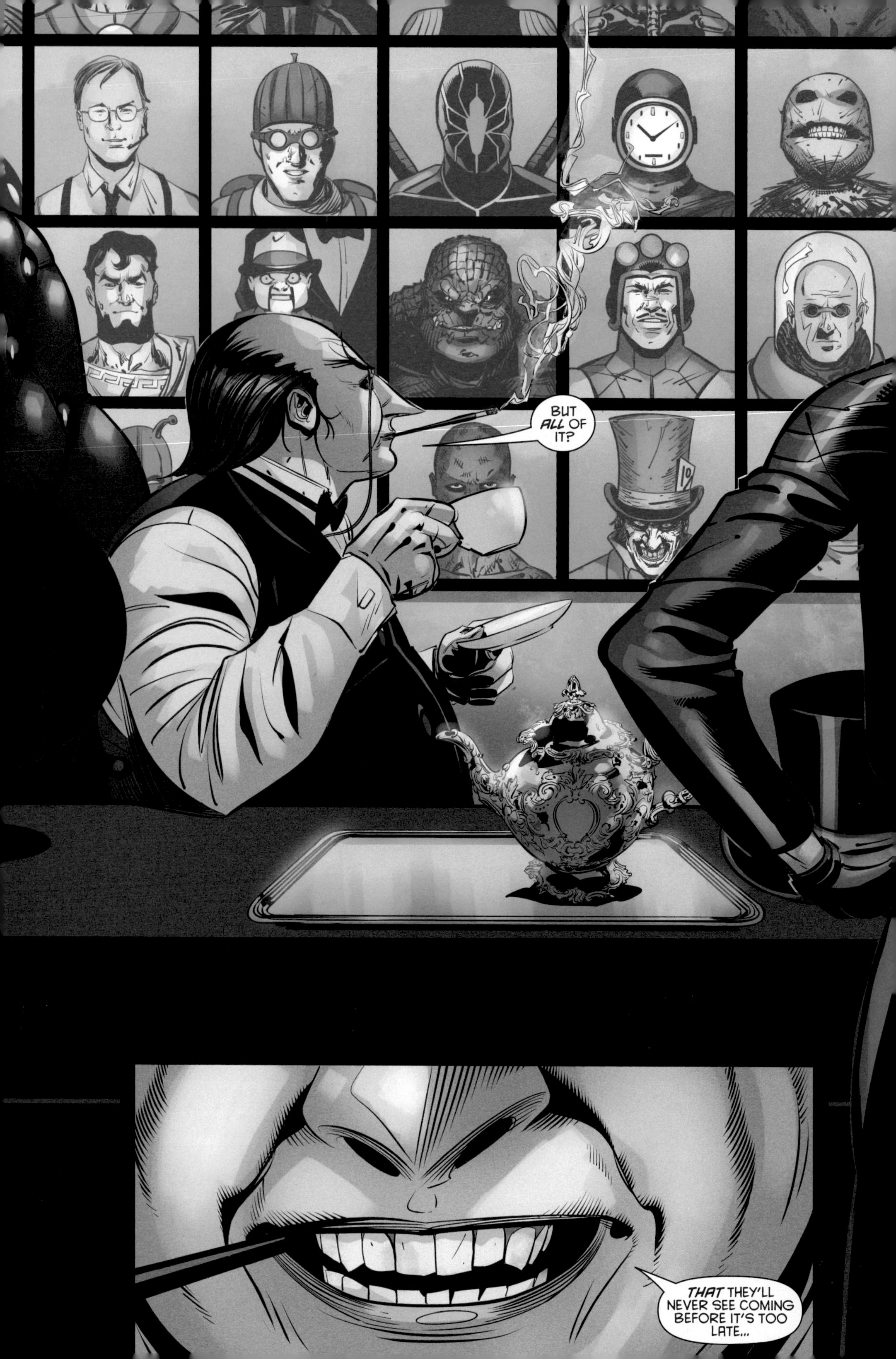
BUT *ALL* OF IT?
*THAT* THEY'LL NEVER SEE COMING BEFORE IT'S TOO LATE...

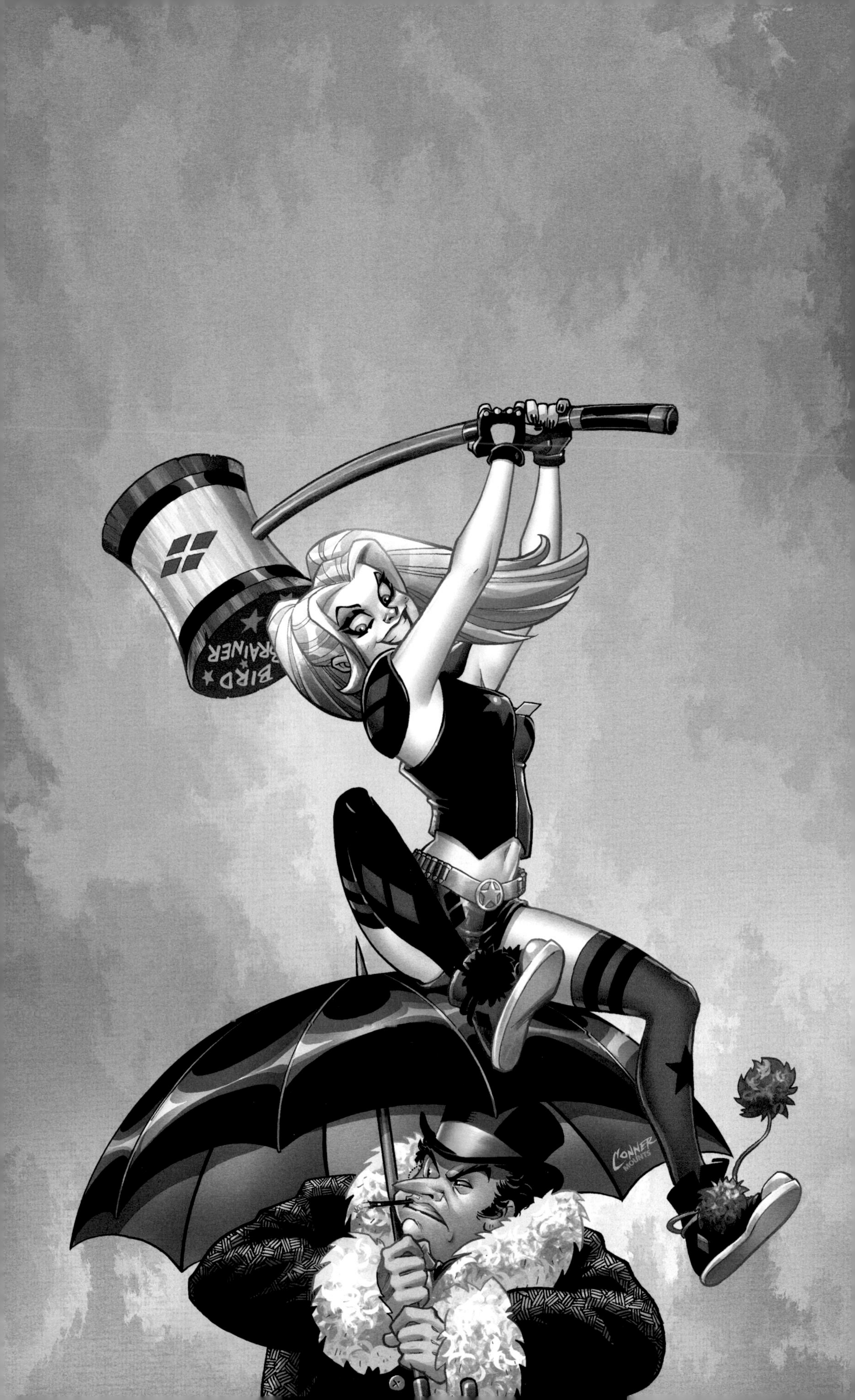
BIRD
RAINER
CONNER
MOUNTS

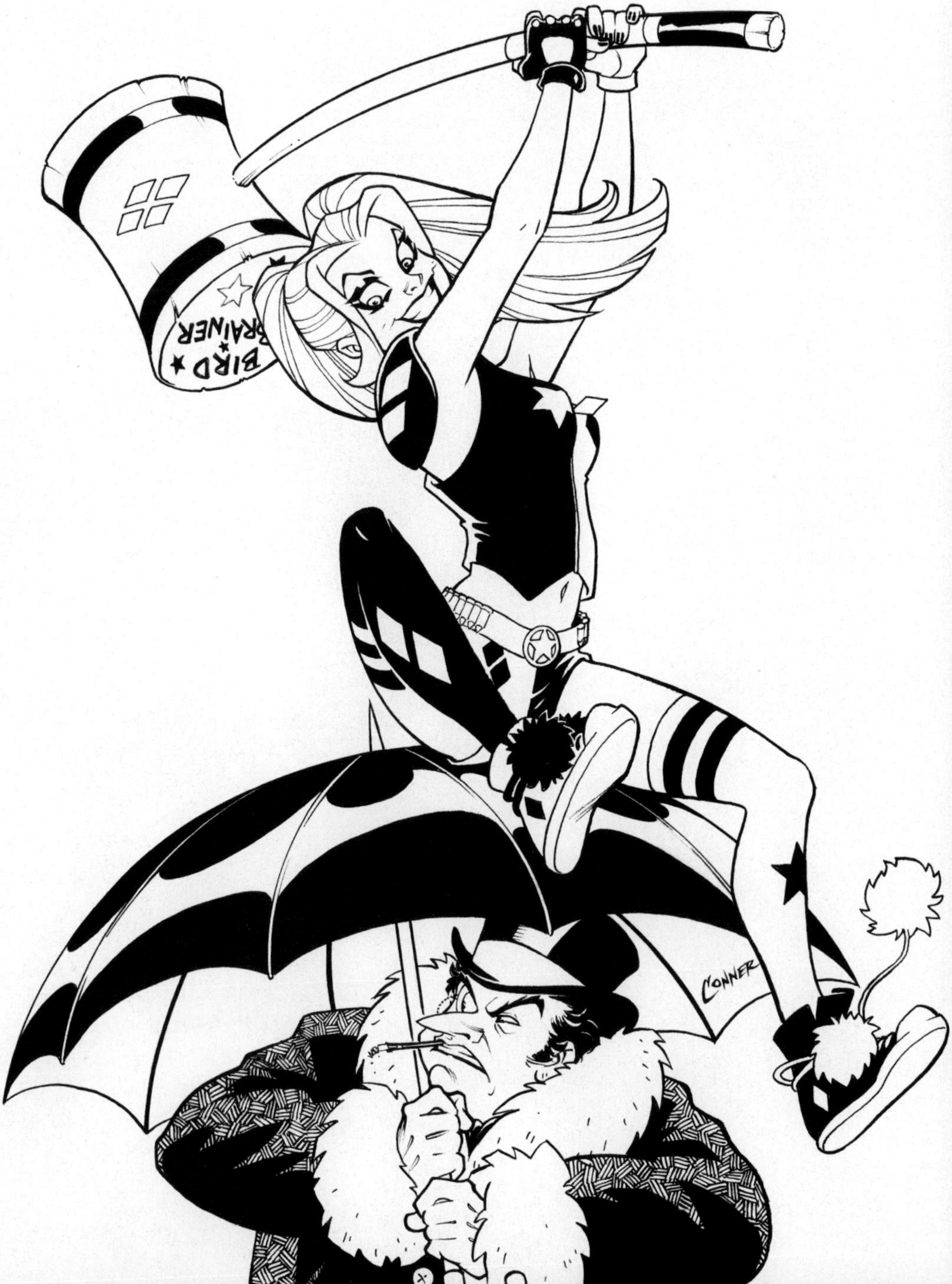
BIRD BRAINER
CONNER

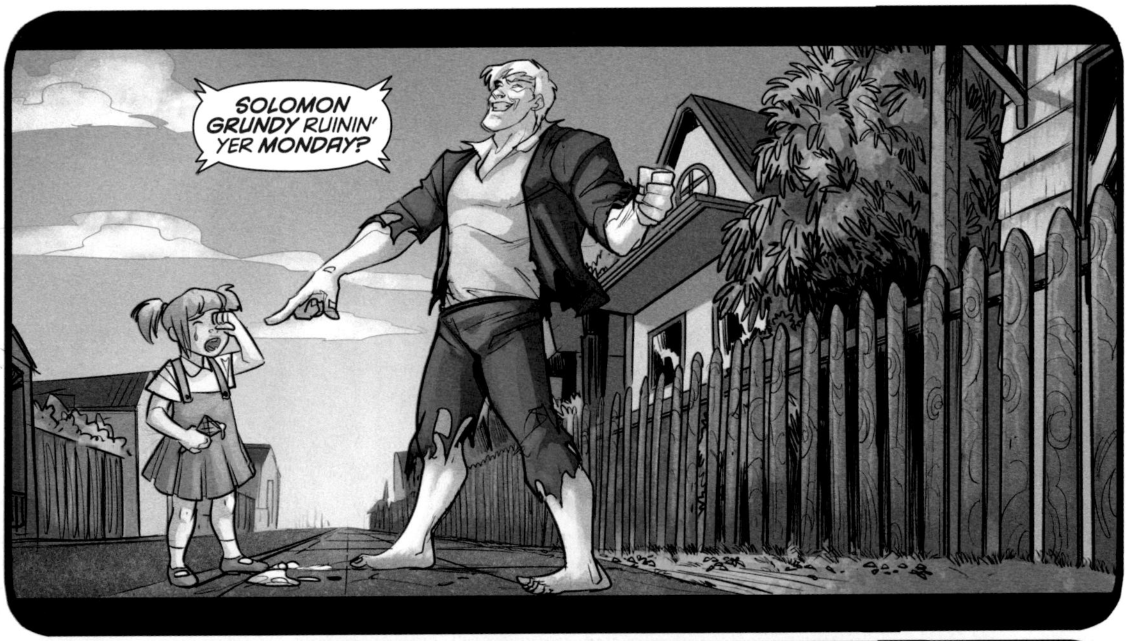
SOLOMON GRUNDY RUININ' YER MONDAY?

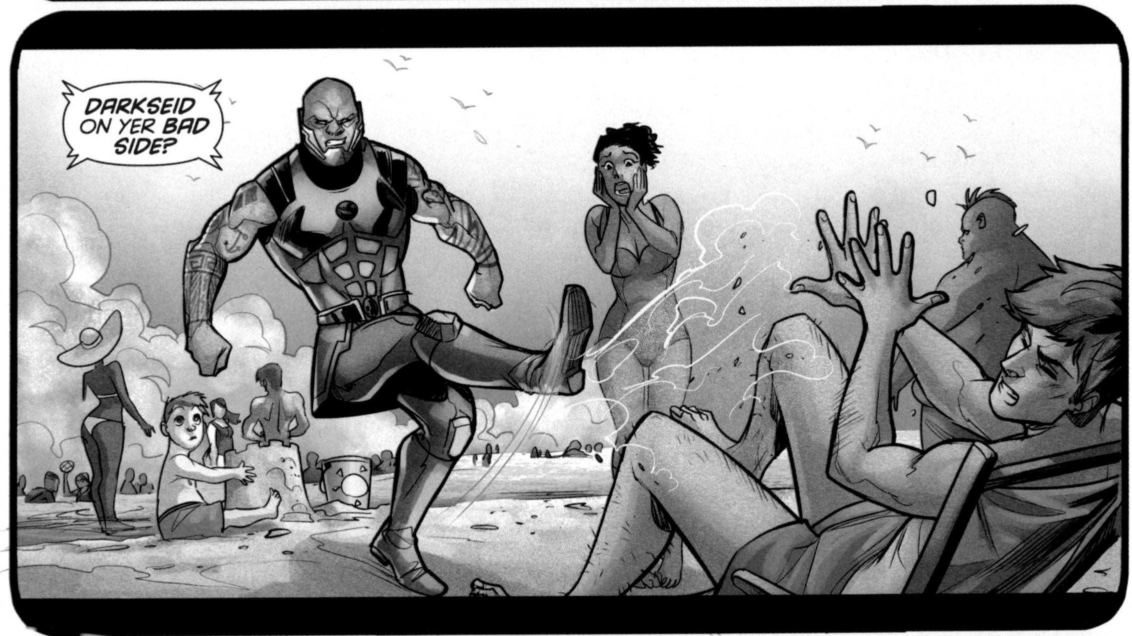
DARKSEID ON YER BAD SIDE?

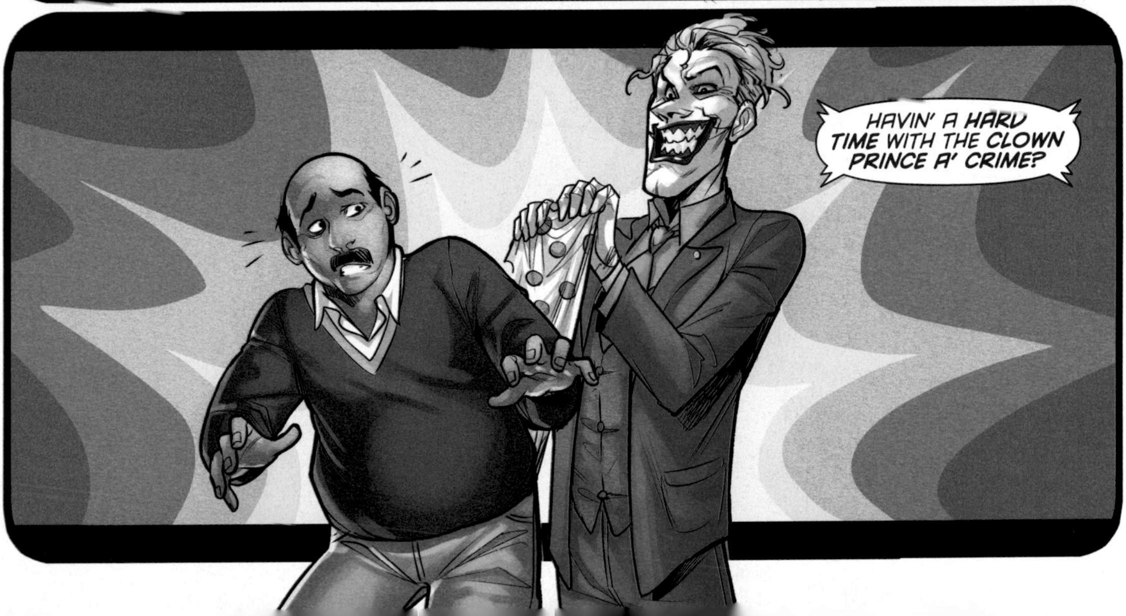
HAVIN' A HARD TIME WITH THE CLOWN PRINCE A' CRIME?

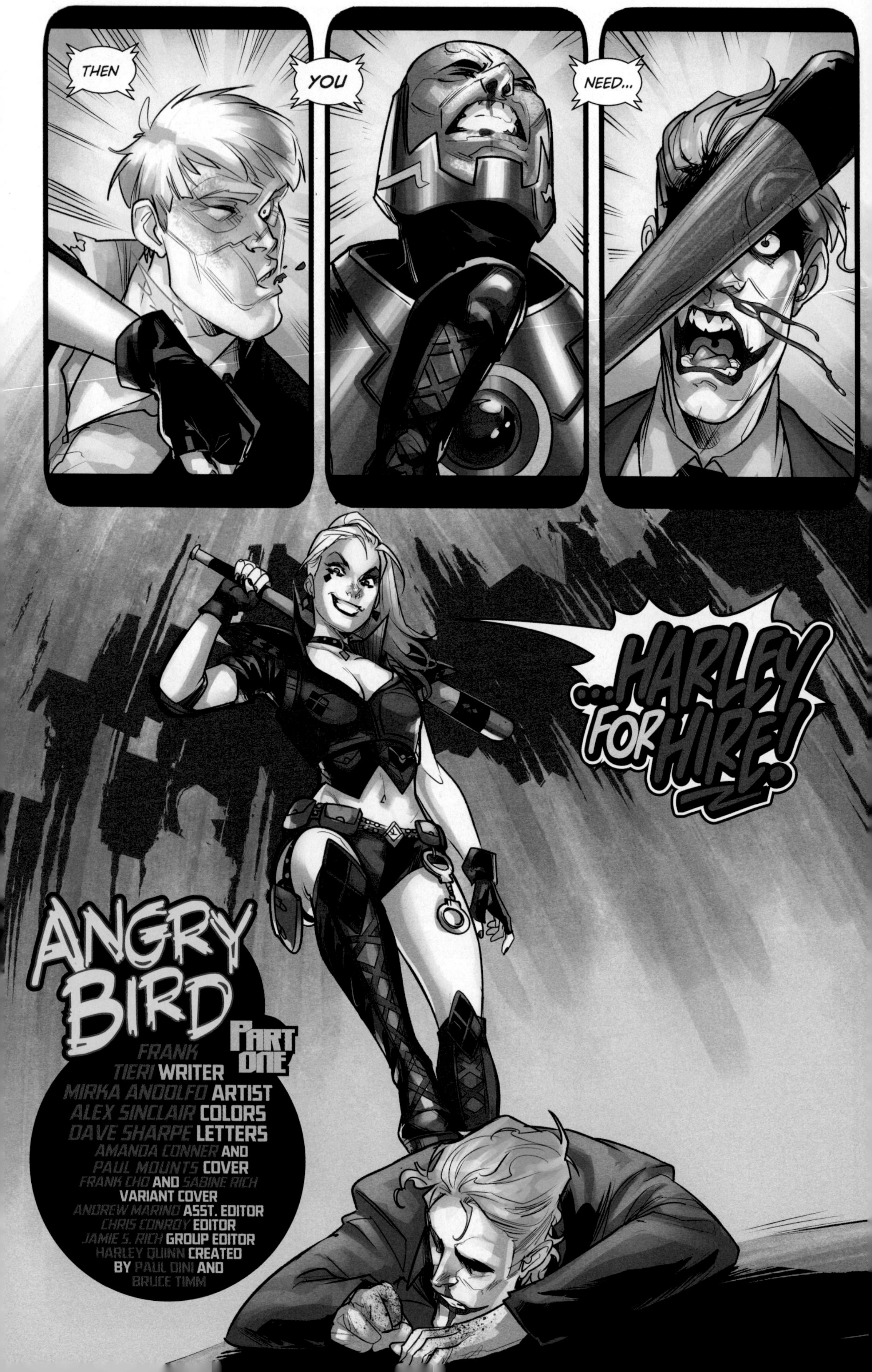
THEN
YOU
NEED...
...HARLEY FOR HIRE!
ANGRY BIRD
PART ONE
FRANK TIERI WRITER
MIRKA ANDOLFO ARTIST
ALEX SINCLAIR COLORS
DAVE SHARPE LETTERS
AMANDA CONNER AND PAUL MOUNTS COVER
FRANK CHO AND SABINE RICH VARIANT COVER
ANDREW MARINO ASST. EDITOR
CHRIS CONROY EDITOR
JAMIE S. RICH GROUP EDITOR
HARLEY QUINN CREATED BY PAUL DINI AND BRUCE TIMM

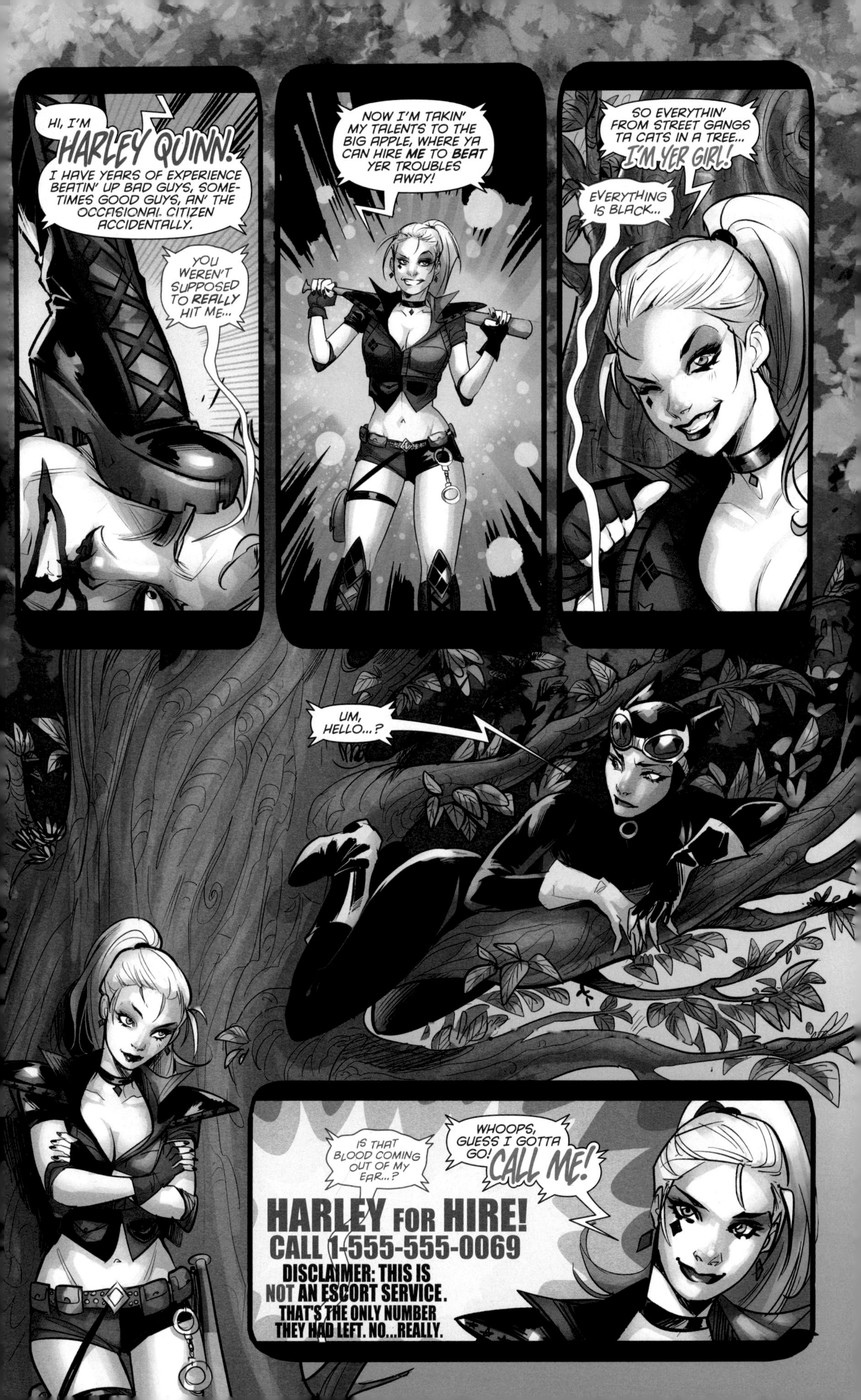
HI, I'M HARLEY QUINN! I HAVE YEARS OF EXPERIENCE BEATIN' UP BAD GUYS, SOME-TIMES GOOD GUYS, AN' THE OCCASIONAL CITIZEN ACCIDENTALLY.
YOU WEREN'T SUPPOSED TO REALLY HIT ME...
NOW I'M TAKIN' MY TALENTS TO THE BIG APPLE, WHERE YA CAN HIRE ME TO BEAT YER TROUBLES AWAY!
SO EVERYTHIN' FROM STREET GANGS TA CATS IN A TREE... I'M YER GIRL!
EVERYTHING IS BLACK...
UM, HELLO...?
IS THAT BLOOD COMING OUT OF MY EAR...?
WHOOPS, GUESS I GOTTA GO! CALL ME!
HARLEY FOR HIRE!
CALL 1-555-555-0069
DISCLAIMER: THIS IS NOT AN ESCORT SERVICE.
THAT'S THE ONLY NUMBER THEY HAD LEFT. NO...REALLY.

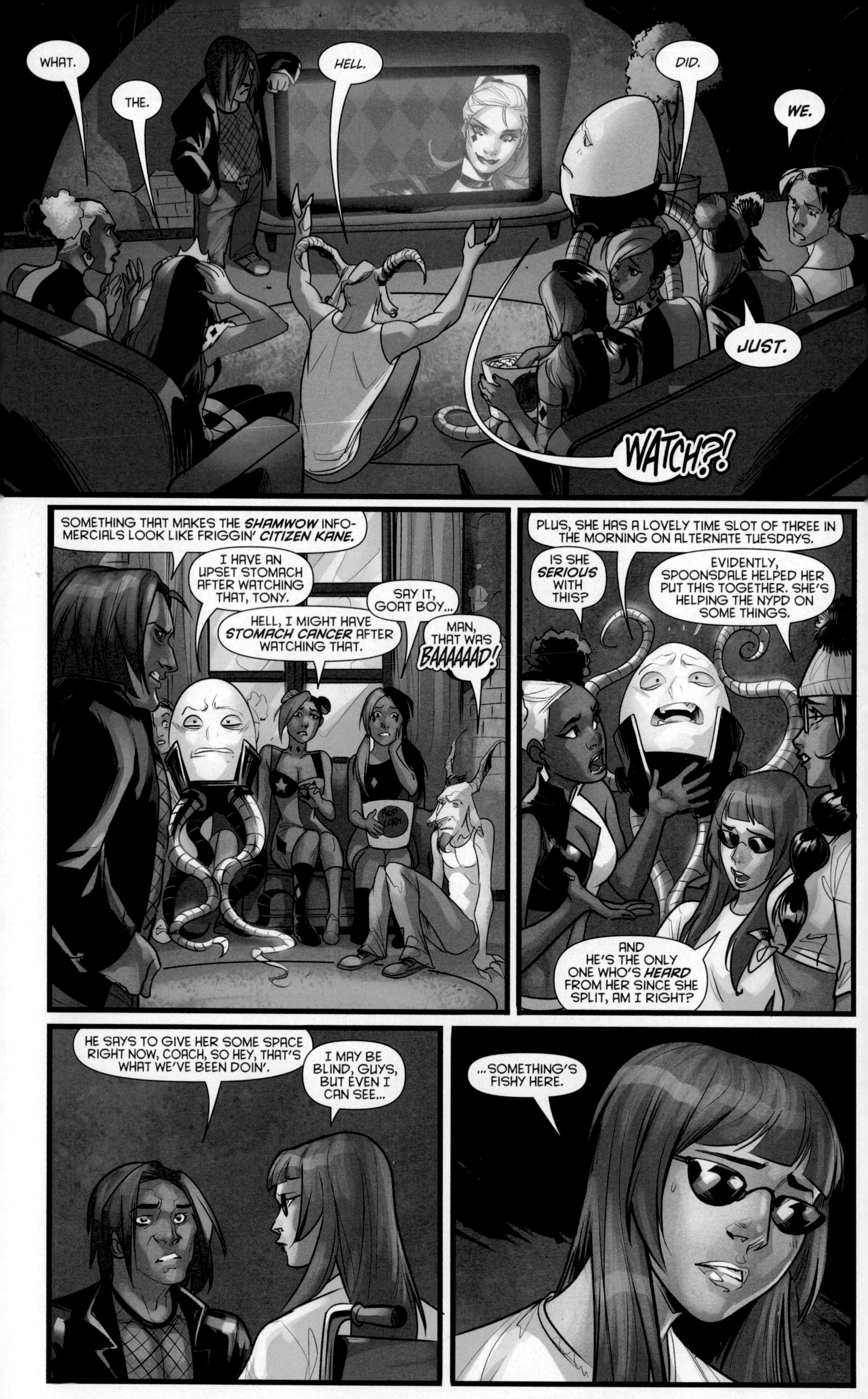
WHAT.
THE.
HELL.
DID.
WE.
JUST.
WATCH?!
SOMETHING THAT MAKES THE SHAMWOW INFO-MERCIALS LOOK LIKE FRIGGIN' CITIZEN KANE.
I HAVE AN UPSET STOMACH AFTER WATCHING THAT, TONY.
HELL, I MIGHT HAVE STOMACH CANCER AFTER WATCHING THAT.
SAY IT, GOAT BOY...
MAN, THAT WAS BAAAAAAD!
PLUS, SHE HAS A LOVELY TIME SLOT OF THREE IN THE MORNING ON ALTERNATE TUESDAYS.
IS SHE SERIOUS WITH THIS?
EVIDENTLY, SPOONSDALE HELPED HER PUT THIS TOGETHER. SHE'S HELPING THE NYPD ON SOME THINGS.
AND HE'S THE ONLY ONE WHO'S HEARD FROM HER SINCE SHE SPLIT, AM I RIGHT?
HE SAYS TO GIVE HER SOME SPACE RIGHT NOW, COACH, SO HEY, THAT'S WHAT WE'VE BEEN DOIN'.
I MAY BE BLIND, GUYS, BUT EVEN I CAN SEE...
...SOMETHING'S FISHY HERE.

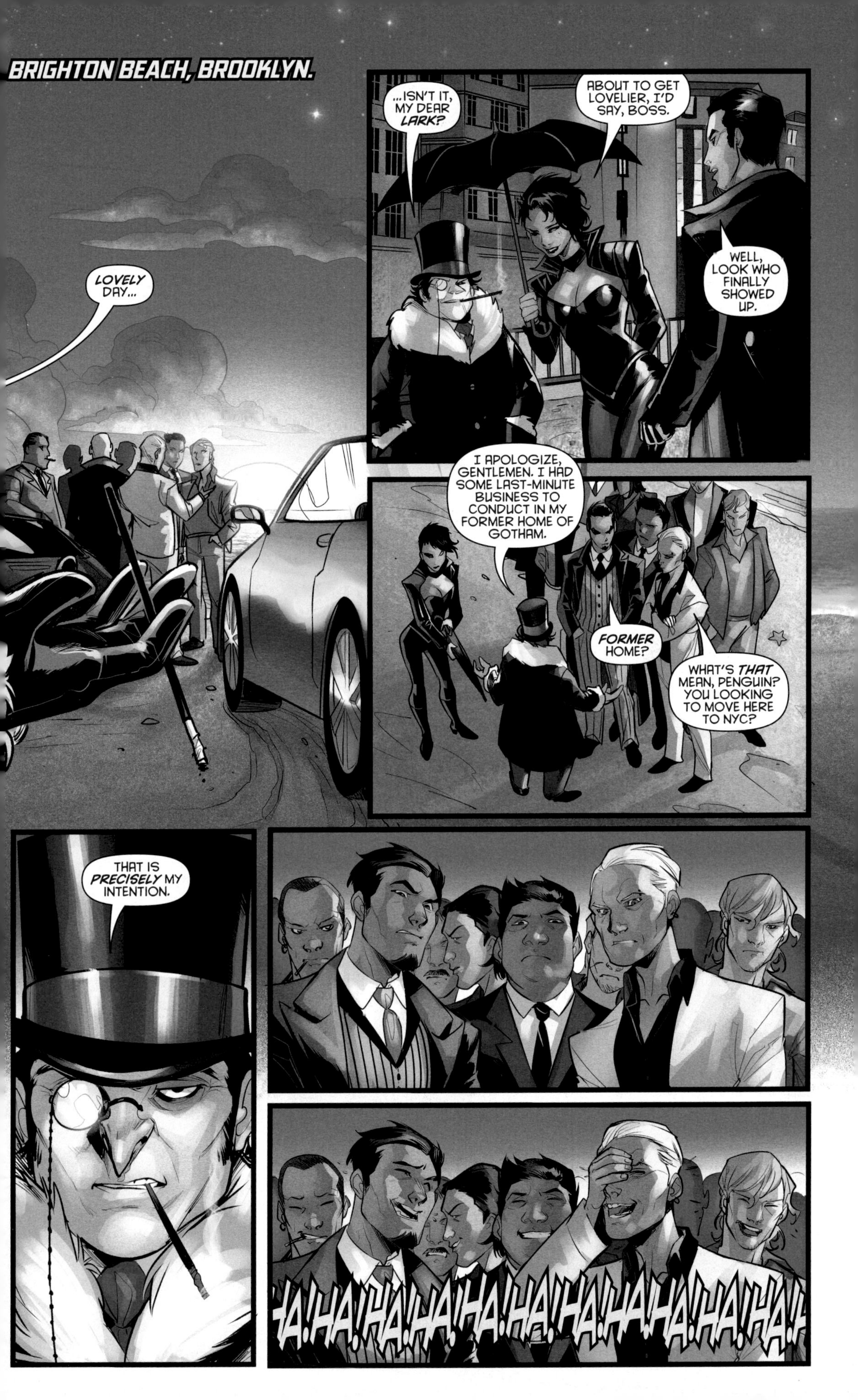
BRIGHTON BEACH, BROOKLYN.
LOVELY DAY...
...ISN'T IT, MY DEAR LARK?
ABOUT TO GET LOVELIER, I'D SAY, BOSS.
WELL, LOOK WHO FINALLY SHOWED UP.
I APOLOGIZE, GENTLEMEN. I HAD SOME LAST-MINUTE BUSINESS TO CONDUCT IN MY FORMER HOME OF GOTHAM.
FORMER HOME?
WHAT'S THAT MEAN, PENGUIN? YOU LOOKING TO MOVE HERE TO NYC?
THAT IS PRECISELY MY INTENTION.
HA! HA! HA! HA! HA! HA! HA! HA! HA! HA! HA!

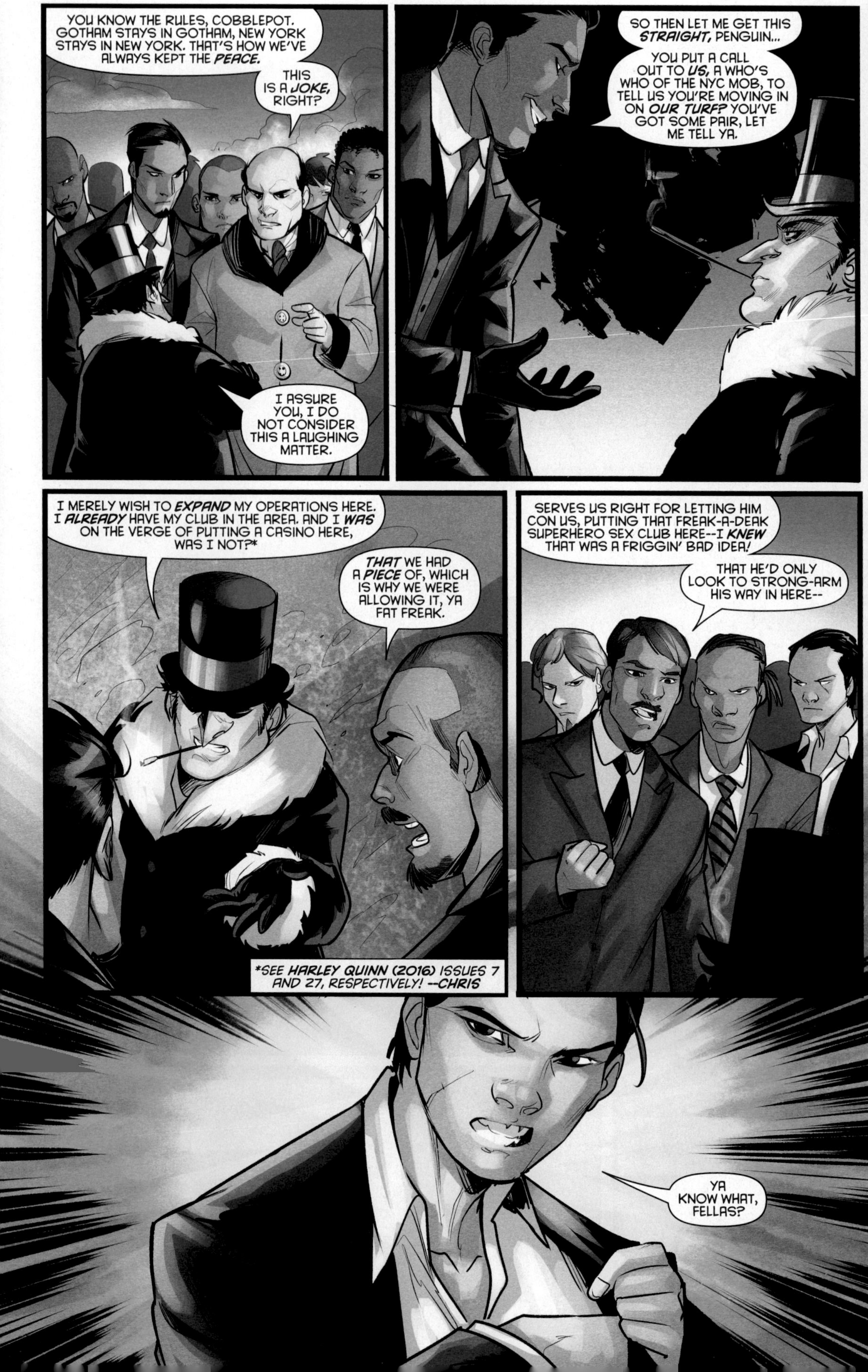
YOU KNOW THE RULES, COBBLEPOT. GOTHAM STAYS IN GOTHAM, NEW YORK STAYS IN NEW YORK. THAT'S HOW WE'VE ALWAYS KEPT THE PEACE.
THIS IS A JOKE, RIGHT?
I ASSURE YOU, I DO NOT CONSIDER THIS A LAUGHING MATTER.
SO THEN LET ME GET THIS STRAIGHT, PENGUIN...
YOU PUT A CALL OUT TO US, A WHO'S WHO OF THE NYC MOB, TO TELL US YOU'RE MOVING IN ON OUR TURF? YOU'VE GOT SOME PAIR, LET ME TELL YA.
I MERELY WISH TO EXPAND MY OPERATIONS HERE. I ALREADY HAVE MY CLUB IN THE AREA. AND I WAS ON THE VERGE OF PUTTING A CASINO HERE, WAS I NOT?*
THAT WE HAD A PIECE OF, WHICH IS WHY WE WERE ALLOWING IT, YA FAT FREAK.
*SEE HARLEY QUINN (2016) ISSUES 7 AND 27, RESPECTIVELY! --CHRIS
SERVES US RIGHT FOR LETTING HIM CON US, PUTTING THAT FREAK-A-DEAK SUPERHERO SEX CLUB HERE--I KNEW THAT WAS A FRIGGIN' BAD IDEA!
THAT HE'D ONLY LOOK TO STRONG-ARM HIS WAY IN HERE--
YA KNOW WHAT, FELLAS?

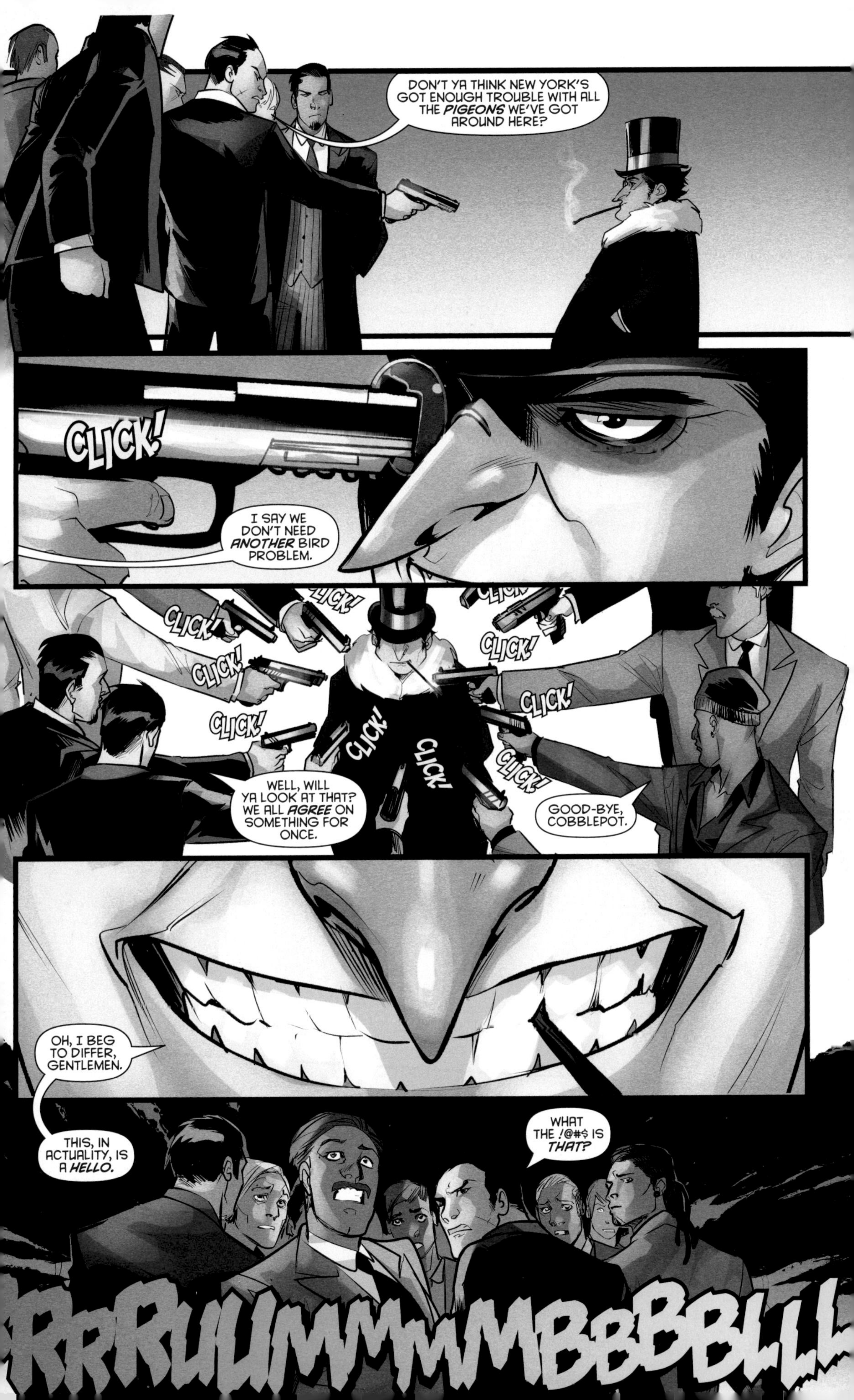
DON'T YA THINK NEW YORK'S GOT ENOUGH TROUBLE WITH ALL THE PIGEONS WE'VE GOT AROUND HERE?
CLICK!
I SAY WE DON'T NEED ANOTHER BIRD PROBLEM.
CLICK!
CLICK!
CLICK!
CLICK!
CLICK!
CLICK!
CLICK!
CLICK!
CLICK!
WELL, WILL YA LOOK AT THAT? WE ALL AGREE ON SOMETHING FOR ONCE.
GOOD-BYE, COBBLEPOT.
OH, I BEG TO DIFFER, GENTLEMEN.
THIS, IN ACTUALITY, IS A HELLO.
WHAT THE !@#$ IS THAT?
RRRUUMMMMMBBBBLLL

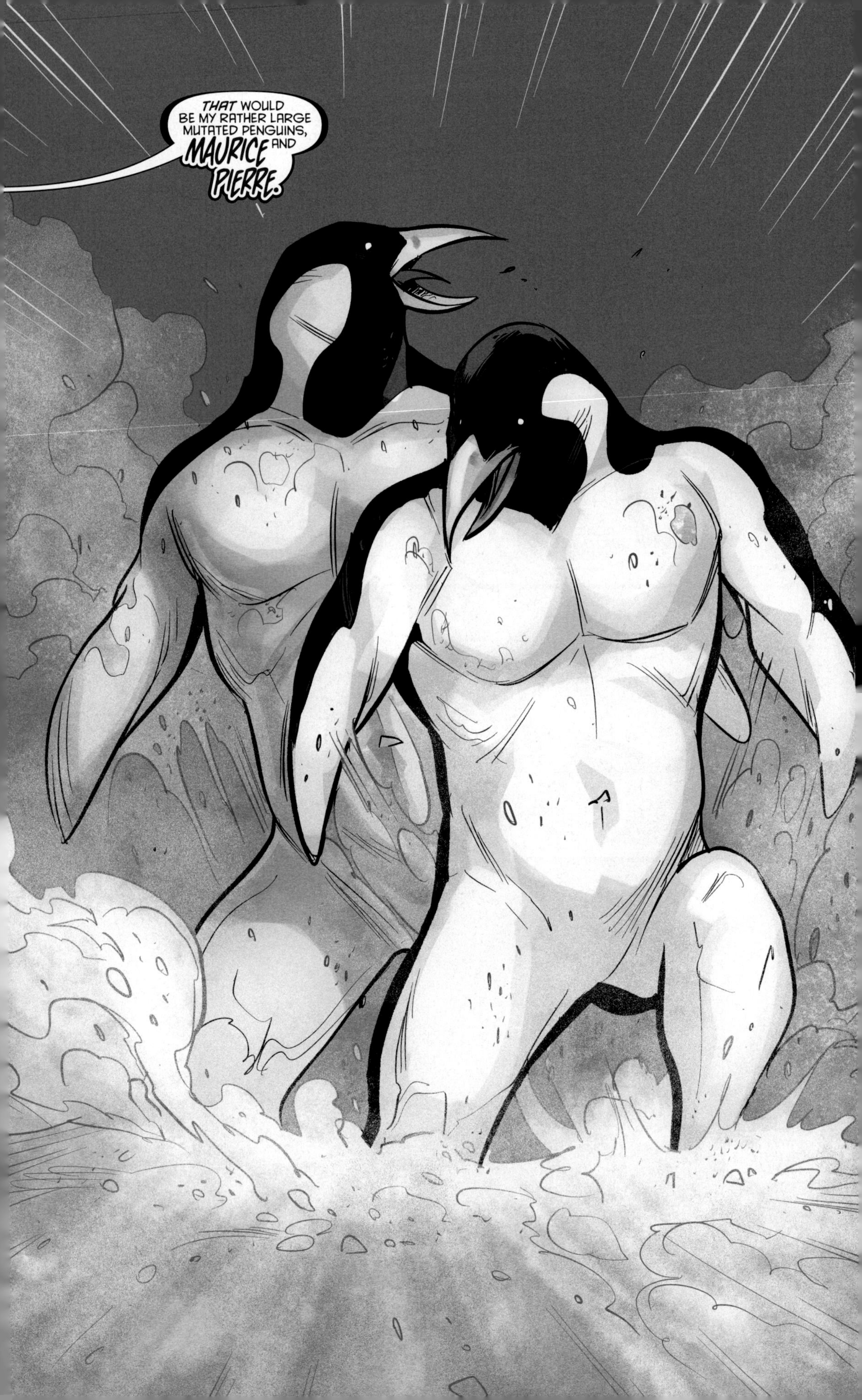
THAT WOULD BE MY RATHER LARGE MUTATED PENGUINS, MAURICE AND PIERRE.

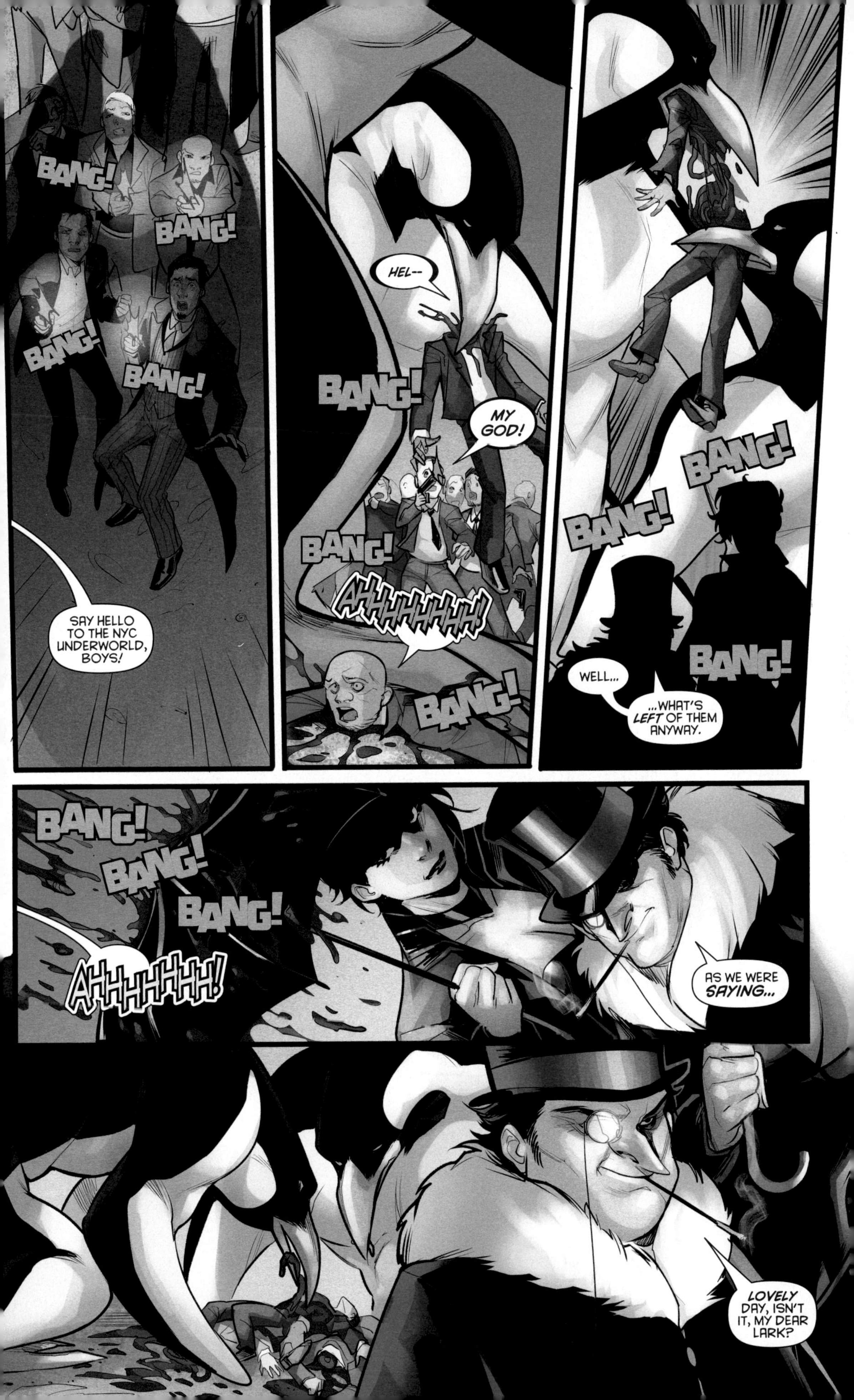
BANG!
BANG!
BANG!
BANG!
SAY HELLO TO THE NYC UNDERWORLD, BOYS!
HEL--
BANG!
MY GOD!
BANG!
AHHHHHHH!
BANG!
BANG!
BANG!
BANG!
WELL...
...WHAT'S LEFT OF THEM ANYWAY.
BANG!
BANG!
BANG!
AHHHHHH!
AS WE WERE SAYING...
LOVELY DAY, ISN'T IT, MY DEAR LARK?

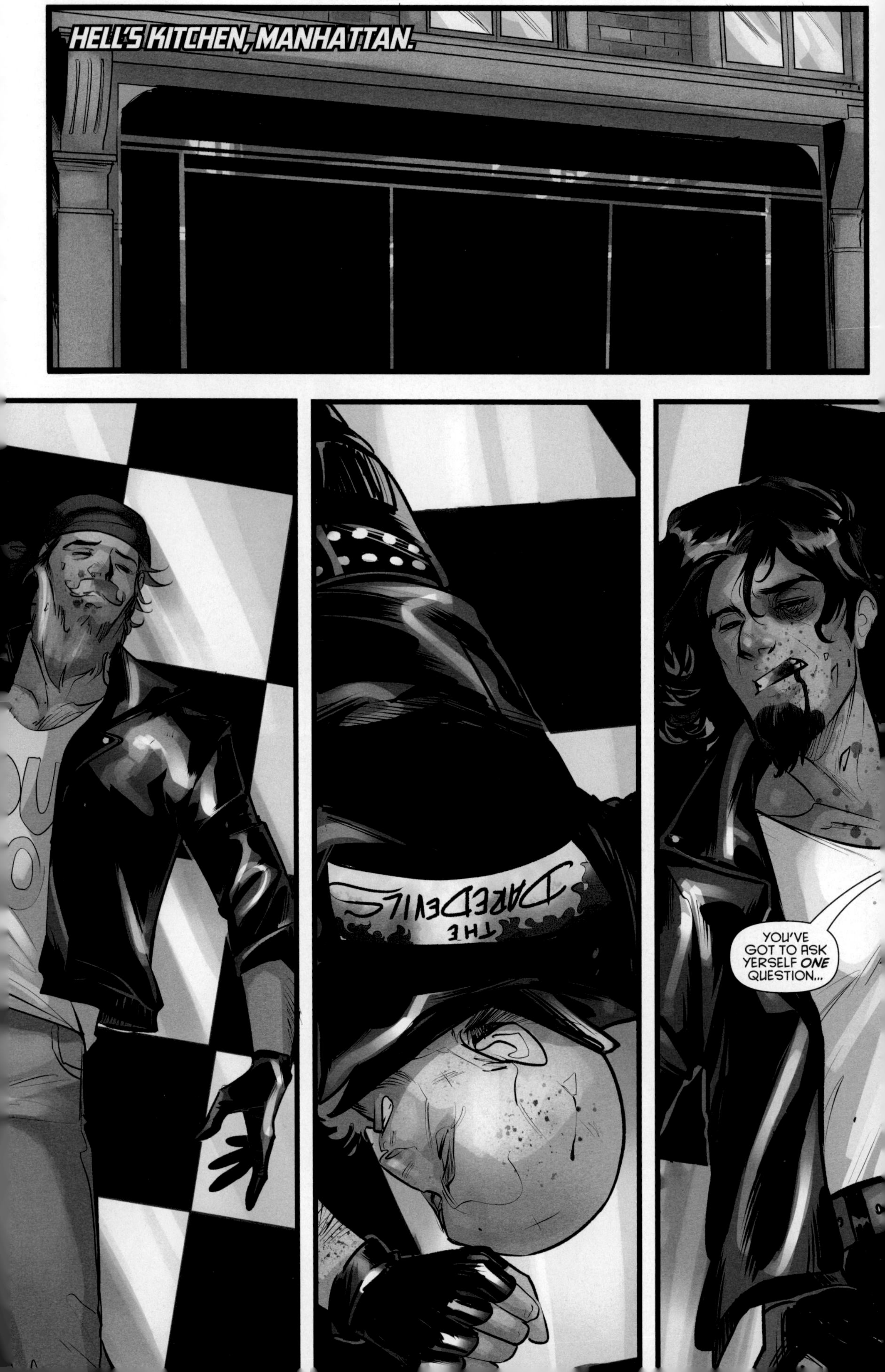
HELL'S KITCHEN, MANHATTAN.
THE DAREDEVILS
YOU'VE GOT TO ASK YERSELF *ONE* QUESTION...

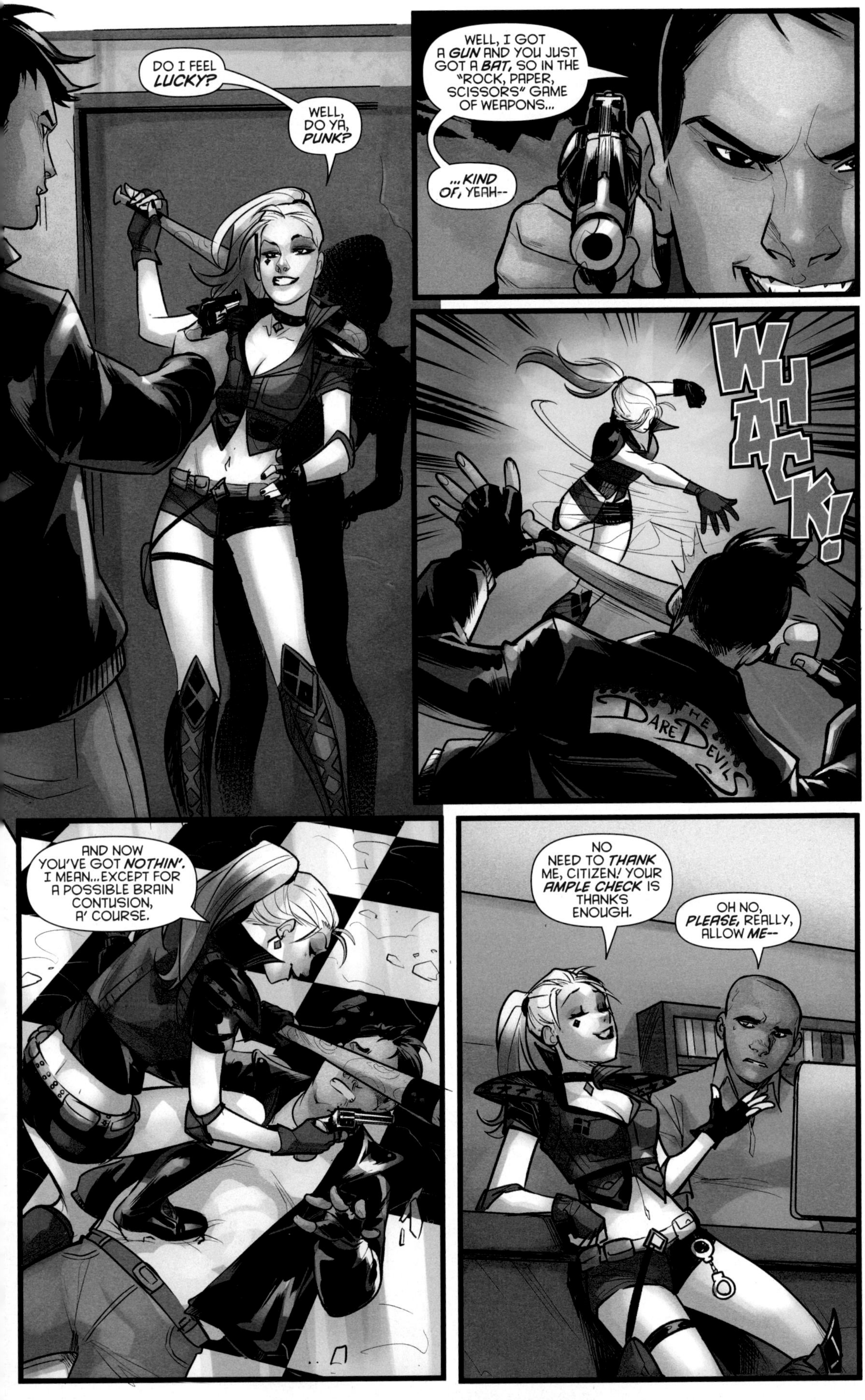
DO I FEEL LUCKY?
WELL, DO YA, PUNK?
WELL, I GOT A GUN AND YOU JUST GOT A BAT, SO IN THE "ROCK, PAPER, SCISSORS" GAME OF WEAPONS...
...KIND OF, YEAH--
WHACK!
THE DAREDEVILS
AND NOW YOU'VE GOT NOTHIN'. I MEAN...EXCEPT FOR A POSSIBLE BRAIN CONTUSION, A' COURSE.
NO NEED TO THANK ME, CITIZEN! YOUR AMPLE CHECK IS THANKS ENOUGH.
OH NO, PLEASE, REALLY, ALLOW ME--

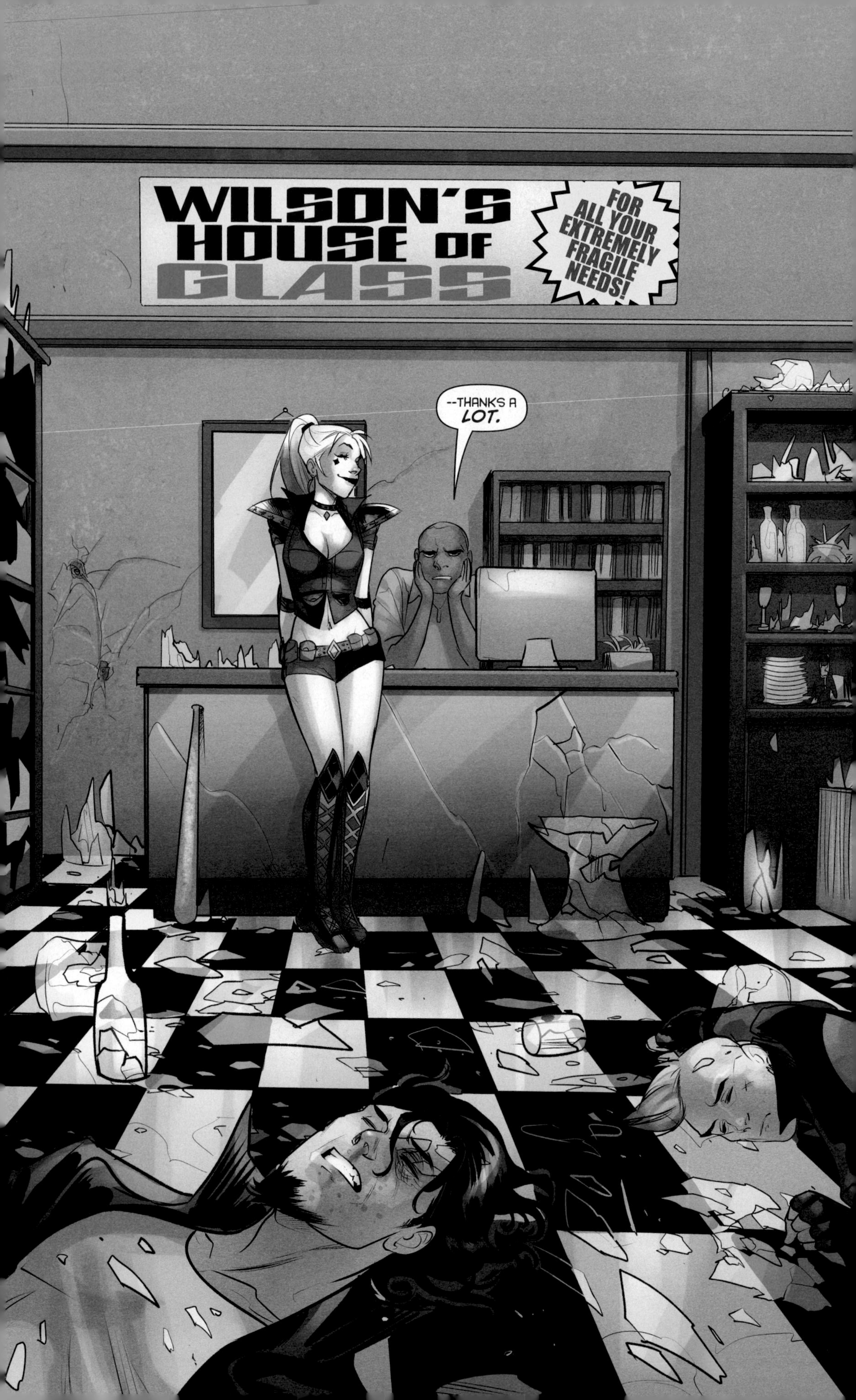
WILSON'S HOUSE OF GLASS
FOR ALL YOUR EXTREMELY FRAGILE NEEDS!
--THANKS A LOT.

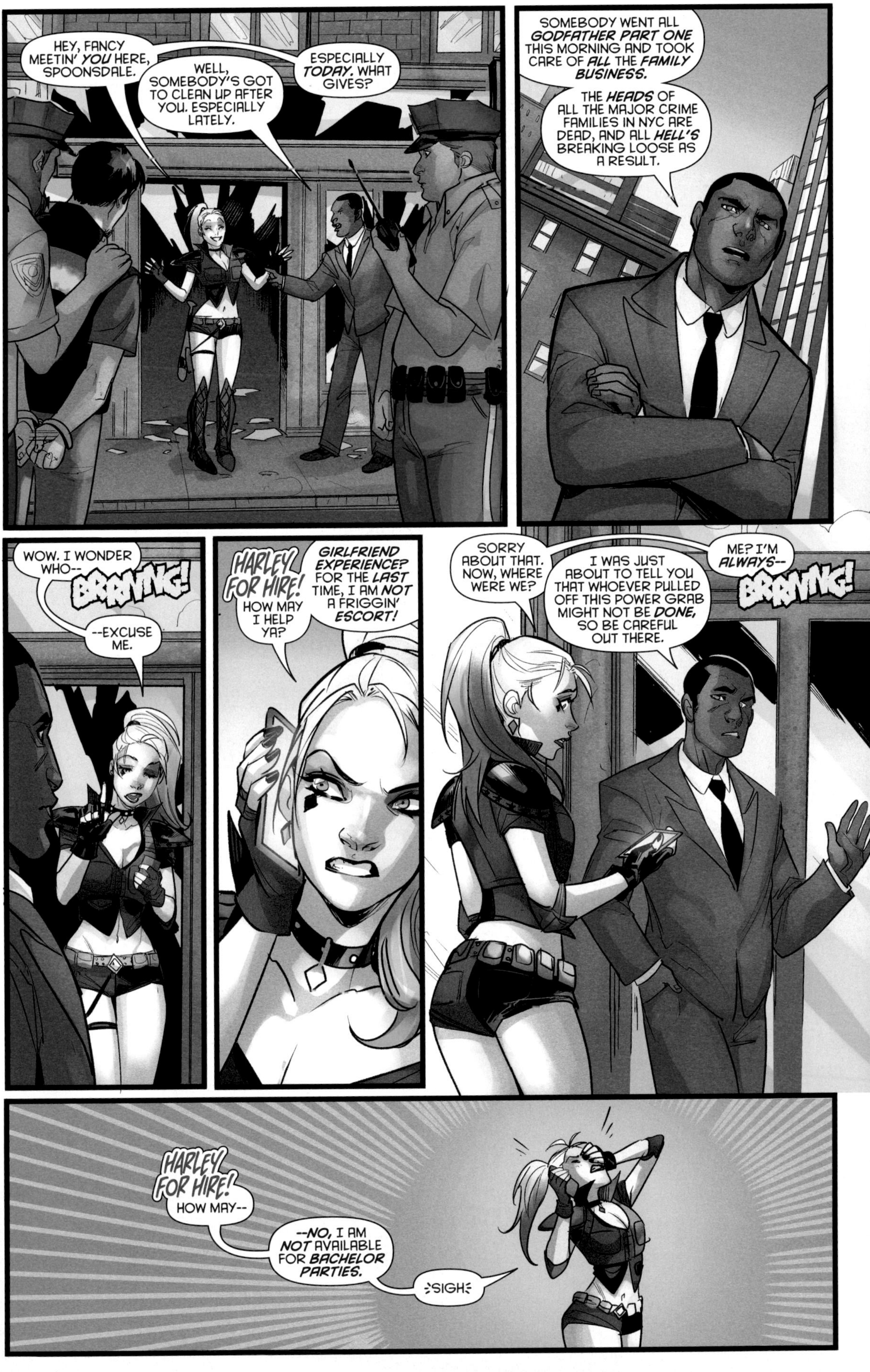
HEY, FANCY MEETIN' YOU HERE, SPOONSDALE.
WELL, SOMEBODY'S GOT TO CLEAN UP AFTER YOU. ESPECIALLY LATELY.
ESPECIALLY TODAY. WHAT GIVES?
SOMEBODY WENT ALL GODFATHER PART ONE THIS MORNING AND TOOK CARE OF ALL THE FAMILY BUSINESS.
THE HEADS OF ALL THE MAJOR CRIME FAMILIES IN NYC ARE DEAD, AND ALL HELL'S BREAKING LOOSE AS A RESULT.
WOW. I WONDER WHO--
BRRING!
--EXCUSE ME.
HARLEY FOR HIRE! HOW MAY I HELP YA?
GIRLFRIEND EXPERIENCE? FOR THE LAST TIME, I AM NOT A FRIGGIN' ESCORT!
SORRY ABOUT THAT. NOW, WHERE WERE WE?
I WAS JUST ABOUT TO TELL YOU THAT WHOEVER PULLED OFF THIS POWER GRAB MIGHT NOT BE DONE, SO BE CAREFUL OUT THERE.
ME? I'M ALWAYS--
BRRING!
HARLEY FOR HIRE! HOW MAY--
--NO, I AM NOT AVAILABLE FOR BACHELOR PARTIES.
SIGH

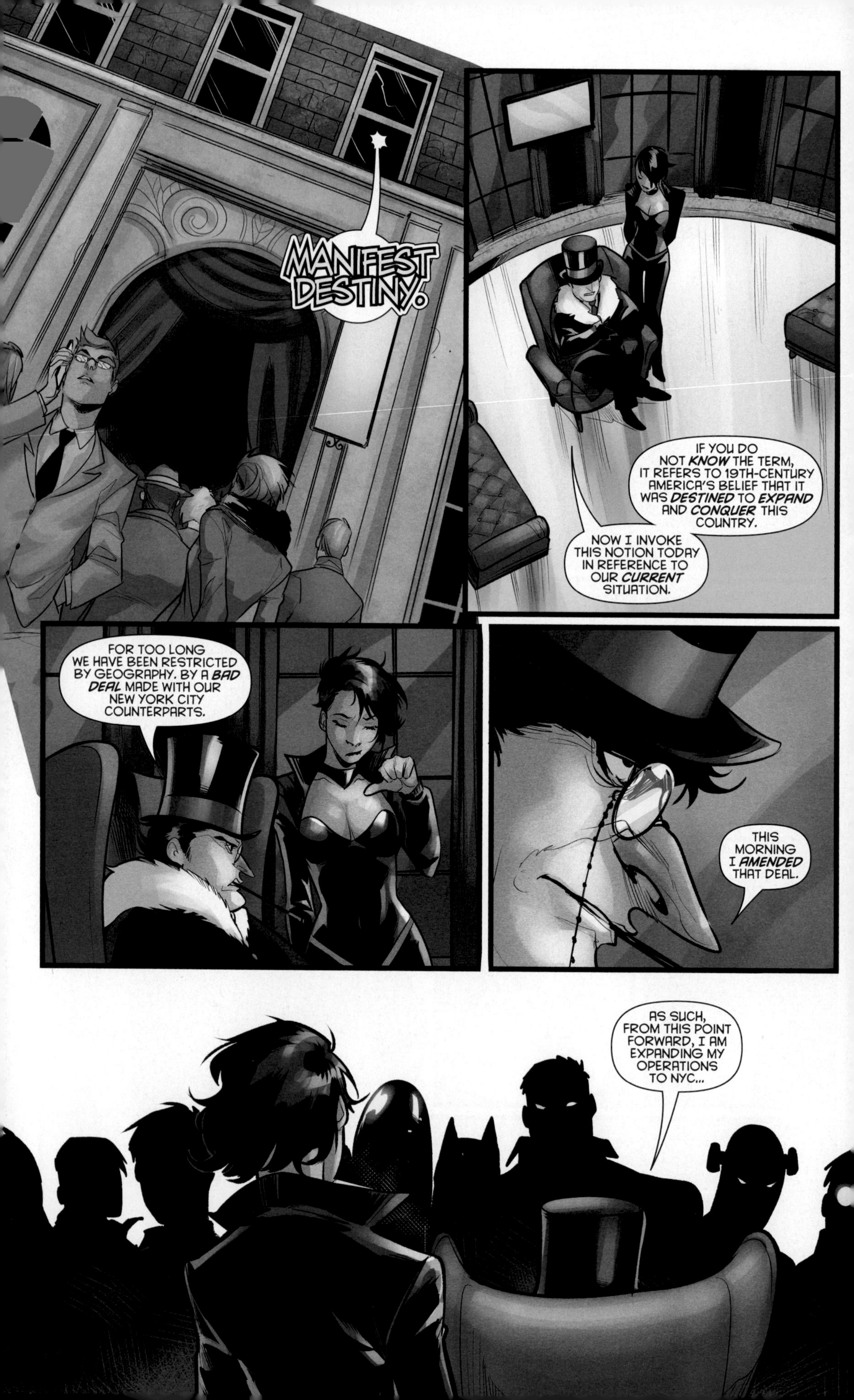
MANIFEST DESTINY.
IF YOU DO NOT KNOW THE TERM, IT REFERS TO 19TH-CENTURY AMERICA'S BELIEF THAT IT WAS DESTINED TO EXPAND AND CONQUER THIS COUNTRY.
NOW I INVOKE THIS NOTION TODAY IN REFERENCE TO OUR CURRENT SITUATION.
FOR TOO LONG WE HAVE BEEN RESTRICTED BY GEOGRAPHY. BY A BAD DEAL MADE WITH OUR NEW YORK CITY COUNTERPARTS.
THIS MORNING I AMENDED THAT DEAL.
AS SUCH, FROM THIS POINT FORWARD, I AM EXPANDING MY OPERATIONS TO NYC...

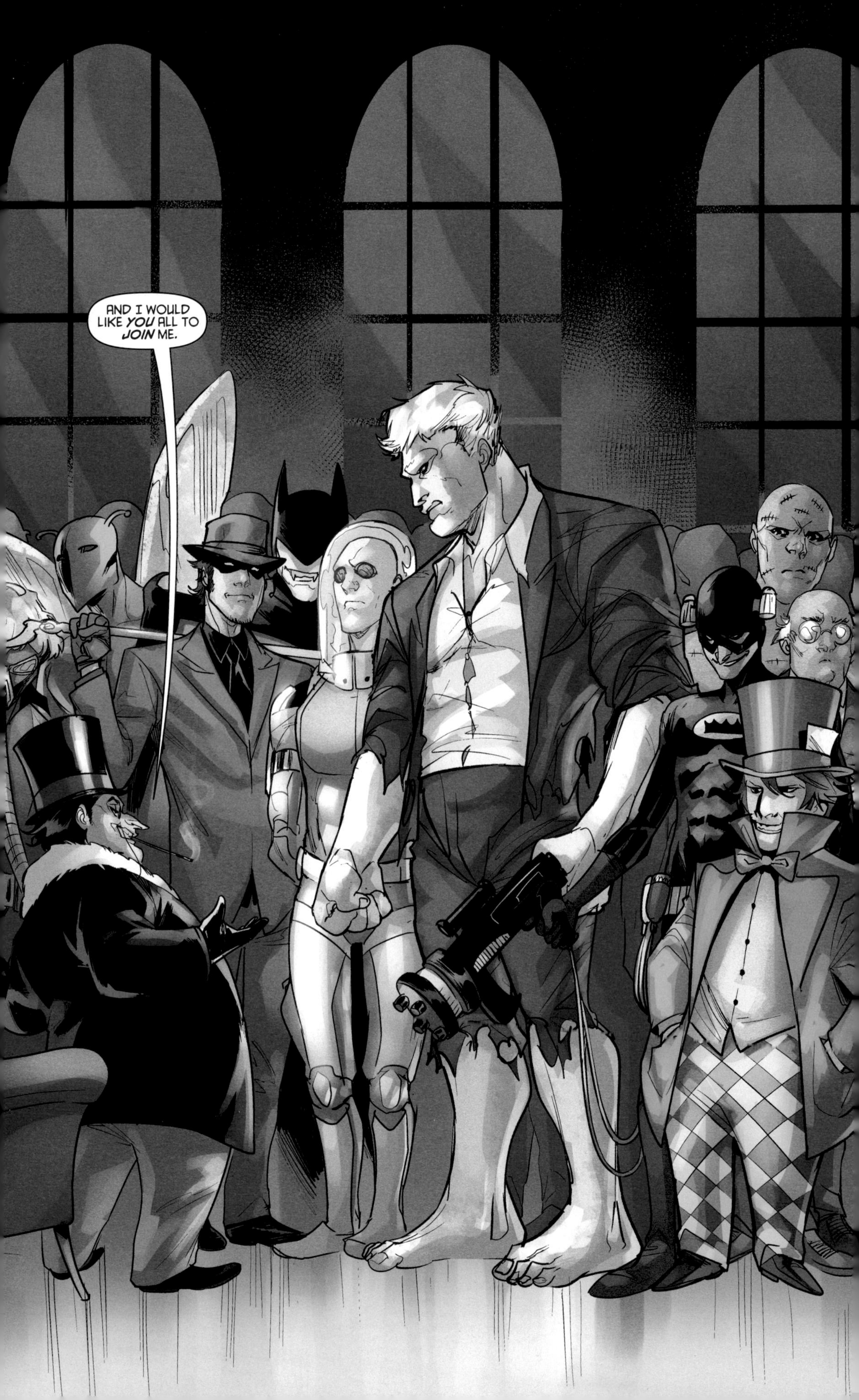
AND I WOULD LIKE *YOU* ALL TO *JOIN* ME.

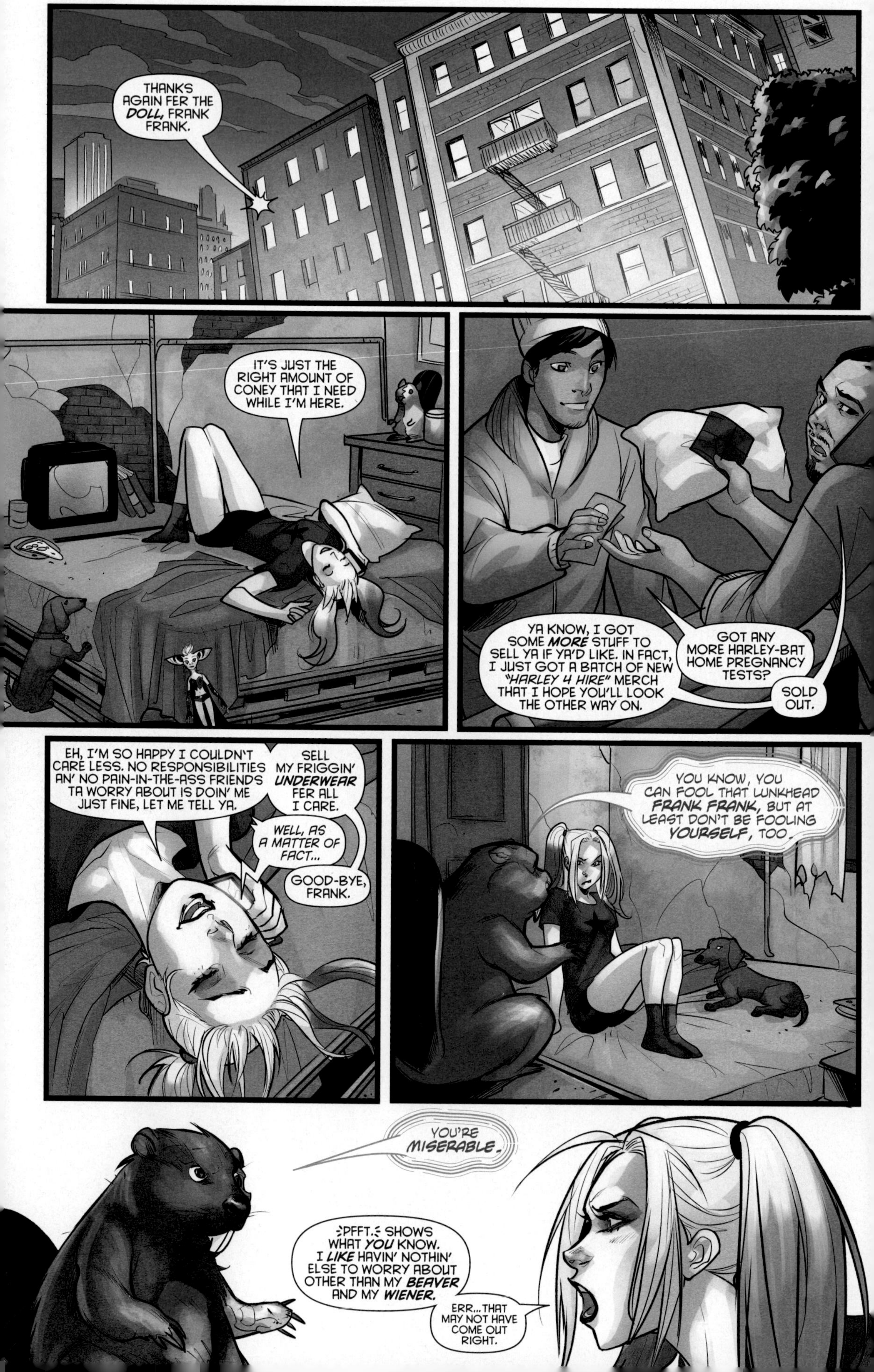
THANKS AGAIN FER THE DOLL, FRANK FRANK.
IT'S JUST THE RIGHT AMOUNT OF CONEY THAT I NEED WHILE I'M HERE.
YA KNOW, I GOT SOME MORE STUFF TO SELL YA IF YA'D LIKE. IN FACT, I JUST GOT A BATCH OF NEW "HARLEY 4 HIRE" MERCH THAT I HOPE YOU'LL LOOK THE OTHER WAY ON.
GOT ANY MORE HARLEY-BAT HOME PREGNANCY TESTS?
SOLD OUT.
EH, I'M SO HAPPY I COULDN'T CARE LESS. NO RESPONSIBILITIES AN' NO PAIN-IN-THE-ASS FRIENDS TA WORRY ABOUT IS DOIN' ME JUST FINE, LET ME TELL YA.
SELL MY FRIGGIN' UNDERWEAR FER ALL I CARE.
WELL, AS A MATTER OF FACT...
GOOD-BYE, FRANK.
YOU KNOW, YOU CAN FOOL THAT LUNKHEAD FRANK FRANK, BUT AT LEAST DON'T BE FOOLING YOURSELF, TOO.
YOU'RE MISERABLE.
PFFT. SHOWS WHAT YOU KNOW. I LIKE HAVIN' NOTHIN' ELSE TO WORRY ABOUT OTHER THAN MY BEAVER AND MY WIENER.
ERR...THAT MAY NOT HAVE COME OUT RIGHT.

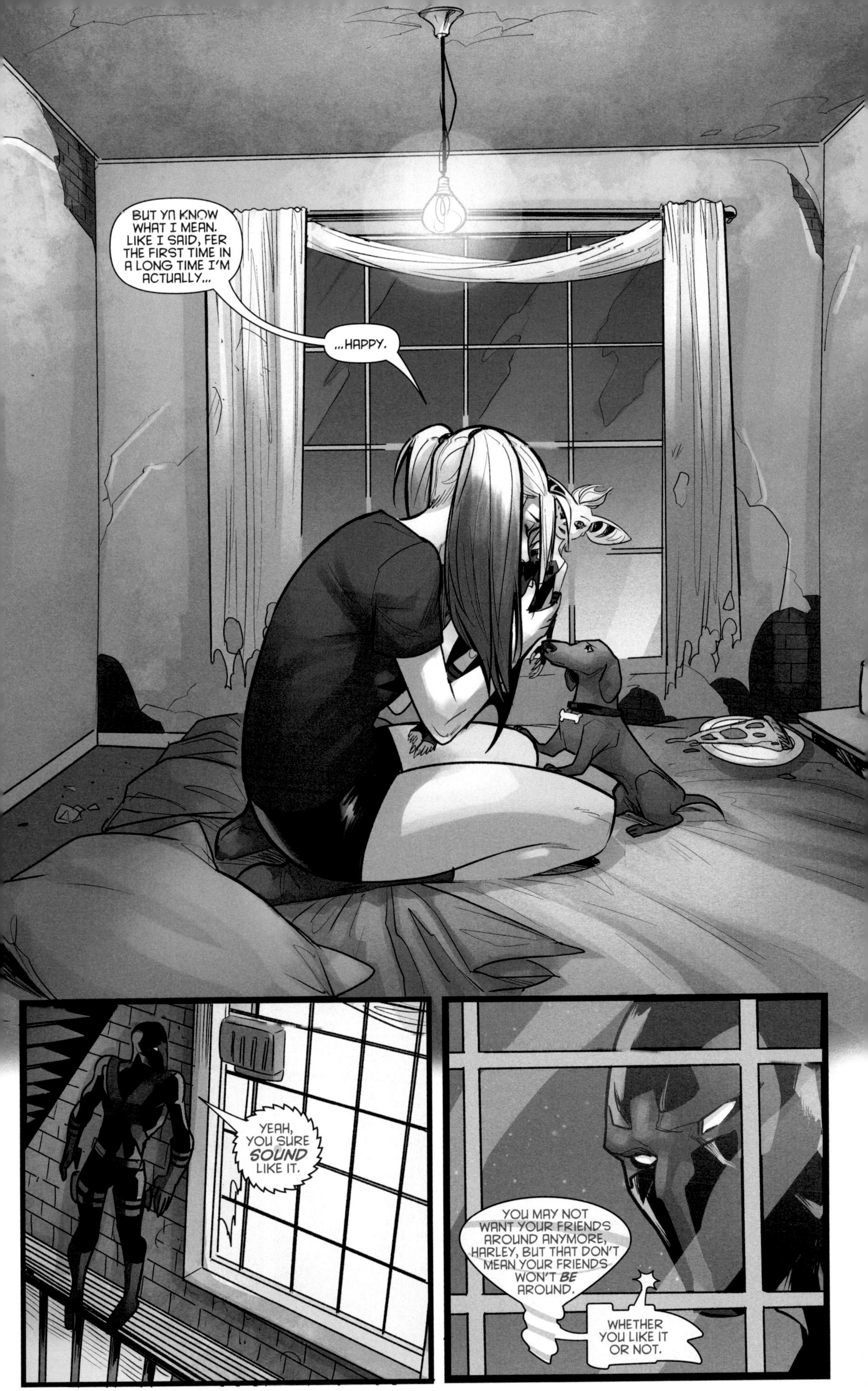

BUT YA KNOW WHAT I MEAN. LIKE I SAID, FER THE FIRST TIME IN A LONG TIME I'M ACTUALLY...
...HAPPY.
YEAH, YOU SURE *SOUND* LIKE IT.
YOU MAY NOT WANT YOUR FRIENDS AROUND ANYMORE, HARLEY, BUT THAT DON'T MEAN YOUR FRIENDS WON'T *BE* AROUND.
WHETHER YOU LIKE IT OR NOT.

SO YOU WOULD ALL BE OPERATING UNDER MY FLAG, WITH A PERCENTAGE KICKING BACK TO ME, AND--

YOU AIN'T EVEN SPELLED OUT THE BEST PART YET, PENGY.

AND THAT'S NO BATMAN.

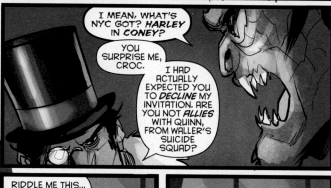

I MEAN, WHAT'S NYC GOT? HARLEY IN CONEY?

YOU SURPRISE ME, CROC.

I HAD ACTUALLY EXPECTED YOU TO DECLINE MY INVITATION. ARE YOU NOT ALLIES WITH QUINN, FROM WALLER'S SUICIDE SQUAD?

RIDDLE ME THIS... WHEN DOES A RAT SMELL LIKE A RAT?

WHEN IT'S A CROC.

EXCUSE ME.

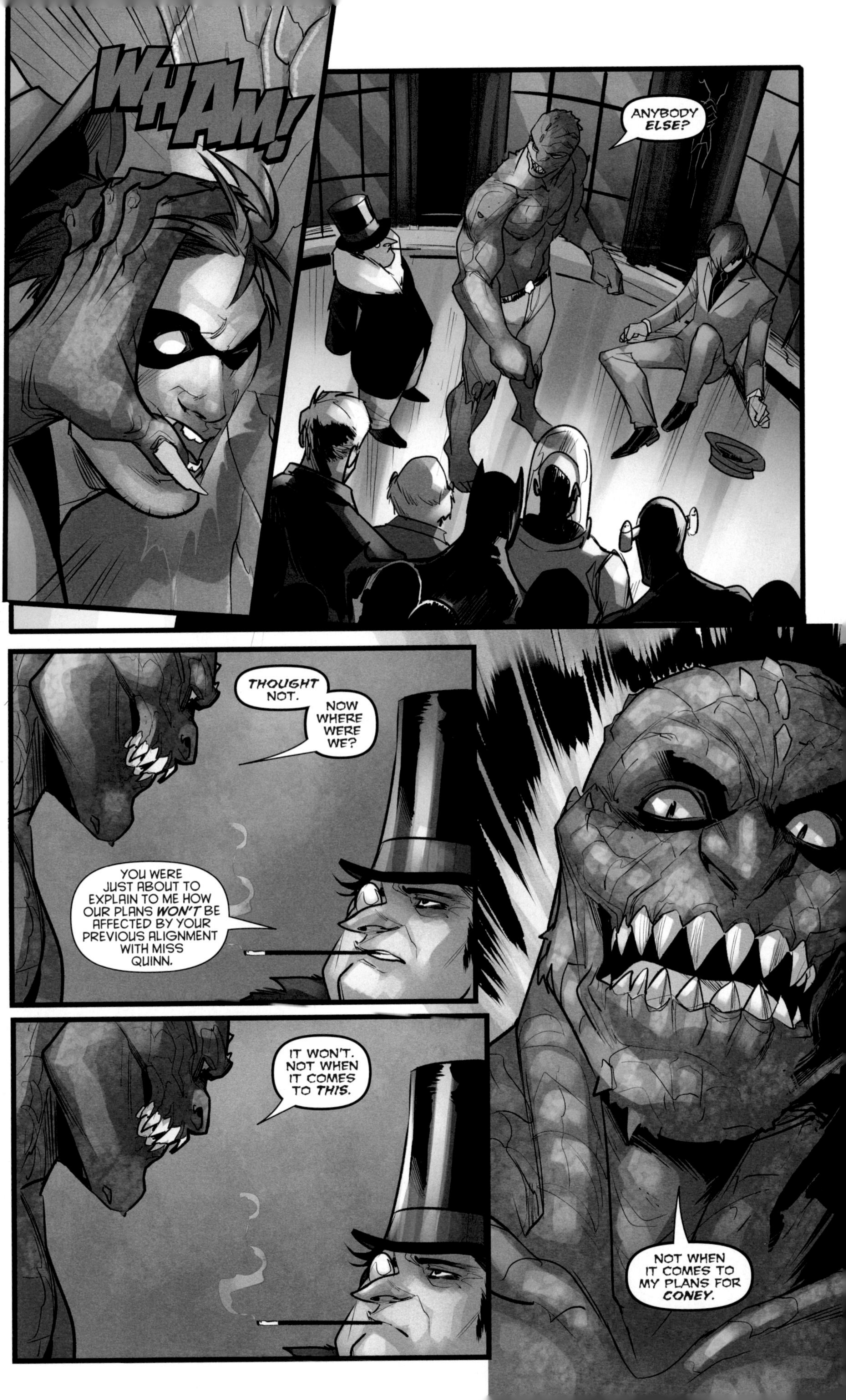
WHAM!
ANYBODY ELSE?
THOUGHT NOT.
NOW WHERE WERE WE?
YOU WERE JUST ABOUT TO EXPLAIN TO ME HOW OUR PLANS WON'T BE AFFECTED BY YOUR PREVIOUS ALIGNMENT WITH MISS QUINN.
IT WON'T. NOT WHEN IT COMES TO THIS.
NOT WHEN IT COMES TO MY PLANS FOR CONEY.

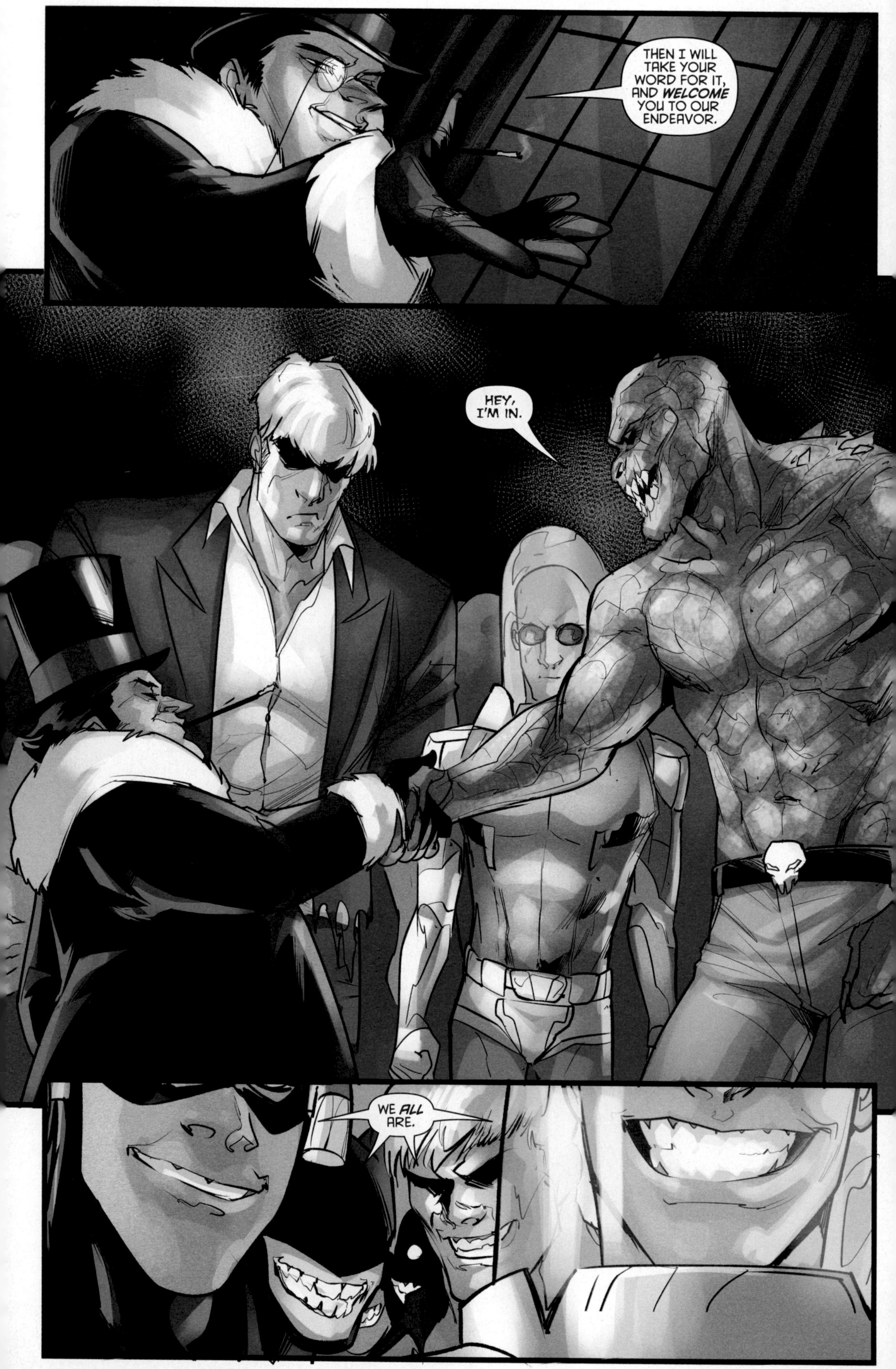
THEN I WILL TAKE YOUR WORD FOR IT, AND *WELCOME* YOU TO OUR ENDEAVOR.
HEY, I'M IN.
WE *ALL* ARE.

AAAAAAAHH!
HOLEE HOWLIN' FOWL PLAY!
RUN!
I ♥ C.I.
Darwyn Conner
MOUNTS

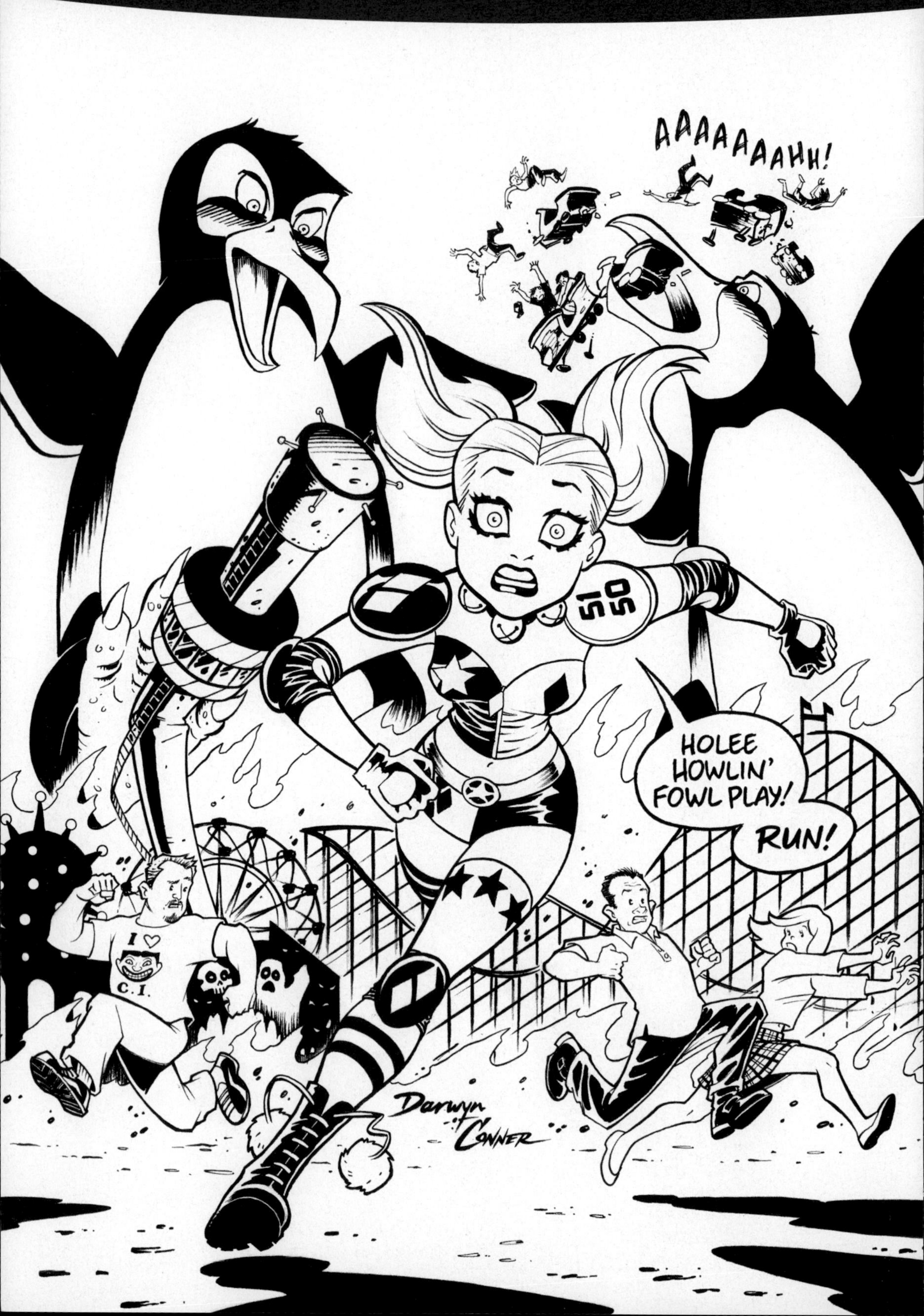
AAAAAAAAHH!
HOLEE HOWLIN' FOWL PLAY!
RUN!
I ♥ C.I.
Darwyn Conner

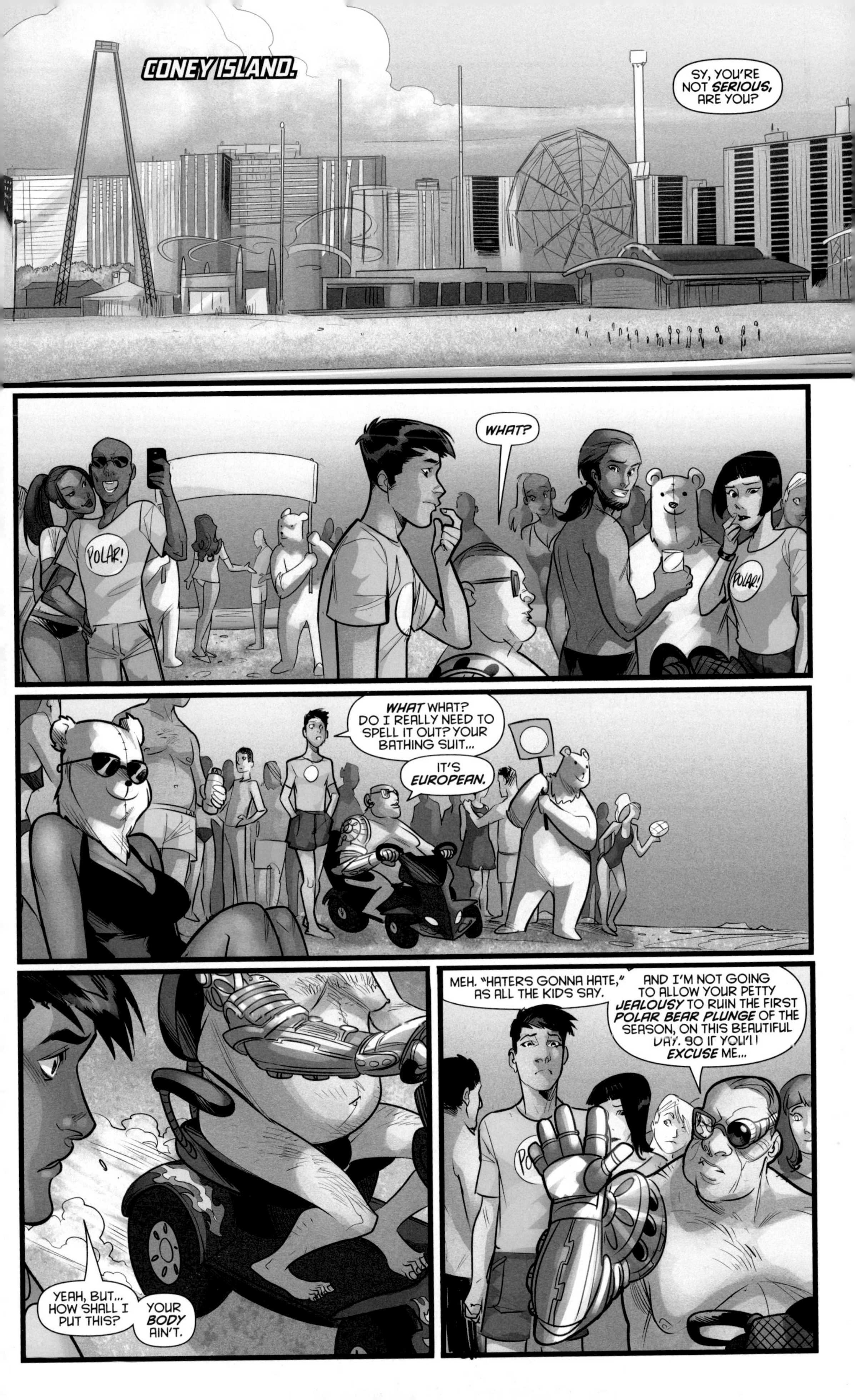
CONEY ISLAND.
SY, YOU'RE NOT SERIOUS, ARE YOU?
POLAR!
WHAT?
POLAR!
WHAT WHAT? DO I REALLY NEED TO SPELL IT OUT? YOUR BATHING SUIT...
IT'S EUROPEAN.
YEAH, BUT... HOW SHALL I PUT THIS?
YOUR BODY AIN'T.
MEH. "HATERS GONNA HATE," AS ALL THE KIDS SAY.
AND I'M NOT GOING TO ALLOW YOUR PETTY JEALOUSY TO RUIN THE FIRST POLAR BEAR PLUNGE OF THE SEASON, ON THIS BEAUTIFUL DAY. SO IF YOU'LL EXCUSE ME...

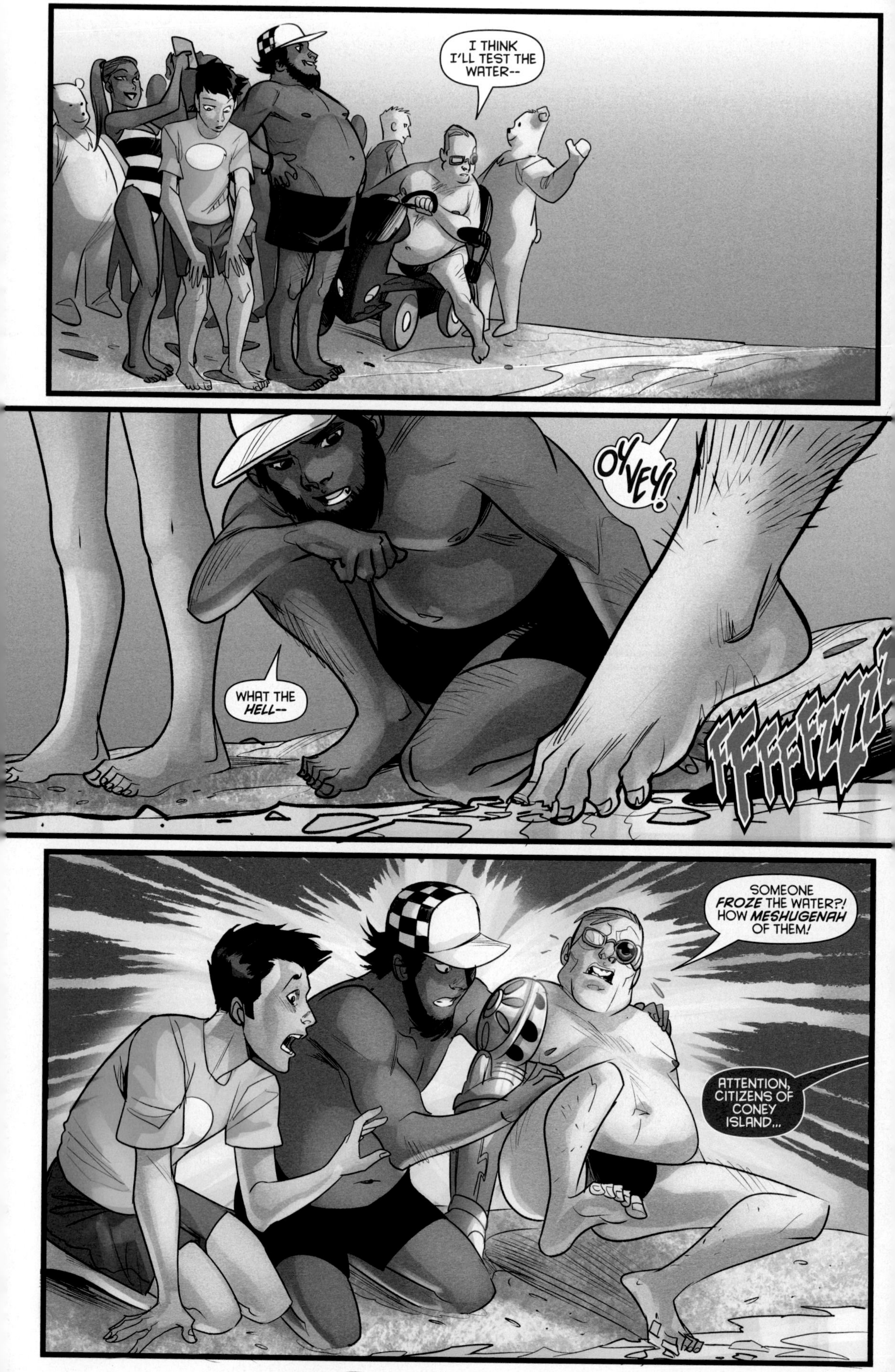
I THINK I'LL TEST THE WATER--
OY VEY!
WHAT THE HELL--
FFFFZZZZ
SOMEONE FROZE THE WATER?! HOW MESHUGENAH OF THEM!
ATTENTION, CITIZENS OF CONEY ISLAND...

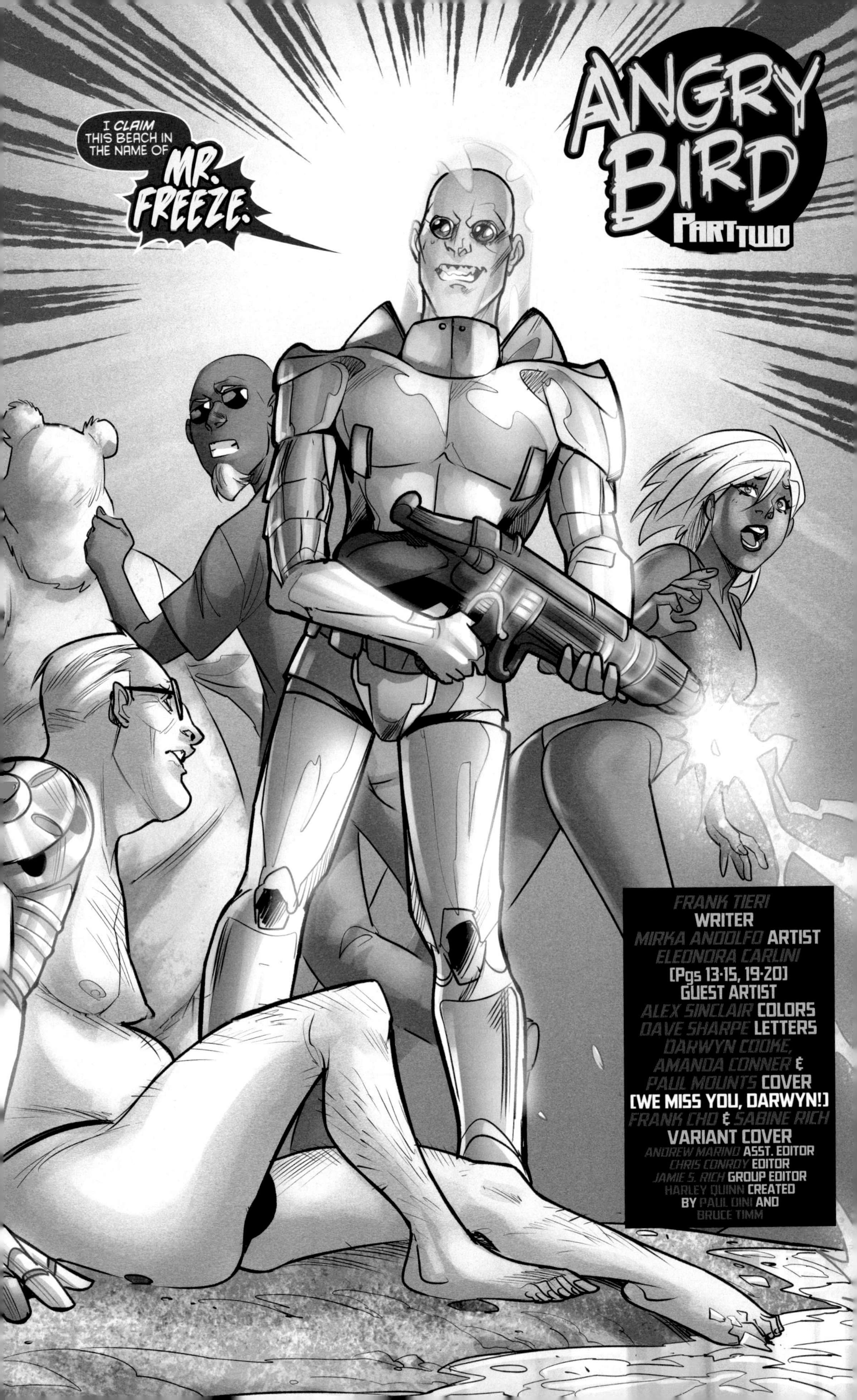
I CLAIM THIS BEACH IN THE NAME OF MR. FREEZE.
ANGRY BIRD
PART TWO
FRANK TIERI WRITER
MIRKA ANDOLFO ARTIST
ELEONORA CARLINI [Pgs 13-15, 19-20] GUEST ARTIST
ALEX SINCLAIR COLORS
DAVE SHARPE LETTERS
DARWYN COOKE, AMANDA CONNER & PAUL MOUNTS COVER
[WE MISS YOU, DARWYN!]
FRANK CHO & SABINE RICH VARIANT COVER
ANDREW MARINO ASST. EDITOR
CHRIS CONROY EDITOR
JAMIE S. RICH GROUP EDITOR
HARLEY QUINN CREATED BY PAUL DINI AND BRUCE TIMM

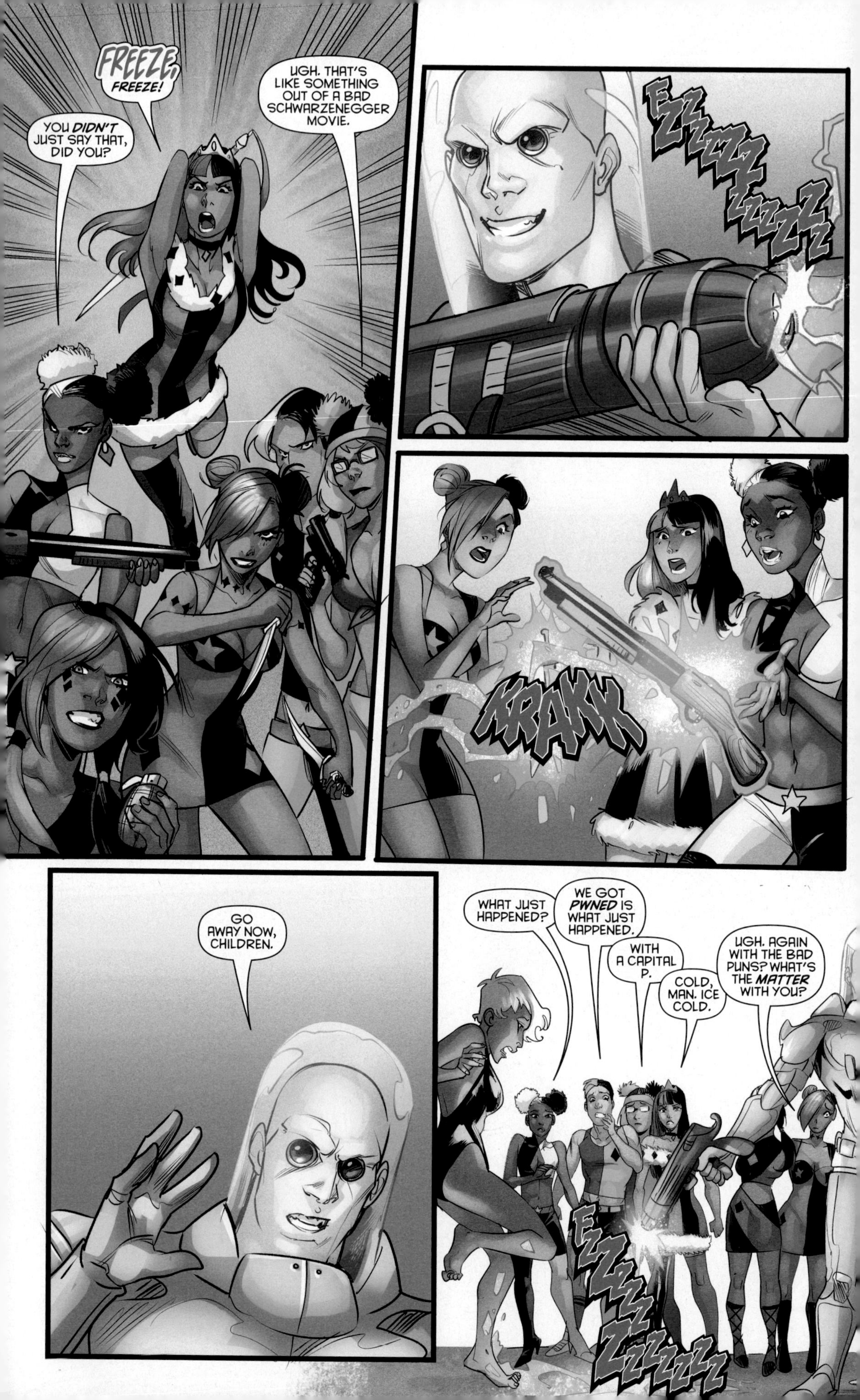
FREEZE, FREEZE!
YOU DIDN'T JUST SAY THAT, DID YOU?
UGH. THAT'S LIKE SOMETHING OUT OF A BAD SCHWARZENEGGER MOVIE.
FZZZZZZZZZZZZ
KRAKK
GO AWAY NOW, CHILDREN.
WHAT JUST HAPPENED?
WE GOT PWNED IS WHAT JUST HAPPENED.
WITH A CAPITAL P.
COLD, MAN. ICE COLD.
UGH. AGAIN WITH THE BAD PUNS? WHAT'S THE MATTER WITH YOU?
FZZZZZZZZZZ

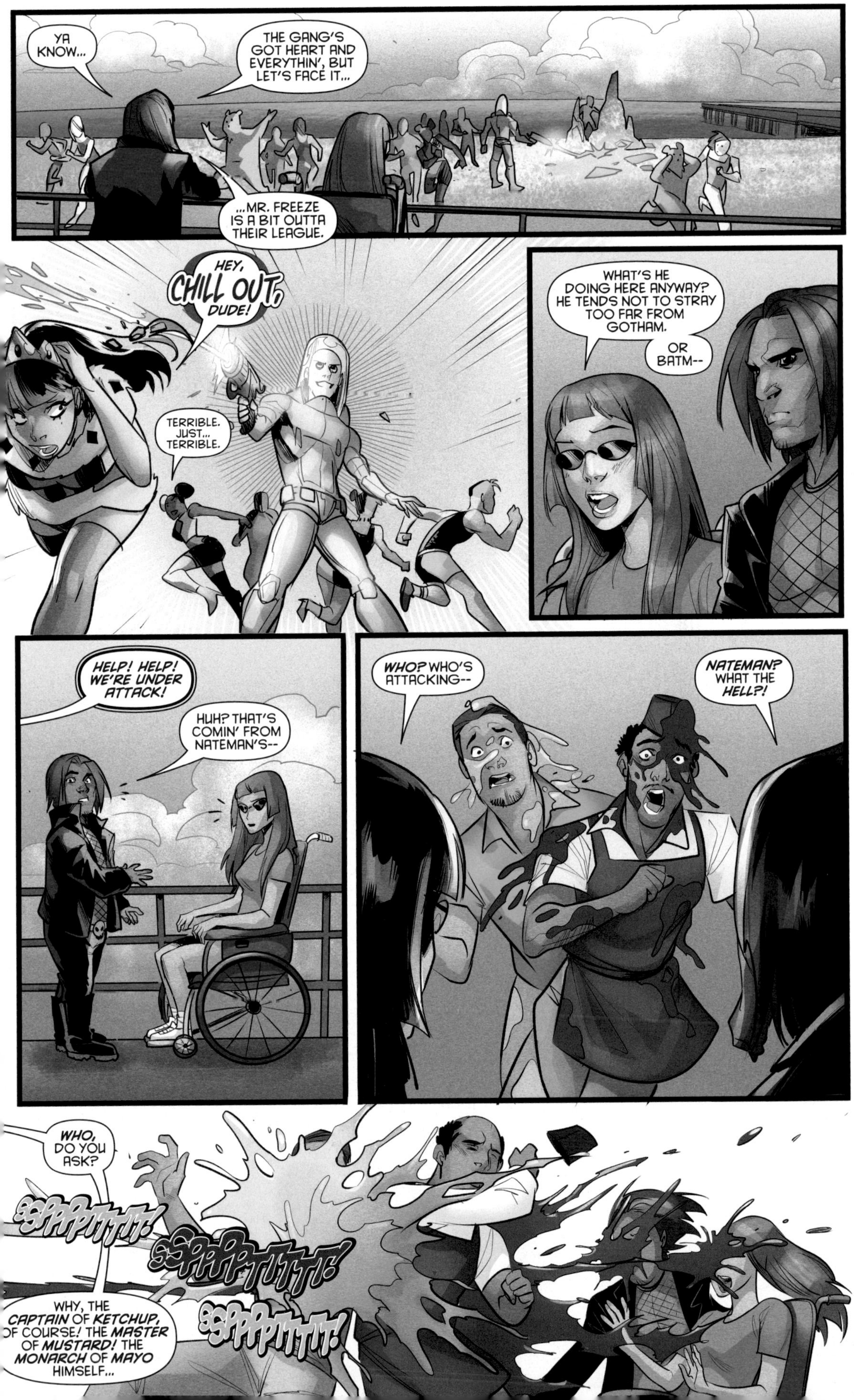
YA KNOW...
THE GANG'S GOT HEART AND EVERYTHIN', BUT LET'S FACE IT...
...MR. FREEZE IS A BIT OUTTA THEIR LEAGUE.
HEY, CHILL OUT, DUDE!
TERRIBLE. JUST... TERRIBLE.
WHAT'S HE DOING HERE ANYWAY? HE TENDS NOT TO STRAY TOO FAR FROM GOTHAM.
OR BATM--
HELP! HELP! WE'RE UNDER ATTACK!
HUH? THAT'S COMIN' FROM NATEMAN'S--
WHO? WHO'S ATTACKING--
NATEMAN? WHAT THE HELL?!
WHO, DO YOU ASK?
SSPPPPTTTTT!
SSPPPPTTTTT!
SSPPPPTTTTT!
WHY, THE CAPTAIN OF KETCHUP, OF COURSE! THE MASTER OF MUSTARD! THE MONARCH OF MAYO HIMSELF...

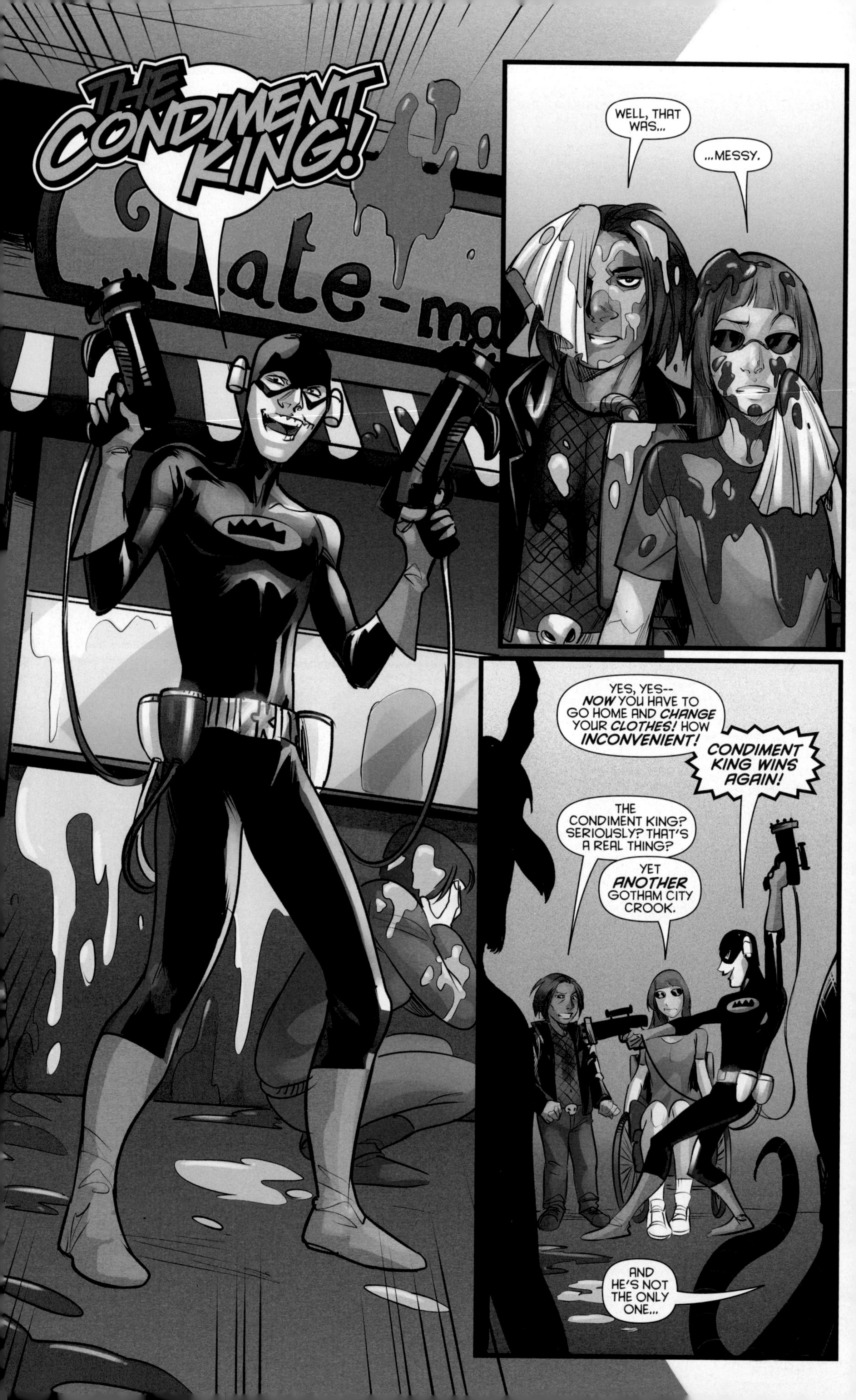
THE CONDIMENT KING!
WELL, THAT WAS...
...MESSY.
YES, YES-- NOW YOU HAVE TO GO HOME AND CHANGE YOUR CLOTHES! HOW INCONVENIENT!
CONDIMENT KING WINS AGAIN!
THE CONDIMENT KING? SERIOUSLY? THAT'S A REAL THING?
YET ANOTHER GOTHAM CITY CROOK.
AND HE'S NOT THE ONLY ONE...

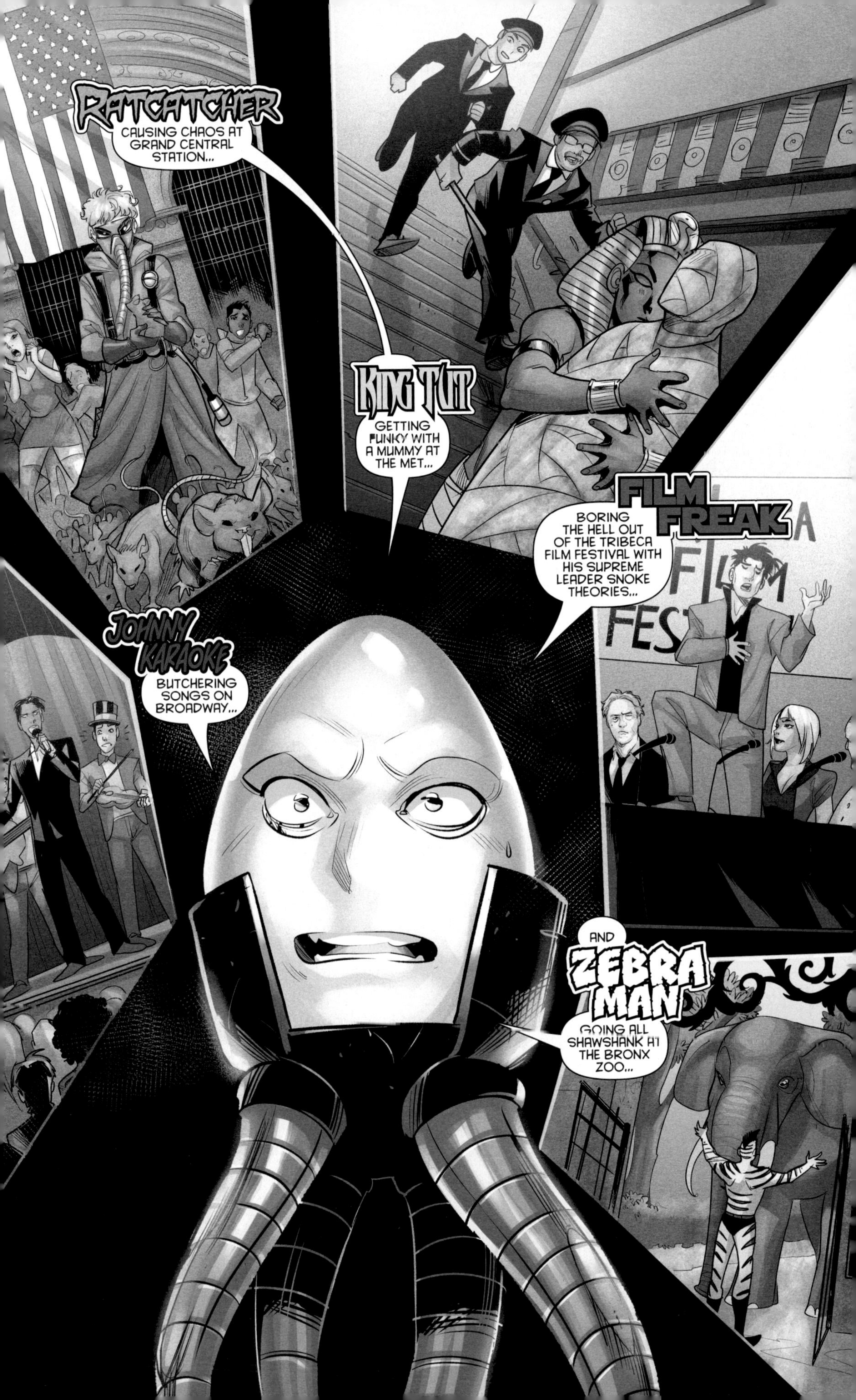
RATCATCHER
CAUSING CHAOS AT GRAND CENTRAL STATION...
KING TUT
GETTING FUNKY WITH A MUMMY AT THE MET...
FILM FREAK
BORING THE HELL OUT OF THE TRIBECA FILM FESTIVAL WITH HIS SUPREME LEADER SNOKE THEORIES...
JOHNNY KARAOKE
BUTCHERING SONGS ON BROADWAY...
AND
ZEBRA MAN
GOING ALL SHAWSHANK AT THE BRONX ZOO...

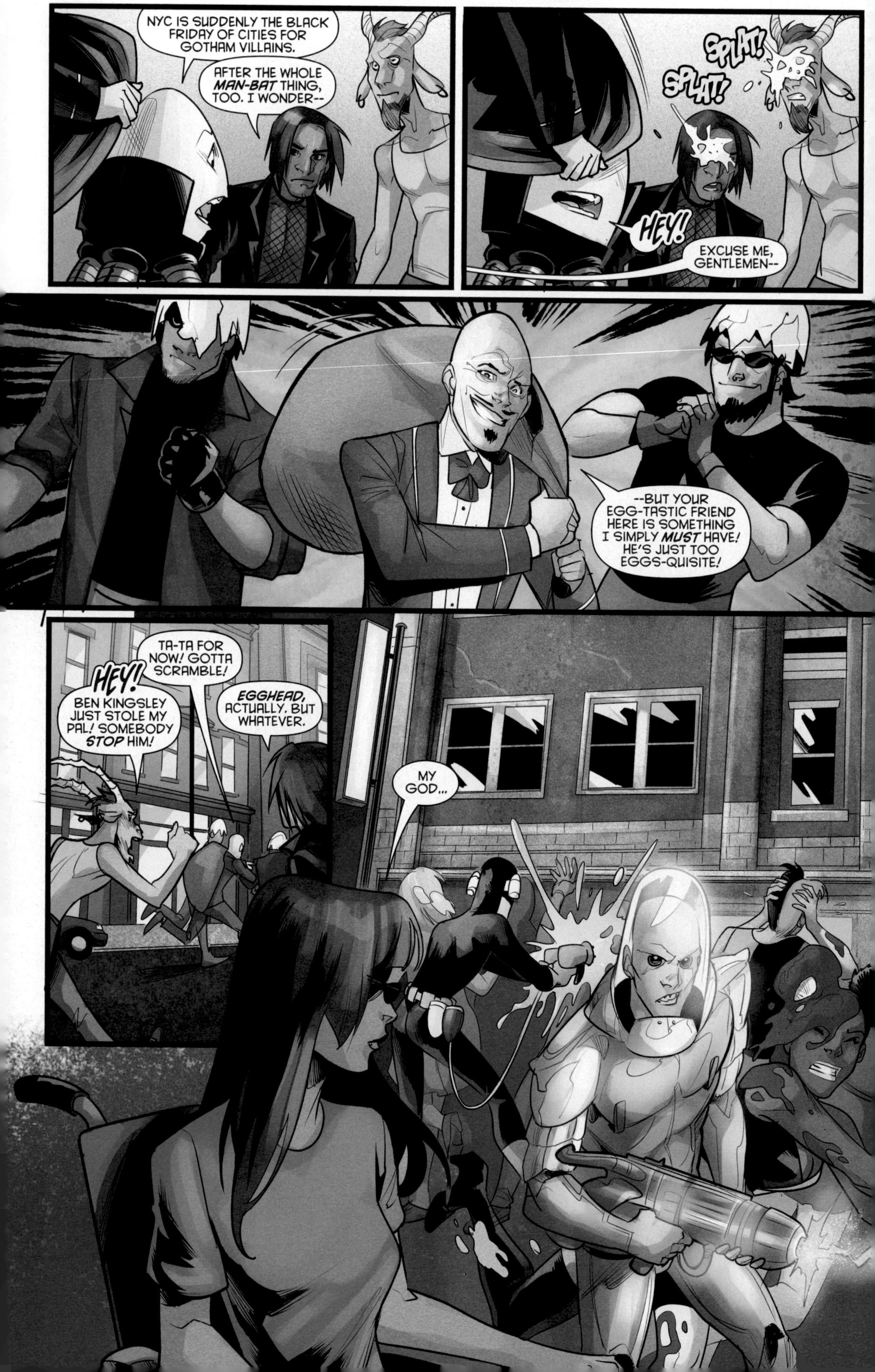
NYC IS SUDDENLY THE BLACK FRIDAY OF CITIES FOR GOTHAM VILLAINS.
AFTER THE WHOLE MAN-BAT THING, TOO. I WONDER--
SPLAT!
SPLAT!
HEY!
EXCUSE ME, GENTLEMEN--
--BUT YOUR EGG-TASTIC FRIEND HERE IS SOMETHING I SIMPLY MUST HAVE! HE'S JUST TOO EGGS-QUISITE!
TA-TA FOR NOW! GOTTA SCRAMBLE!
HEY!
BEN KINGSLEY JUST STOLE MY PAL! SOMEBODY STOP HIM!
EGGHEAD, ACTUALLY. BUT WHATEVER.
MY GOD...

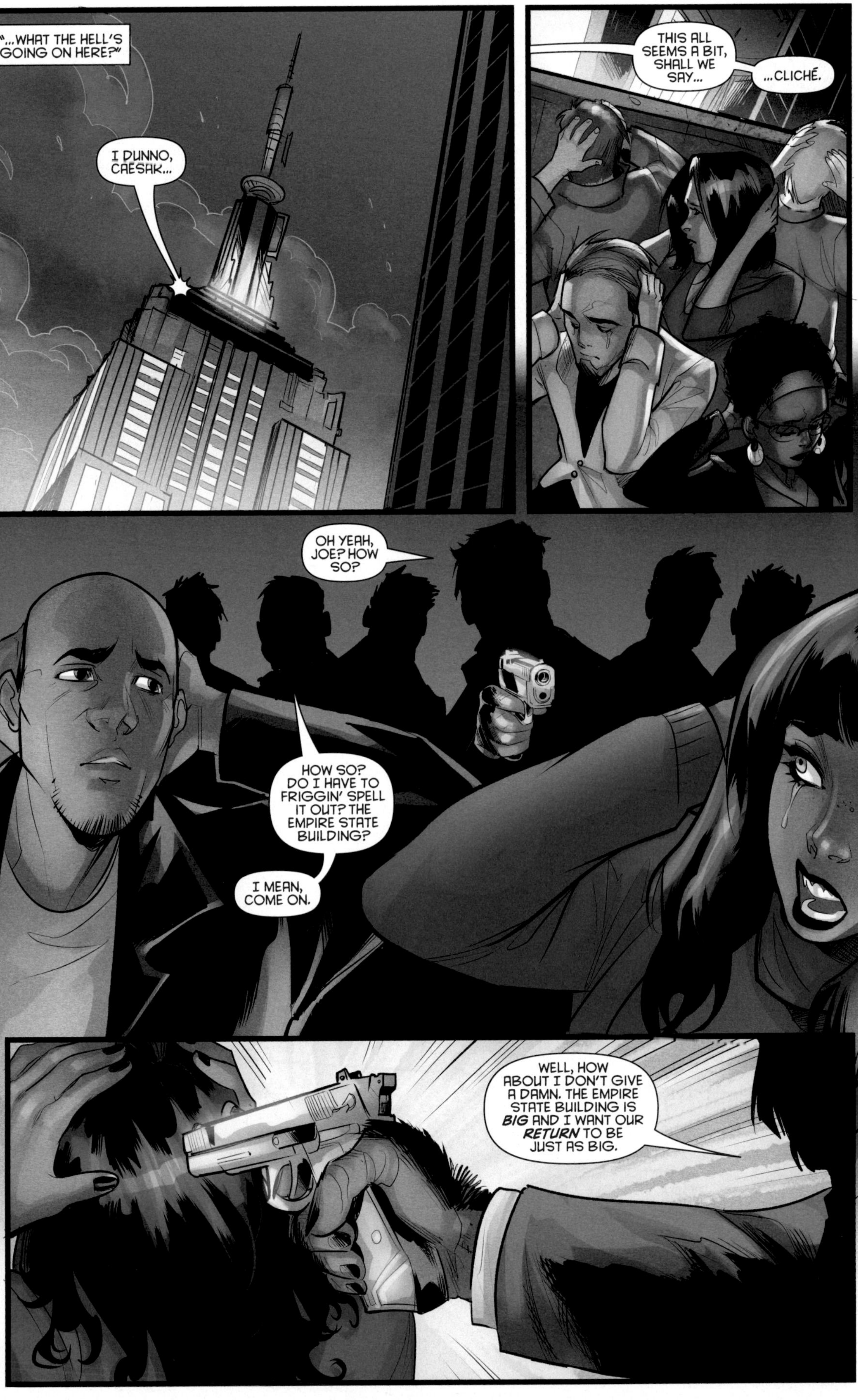
"...WHAT THE HELL'S GOING ON HERE?"
I DUNNO, CAESAR...
THIS ALL SEEMS A BIT, SHALL WE SAY...
...CLICHÉ.
OH YEAH, JOE? HOW SO?
HOW SO? DO I HAVE TO FRIGGIN' SPELL IT OUT? THE EMPIRE STATE BUILDING?
I MEAN, COME ON.
WELL, HOW ABOUT I DON'T GIVE A DAMN. THE EMPIRE STATE BUILDING IS *BIG* AND I WANT OUR *RETURN* TO BE JUST AS BIG.

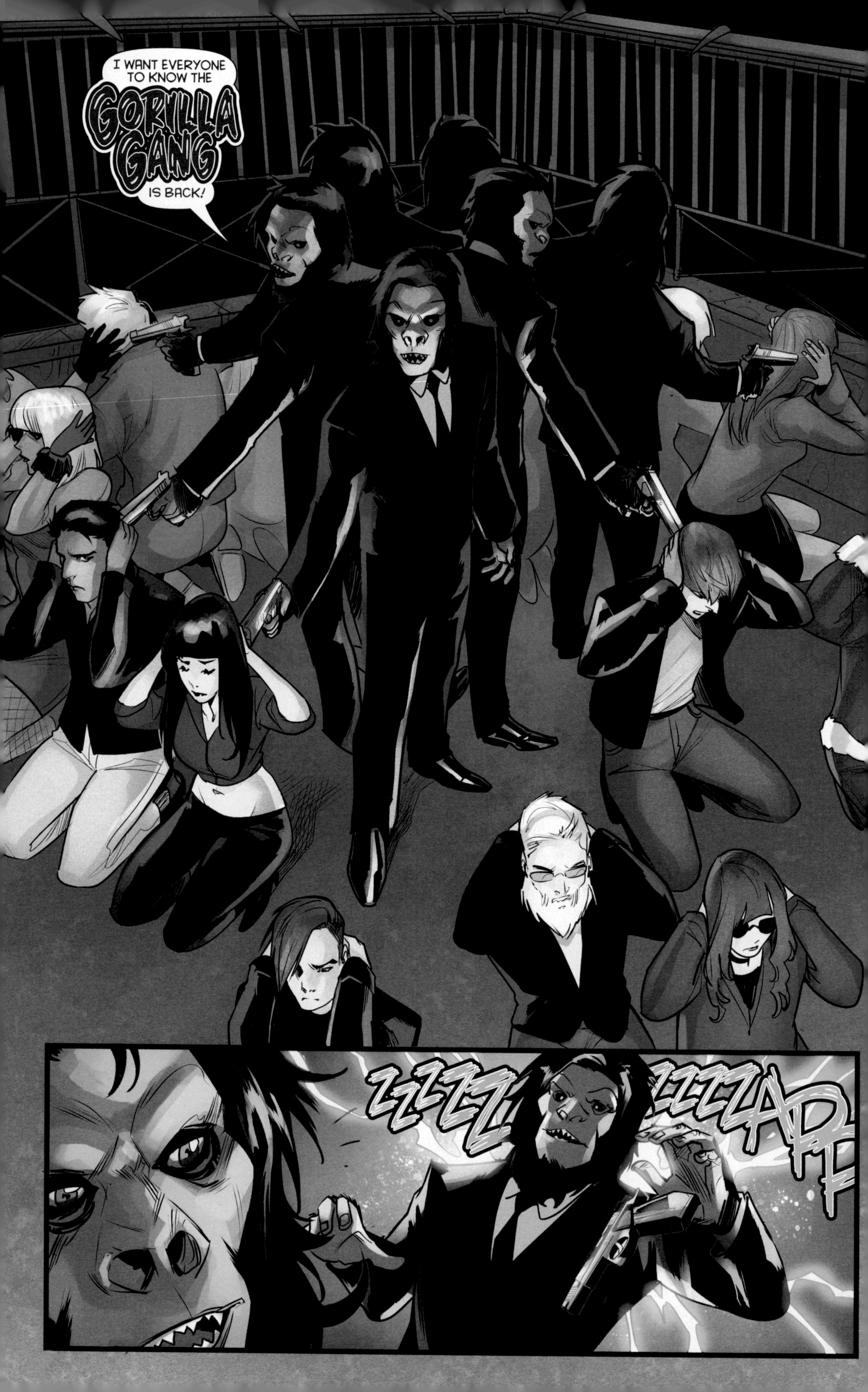
I WANT EVERYONE TO KNOW THE GORILLA GANG IS BACK!
ZZZZZ ZZZZZAP

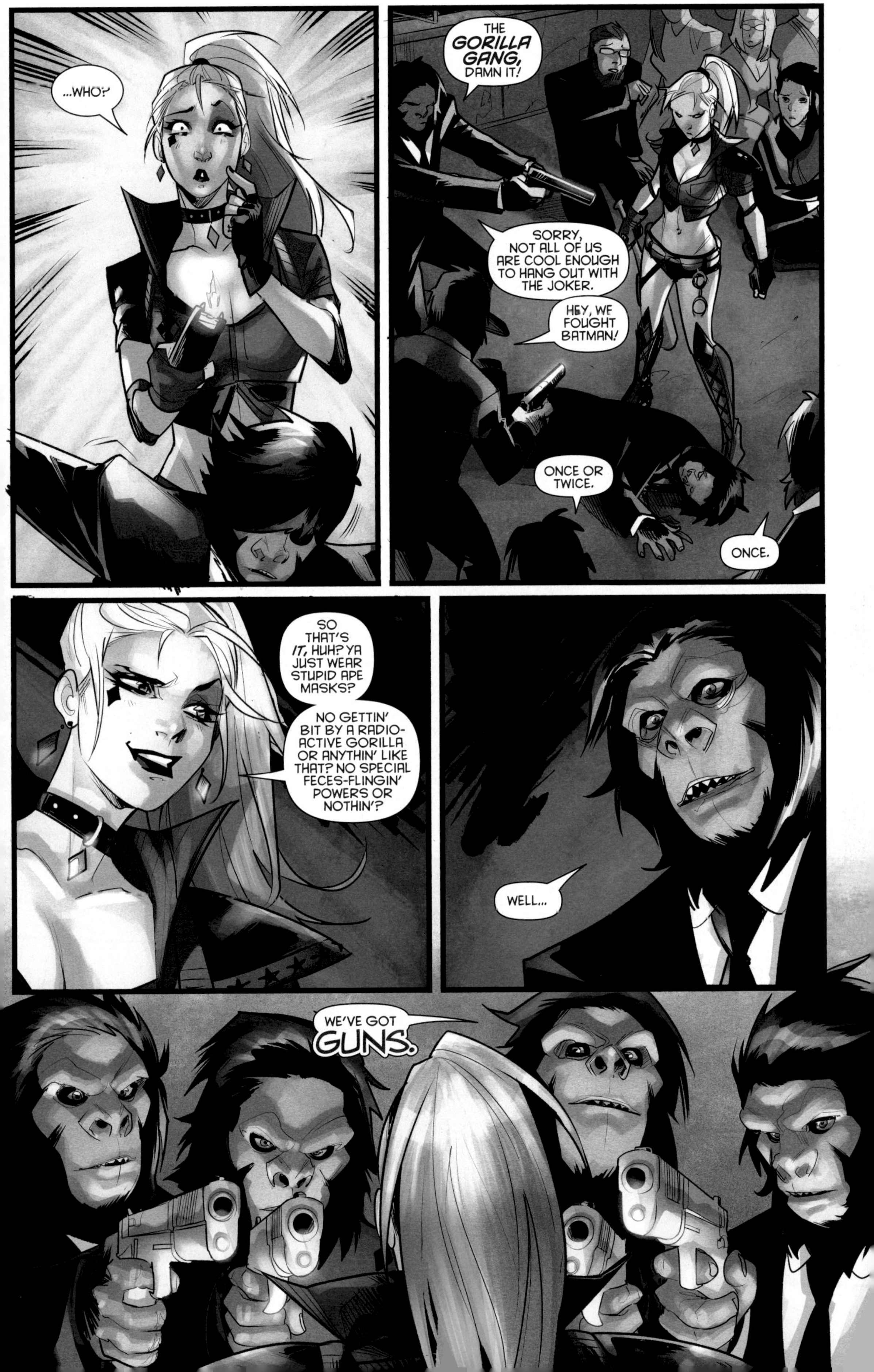
...WHO?
THE GORILLA GANG, DAMN IT!
SORRY, NOT ALL OF US ARE COOL ENOUGH TO HANG OUT WITH THE JOKER.
HEY, WE FOUGHT BATMAN!
ONCE OR TWICE.
ONCE.
SO THAT'S IT, HUH? YA JUST WEAR STUPID APE MASKS?
NO GETTIN' BIT BY A RADIO-ACTIVE GORILLA OR ANYTHIN' LIKE THAT? NO SPECIAL FECES-FLINGIN' POWERS OR NOTHIN'?
WELL...
WE'VE GOT GUNS.

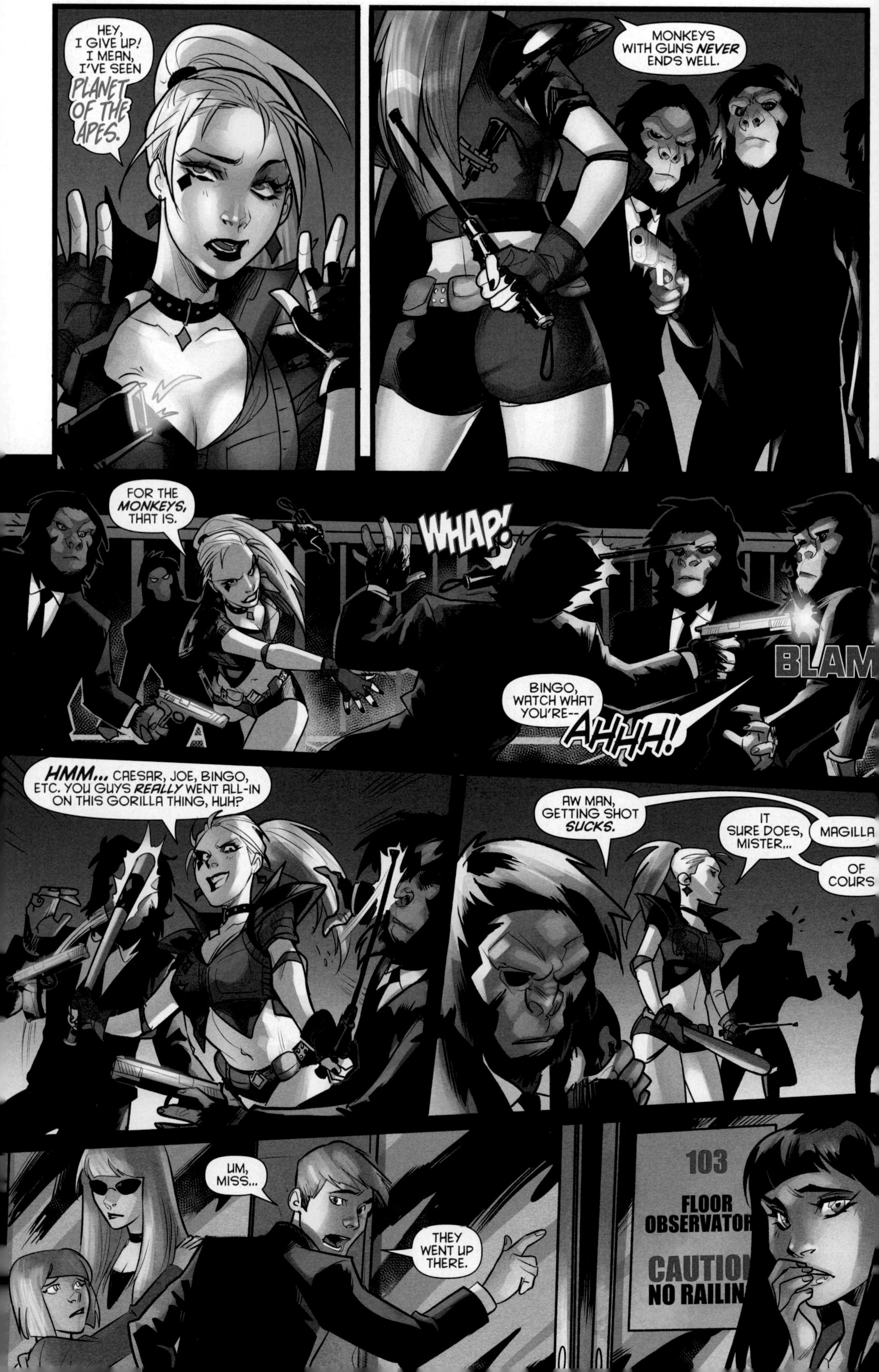

HEY, I GIVE UP! I MEAN, I'VE SEEN PLANET OF THE APES.
MONKEYS WITH GUNS NEVER ENDS WELL.
FOR THE MONKEYS, THAT IS.
WHAP!
BLAM
BINGO, WATCH WHAT YOU'RE-- AHHH!
HMM... CAESAR, JOE, BINGO, ETC. YOU GUYS REALLY WENT ALL-IN ON THIS GORILLA THING, HUH?
AW MAN, GETTING SHOT SUCKS.
IT SURE DOES, MISTER...
MAGILLA
OF COURS
UM, MISS...
THEY WENT UP THERE.
103
FLOOR OBSERVATOR
CAUTIO
NO RAILIN

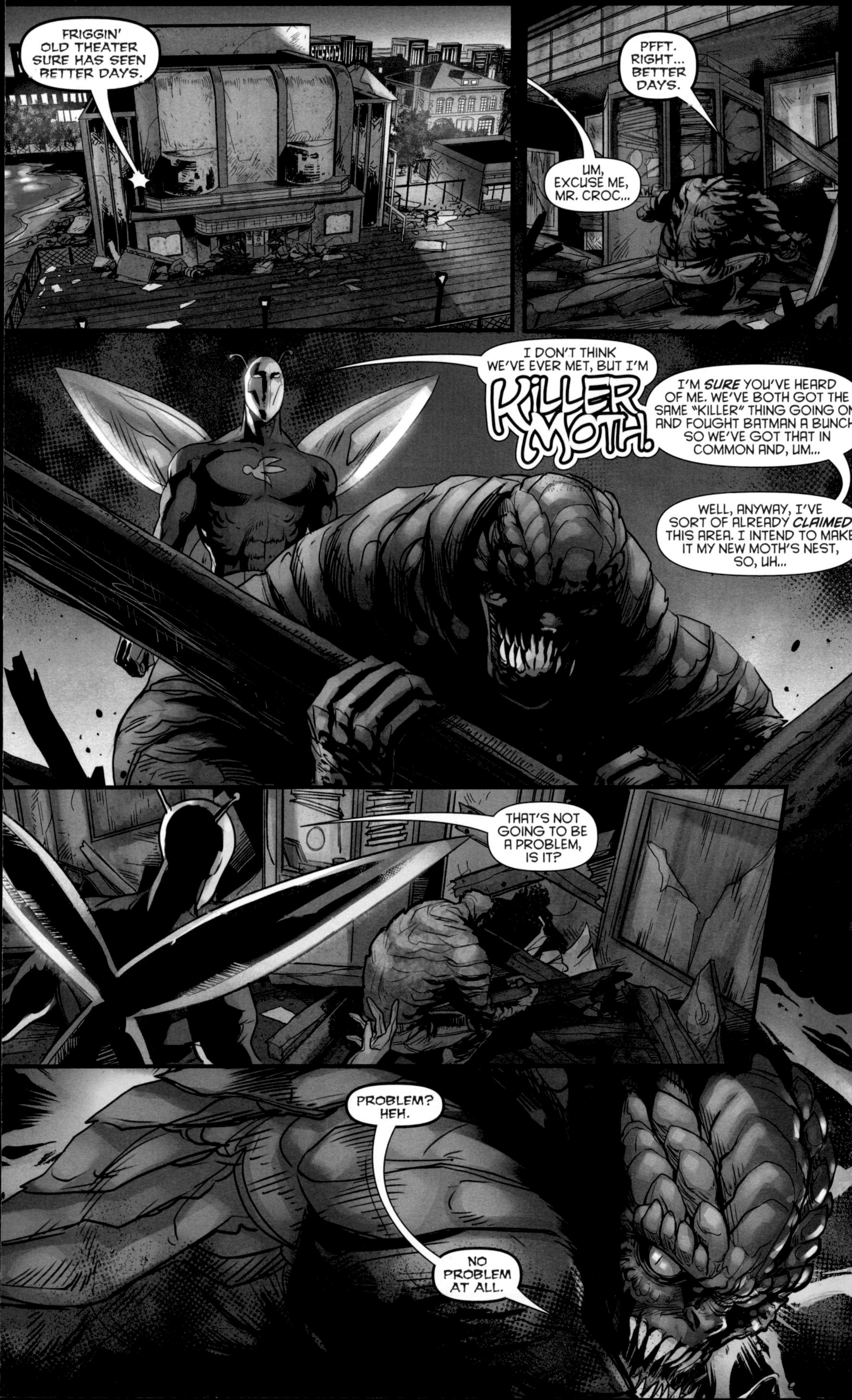
FRIGGIN' OLD THEATER SURE HAS SEEN BETTER DAYS.
PFFT. RIGHT... BETTER DAYS.
UM, EXCUSE ME, MR. CROC...
I DON'T THINK WE'VE EVER MET, BUT I'M
KILLER MOTH.
I'M SURE YOU'VE HEARD OF ME. WE'VE BOTH GOT THE SAME "KILLER" THING GOING ON, AND FOUGHT BATMAN A BUNCH, SO WE'VE GOT THAT IN COMMON AND, UM...
WELL, ANYWAY, I'VE SORT OF ALREADY CLAIMED THIS AREA. I INTEND TO MAKE IT MY NEW MOTH'S NEST, SO, UH...
THAT'S NOT GOING TO BE A PROBLEM, IS IT?
PROBLEM? HEH.
NO PROBLEM AT ALL.

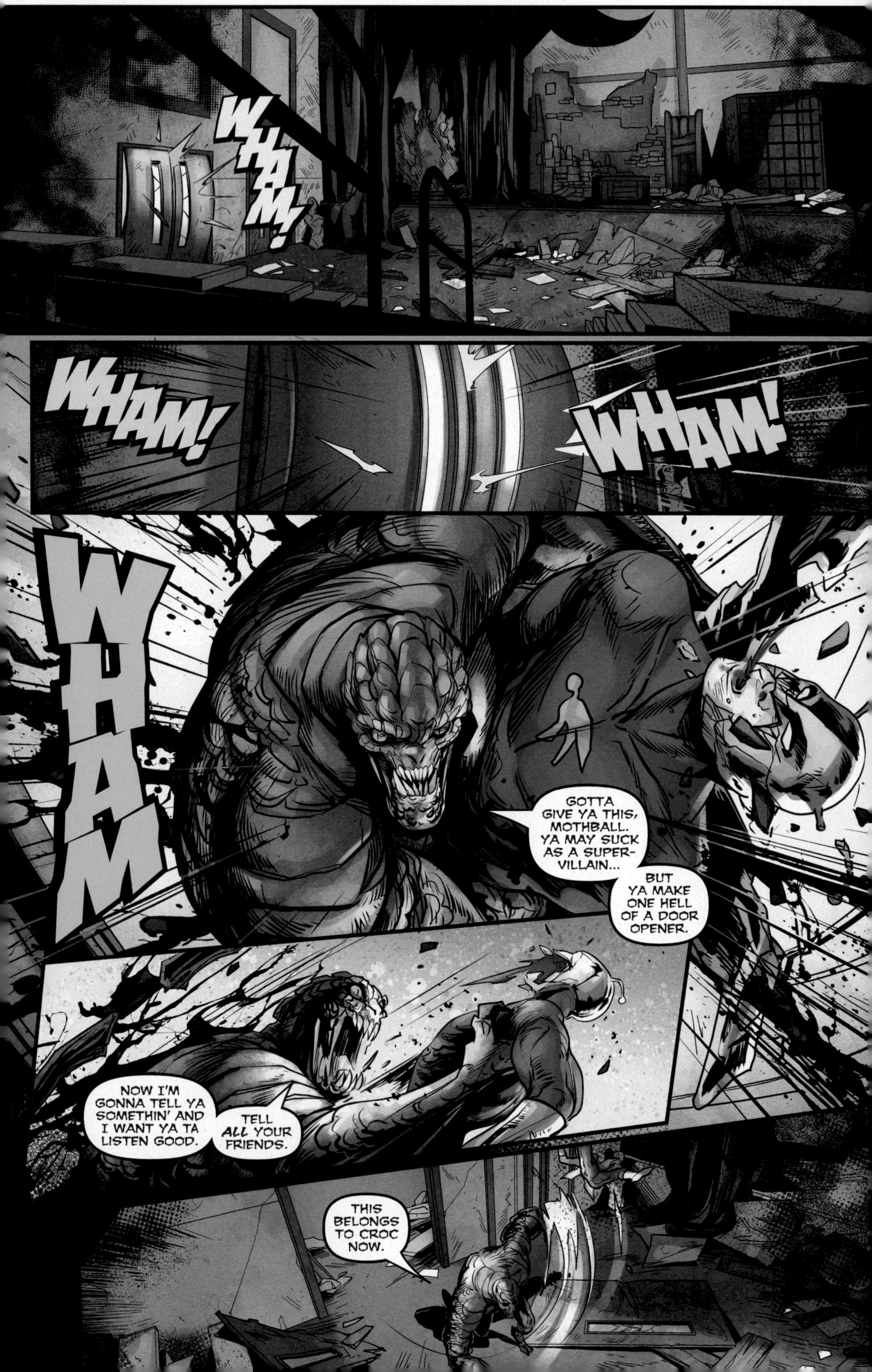
WHAM!
WHAM!
WHAM!
WHAM
GOTTA GIVE YA THIS, MOTHBALL. YA MAY SUCK AS A SUPER-VILLAIN...
BUT YA MAKE ONE HELL OF A DOOR OPENER.
NOW I'M GONNA TELL YA SOMETHIN' AND I WANT YA TA LISTEN GOOD.
TELL ALL YOUR FRIENDS.
THIS BELONGS TO CROC NOW.

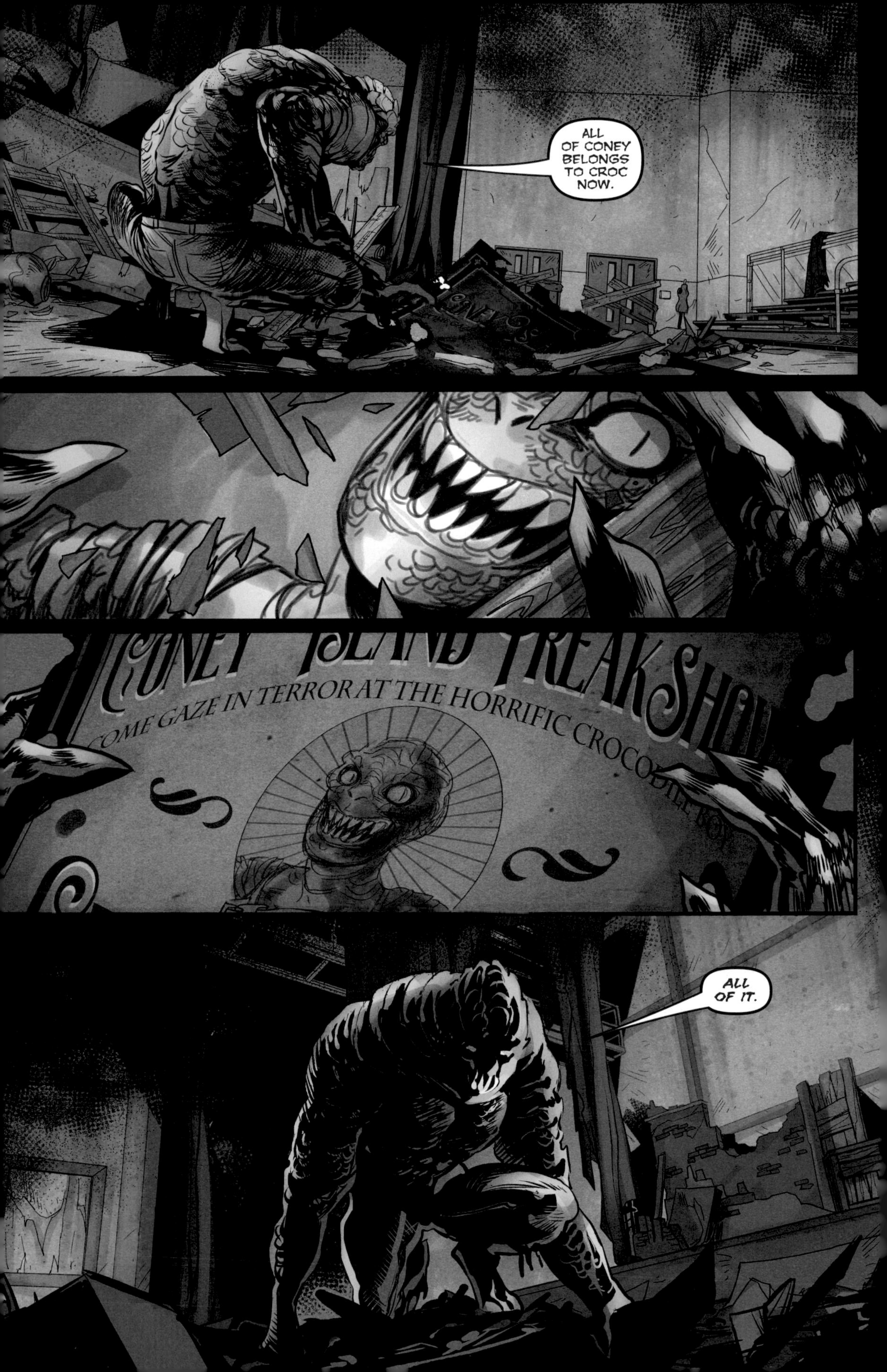
ALL OF CONEY BELONGS TO CROC NOW.
COME GAZE IN TERROR AT THE HORRIFIC
ALL OF IT.

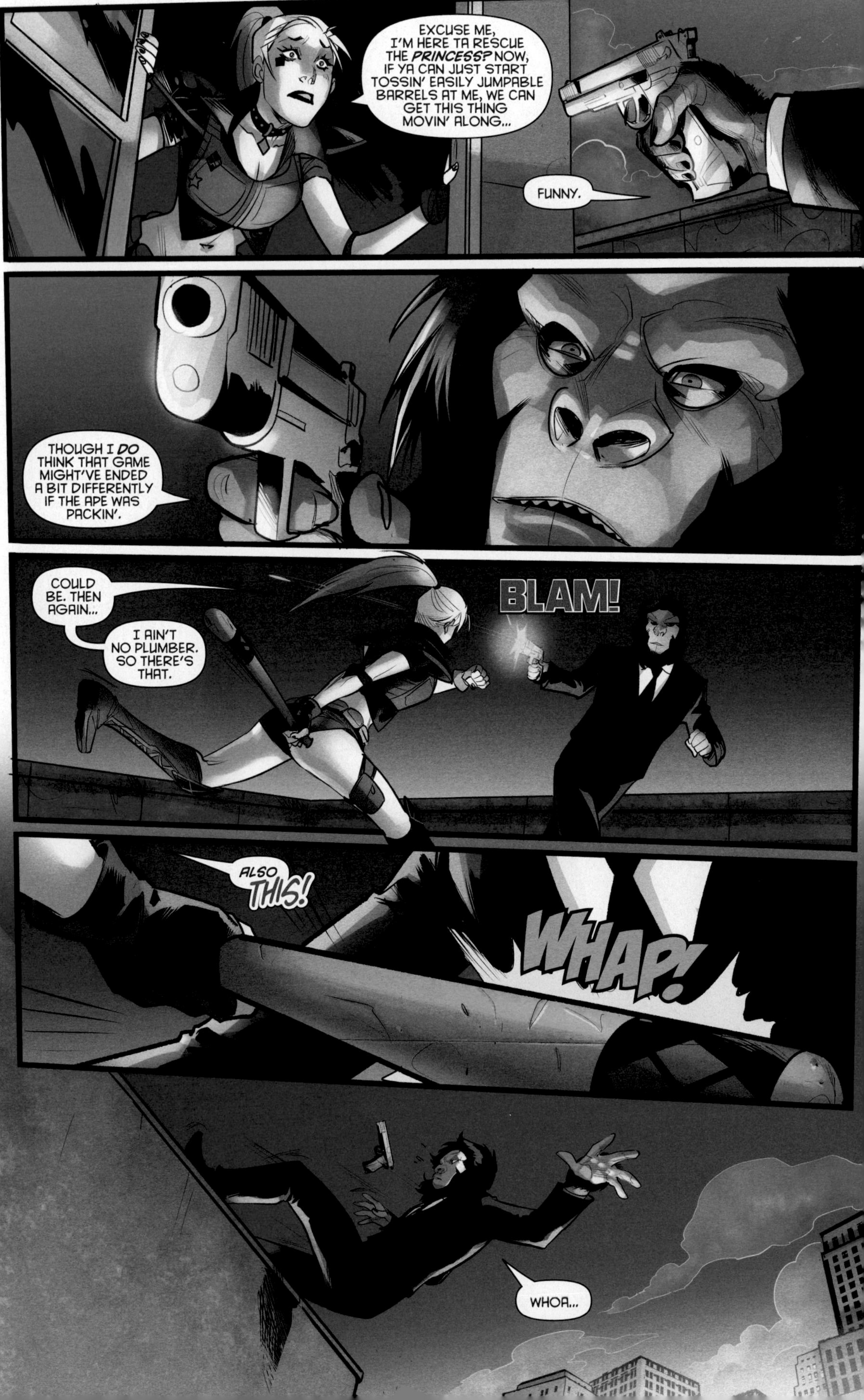
EXCUSE ME, I'M HERE TA RESCUE THE PRINCESS? NOW, IF YA CAN JUST START TOSSIN' EASILY JUMPABLE BARRELS AT ME, WE CAN GET THIS THING MOVIN' ALONG...
FUNNY.
THOUGH I DO THINK THAT GAME MIGHT'VE ENDED A BIT DIFFERENTLY IF THE APE WAS PACKIN'.
COULD BE. THEN AGAIN...
I AIN'T NO PLUMBER. SO THERE'S THAT.
BLAM!
ALSO THIS!
WHAP!
WHOA...

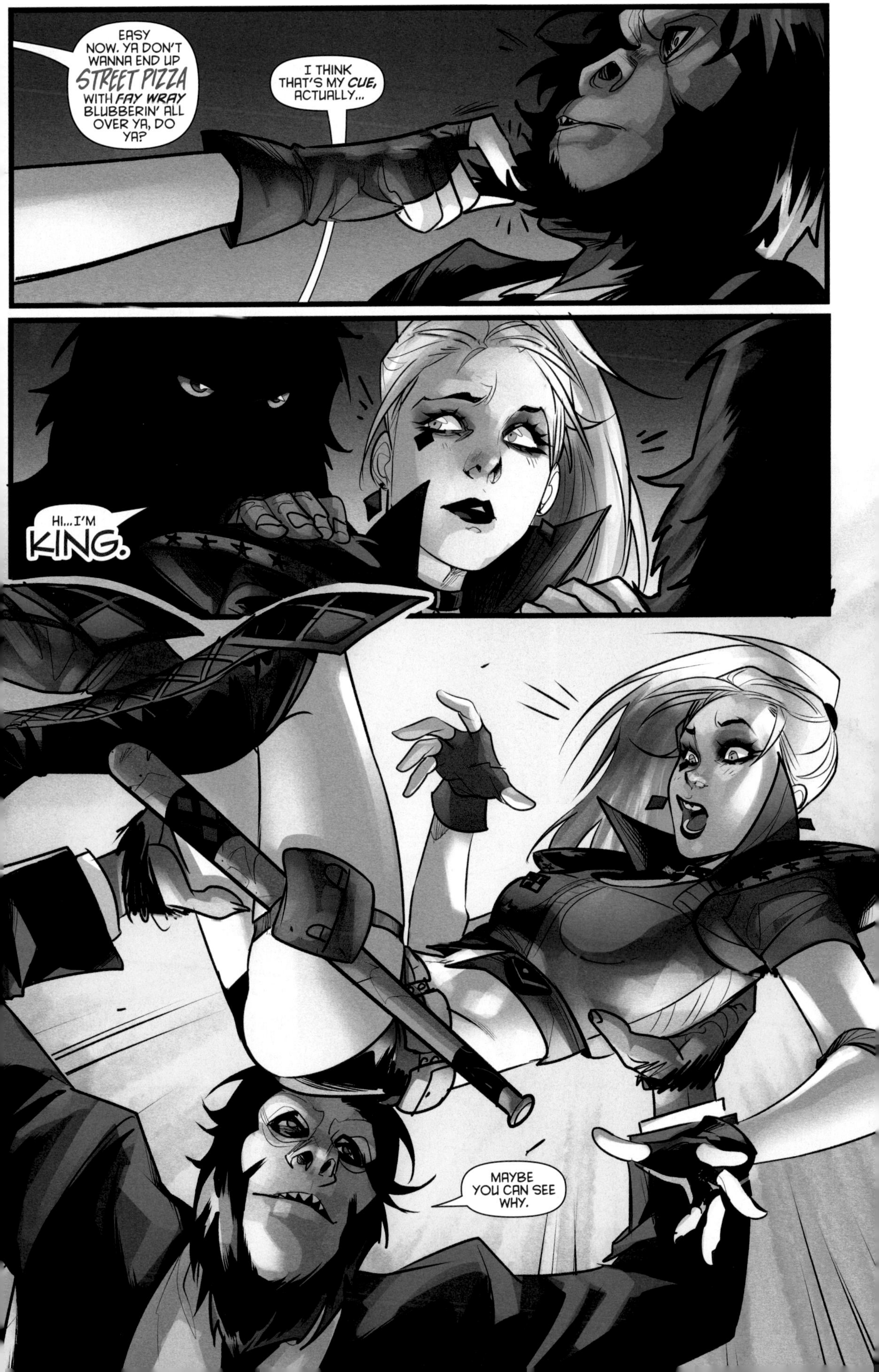
EASY NOW. YA DON'T WANNA END UP STREET PIZZA WITH FAY WRAY BLUBBERIN' ALL OVER YA, DO YA?
I THINK THAT'S MY CUE, ACTUALLY...
HI...I'M KING.
MAYBE YOU CAN SEE WHY.

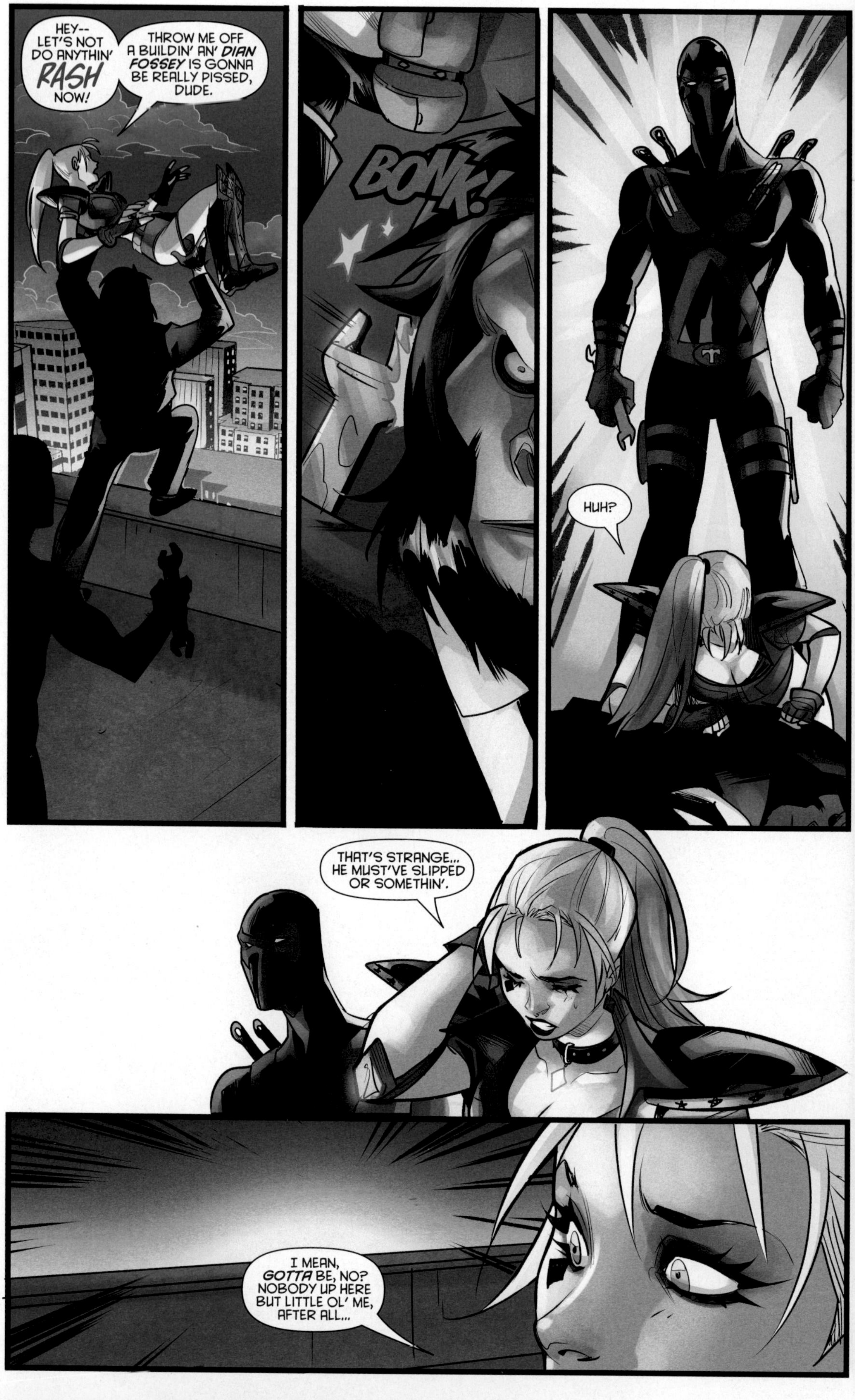
HEY-- LET'S NOT DO ANYTHIN' RASH NOW!
THROW ME OFF A BUILDIN' AN' DIAN FOSSEY IS GONNA BE REALLY PISSED, DUDE.
BONK!
HUH?
THAT'S STRANGE... HE MUST'VE SLIPPED OR SOMETHIN'.
I MEAN, GOTTA BE, NO? NOBODY UP HERE BUT LITTLE OL' ME, AFTER ALL...

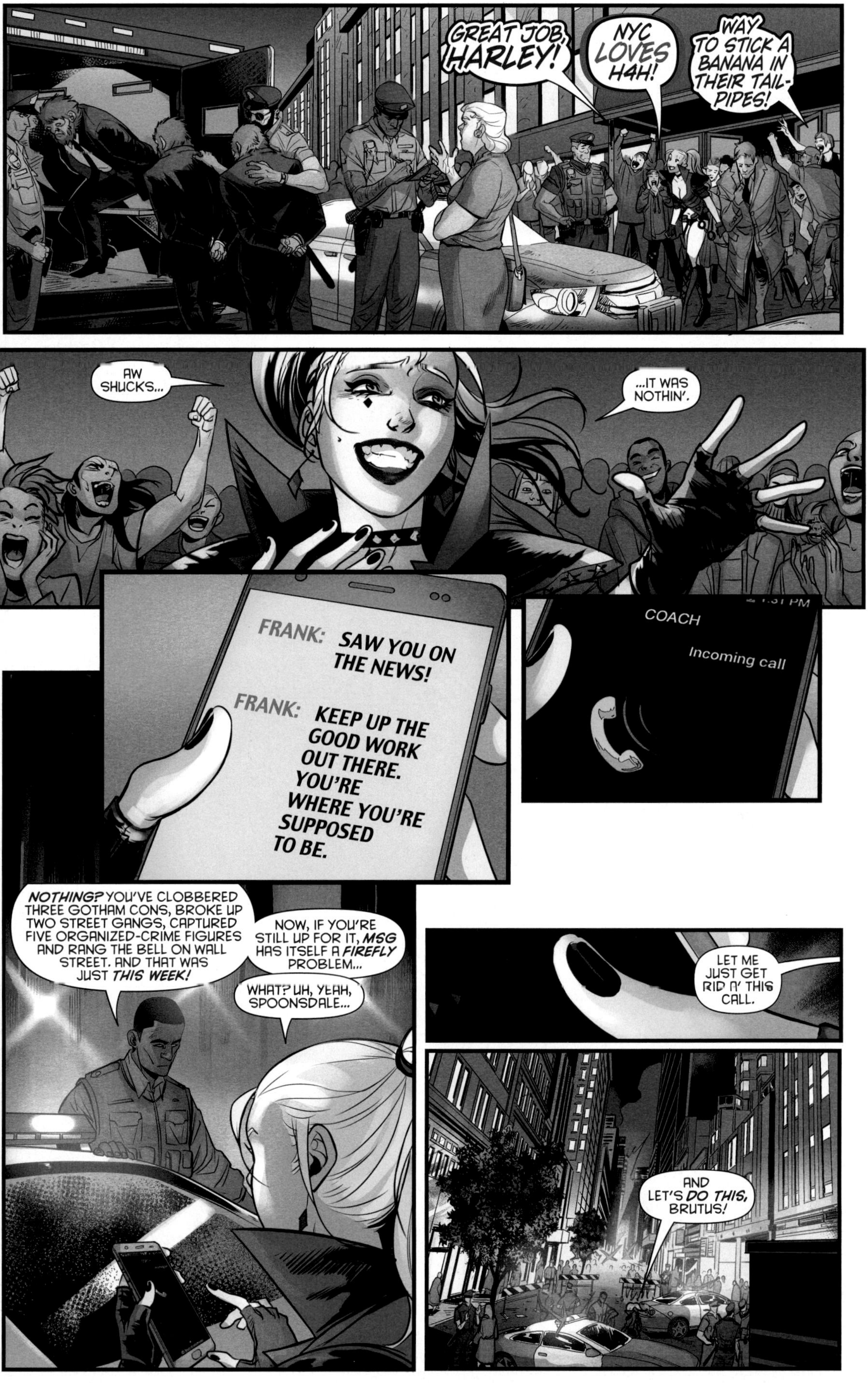

GREAT JOB, HARLEY!
NYC LOVES H4H!
WAY TO STICK A BANANA IN THEIR TAIL-PIPES!
AW SHUCKS...
...IT WAS NOTHIN'.
FRANK: SAW YOU ON THE NEWS!
FRANK: KEEP UP THE GOOD WORK OUT THERE. YOU'RE WHERE YOU'RE SUPPOSED TO BE.
COACH
Incoming call
NOTHING? YOU'VE CLOBBERED THREE GOTHAM CONS, BROKE UP TWO STREET GANGS, CAPTURED FIVE ORGANIZED-CRIME FIGURES AND RANG THE BELL ON WALL STREET. AND THAT WAS JUST THIS WEEK!
NOW, IF YOU'RE STILL UP FOR IT, MSG HAS ITSELF A FIREFLY PROBLEM...
WHAT? UH, YEAH, SPOONSDALE...
LET ME JUST GET RID A' THIS CALL.
AND LET'S DO THIS, BRUTUS!

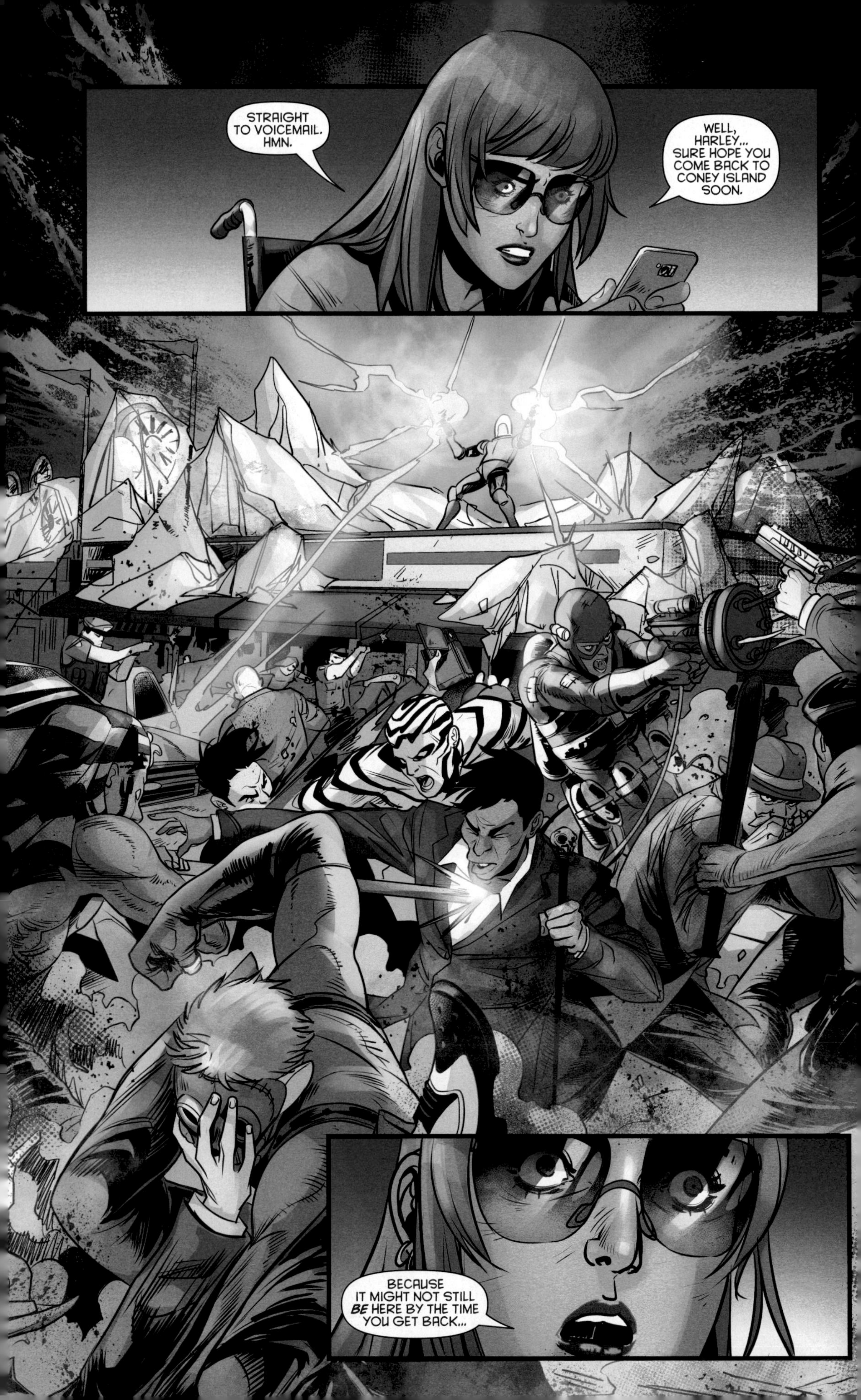
STRAIGHT TO VOICEMAIL. HMN.
WELL, HARLEY... SURE HOPE YOU COME BACK TO CONEY ISLAND SOON.
BECAUSE IT MIGHT NOT STILL *BE* HERE BY THE TIME YOU GET BACK...

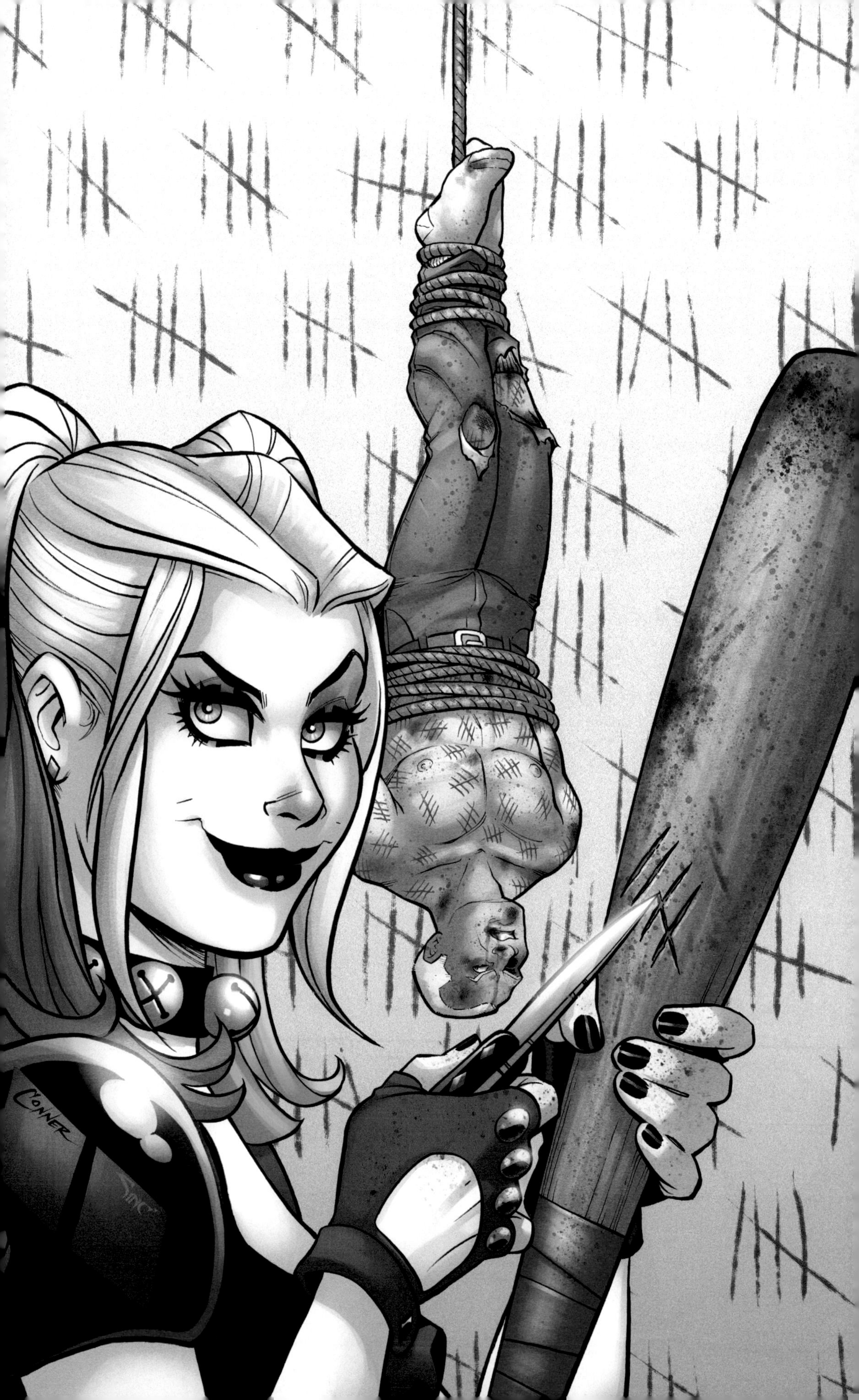
CONNER

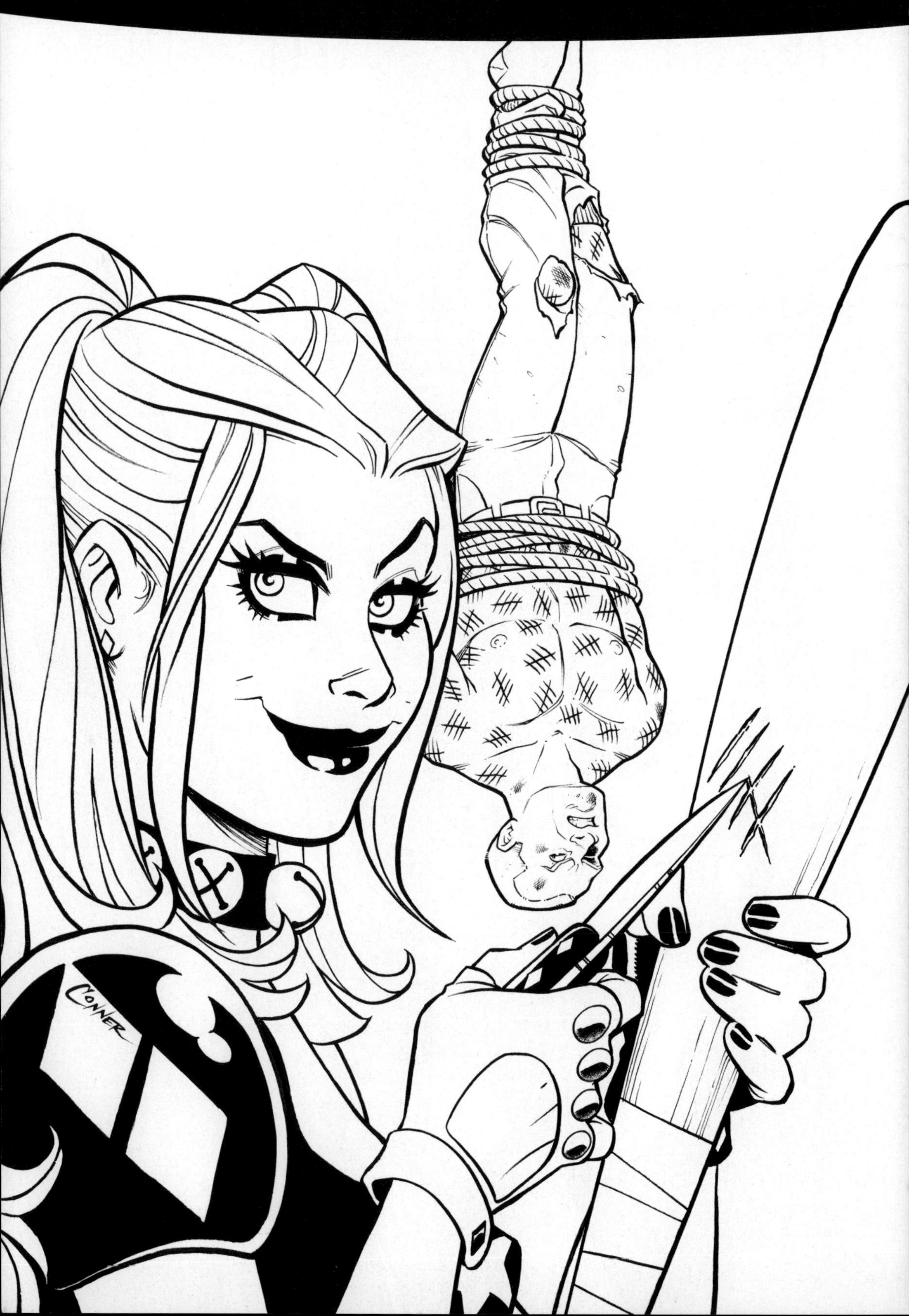
CONNER

DON'T KNOW WHY WE'RE *BOTHERING* TO BUILD THIS ALL UP AFTER THE HURRICANE...

...WHAT WITH EVERYTHING IN CONEY GETTING *TORN DOWN* ALL AROUND US.

HEY KIDS FISH!

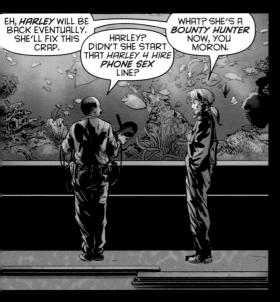

EH, *HARLEY* WILL BE BACK EVENTUALLY. SHE'LL FIX THIS CRAP.

HARLEY? DIDN'T SHE START THAT *HARLEY 4 HIRE PHONE SEX* LINE?

WHAT? SHE'S A *BOUNTY HUNTER* NOW, YOU MORON.

HMM. NO *WONDER* SHE THREATENED TO SET MY TESTICLES ON FIRE WHEN I STARTED BREATHIN' HEAVY. AND HERE I THOUGHT THAT WAS JUST SEXY TALK.

WHAT'S THE *MATTER* WITH YOU?

HEY, MAN, I GET LONELY. I'M HERE WITH NOTHING BUT *YOU* AND *FISH* TO TALK TO ALL DAY. AND YOU AIN'T MY TYPE.

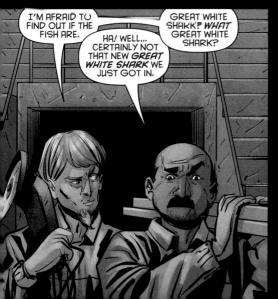

I'M AFRAID TO FIND OUT IF THE FISH ARE.

HA! WELL... CERTAINLY NOT THAT NEW *GREAT WHITE SHARK* WE JUST GOT IN.

*GREAT WHITE SHARK? WHAT* GREAT WHITE SHARK?

*THAT* ONE.

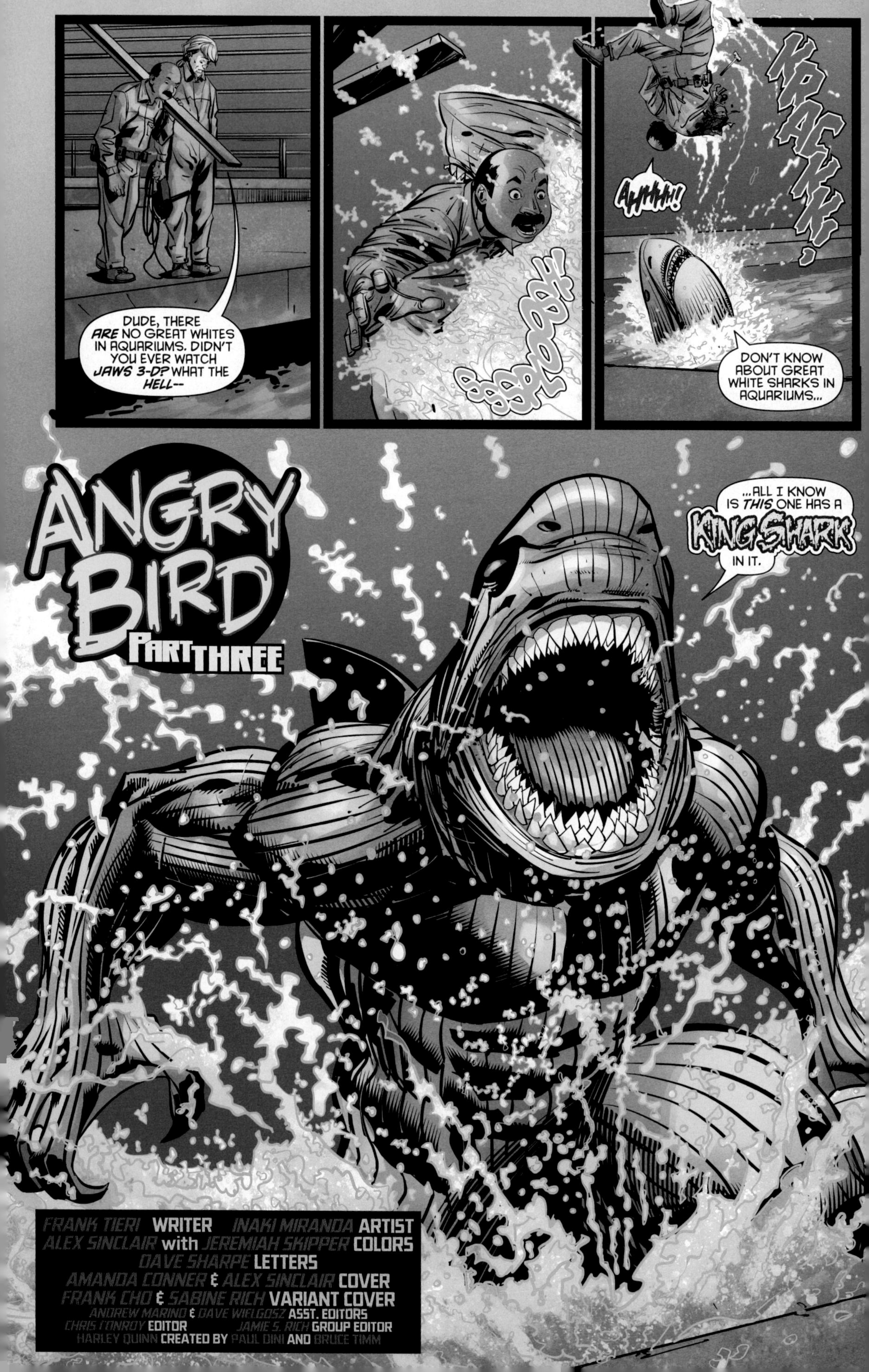

DUDE, THERE ARE NO GREAT WHITES IN AQUARIUMS. DIDN'T YOU EVER WATCH JAWS 3-D? WHAT THE HELL--
SSSPLOOSH!
AHHHH!
KRACKK!
DON'T KNOW ABOUT GREAT WHITE SHARKS IN AQUARIUMS...
ANGRY BIRD
PART THREE
...ALL I KNOW IS THIS ONE HAS A KING SHARK IN IT.
FRANK TIERI WRITER INAKI MIRANDA ARTIST
ALEX SINCLAIR with JEREMIAH SKIPPER COLORS
DAVE SHARPE LETTERS
AMANDA CONNER & ALEX SINCLAIR COVER
FRANK CHO & SABINE RICH VARIANT COVER
ANDREW MARINO & DAVE WIELGOSZ ASST. EDITORS
CHRIS CONROY EDITOR JAMIE S. RICH GROUP EDITOR
HARLEY QUINN CREATED BY PAUL DINI AND BRUCE TIMM

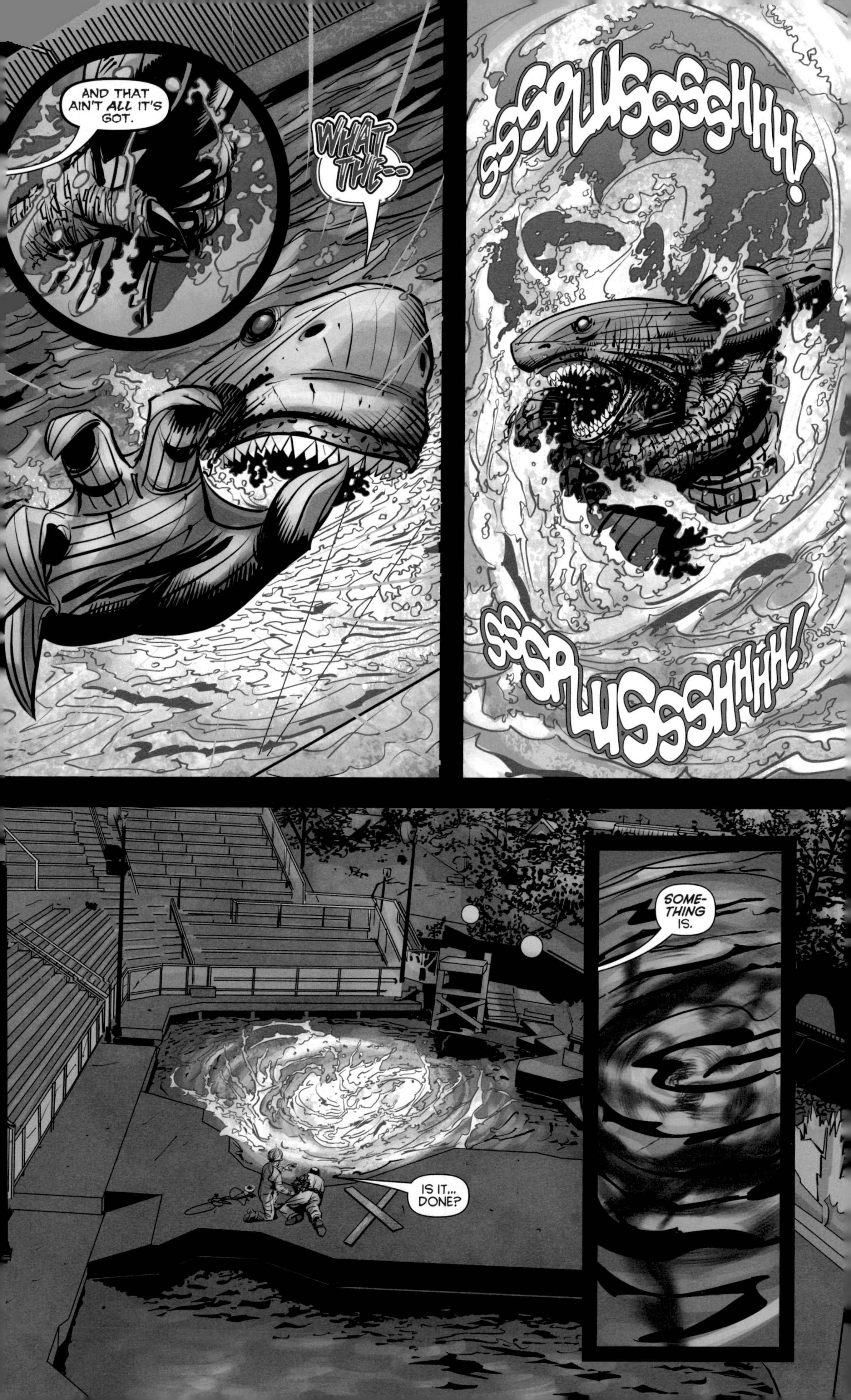
AND THAT AIN'T ALL IT'S GOT.
WHAT THE--
SSSPLUSSSSHHH!
SSSPLUSSSHHH!
IS IT... DONE?
SOME-THING IS.

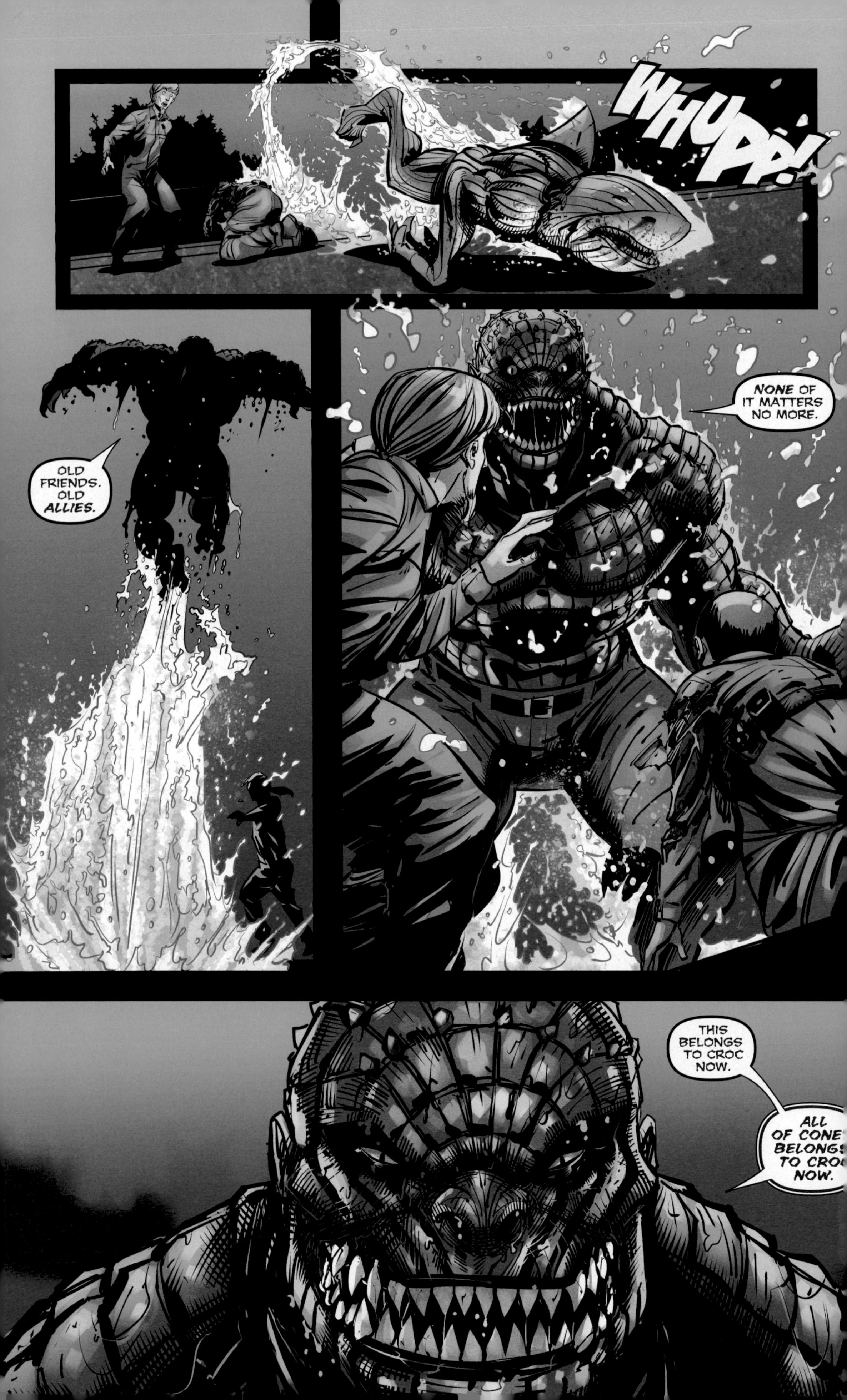
WHUDD!
OLD FRIENDS. OLD ALLIES.
NONE OF IT MATTERS NO MORE.
THIS BELONGS TO CROC NOW.
ALL OF CONE BELONGS TO CROC NOW.

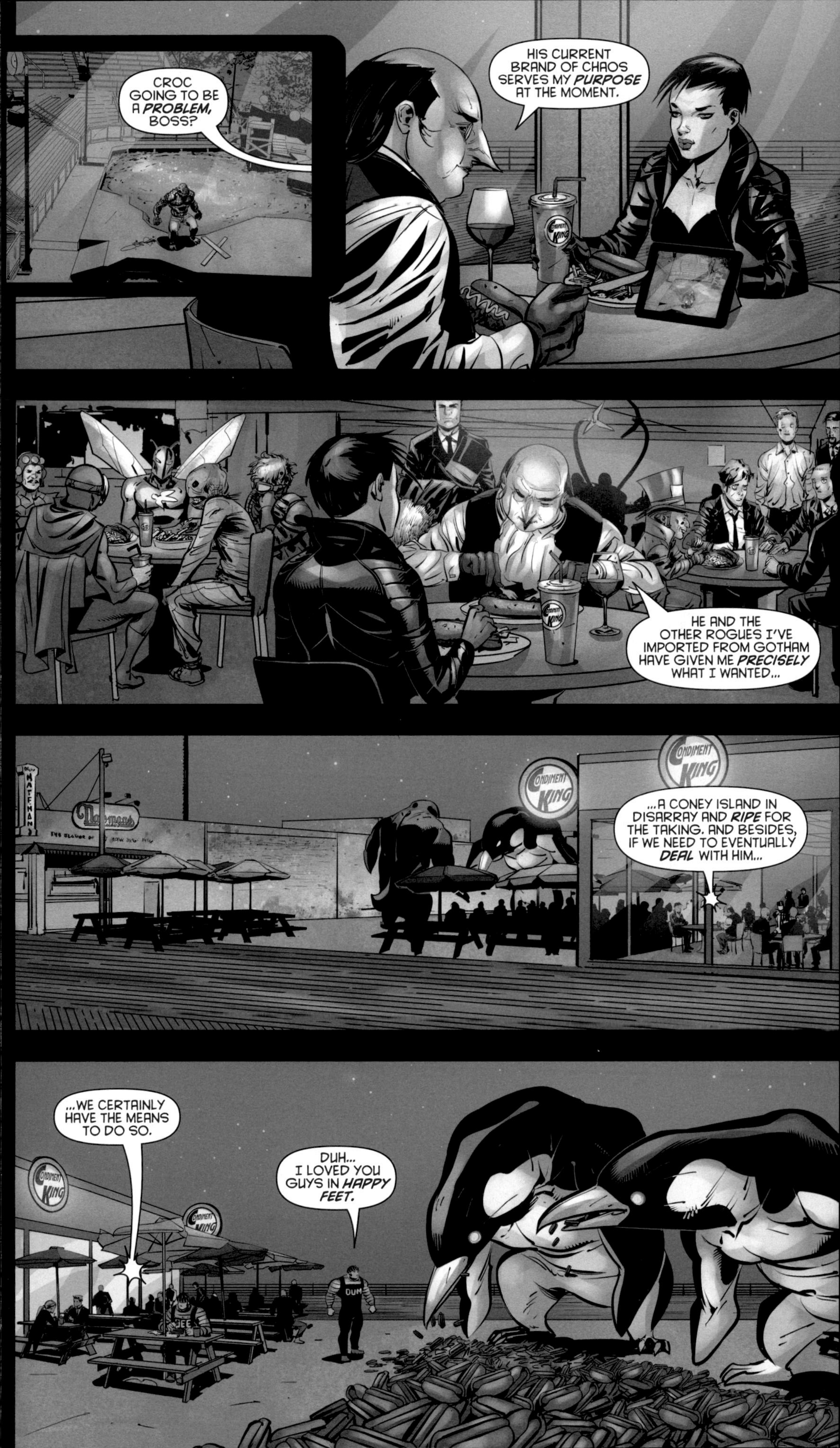
CROC GOING TO BE A PROBLEM, BOSS?
HIS CURRENT BRAND OF CHAOS SERVES MY PURPOSE AT THE MOMENT.
HE AND THE OTHER ROGUES I'VE IMPORTED FROM GOTHAM HAVE GIVEN ME PRECISELY WHAT I WANTED...
...A CONEY ISLAND IN DISARRAY AND RIPE FOR THE TAKING. AND BESIDES, IF WE NEED TO EVENTUALLY DEAL WITH HIM...
...WE CERTAINLY HAVE THE MEANS TO DO SO.
DUH... I LOVED YOU GUYS IN HAPPY FEET.
CONDIMENT KING
DUM

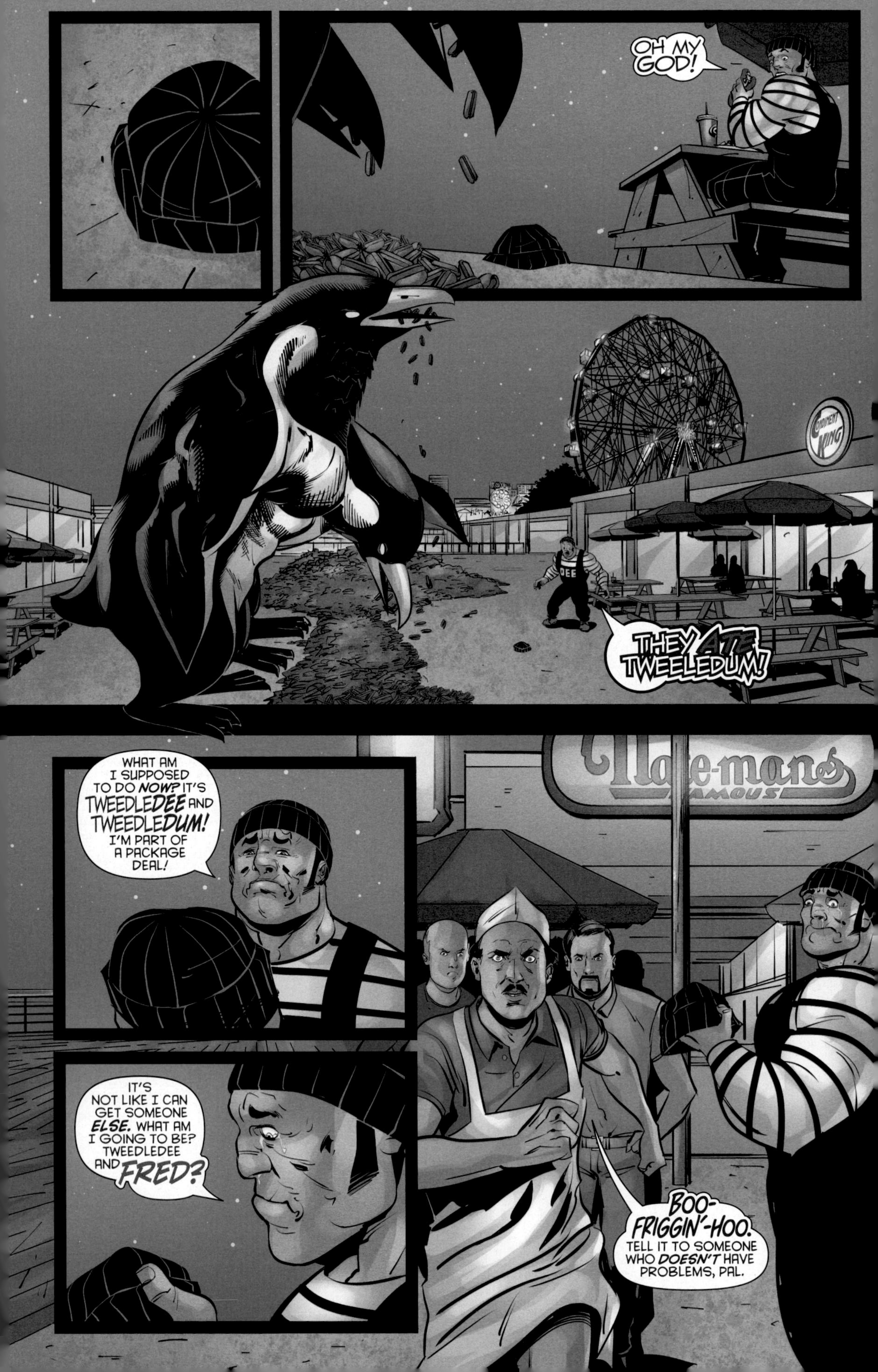
OH MY GOD!
THEY ATE TWEELEDUM!
WHAT AM I SUPPOSED TO DO NOW? IT'S TWEEDLEDEE AND TWEEDLEDUM! I'M PART OF A PACKAGE DEAL!
IT'S NOT LIKE I CAN GET SOMEONE ELSE. WHAT AM I GOING TO BE? TWEEDLEDEE AND FRED?
BOO-FRIGGIN'-HOO. TELL IT TO SOMEONE WHO DOESN'T HAVE PROBLEMS, PAL.

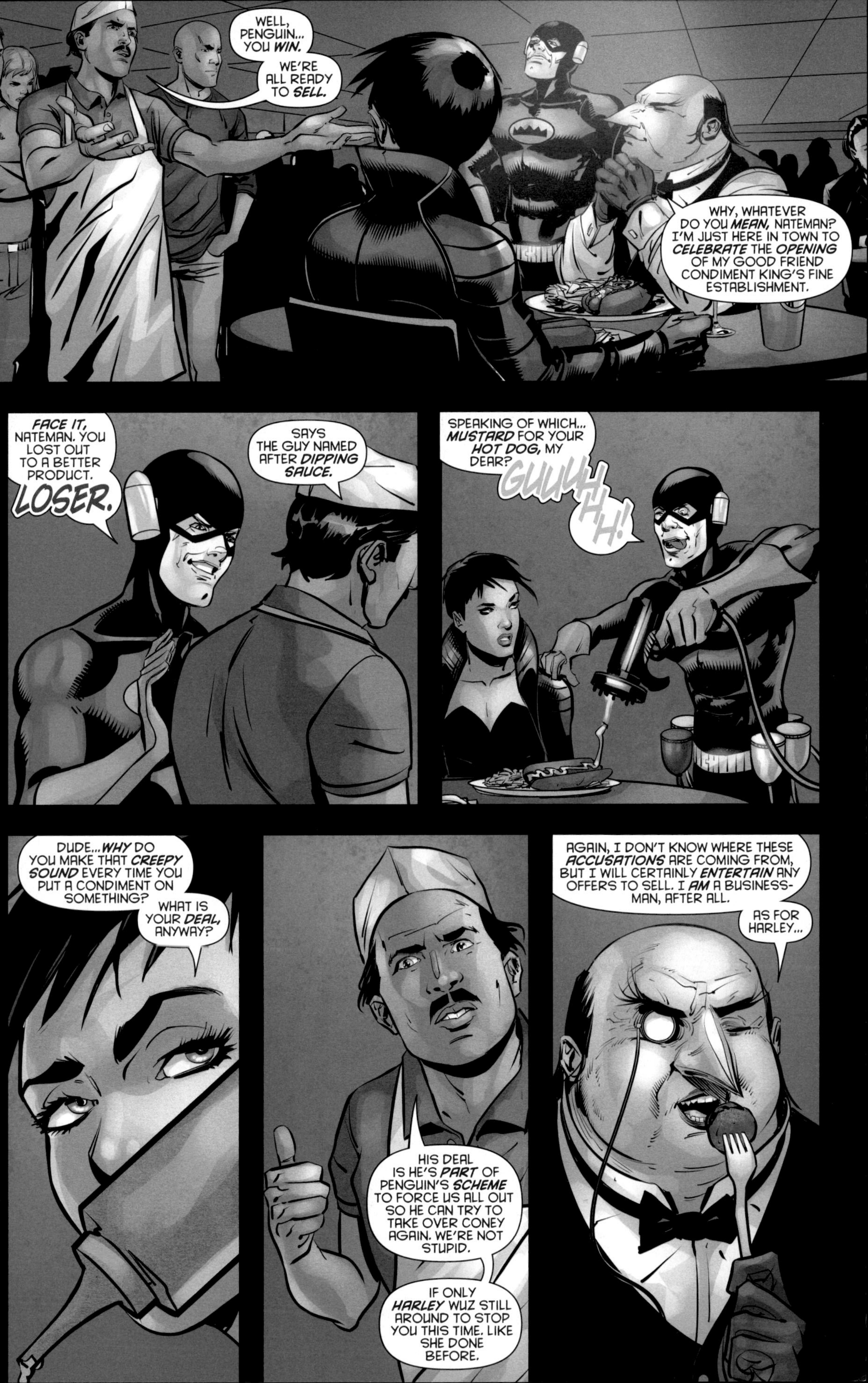
WELL, PENGUIN... YOU WIN.
WE'RE ALL READY TO SELL.
WHY, WHATEVER DO YOU MEAN, NATEMAN? I'M JUST HERE IN TOWN TO CELEBRATE THE OPENING OF MY GOOD FRIEND CONDIMENT KING'S FINE ESTABLISHMENT.
FACE IT, NATEMAN. YOU LOST OUT TO A BETTER PRODUCT. LOSER.
SAYS THE GUY NAMED AFTER DIPPING SAUCE.
SPEAKING OF WHICH... MUSTARD FOR YOUR HOT DOG, MY DEAR?
GUUUHHH!
DUDE...WHY DO YOU MAKE THAT CREEPY SOUND EVERY TIME YOU PUT A CONDIMENT ON SOMETHING?
WHAT IS YOUR DEAL, ANYWAY?
HIS DEAL IS HE'S PART OF PENGUIN'S SCHEME TO FORCE US ALL OUT SO HE CAN TRY TO TAKE OVER CONEY AGAIN. WE'RE NOT STUPID.
IF ONLY HARLEY WUZ STILL AROUND TO STOP YOU THIS TIME. LIKE SHE DONE BEFORE.
AGAIN, I DON'T KNOW WHERE THESE ACCUSATIONS ARE COMING FROM, BUT I WILL CERTAINLY ENTERTAIN ANY OFFERS TO SELL. I AM A BUSINESS-MAN, AFTER ALL.
AS FOR HARLEY...

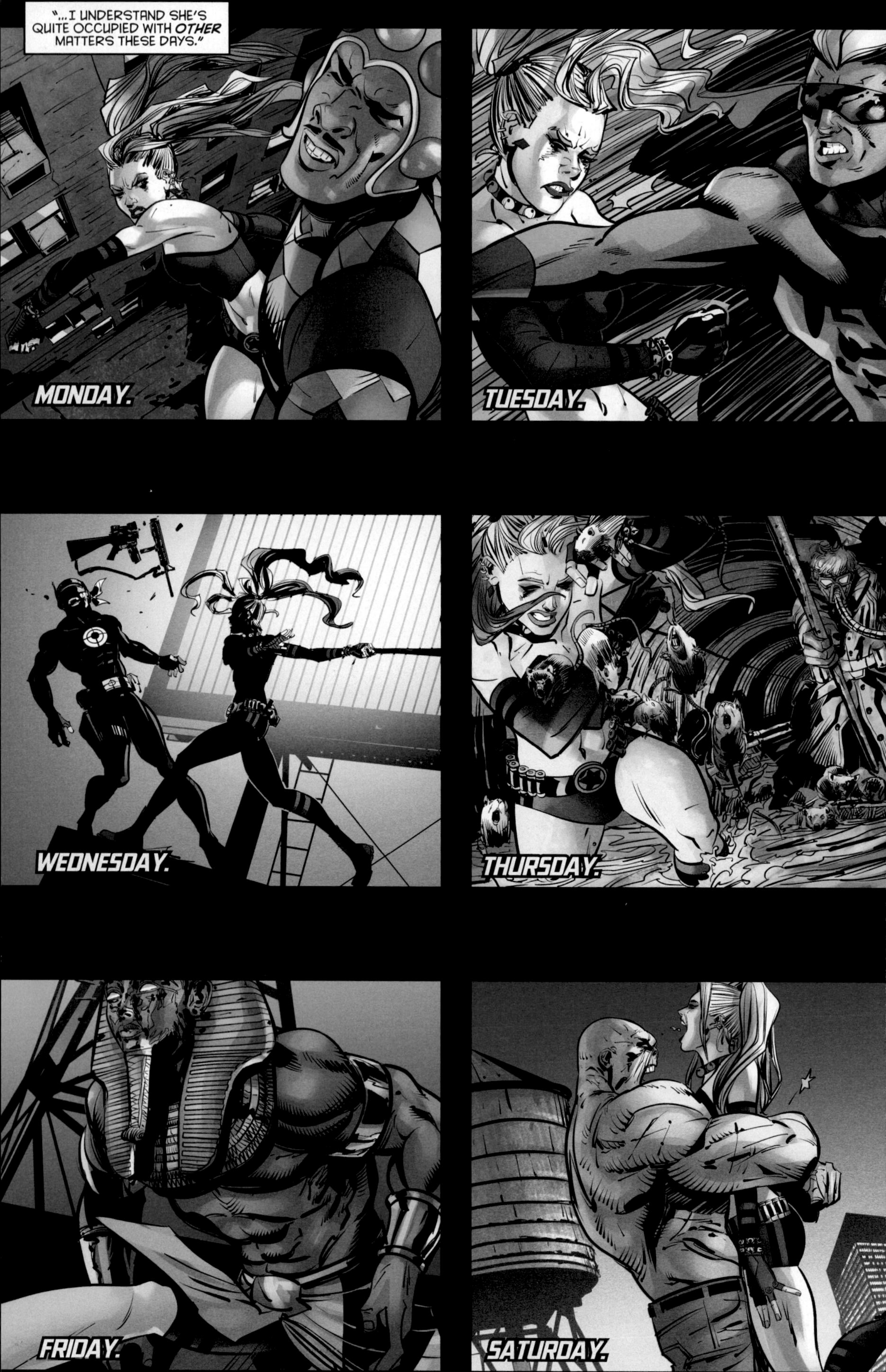
"...I UNDERSTAND SHE'S QUITE OCCUPIED WITH OTHER MATTERS THESE DAYS."
MONDAY.
TUESDAY.
WEDNESDAY.
THURSDAY.
FRIDAY.
SATURDAY.

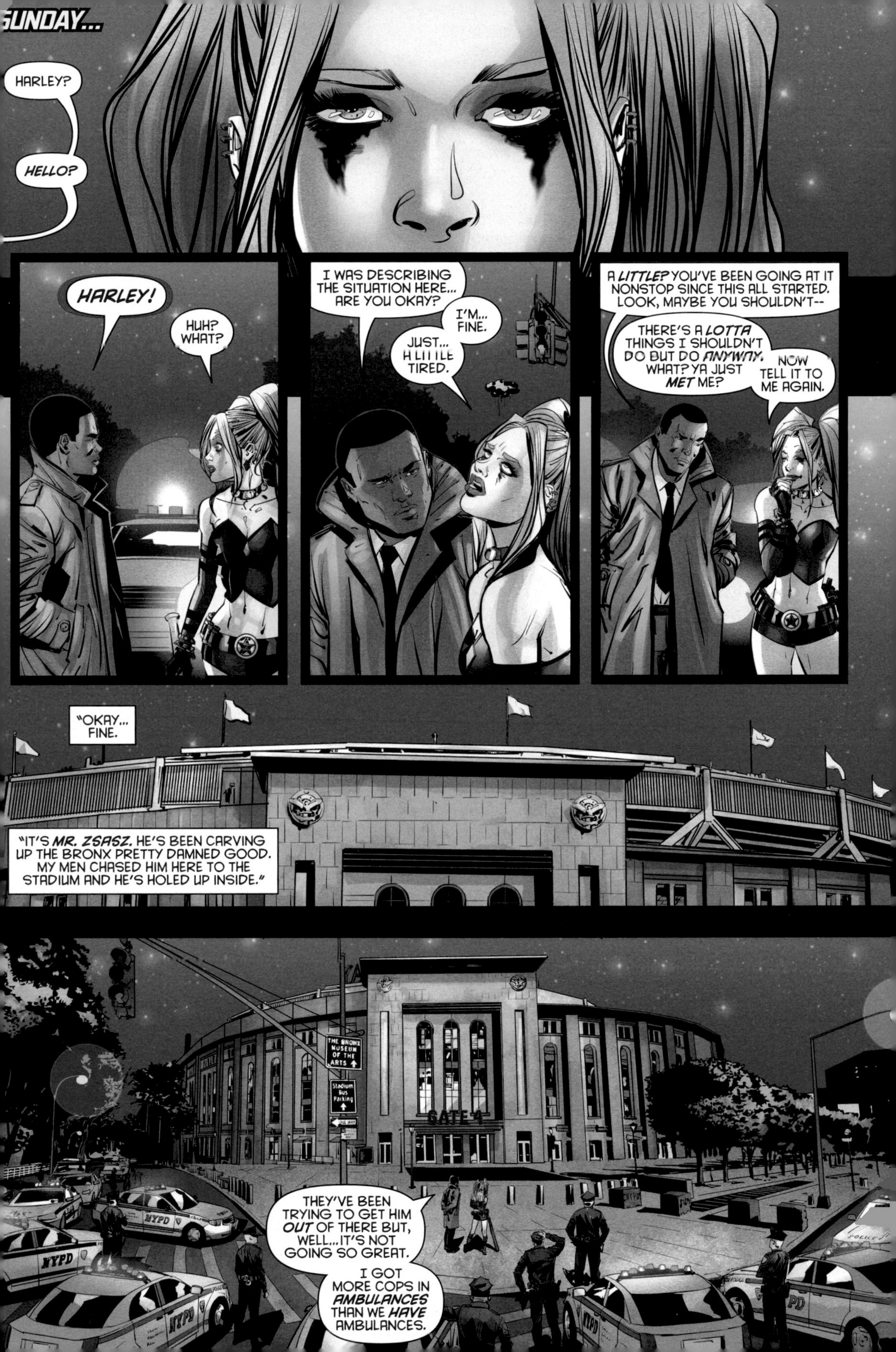
SUNDAY...
HARLEY?
HELLO?
HARLEY!
HUH? WHAT?
I WAS DESCRIBING THE SITUATION HERE... ARE YOU OKAY?
I'M... FINE.
JUST... A LITTLE TIRED.
A LITTLE? YOU'VE BEEN GOING AT IT NONSTOP SINCE THIS ALL STARTED. LOOK, MAYBE YOU SHOULDN'T--
THERE'S A LOTTA THINGS I SHOULDN'T DO BUT DO ANYWAY. WHAT? YA JUST MET ME?
NOW TELL IT TO ME AGAIN.
"OKAY... FINE.
"IT'S MR. ZSASZ. HE'S BEEN CARVING UP THE BRONX PRETTY DAMNED GOOD. MY MEN CHASED HIM HERE TO THE STADIUM AND HE'S HOLED UP INSIDE."
THE BRONX MUSEUM OF THE ARTS
Stadium Bus Parking
ONE WAY
GATE 4
NYPD
THEY'VE BEEN TRYING TO GET HIM OUT OF THERE BUT, WELL...IT'S NOT GOING SO GREAT.
I GOT MORE COPS IN AMBULANCES THAN WE HAVE AMBULANCES.

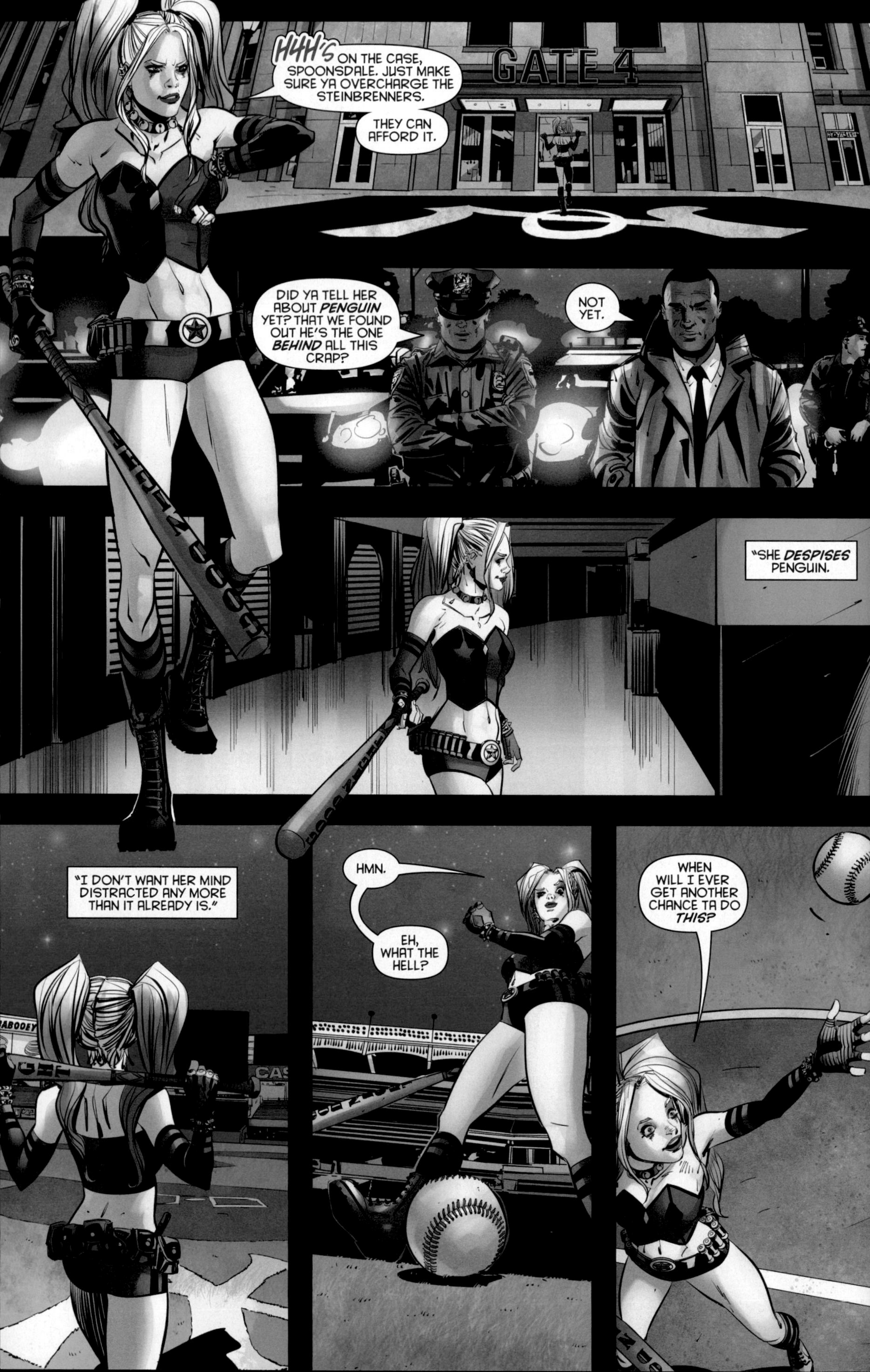
H4H'S ON THE CASE, SPOONSDALE. JUST MAKE SURE YA OVERCHARGE THE STEINBRENNERS.
THEY CAN AFFORD IT.
GATE 4
DID YA TELL HER ABOUT PENGUIN YET? THAT WE FOUND OUT HE'S THE ONE BEHIND ALL THIS CRAP?
NOT YET.
"SHE DESPISES PENGUIN.
"I DON'T WANT HER MIND DISTRACTED ANY MORE THAN IT ALREADY IS."
HMN.
EH, WHAT THE HELL?
WHEN WILL I EVER GET ANOTHER CHANCE TA DO THIS?

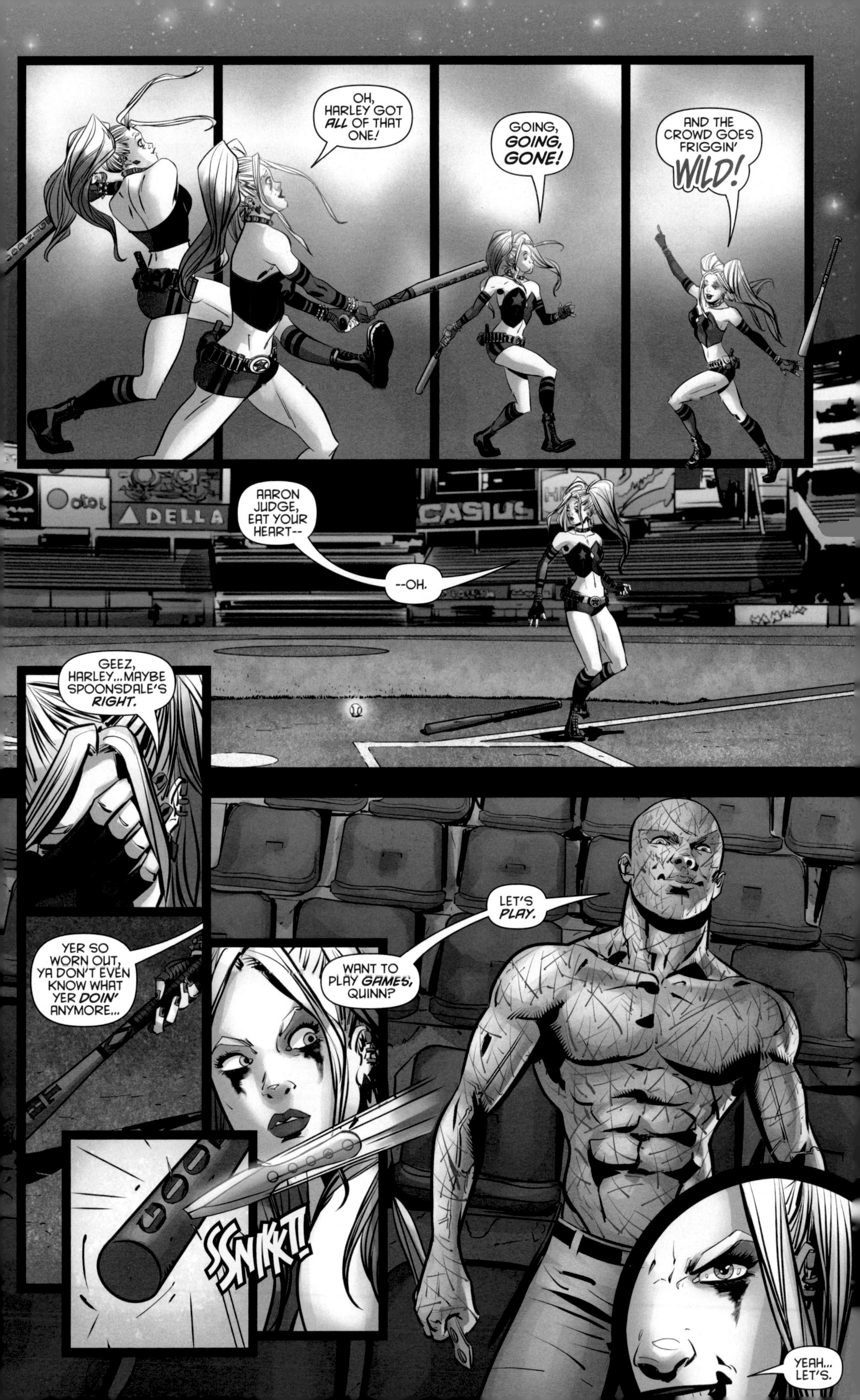

OH, HARLEY GOT ALL OF THAT ONE!
GOING, GOING, GONE!
AND THE CROWD GOES FRIGGIN' WILD!
AARON JUDGE, EAT YOUR HEART--
--OH.
DELLA
CASIUS
GEEZ, HARLEY...MAYBE SPOONSDALE'S RIGHT.
YER SO WORN OUT, YA DON'T EVEN KNOW WHAT YER DOIN' ANYMORE...
SSNIKT!
WANT TO PLAY GAMES, QUINN?
LET'S PLAY.
YEAH... LET'S.

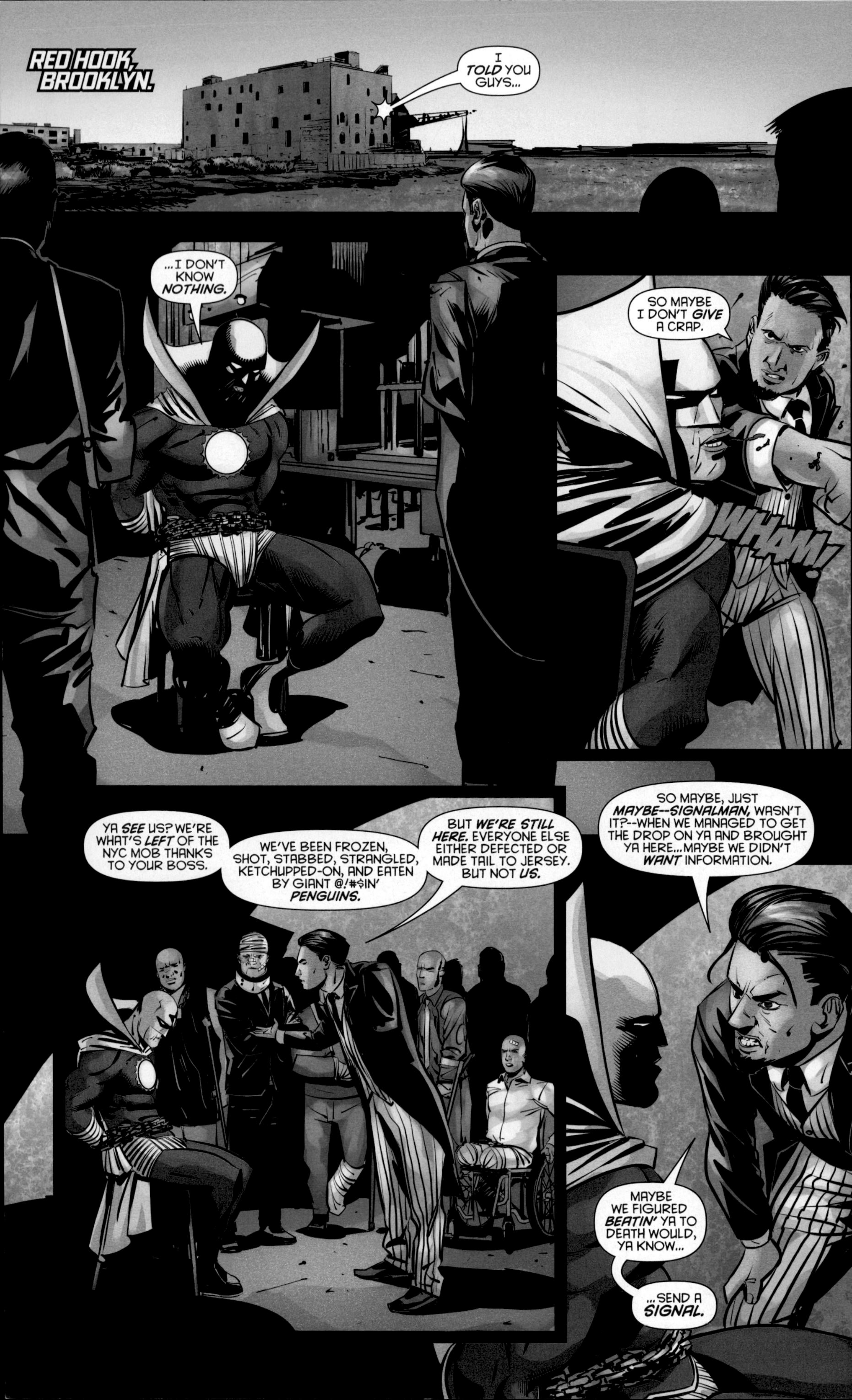
RED HOOK, BROOKLYN.
I TOLD YOU GUYS...
...I DON'T KNOW NOTHING.
SO MAYBE I DON'T GIVE A CRAP.
WHAM!
YA SEE US? WE'RE WHAT'S LEFT OF THE NYC MOB THANKS TO YOUR BOSS.
WE'VE BEEN FROZEN, SHOT, STABBED, STRANGLED, KETCHUPPED-ON, AND EATEN BY GIANT @!#$IN' PENGUINS.
BUT WE'RE STILL HERE. EVERYONE ELSE EITHER DEFECTED OR MADE TAIL TO JERSEY. BUT NOT US.
SO MAYBE, JUST MAYBE--SIGNALMAN, WASN'T IT?--WHEN WE MANAGED TO GET THE DROP ON YA AND BROUGHT YA HERE...MAYBE WE DIDN'T WANT INFORMATION.
MAYBE WE FIGURED BEATIN' YA TO DEATH WOULD, YA KNOW...
...SEND A SIGNAL.

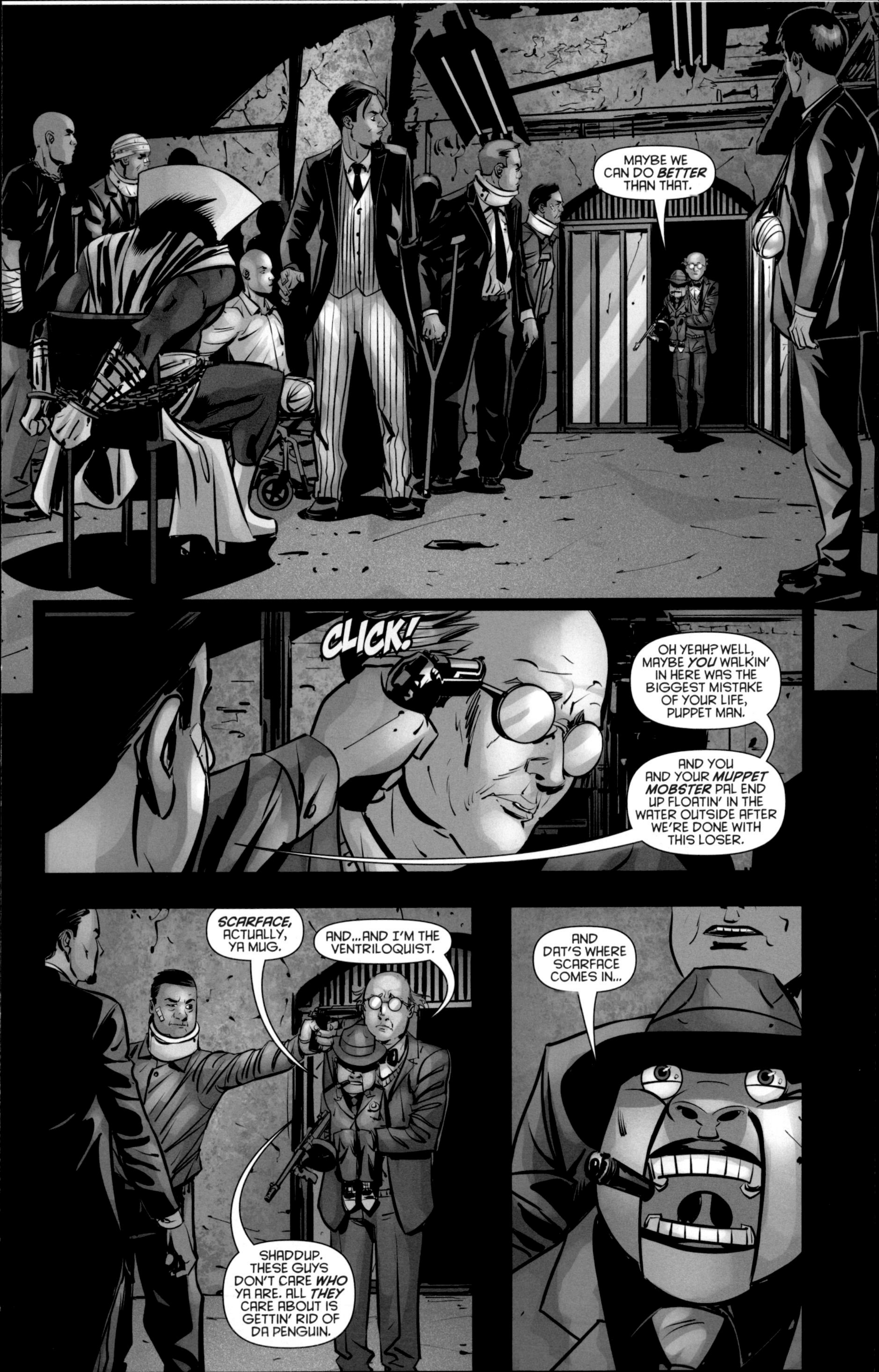
MAYBE WE CAN DO *BETTER* THAN THAT.
CLICK!
OH YEAH? WELL, MAYBE *YOU* WALKIN' IN HERE WAS THE BIGGEST MISTAKE OF YOUR LIFE, PUPPET MAN.
AND YOU AND YOUR *MUPPET MOBSTER* PAL END UP FLOATIN' IN THE WATER OUTSIDE AFTER WE'RE DONE WITH THIS LOSER.
*SCARFACE,* ACTUALLY, YA MUG.
AND...AND I'M THE VENTRILOQUIST.
SHADDUP. THESE GUYS DON'T CARE *WHO* YA ARE. ALL *THEY* CARE ABOUT IS GETTIN' RID OF DA PENGUIN.
AND DAT'S WHERE SCARFACE COMES IN...

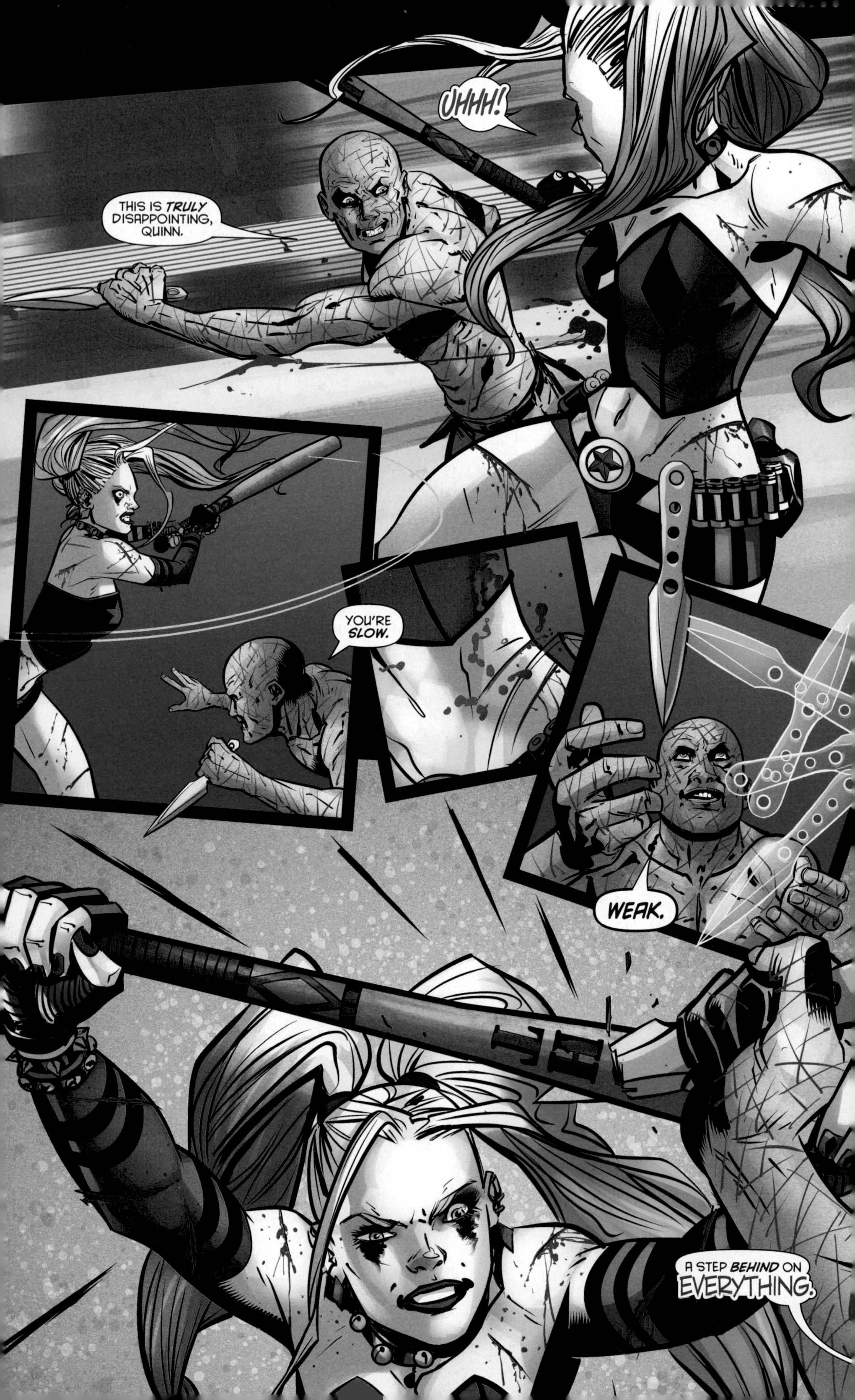
UHHH!
THIS IS TRULY DISAPPOINTING, QUINN.
YOU'RE SLOW.
WEAK.
A STEP BEHIND ON EVERYTHING.

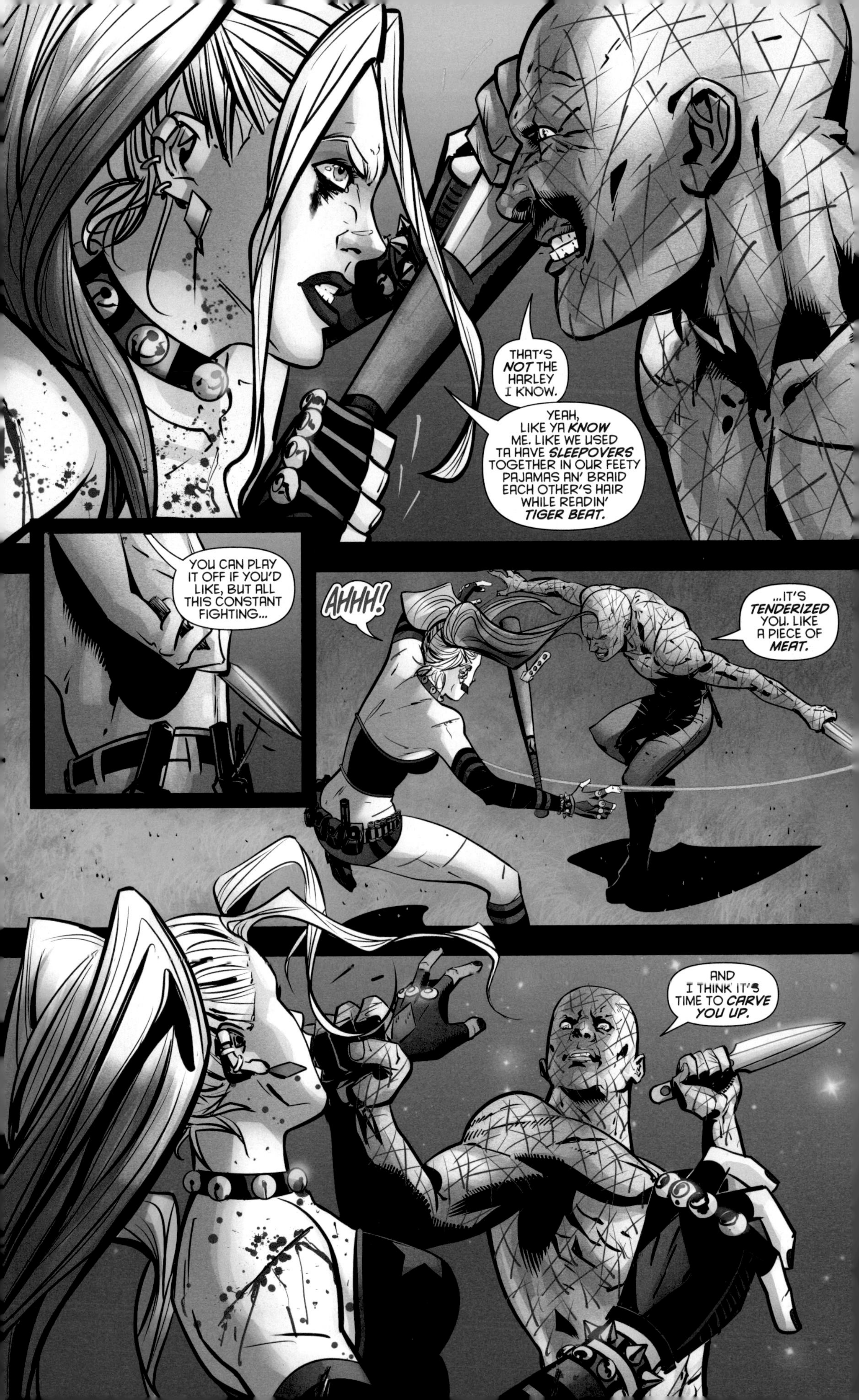
THAT'S NOT THE HARLEY I KNOW.
YEAH, LIKE YA KNOW ME. LIKE WE USED TA HAVE SLEEPOVERS TOGETHER IN OUR FEETY PAJAMAS AN' BRAID EACH OTHER'S HAIR WHILE READIN' TIGER BEAT.
YOU CAN PLAY IT OFF IF YOU'D LIKE, BUT ALL THIS CONSTANT FIGHTING...
AHHH!
...IT'S TENDERIZED YOU. LIKE A PIECE OF MEAT.
AND I THINK IT'S TIME TO CARVE YOU UP.

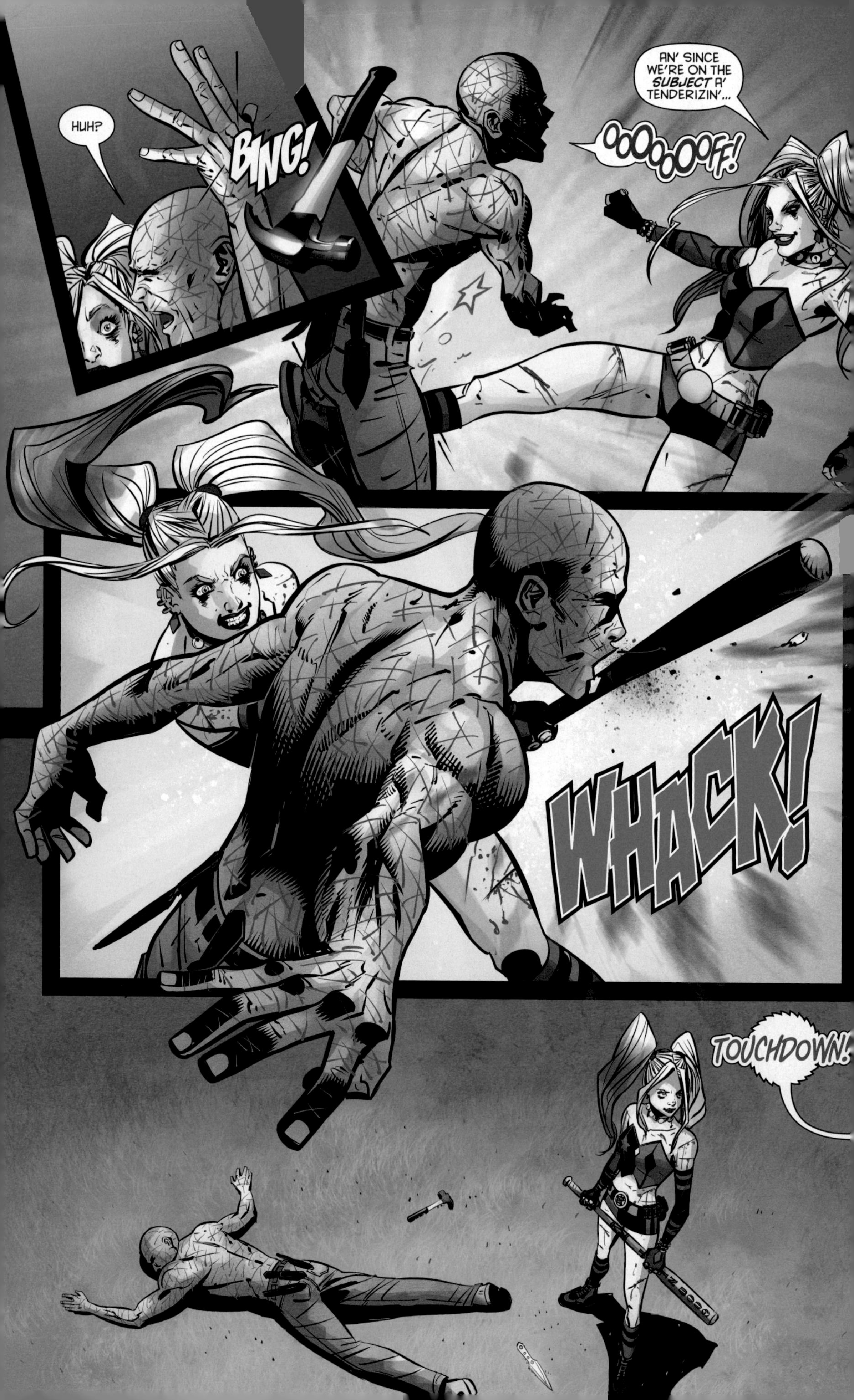
HUH?
BING!
AN' SINCE WE'RE ON THE SUBJECT A' TENDERIZIN'...
OOOOOOOFF!
WHACK!
TOUCHDOWN!

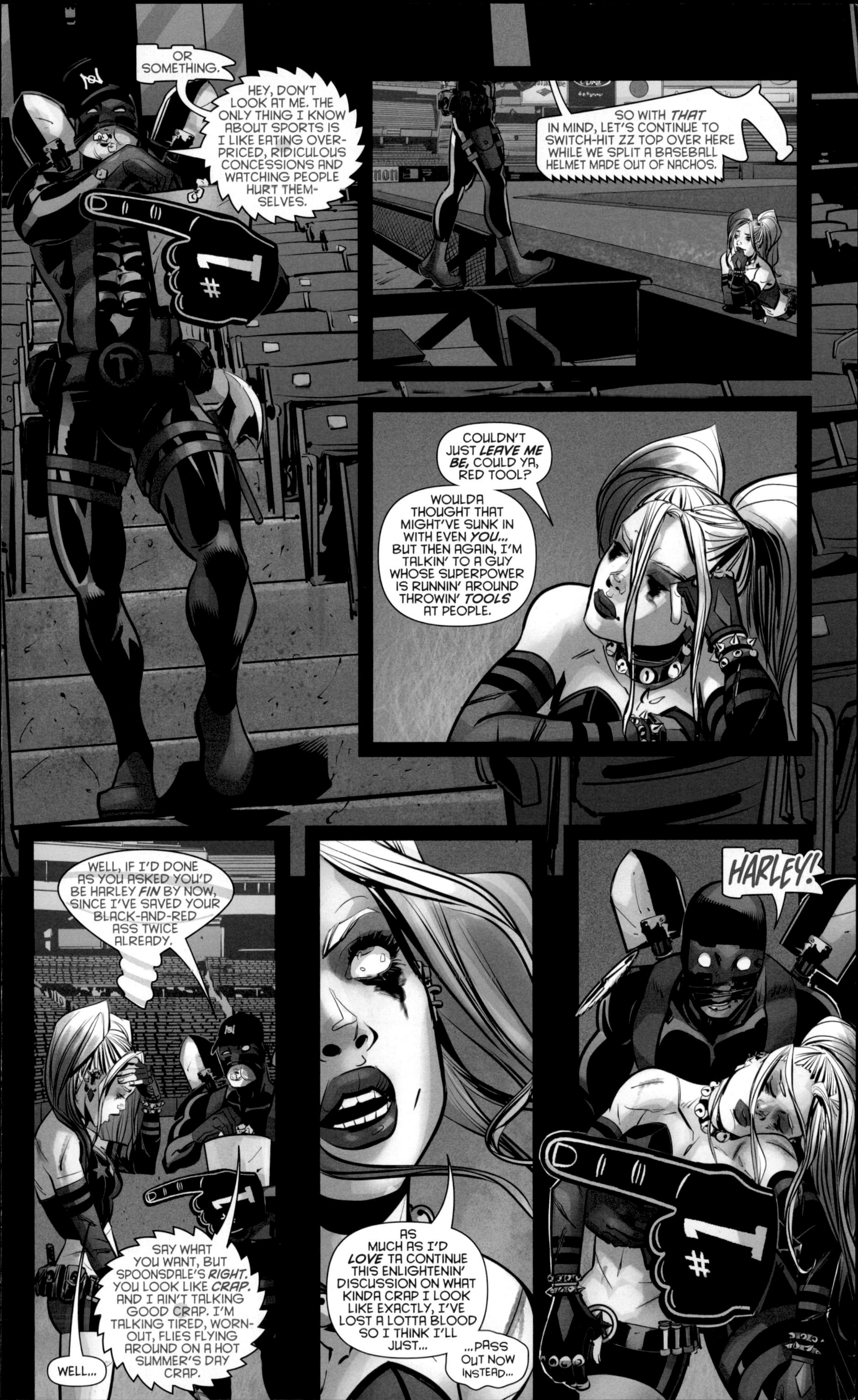
OR SOMETHING.
HEY, DON'T LOOK AT ME. THE ONLY THING I KNOW ABOUT SPORTS IS I LIKE EATING OVER-PRICED, RIDICULOUS CONCESSIONS AND WATCHING PEOPLE HURT THEM-SELVES.
SO WITH THAT IN MIND, LET'S CONTINUE TO SWITCH-HIT ZZ TOP OVER HERE WHILE WE SPLIT A BASEBALL HELMET MADE OUT OF NACHOS.
COULDN'T JUST LEAVE ME BE, COULD YA, RED TOOL?
WOULDA THOUGHT THAT MIGHT'VE SUNK IN WITH EVEN YOU... BUT THEN AGAIN, I'M TALKIN' TO A GUY WHOSE SUPERPOWER IS RUNNIN' AROUND THROWIN' TOOLS AT PEOPLE.
WELL, IF I'D DONE AS YOU ASKED YOU'D BE HARLEY FIN BY NOW, SINCE I'VE SAVED YOUR BLACK-AND-RED ASS TWICE ALREADY.
SAY WHAT YOU WANT, BUT SPOONSDALE'S RIGHT. YOU LOOK LIKE CRAP. AND I AIN'T TALKING GOOD CRAP. I'M TALKING TIRED, WORN-OUT, FLIES FLYING AROUND ON A HOT SUMMER'S DAY CRAP.
WELL...
AS MUCH AS I'D LOVE TA CONTINUE THIS ENLIGHTENIN' DISCUSSION ON WHAT KINDA CRAP I LOOK LIKE EXACTLY, I'VE LOST A LOTTA BLOOD SO I THINK I'LL JUST...
...PASS OUT NOW INSTEAD...
HARLEY!!

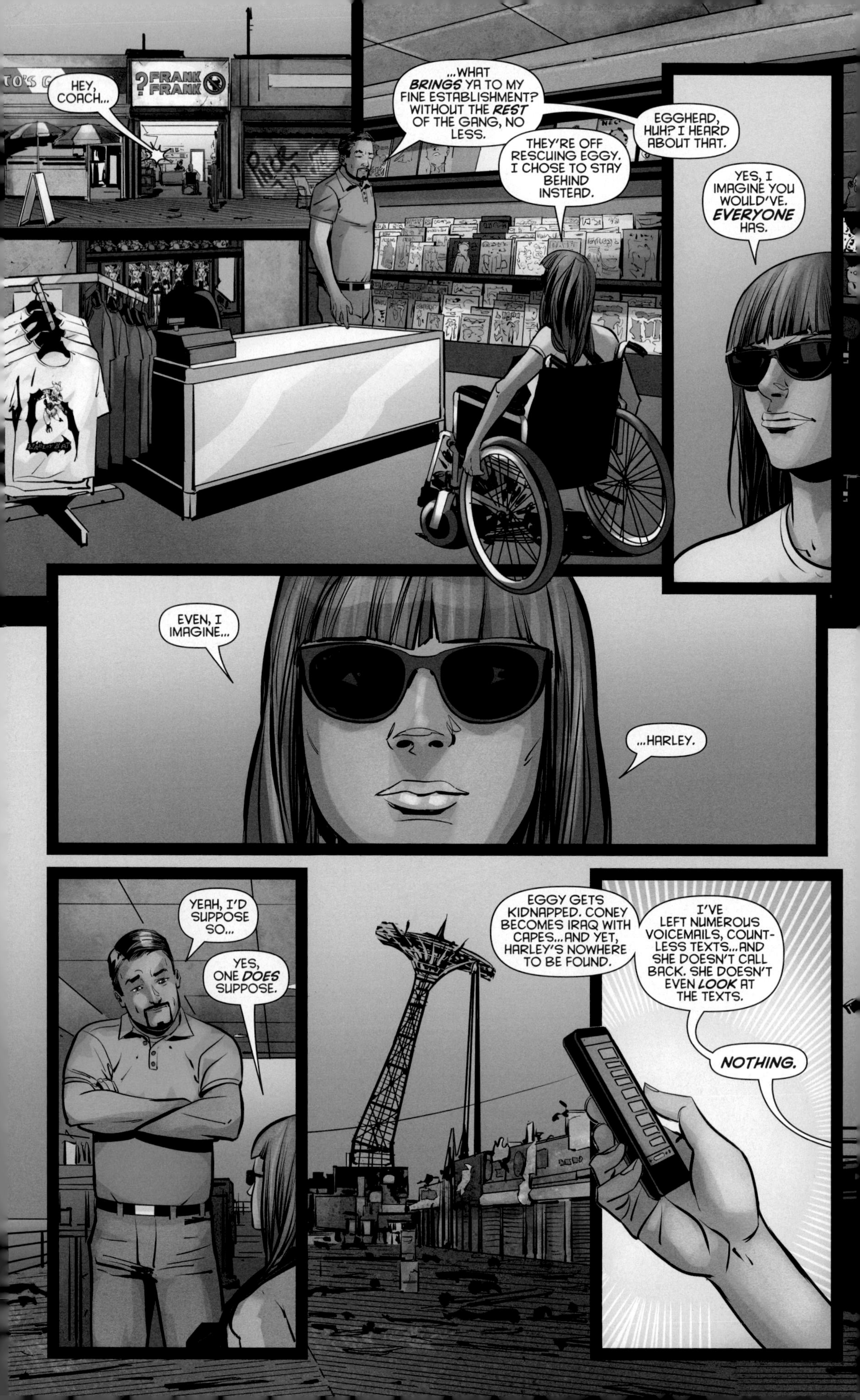
FRANK FRANK
HEY, COACH...
...WHAT BRINGS YA TO MY FINE ESTABLISHMENT? WITHOUT THE REST OF THE GANG, NO LESS.
THEY'RE OFF RESCUING EGGY. I CHOSE TO STAY BEHIND INSTEAD.
EGGHEAD, HUH? I HEARD ABOUT THAT.
YES, I IMAGINE YOU WOULD'VE. EVERYONE HAS.
EVEN, I IMAGINE...
...HARLEY.
YEAH, I'D SUPPOSE SO...
YES, ONE DOES SUPPOSE.
EGGY GETS KIDNAPPED. CONEY BECOMES IRAQ WITH CAPES...AND YET, HARLEY'S NOWHERE TO BE FOUND.
I'VE LEFT NUMEROUS VOICEMAILS, COUNT-LESS TEXTS...AND SHE DOESN'T CALL BACK. SHE DOESN'T EVEN LOOK AT THE TEXTS.
NOTHING.

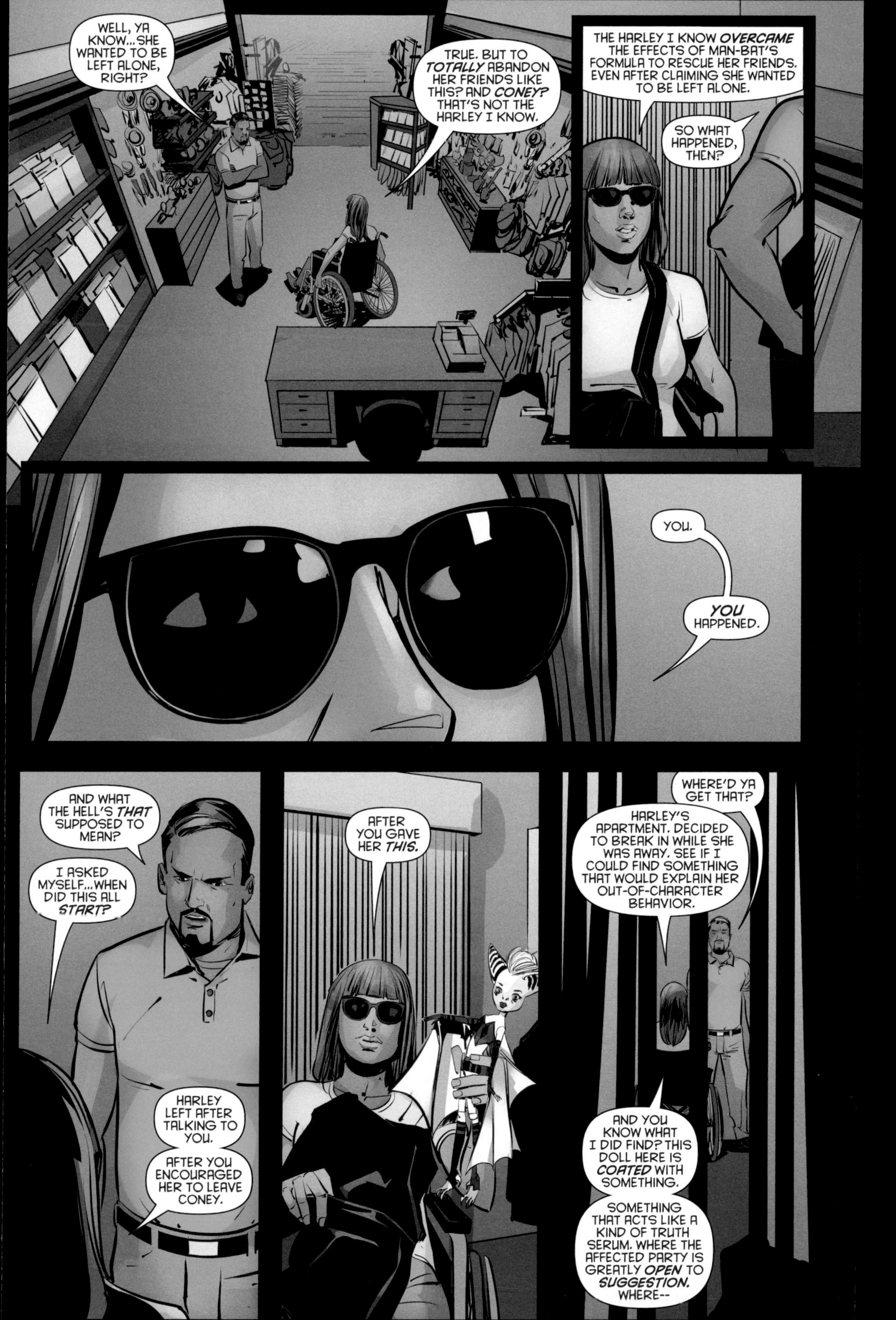

WELL, YA KNOW...SHE WANTED TO BE LEFT ALONE, RIGHT?
TRUE. BUT TO *TOTALLY* ABANDON HER FRIENDS LIKE THIS? AND *CONEY?* THAT'S NOT THE HARLEY I KNOW.
THE HARLEY I KNOW *OVERCAME* THE EFFECTS OF MAN-BAT'S FORMULA TO RESCUE HER FRIENDS. EVEN AFTER CLAIMING SHE WANTED TO BE LEFT ALONE.
SO WHAT HAPPENED, THEN?
YOU.
*YOU* HAPPENED.
AND WHAT THE HELL'S *THAT* SUPPOSED TO MEAN?
I ASKED MYSELF...WHEN DID THIS ALL *START?*
HARLEY LEFT AFTER TALKING TO YOU.
AFTER YOU ENCOURAGED HER TO LEAVE CONEY.
AFTER YOU GAVE HER *THIS.*
WHERE'D YA GET THAT?
HARLEY'S APARTMENT. DECIDED TO BREAK IN WHILE SHE WAS AWAY. SEE IF I COULD FIND SOMETHING THAT WOULD EXPLAIN HER OUT-OF-CHARACTER BEHAVIOR.
AND YOU KNOW WHAT I DID FIND? THIS DOLL HERE IS *COATED* WITH SOMETHING.
SOMETHING THAT ACTS LIKE A KIND OF TRUTH SERUM. WHERE THE AFFECTED PARTY IS GREATLY *OPEN* TO *SUGGESTION.* WHERE--

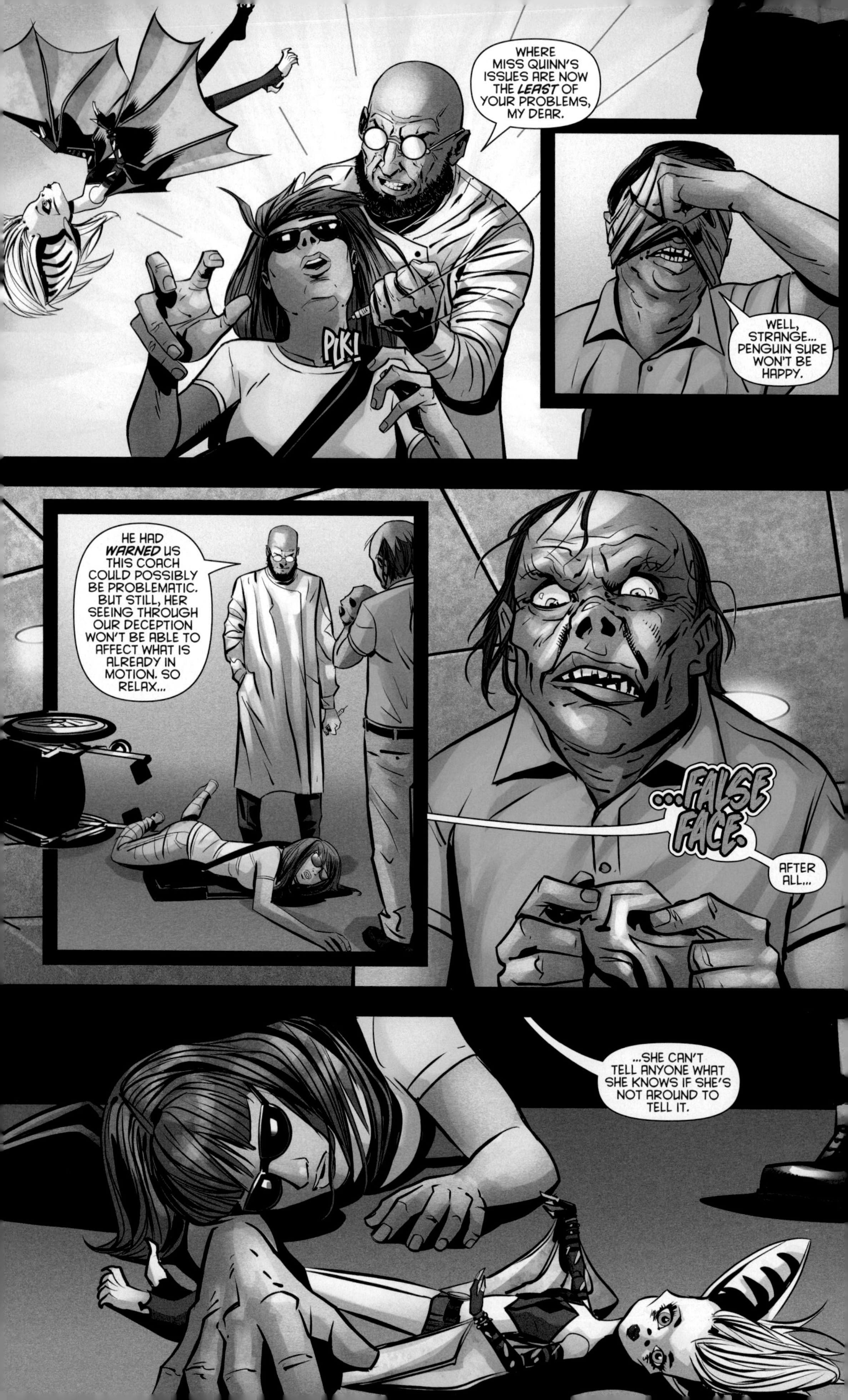
WHERE MISS QUINN'S ISSUES ARE NOW THE LEAST OF YOUR PROBLEMS, MY DEAR.
PLK!
WELL, STRANGE... PENGUIN SURE WON'T BE HAPPY.
HE HAD WARNED US THIS COACH COULD POSSIBLY BE PROBLEMATIC. BUT STILL, HER SEEING THROUGH OUR DECEPTION WON'T BE ABLE TO AFFECT WHAT IS ALREADY IN MOTION. SO RELAX...
...FALSE FACE.
AFTER ALL...
...SHE CAN'T TELL ANYONE WHAT SHE KNOWS IF SHE'S NOT AROUND TO TELL IT.

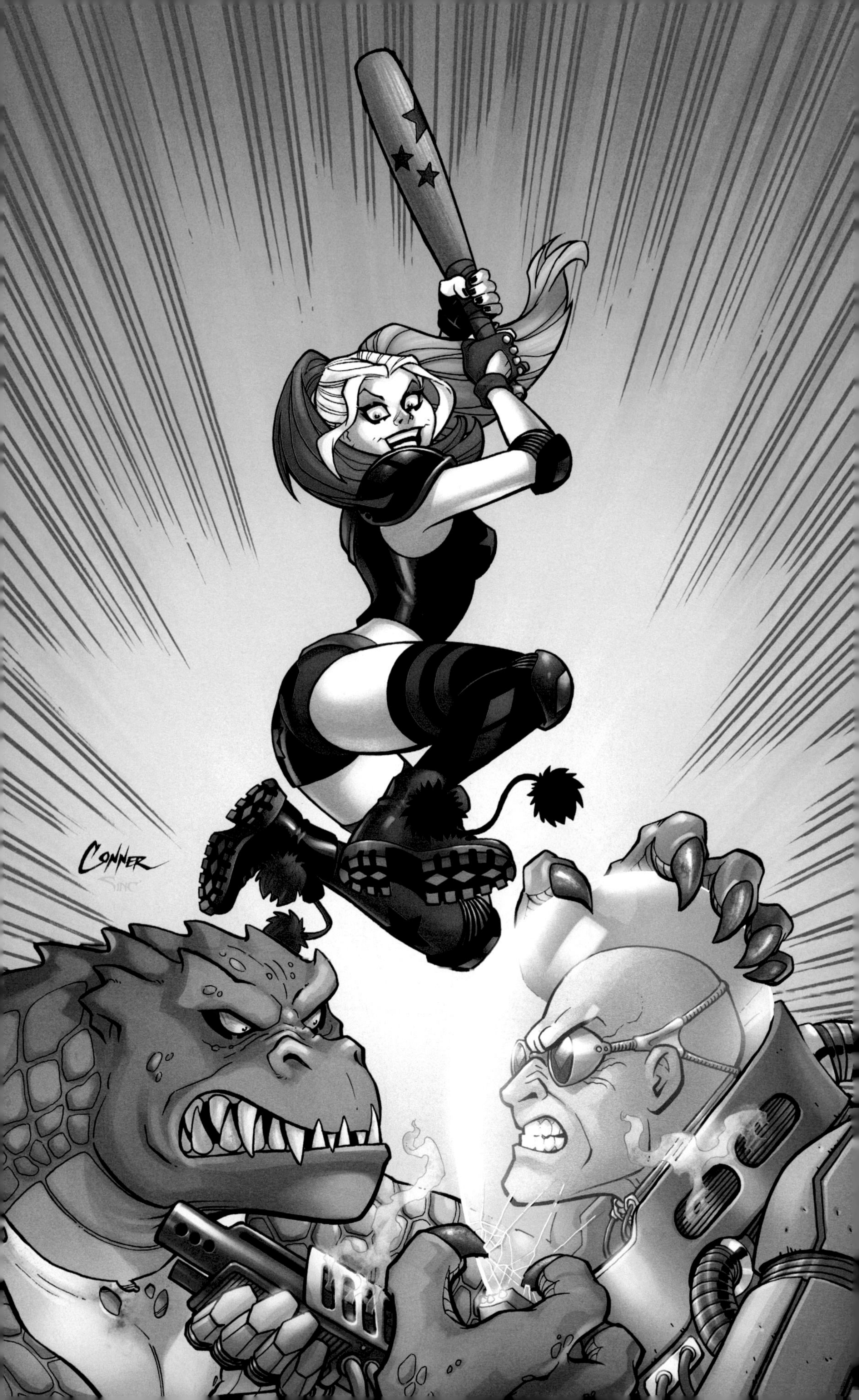
CONNER

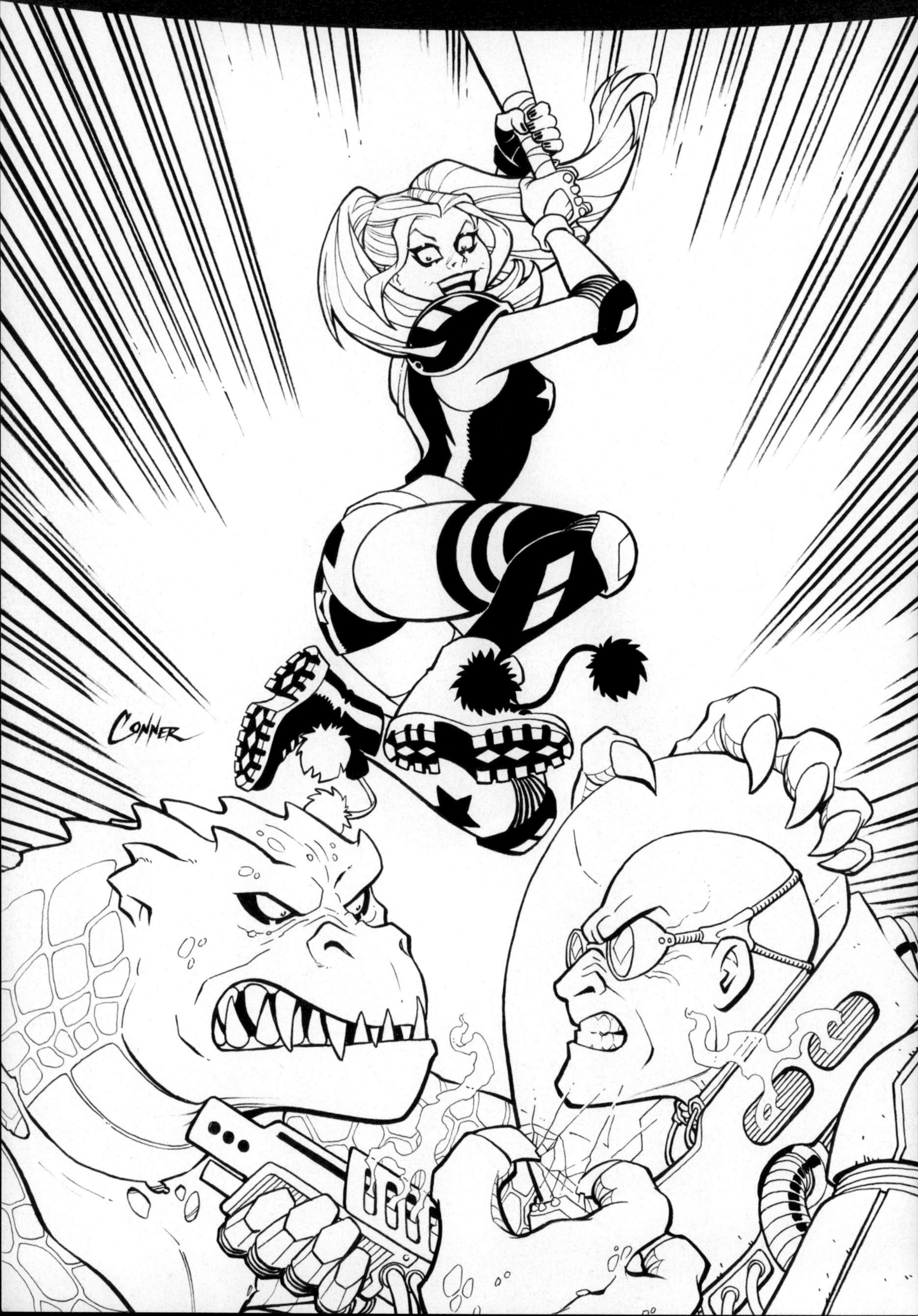
CONNER

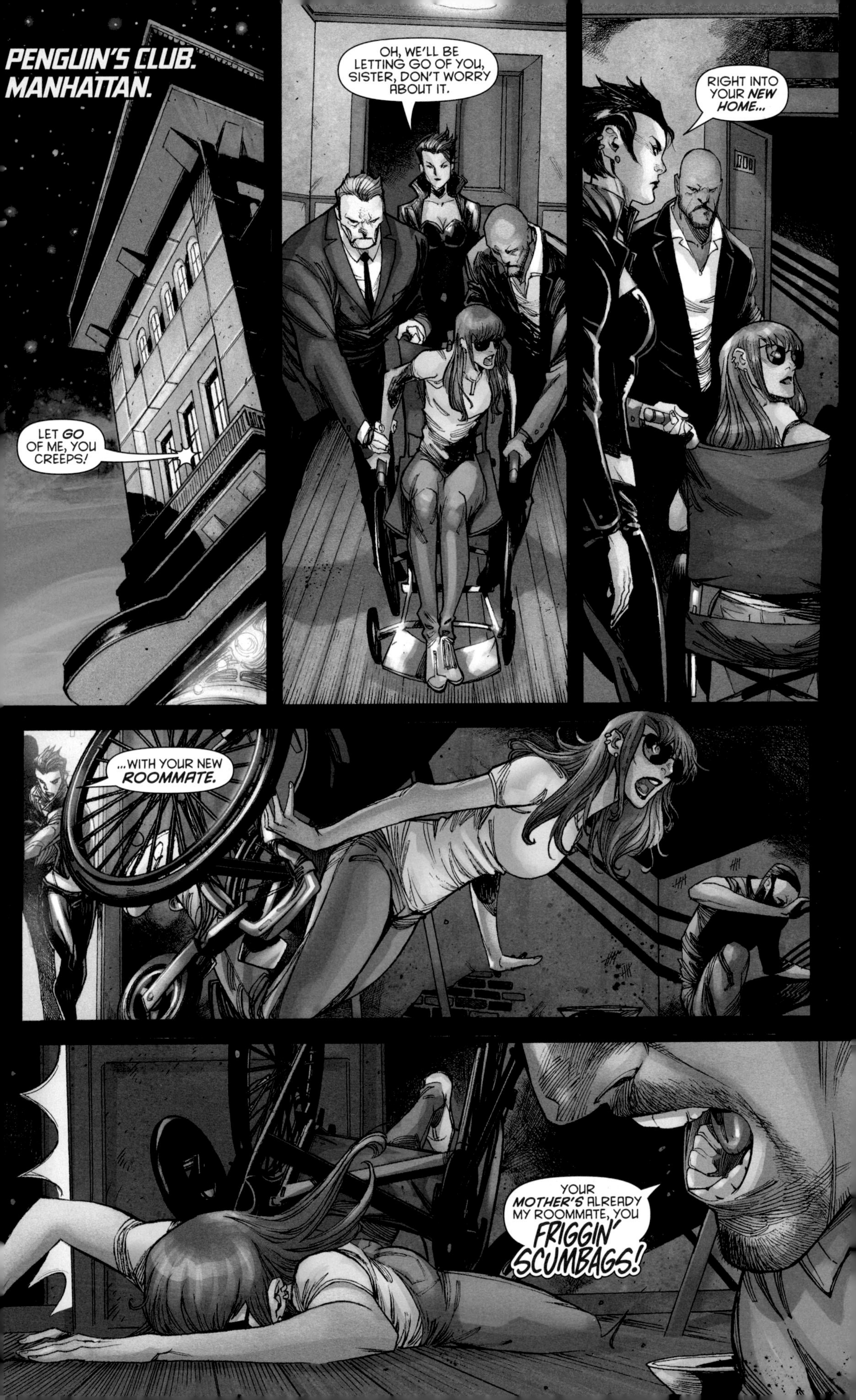
PENGUIN'S CLUB. MANHATTAN.
LET GO OF ME, YOU CREEPS!
OH, WE'LL BE LETTING GO OF YOU, SISTER, DON'T WORRY ABOUT IT.
RIGHT INTO YOUR NEW HOME...
...WITH YOUR NEW ROOMMATE.
YOUR MOTHER'S ALREADY MY ROOMMATE, YOU FRIGGIN' SCUMBAGS!

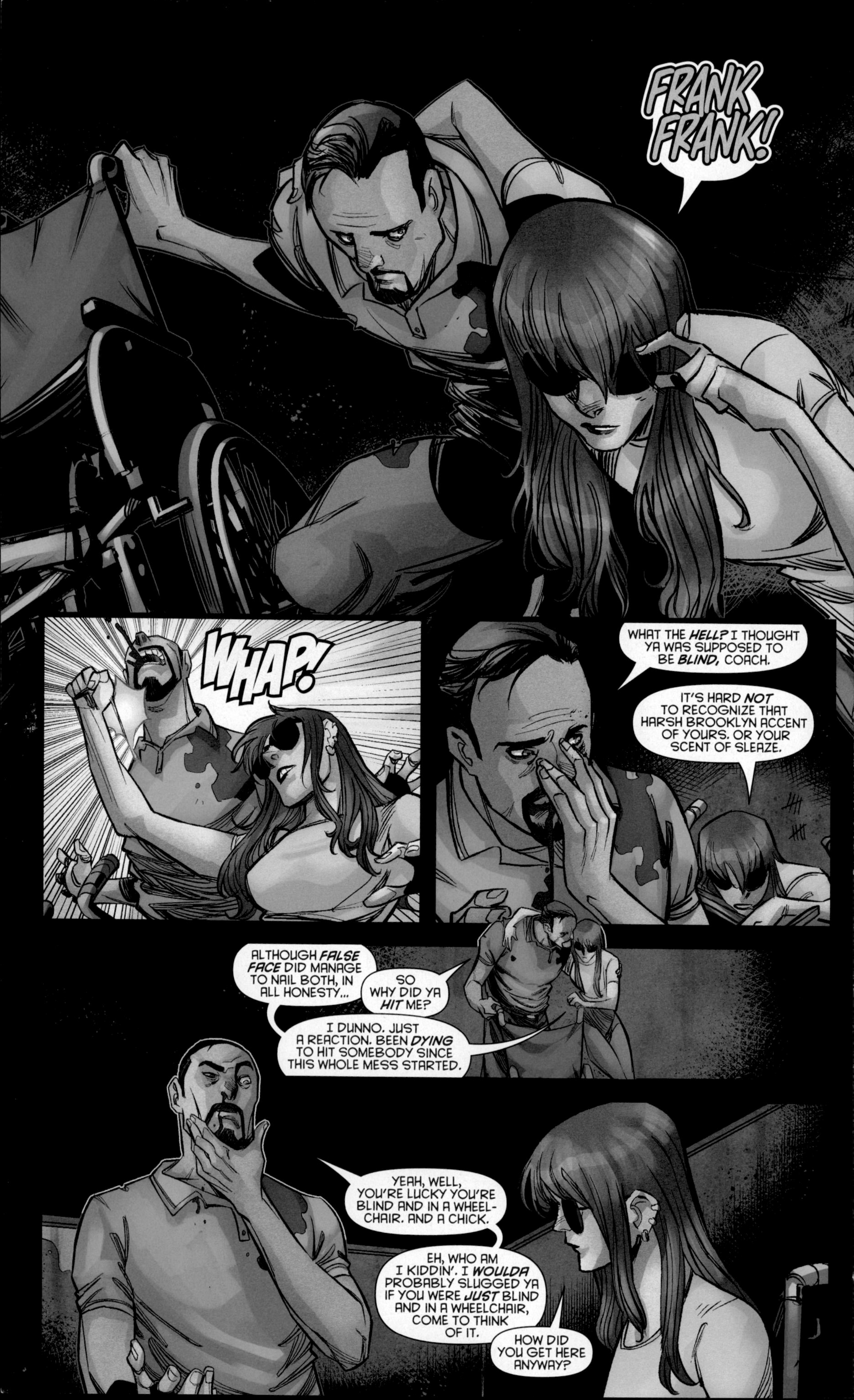
FRANK FRANK!
WHAP!
WHAT THE HELL? I THOUGHT YA WAS SUPPOSED TO BE BLIND, COACH.
IT'S HARD NOT TO RECOGNIZE THAT HARSH BROOKLYN ACCENT OF YOURS. OR YOUR SCENT OF SLEAZE.
ALTHOUGH FALSE FACE DID MANAGE TO NAIL BOTH, IN ALL HONESTY...
SO WHY DID YA HIT ME?
I DUNNO. JUST A REACTION. BEEN DYING TO HIT SOMEBODY SINCE THIS WHOLE MESS STARTED.
YEAH, WELL, YOU'RE LUCKY YOU'RE BLIND AND IN A WHEEL-CHAIR. AND A CHICK.
EH, WHO AM I KIDDIN'. I WOULDA PROBABLY SLUGGED YA IF YOU WERE JUST BLIND AND IN A WHEELCHAIR, COME TO THINK OF IT.
HOW DID YOU GET HERE ANYWAY?

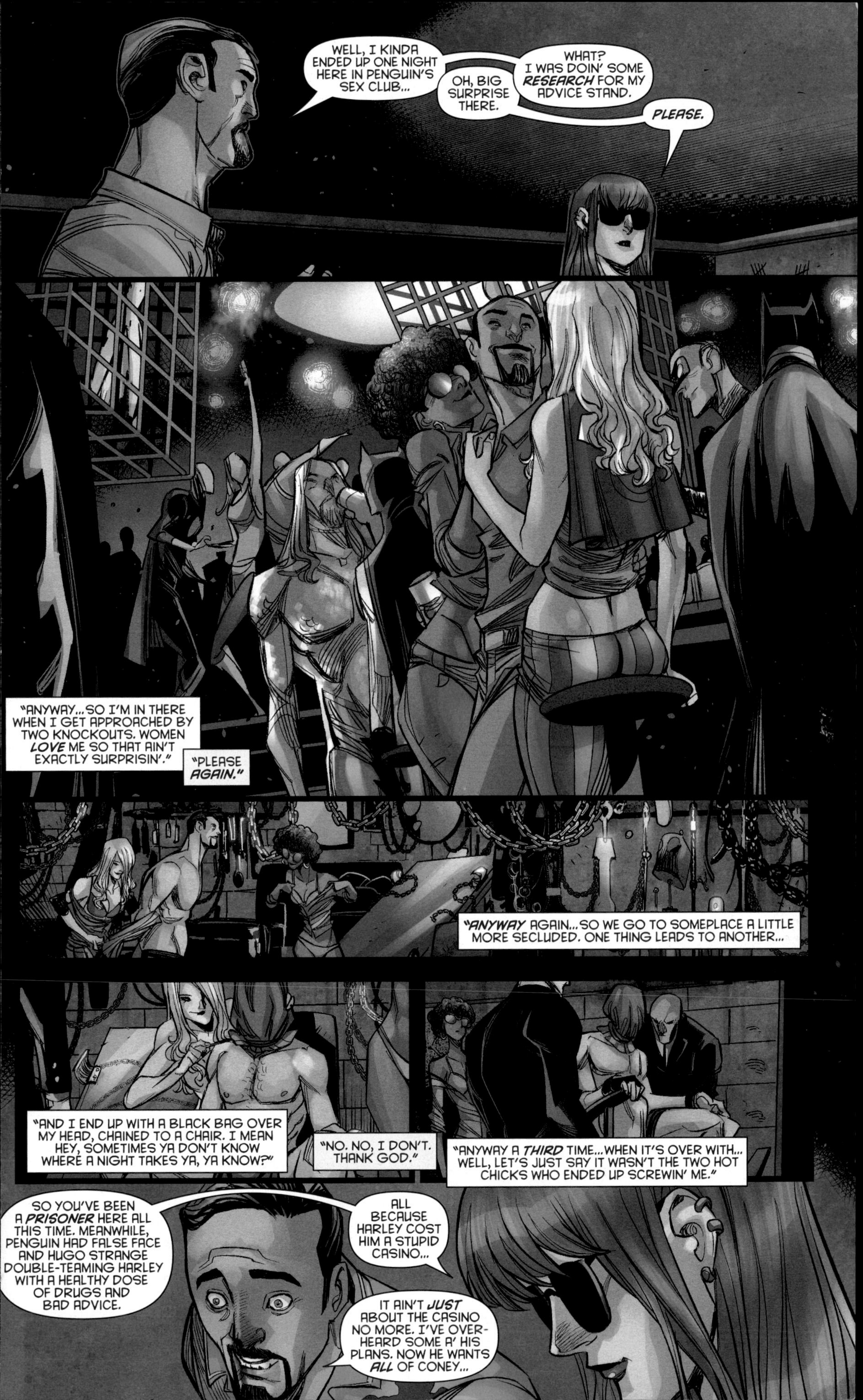

WELL, I KINDA ENDED UP ONE NIGHT HERE IN PENGUIN'S SEX CLUB...
OH, BIG SURPRISE THERE.
WHAT? I WAS DOIN' SOME RESEARCH FOR MY ADVICE STAND.
PLEASE.
"ANYWAY... SO I'M IN THERE WHEN I GET APPROACHED BY TWO KNOCKOUTS. WOMEN LOVE ME SO THAT AIN'T EXACTLY SURPRISIN'."
"PLEASE AGAIN."
"ANYWAY AGAIN... SO WE GO TO SOMEPLACE A LITTLE MORE SECLUDED. ONE THING LEADS TO ANOTHER...
"AND I END UP WITH A BLACK BAG OVER MY HEAD, CHAINED TO A CHAIR. I MEAN HEY, SOMETIMES YA DON'T KNOW WHERE A NIGHT TAKES YA, YA KNOW?"
"NO. NO, I DON'T. THANK GOD."
"ANYWAY A THIRD TIME... WHEN IT'S OVER WITH... WELL, LET'S JUST SAY IT WASN'T THE TWO HOT CHICKS WHO ENDED UP SCREWIN' ME."
SO YOU'VE BEEN A PRISONER HERE ALL THIS TIME. MEANWHILE, PENGUIN HAD FALSE FACE AND HUGO STRANGE DOUBLE-TEAMING HARLEY WITH A HEALTHY DOSE OF DRUGS AND BAD ADVICE.
ALL BECAUSE HARLEY COST HIM A STUPID CASINO...
IT AIN'T JUST ABOUT THE CASINO NO MORE. I'VE OVER-HEARD SOME A' HIS PLANS. NOW HE WANTS ALL OF CONEY...

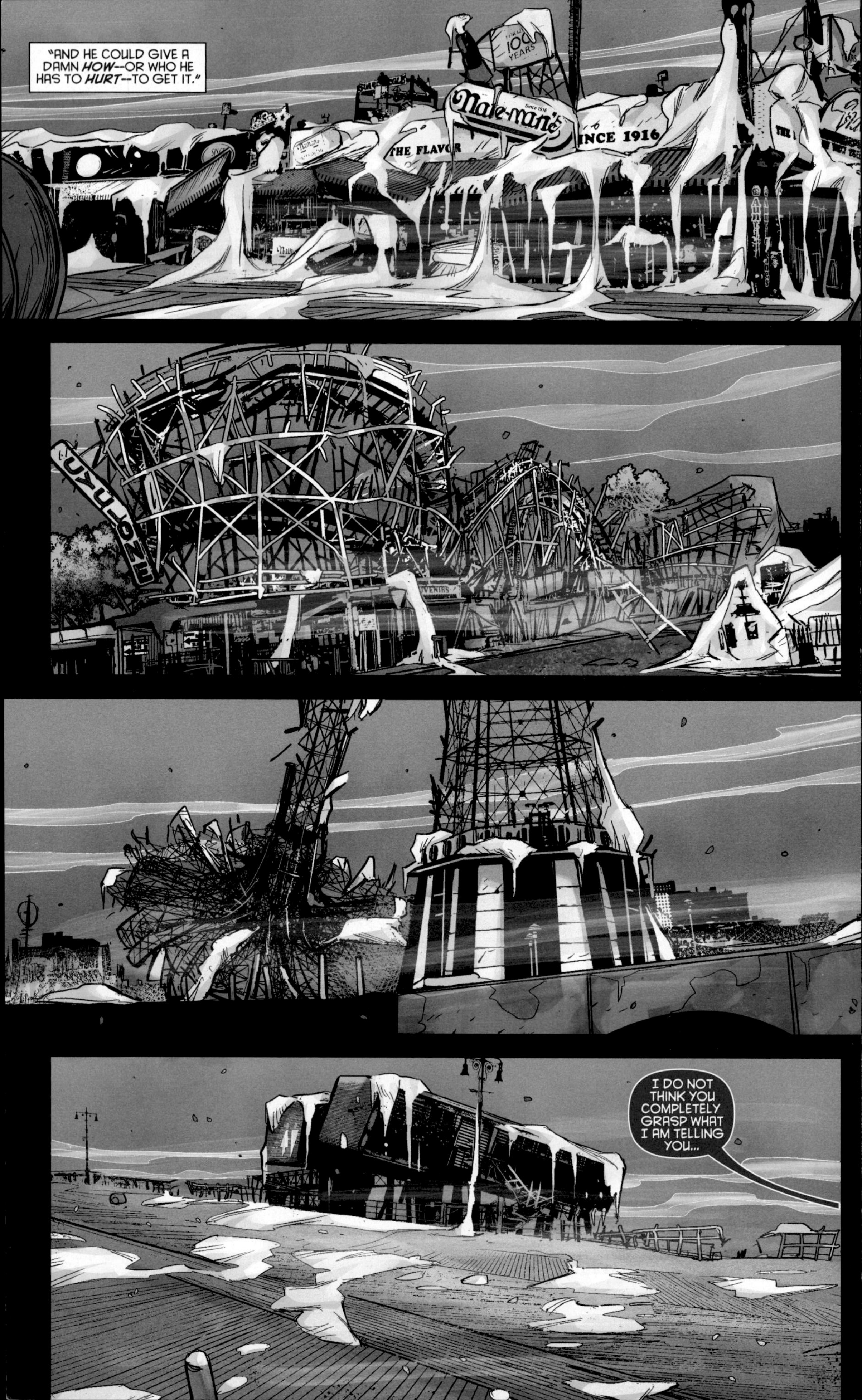
"AND HE COULD GIVE A DAMN *HOW*--OR WHO HE HAS TO *HURT*--TO GET IT."
I DO NOT THINK YOU COMPLETELY GRASP WHAT I AM TELLING YOU...

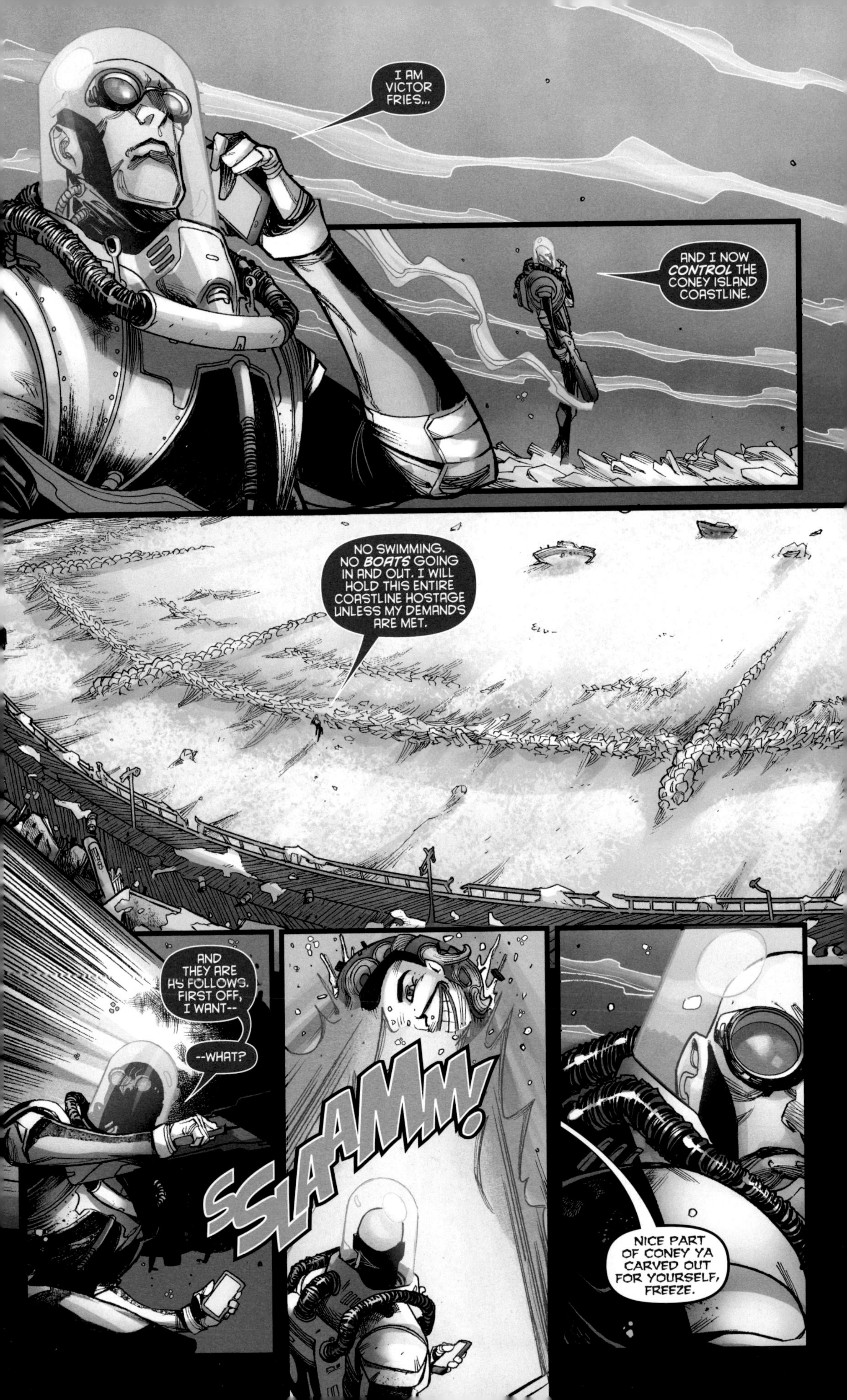
I AM VICTOR FRIES...
AND I NOW CONTROL THE CONEY ISLAND COASTLINE.
NO SWIMMING. NO BOATS GOING IN AND OUT. I WILL HOLD THIS ENTIRE COASTLINE HOSTAGE UNLESS MY DEMANDS ARE MET.
AND THEY ARE AS FOLLOWS. FIRST OFF, I WANT--
--WHAT?
SSLAAMM!
NICE PART OF CONEY YA CARVED OUT FOR YOURSELF, FREEZE.

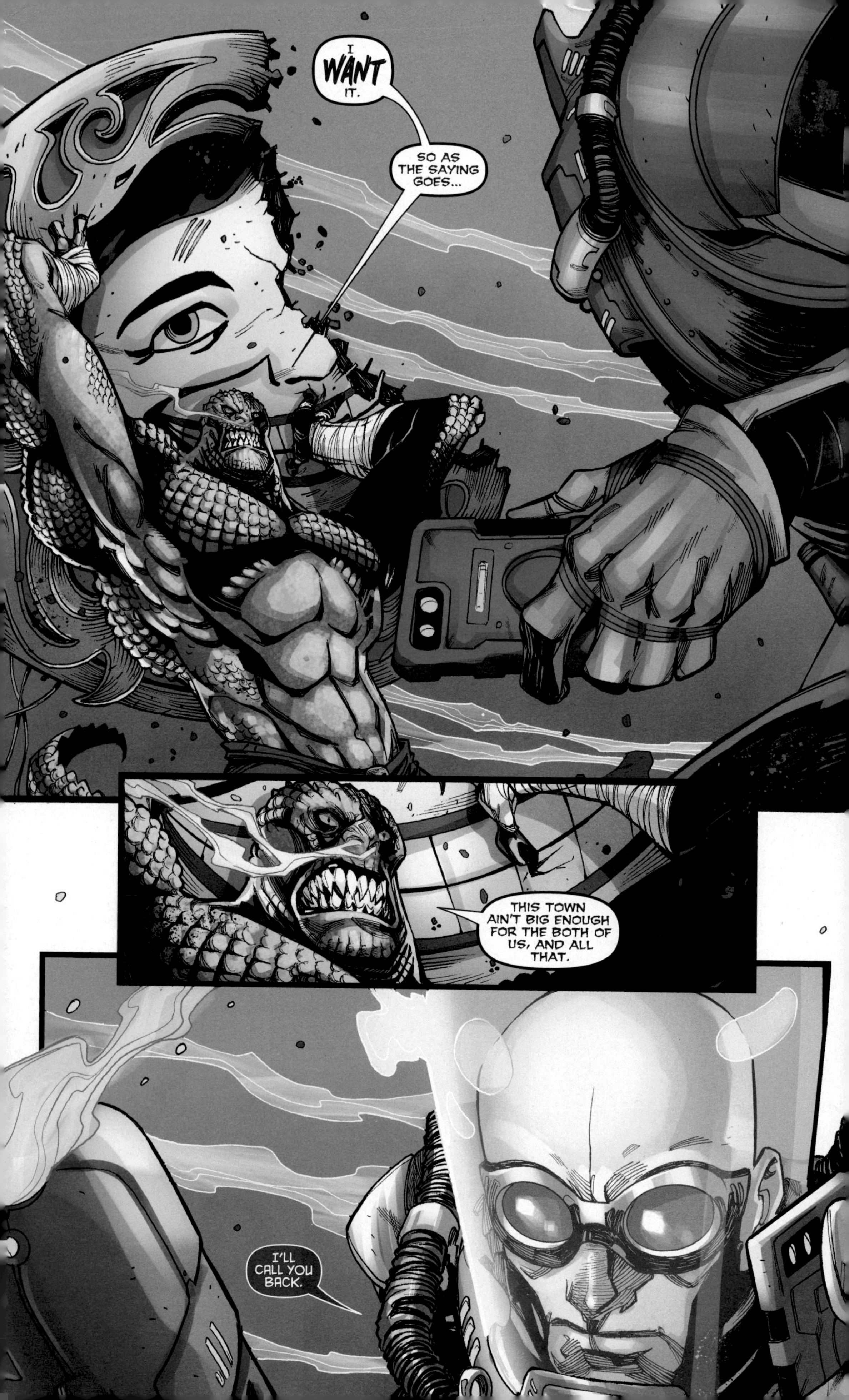
I WANT IT.
SO AS THE SAYING GOES...
THIS TOWN AIN'T BIG ENOUGH FOR THE BOTH OF US, AND ALL THAT.
I'LL CALL YOU BACK.

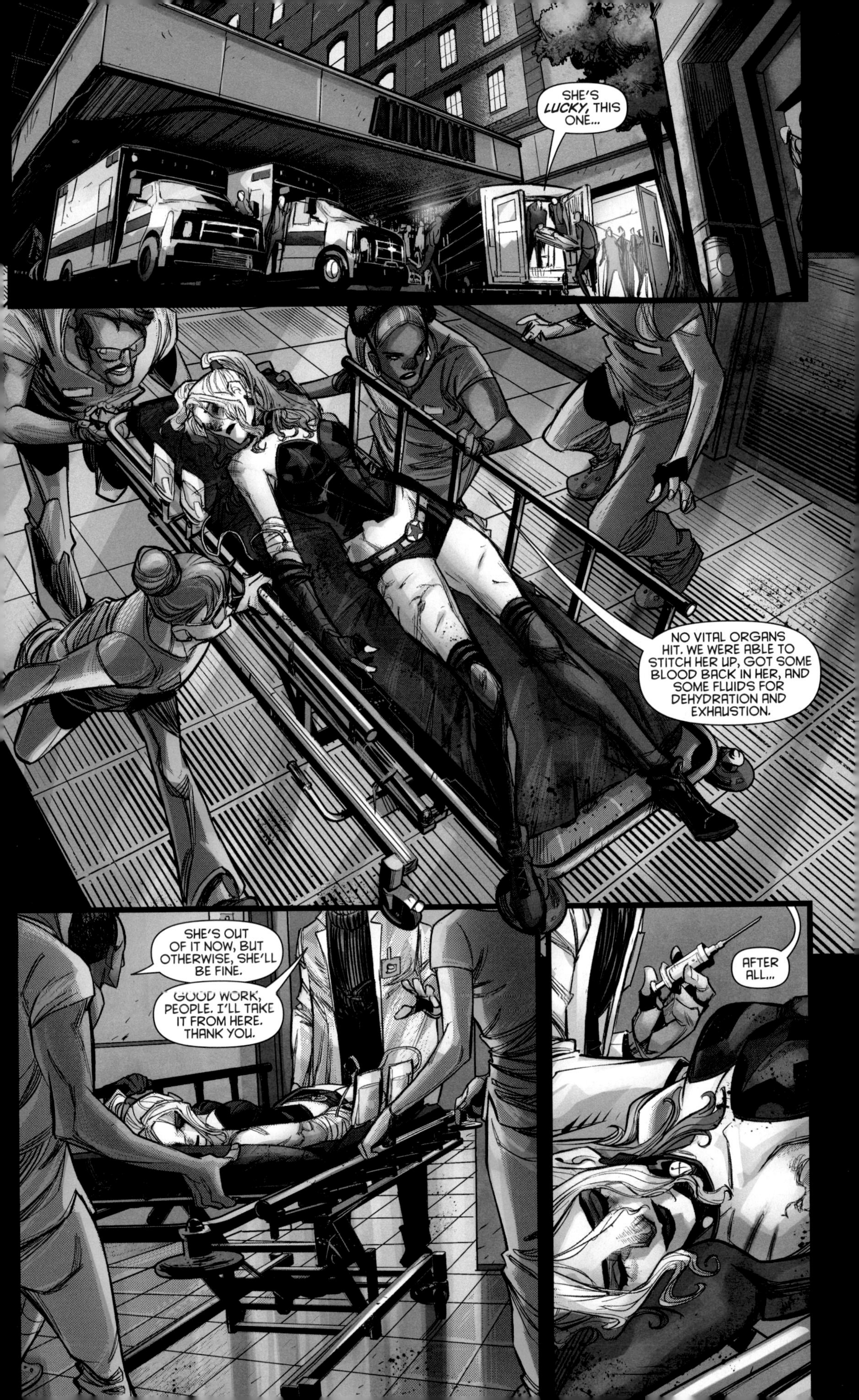
SHE'S *LUCKY,* THIS ONE...
NO VITAL ORGANS HIT. WE WERE ABLE TO STITCH HER UP, GOT SOME BLOOD BACK IN HER, AND SOME FLUIDS FOR DEHYDRATION AND EXHAUSTION.
SHE'S OUT OF IT NOW, BUT OTHERWISE, SHE'LL BE FINE.
GOOD WORK, PEOPLE. I'LL TAKE IT FROM HERE. THANK YOU.
AFTER ALL...

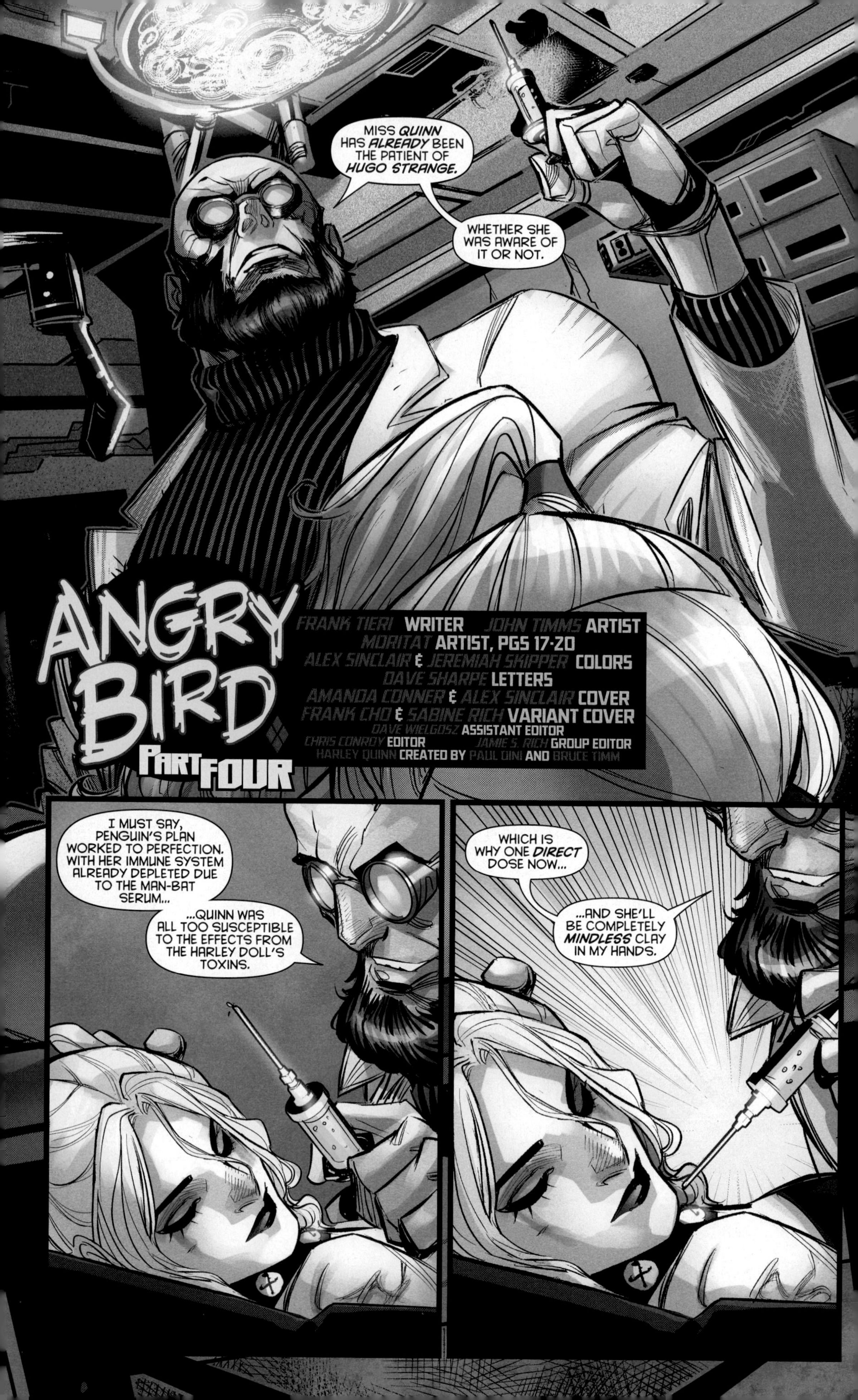

MISS QUINN HAS ALREADY BEEN THE PATIENT OF HUGO STRANGE.
WHETHER SHE WAS AWARE OF IT OR NOT.
ANGRY BIRD
PART FOUR
FRANK TIERI WRITER JOHN TIMMS ARTIST
MORITAT ARTIST, PGS 17-20
ALEX SINCLAIR & JEREMIAH SKIPPER COLORS
DAVE SHARPE LETTERS
AMANDA CONNER & ALEX SINCLAIR COVER
FRANK CHO & SABINE RICH VARIANT COVER
DAVE WIELGOSZ ASSISTANT EDITOR
CHRIS CONROY EDITOR JAMIE S. RICH GROUP EDITOR
HARLEY QUINN CREATED BY PAUL DINI AND BRUCE TIMM
I MUST SAY, PENGUIN'S PLAN WORKED TO PERFECTION. WITH HER IMMUNE SYSTEM ALREADY DEPLETED DUE TO THE MAN-BAT SERUM...
...QUINN WAS ALL TOO SUSCEPTIBLE TO THE EFFECTS FROM THE HARLEY DOLL'S TOXINS.
WHICH IS WHY ONE DIRECT DOSE NOW...
...AND SHE'LL BE COMPLETELY MINDLESS CLAY IN MY HANDS.

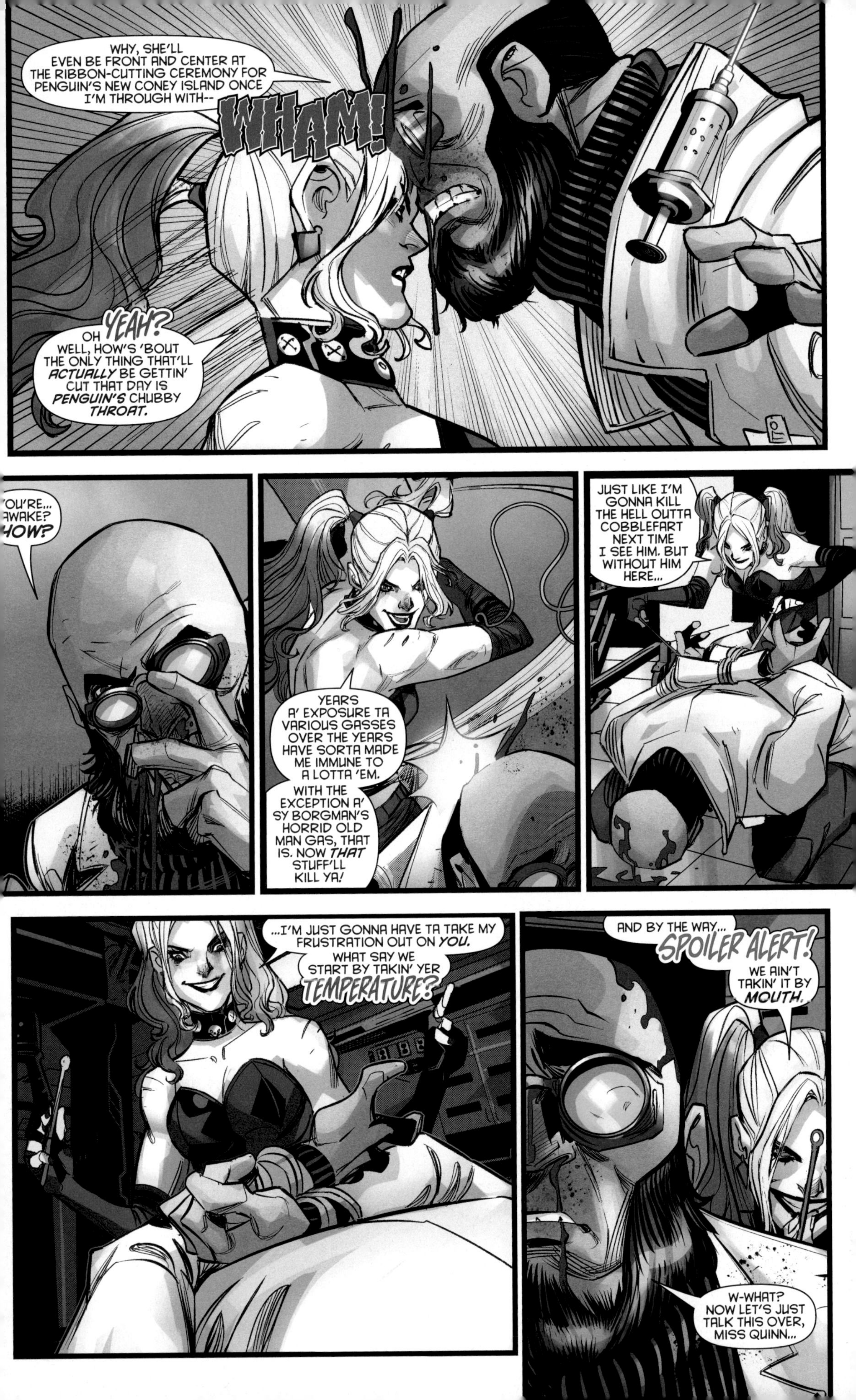
WHY, SHE'LL EVEN BE FRONT AND CENTER AT THE RIBBON-CUTTING CEREMONY FOR PENGUIN'S NEW CONEY ISLAND ONCE I'M THROUGH WITH--
WHAM!
OH YEAH? WELL, HOW'S 'BOUT THE ONLY THING THAT'LL ACTUALLY BE GETTIN' CUT THAT DAY IS PENGUIN'S CHUBBY THROAT.
OU'RE... AWAKE? HOW?
YEARS A' EXPOSURE TA VARIOUS GASSES OVER THE YEARS HAVE SORTA MADE ME IMMUNE TO A LOTTA 'EM.
WITH THE EXCEPTION A' SY BORGMAN'S HORRID OLD MAN GAS, THAT IS. NOW THAT STUFF'LL KILL YA!
JUST LIKE I'M GONNA KILL THE HELL OUTTA COBBLEFART NEXT TIME I SEE HIM. BUT WITHOUT HIM HERE...
...I'M JUST GONNA HAVE TA TAKE MY FRUSTRATION OUT ON YOU. WHAT SAY WE START BY TAKIN' YER TEMPERATURE?
AND BY THE WAY... SPOILER ALERT! WE AIN'T TAKIN' IT BY MOUTH.
W-WHAT? NOW LET'S JUST TALK THIS OVER, MISS QUINN...

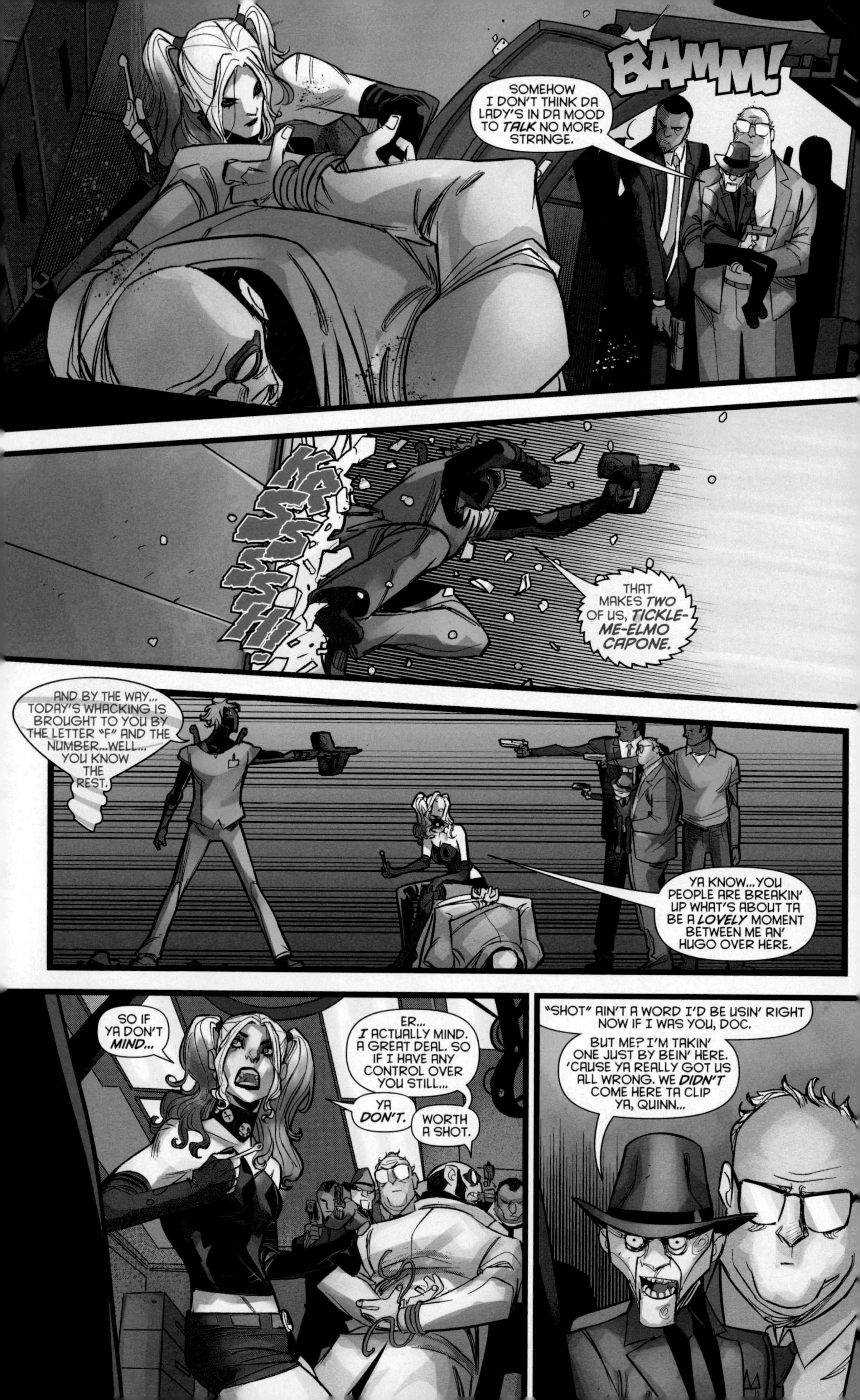
BAMM!
SOMEHOW I DON'T THINK DA LADY'S IN DA MOOD TO TALK NO MORE, STRANGE.
KRSSSHH!
THAT MAKES TWO OF US, TICKLE-ME-ELMO CAPONE.
AND BY THE WAY... TODAY'S WHACKING IS BROUGHT TO YOU BY THE LETTER "F" AND THE NUMBER...WELL... YOU KNOW THE REST.
YA KNOW...YOU PEOPLE ARE BREAKIN' UP WHAT'S ABOUT TA BE A LOVELY MOMENT BETWEEN ME AN' HUGO OVER HERE.
SO IF YA DON'T MIND...
ER... I ACTUALLY MIND. A GREAT DEAL. SO IF I HAVE ANY CONTROL OVER YOU STILL...
YA DON'T.
WORTH A SHOT.
"SHOT" AIN'T A WORD I'D BE USIN' RIGHT NOW IF I WAS YOU, DOC.
BUT ME? I'M TAKIN' ONE JUST BY BEIN' HERE. 'CAUSE YA REALLY GOT US ALL WRONG. WE DIDN'T COME HERE TA CLIP YA, QUINN...

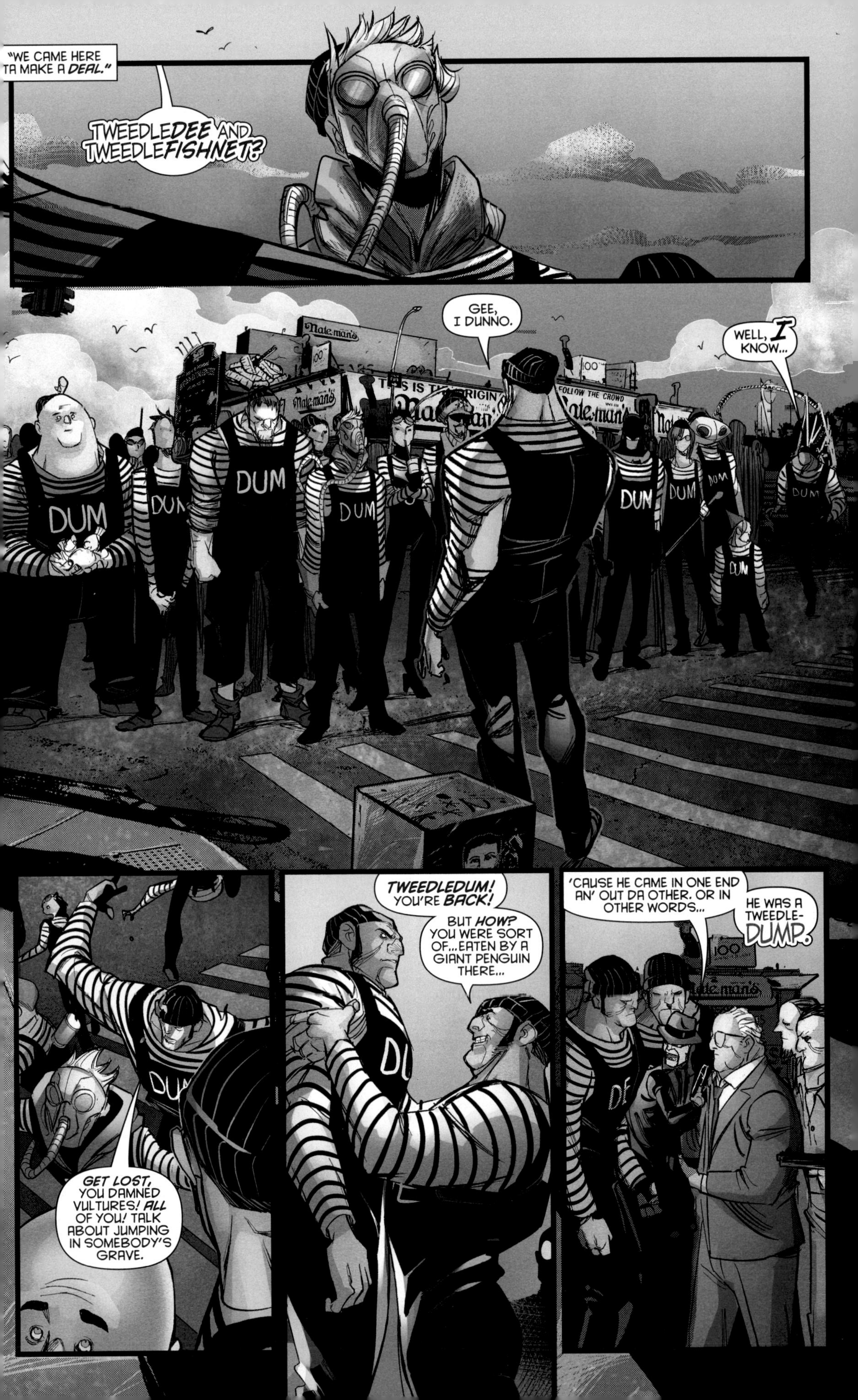
"WE CAME HERE TA MAKE A DEAL."
TWEEDLEDEE AND TWEEDLEFISHNET?
GEE, I DUNNO.
WELL, I KNOW...
DUM
Nate·man's
FOLLOW THE CROWD
GET LOST, YOU DAMNED VULTURES! ALL OF YOU! TALK ABOUT JUMPING IN SOMEBODY'S GRAVE.
TWEEDLEDUM! YOU'RE BACK!
BUT HOW? YOU WERE SORT OF...EATEN BY A GIANT PENGUIN THERE...
'CAUSE HE CAME IN ONE END AN' OUT DA OTHER. OR IN OTHER WORDS...
HE WAS A TWEEDLE-DUMP.

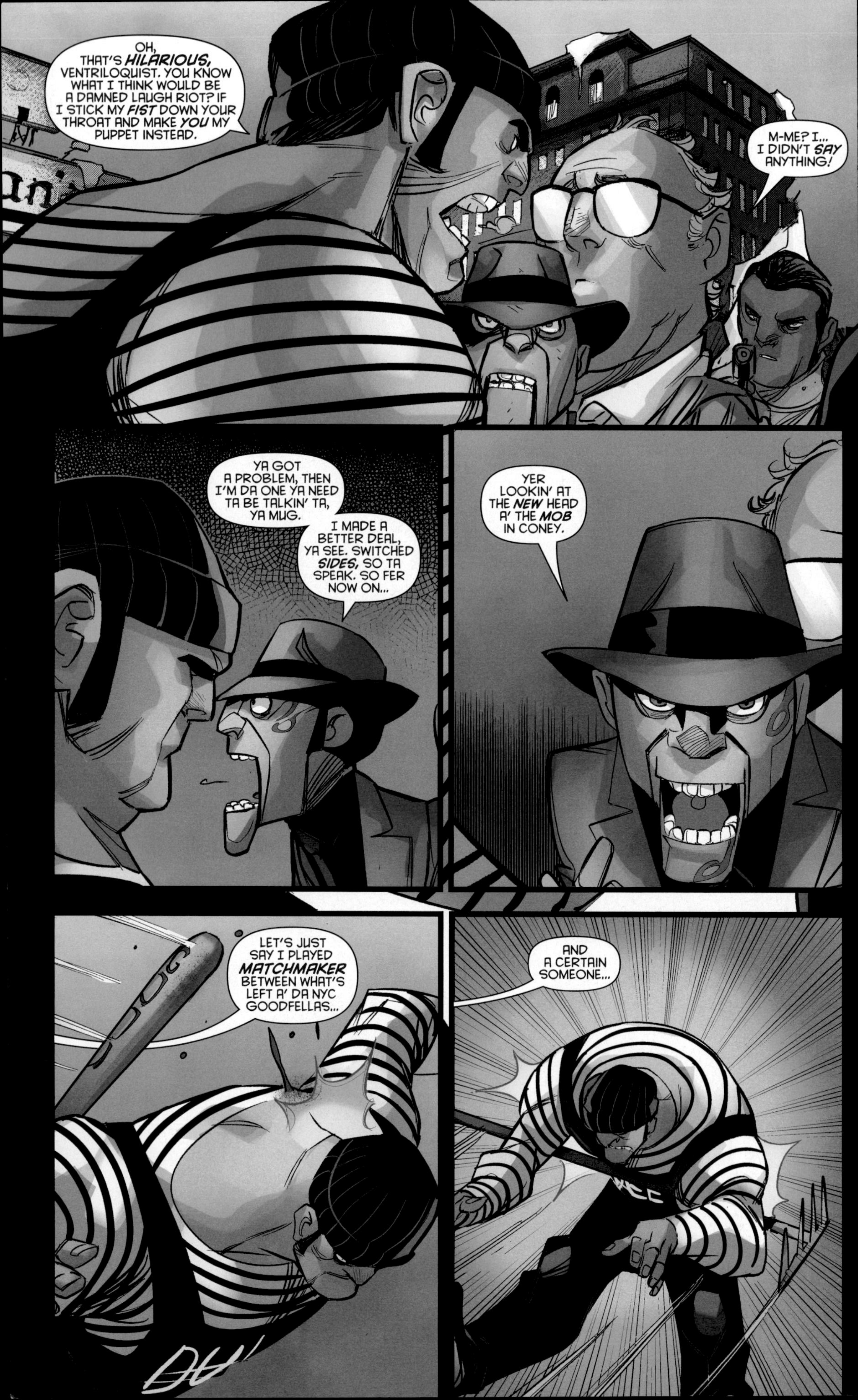
OH, THAT'S HILARIOUS, VENTRILOQUIST. YOU KNOW WHAT I THINK WOULD BE A DAMNED LAUGH RIOT? IF I STICK MY FIST DOWN YOUR THROAT AND MAKE YOU MY PUPPET INSTEAD.
M-ME? I... I DIDN'T SAY ANYTHING!
YA GOT A PROBLEM, THEN I'M DA ONE YA NEED TA BE TALKIN' TA, YA MUG.
I MADE A BETTER DEAL, YA SEE. SWITCHED SIDES, SO TA SPEAK. SO FER NOW ON...
YER LOOKIN' AT THE NEW HEAD A' THE MOB IN CONEY.
LET'S JUST SAY I PLAYED MATCHMAKER BETWEEN WHAT'S LEFT A' DA NYC GOODFELLAS...
AND A CERTAIN SOMEONE...

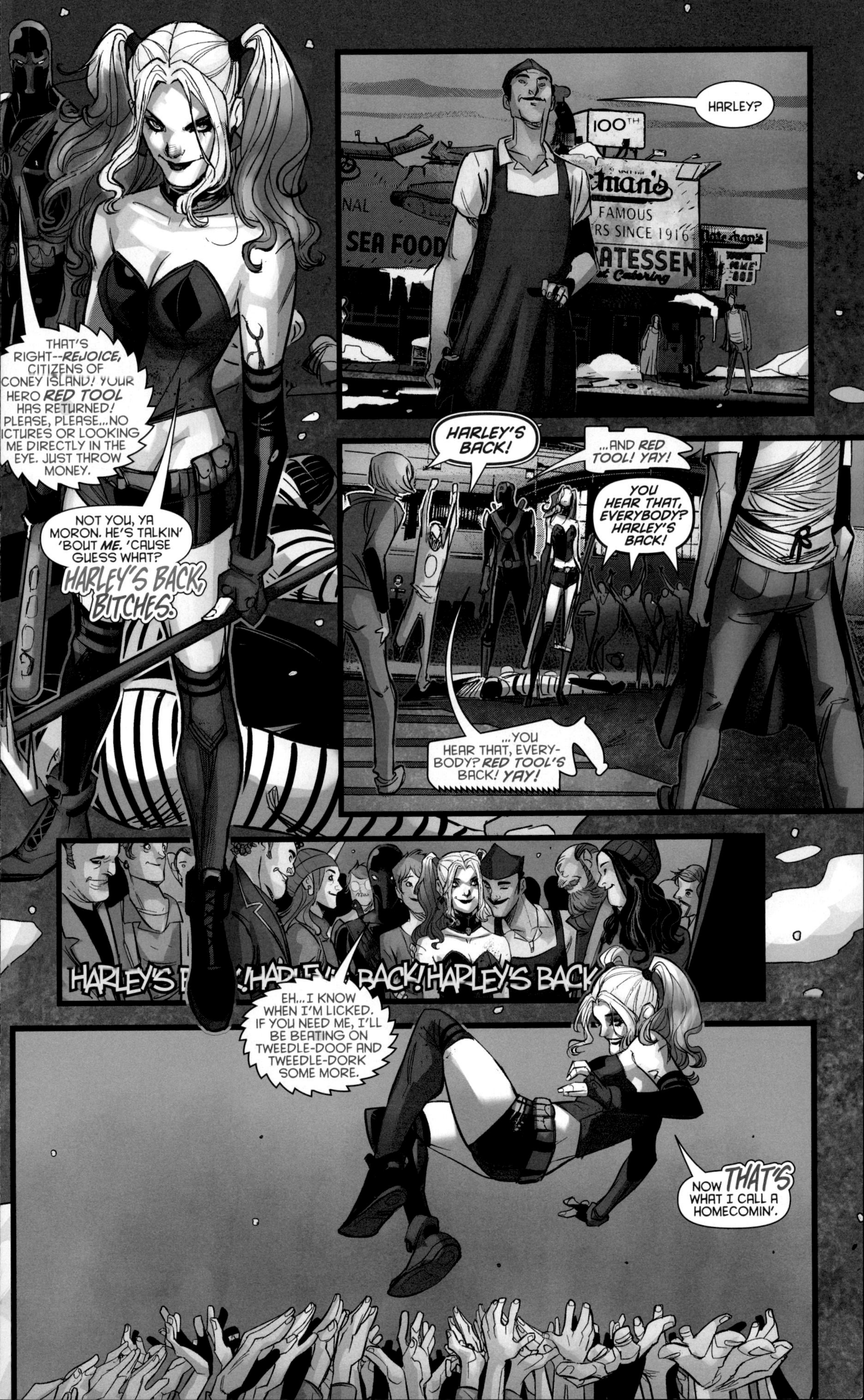
THAT'S RIGHT--*REJOICE,* CITIZENS OF CONEY ISLAND! YOUR HERO *RED TOOL* HAS RETURNED! PLEASE, PLEASE...NO ICTURES OR LOOKING ME DIRECTLY IN THE EYE. JUST THROW MONEY.
NOT YOU, YA MORON. HE'S TALKIN' 'BOUT *ME.* 'CAUSE GUESS WHAT?
HARLEY'S BACK, BITCHES.
HARLEY?
100TH
FAMOUS
SEA FOOD
HARLEY'S BACK!
...AND *RED* TOOL! YAY!
YOU HEAR THAT, EVERYBODY? HARLEY'S BACK!
...YOU HEAR THAT, EVERY-BODY? *RED TOOL'S* BACK! *YAY!*
BACK! HARLEY'S BACK
EH...I KNOW WHEN I'M LICKED. IF YOU NEED ME, I'LL BE BEATING ON TWEEDLE-DOOF AND TWEEDLE-DORK SOME MORE.
NOW *THAT'S* WHAT I CALL A HOMECOMIN'.

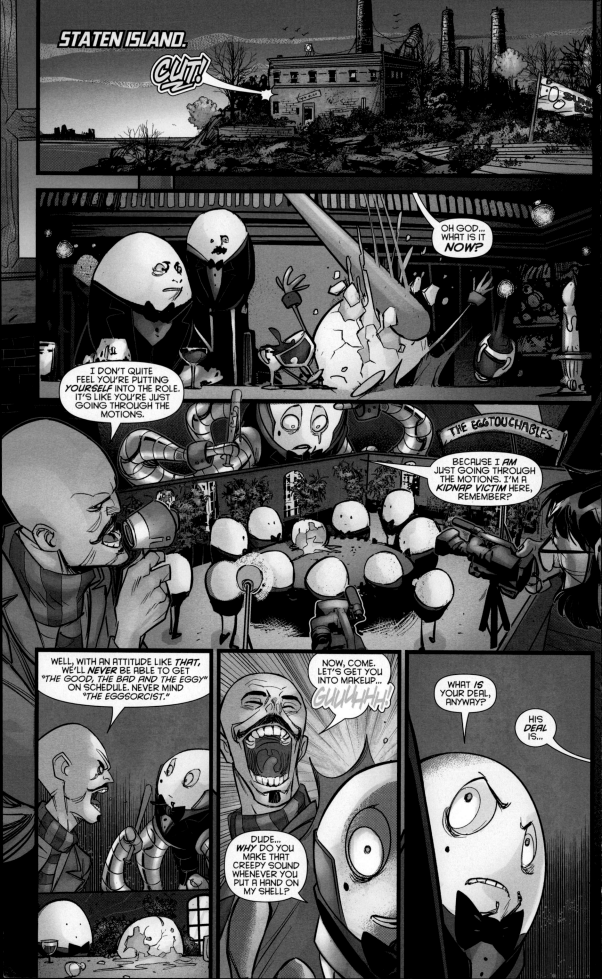

STATEN ISLAND.

CUT!

OH GOD... WHAT IS IT *NOW?*

I DON'T QUITE FEEL YOU'RE PUTTING *YOURSELF* INTO THE ROLE. IT'S LIKE YOU'RE JUST GOING THROUGH THE MOTIONS.

THE EGGTOUCHABLES

BECAUSE I *AM* JUST GOING THROUGH THE MOTIONS. I'M A *KIDNAP VICTIM* HERE, REMEMBER?

WELL, WITH AN ATTITUDE LIKE *THAT*, WE'LL *NEVER* BE ABLE TO GET *"THE GOOD, THE BAD AND THE EGGY"* ON SCHEDULE. NEVER MIND *"THE EGGSORCIST."*

NOW, COME. LET'S GET YOU INTO MAKEUP... GUUUHHH!

WHAT *IS* YOUR DEAL, ANYWAY?

HIS *DEAL* IS...

DUDE... *WHY* DO YOU MAKE THAT CREEPY SOUND WHENEVER YOU PUT A HAND ON MY SHELL?

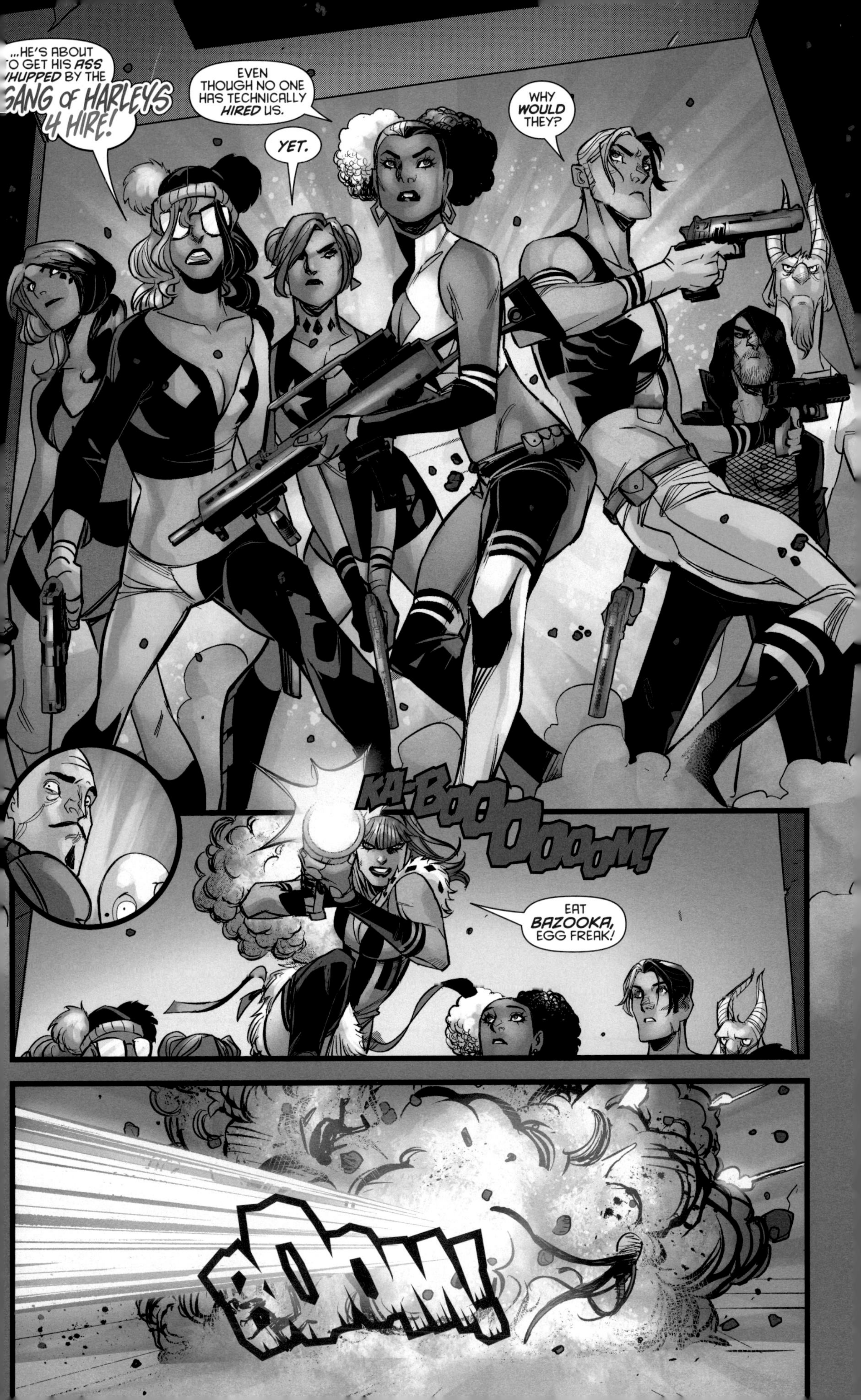
...HE'S ABOUT TO GET HIS ASS WHUPPED BY THE GANG OF HARLEYS 4 HIRE!
EVEN THOUGH NO ONE HAS TECHNICALLY HIRED US.
YET.
WHY WOULD THEY?
KA-BOOOOOOOM!
EAT BAZOOKA, EGG FREAK!
BOOM!

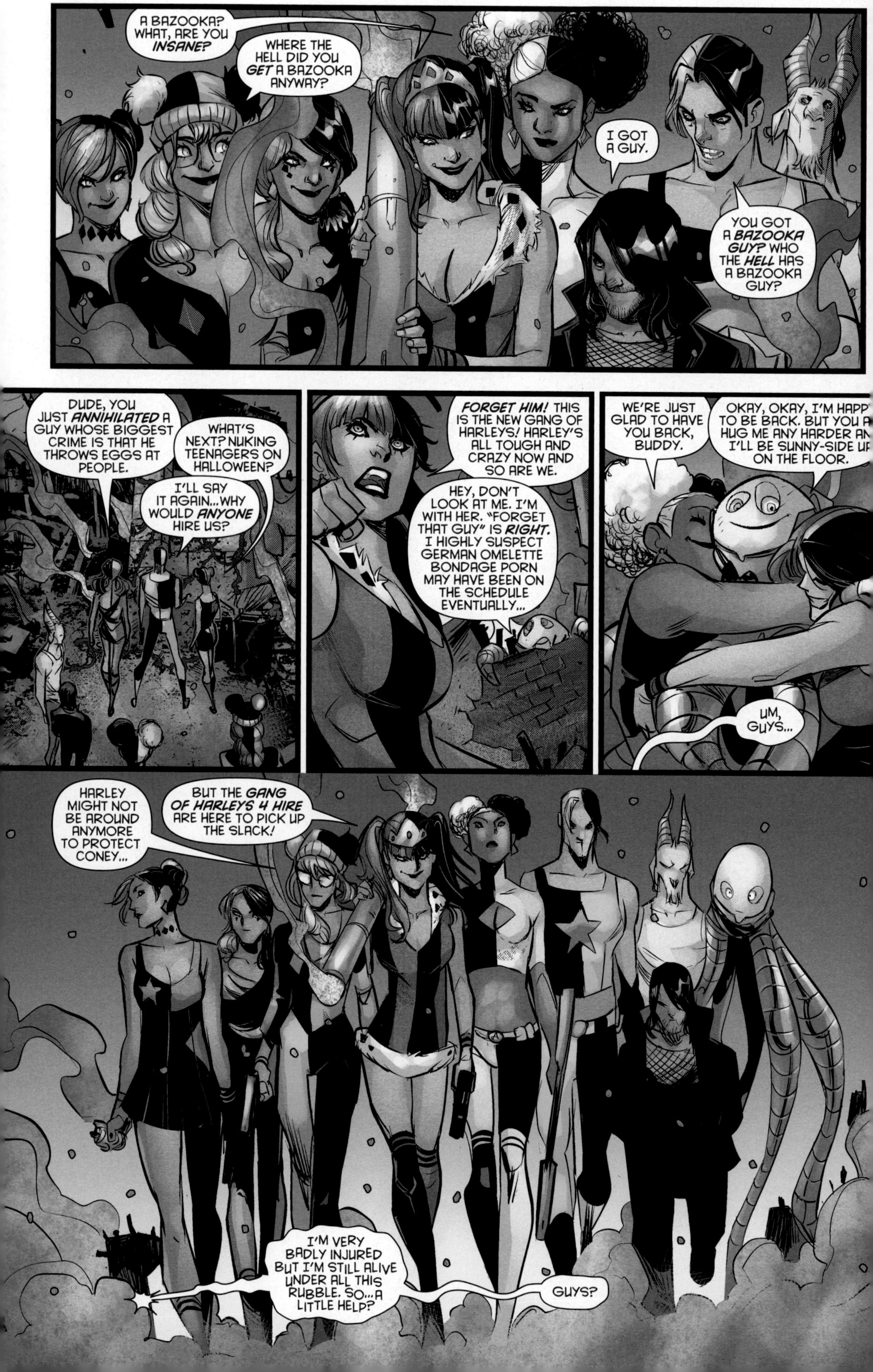
A BAZOOKA? WHAT, ARE YOU INSANE?
WHERE THE HELL DID YOU GET A BAZOOKA ANYWAY?
I GOT A GUY.
YOU GOT A BAZOOKA GUY? WHO THE HELL HAS A BAZOOKA GUY?
DUDE, YOU JUST ANNIHILATED A GUY WHOSE BIGGEST CRIME IS THAT HE THROWS EGGS AT PEOPLE.
WHAT'S NEXT? NUKING TEENAGERS ON HALLOWEEN?
I'LL SAY IT AGAIN...WHY WOULD ANYONE HIRE US?
FORGET HIM! THIS IS THE NEW GANG OF HARLEYS! HARLEY'S ALL TOUGH AND CRAZY NOW AND SO ARE WE.
HEY, DON'T LOOK AT ME. I'M WITH HER. "FORGET THAT GUY" IS RIGHT. I HIGHLY SUSPECT GERMAN OMELETTE BONDAGE PORN MAY HAVE BEEN ON THE SCHEDULE EVENTUALLY...
WE'RE JUST GLAD TO HAVE YOU BACK, BUDDY.
OKAY, OKAY, I'M HAPPY TO BE BACK. BUT YOU A HUG ME ANY HARDER AN I'LL BE SUNNY-SIDE UP ON THE FLOOR.
UM, GUYS...
HARLEY MIGHT NOT BE AROUND ANYMORE TO PROTECT CONEY...
BUT THE GANG OF HARLEYS 4 HIRE ARE HERE TO PICK UP THE SLACK!
I'M VERY BADLY INJURED BUT I'M STILL ALIVE UNDER ALL THIS RUBBLE. SO...A LITTLE HELP?
GUYS?

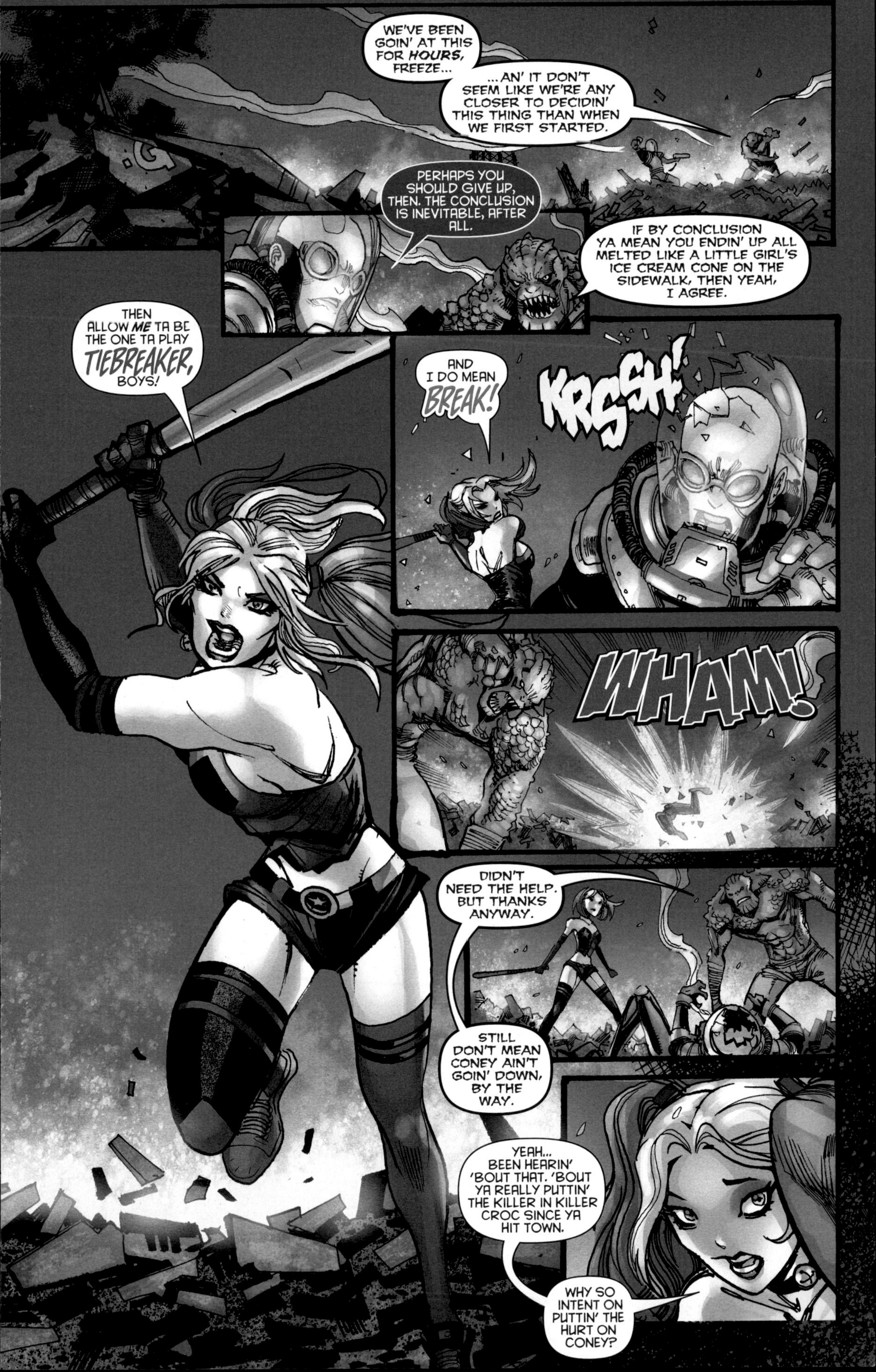
WE'VE BEEN GOIN' AT THIS FOR HOURS, FREEZE...
...AN' IT DON'T SEEM LIKE WE'RE ANY CLOSER TO DECIDIN' THIS THING THAN WHEN WE FIRST STARTED.
PERHAPS YOU SHOULD GIVE UP, THEN. THE CONCLUSION IS INEVITABLE, AFTER ALL.
IF BY CONCLUSION YA MEAN YOU ENDIN' UP ALL MELTED LIKE A LITTLE GIRL'S ICE CREAM CONE ON THE SIDEWALK, THEN YEAH, I AGREE.
THEN ALLOW ME TA BE THE ONE TA PLAY TIEBREAKER, BOYS!
AND I DO MEAN BREAK!
KRSSH!
WHAM!
DIDN'T NEED THE HELP. BUT THANKS ANYWAY.
STILL DON'T MEAN CONEY AIN'T GOIN' DOWN, BY THE WAY.
YEAH... BEEN HEARIN' 'BOUT THAT. 'BOUT YA REALLY PUTTIN' THE KILLER IN KILLER CROC SINCE YA HIT TOWN.
WHY SO INTENT ON PUTTIN' THE HURT ON CONEY?

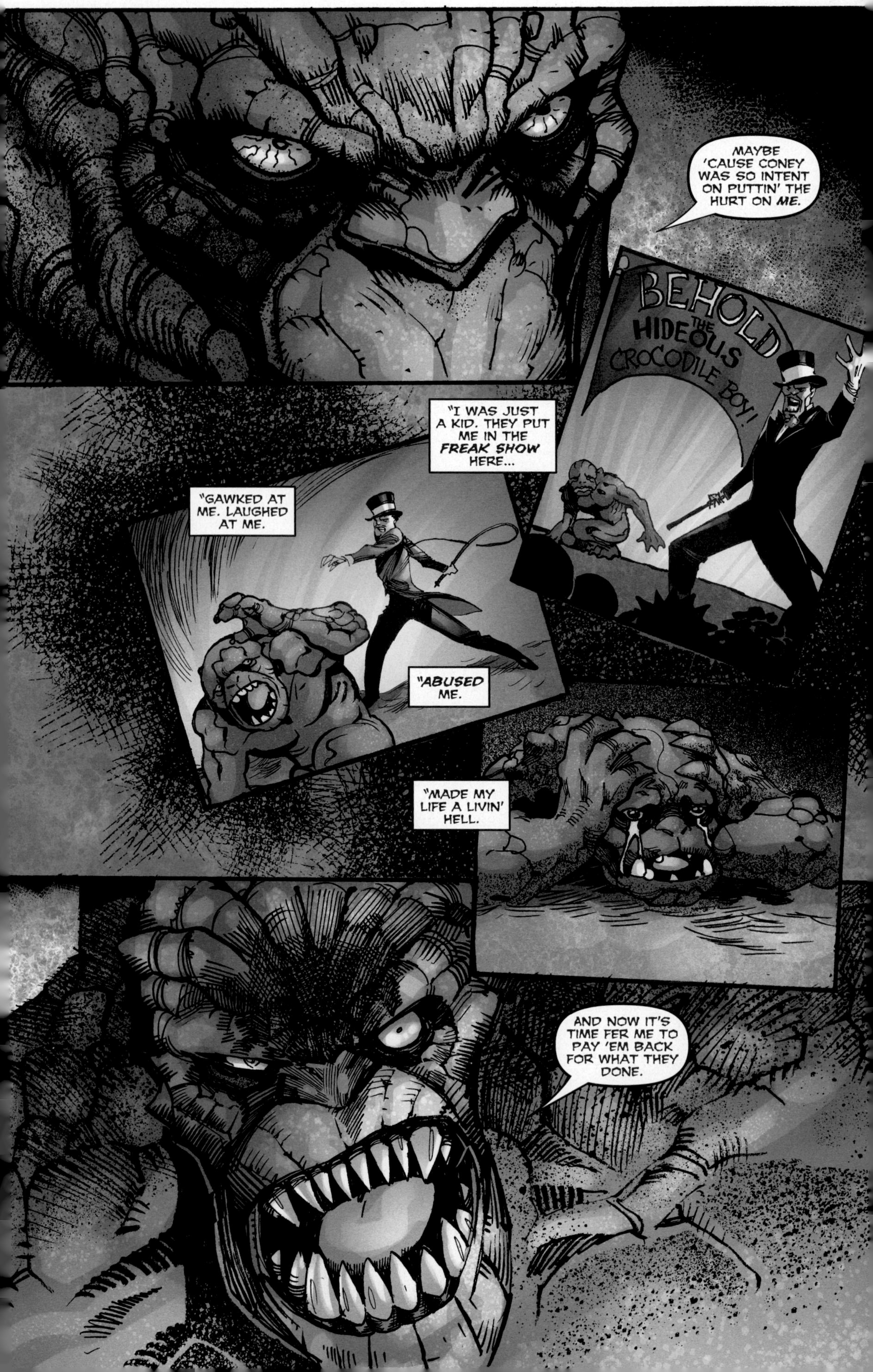
MAYBE 'CAUSE CONEY WAS SO INTENT ON PUTTIN' THE HURT ON *ME*.
BEHOLD THE HIDEOUS CROCODILE BOY!
"I WAS JUST A KID. THEY PUT ME IN THE *FREAK SHOW* HERE...
"GAWKED AT ME. LAUGHED AT ME.
"*ABUSED* ME.
"MADE MY LIFE A LIVIN' HELL.
AND NOW IT'S TIME FER ME TO PAY 'EM BACK FOR WHAT THEY DONE.

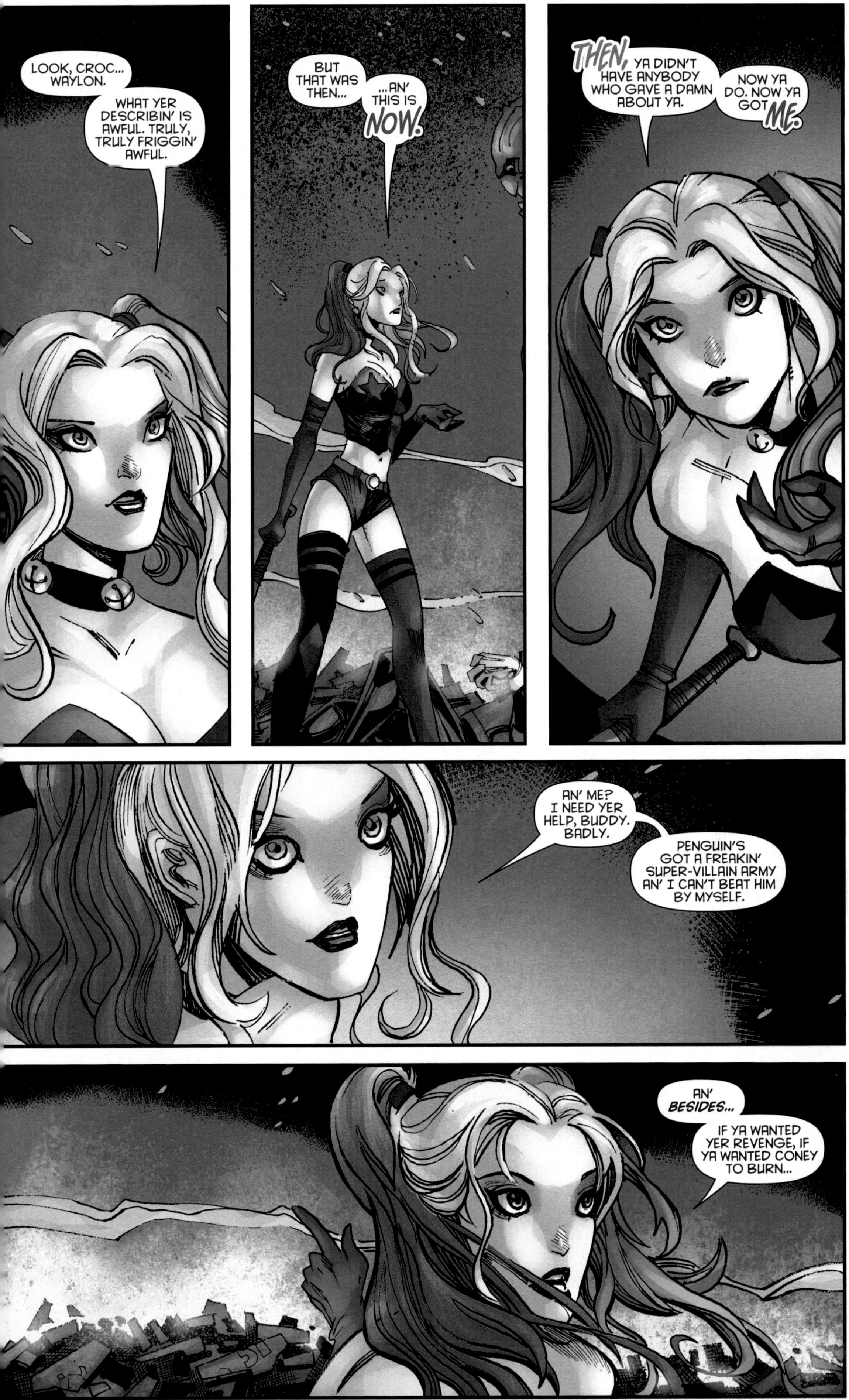
LOOK, CROC... WAYLON.
WHAT YER DESCRIBIN' IS AWFUL. TRULY, TRULY FRIGGIN' AWFUL.
BUT THAT WAS THEN...
...AN' THIS IS NOW.
THEN, YA DIDN'T HAVE ANYBODY WHO GAVE A DAMN ABOUT YA.
NOW YA DO. NOW YA GOT ME.
AN' ME? I NEED YER HELP, BUDDY. BADLY.
PENGUIN'S GOT A FREAKIN' SUPER-VILLAIN ARMY AN' I CAN'T BEAT HIM BY MYSELF.
AN' BESIDES...
IF YA WANTED YER REVENGE, IF YA WANTED CONEY TO BURN...

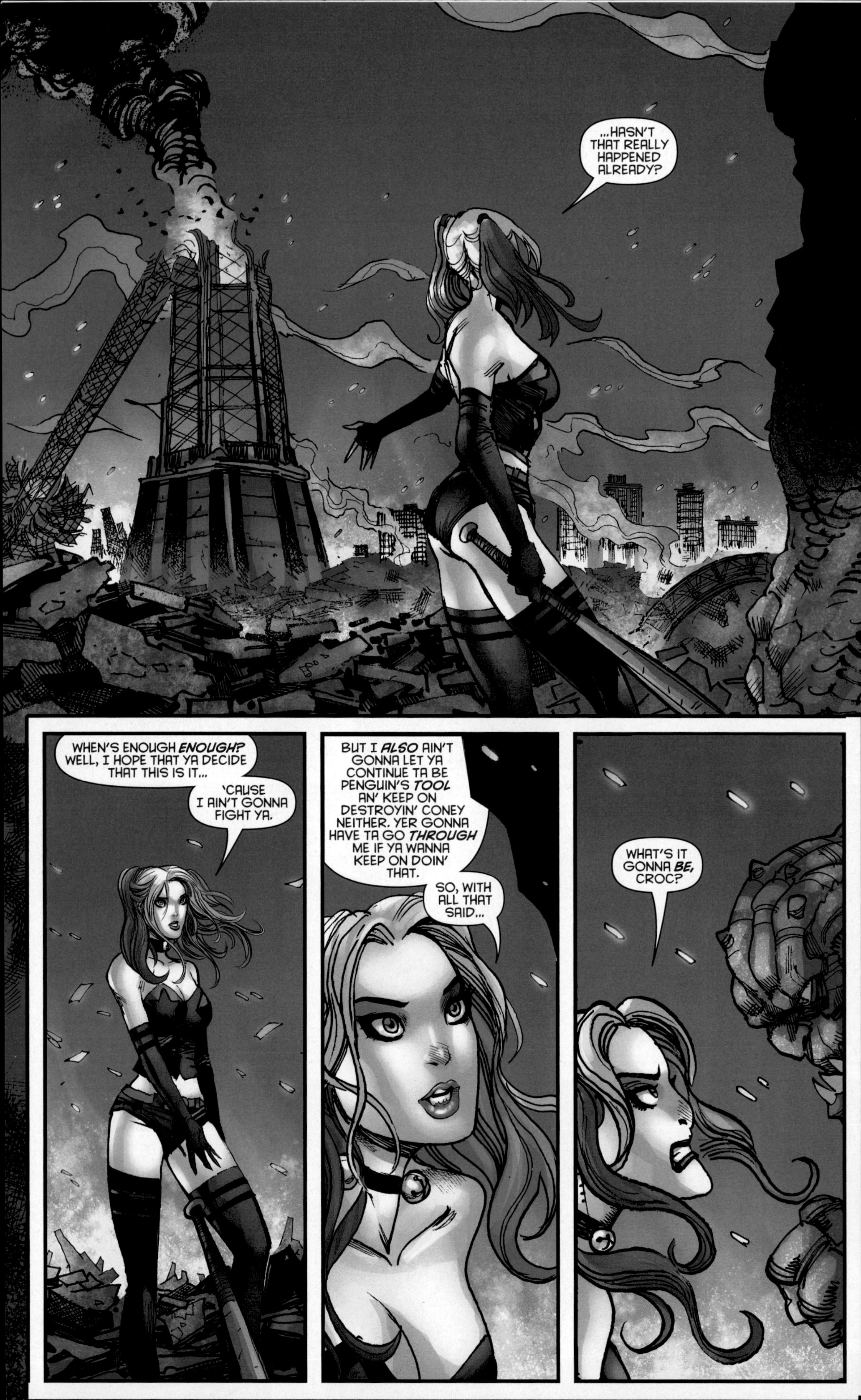
...HASN'T THAT REALLY HAPPENED ALREADY?
WHEN'S ENOUGH *ENOUGH?* WELL, I HOPE THAT YA DECIDE THAT THIS IS IT...
'CAUSE I AIN'T GONNA FIGHT YA.
BUT I *ALSO* AIN'T GONNA LET YA CONTINUE TA BE PENGUIN'S *TOOL* AN' KEEP ON DESTROYIN' CONEY NEITHER. YER GONNA HAVE TA GO *THROUGH* ME IF YA WANNA KEEP ON DOIN' THAT.
SO, WITH ALL THAT SAID...
WHAT'S IT GONNA *BE,* CROC?

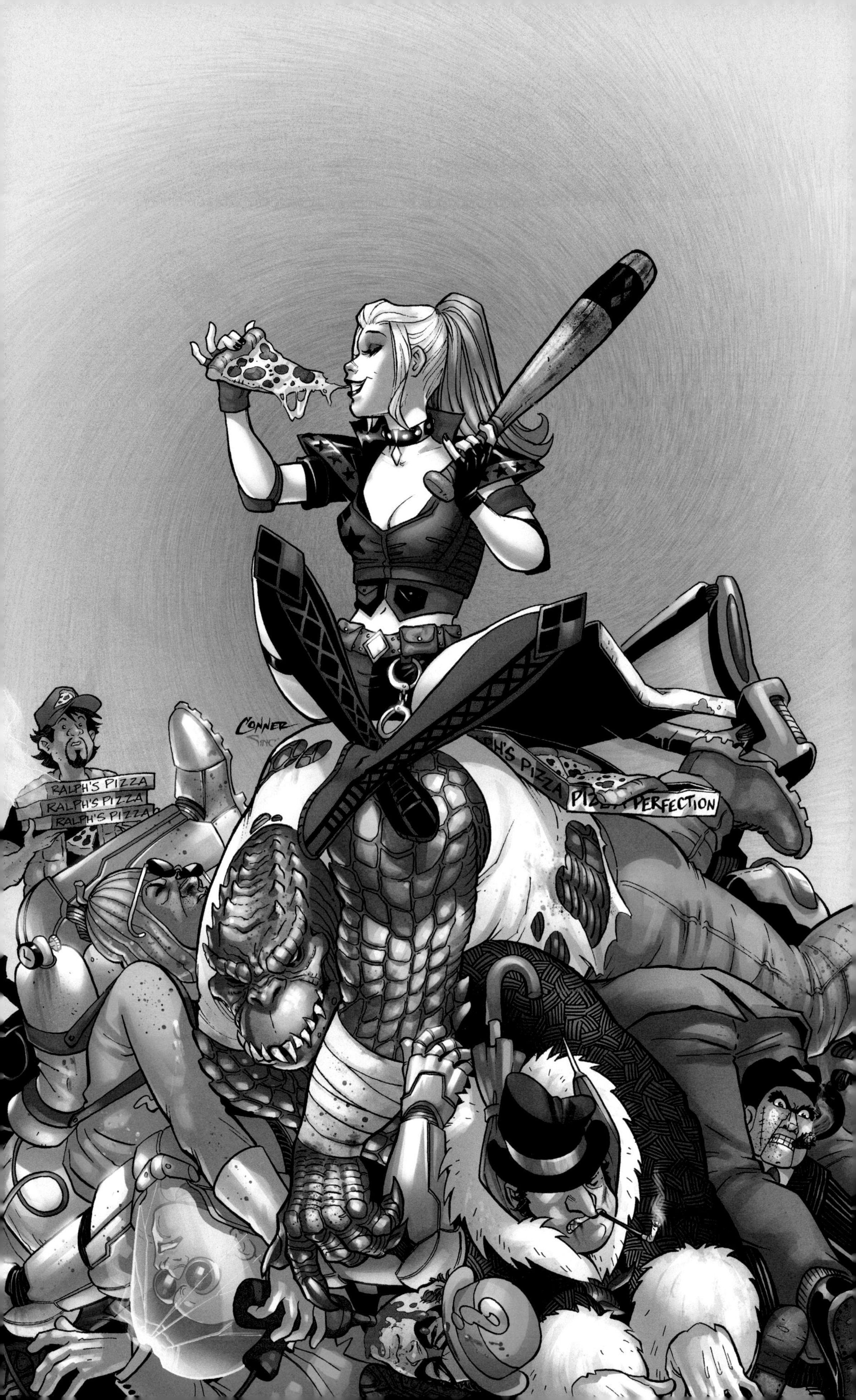
CONNER
RALPH'S PIZZA
RALPH'S PIZZA
RALPH'S PIZZA
PERFECTION

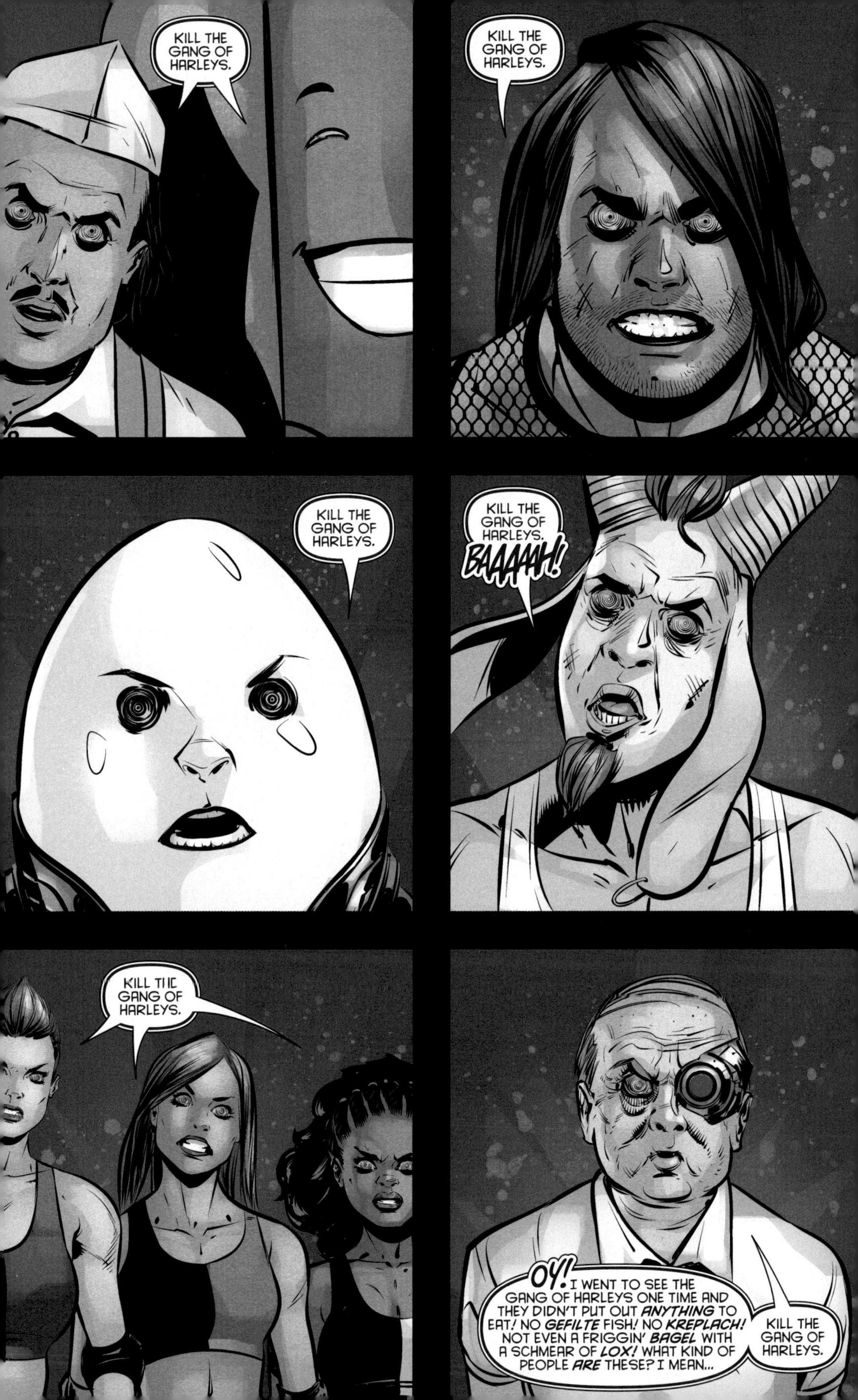
KILL THE GANG OF HARLEYS.
KILL THE GANG OF HARLEYS.
KILL THE GANG OF HARLEYS.
KILL THE GANG OF HARLEYS.
BAAAAAH!
KILL THE GANG OF HARLEYS.
OY! I WENT TO SEE THE GANG OF HARLEYS ONE TIME AND THEY DIDN'T PUT OUT ANYTHING TO EAT! NO GEFILTE FISH! NO KREPLACH! NOT EVEN A FRIGGIN' BAGEL WITH A SCHMEAR OF LOX! WHAT KIND OF PEOPLE ARE THESE? I MEAN...
KILL THE GANG OF HARLEYS.

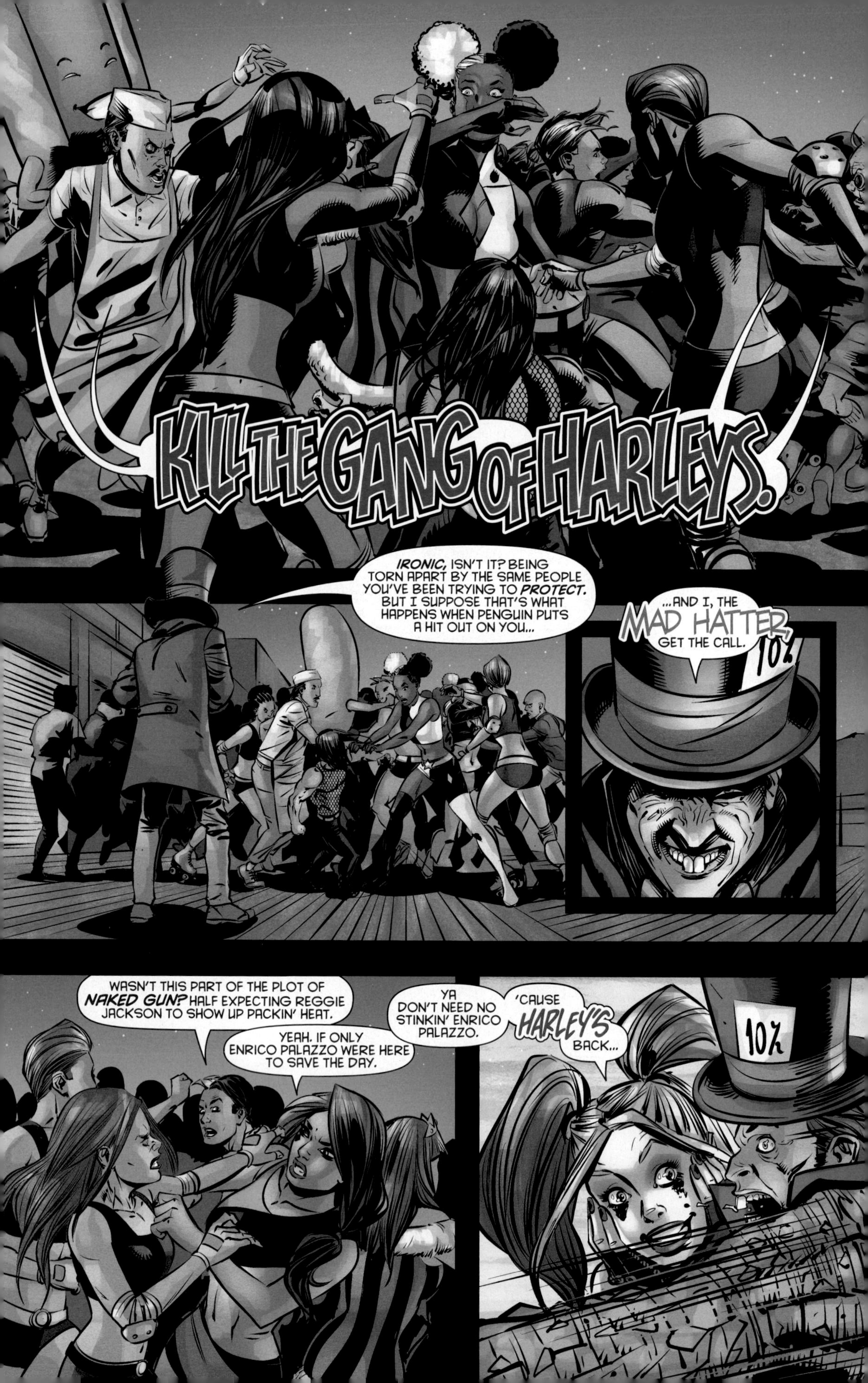
KILL THE GANG OF HARLEYS.
IRONIC, ISN'T IT? BEING TORN APART BY THE SAME PEOPLE YOU'VE BEEN TRYING TO PROTECT. BUT I SUPPOSE THAT'S WHAT HAPPENS WHEN PENGUIN PUTS A HIT OUT ON YOU...
...AND I, THE MAD HATTER GET THE CALL.
10/6
WASN'T THIS PART OF THE PLOT OF NAKED GUN? HALF EXPECTING REGGIE JACKSON TO SHOW UP PACKIN' HEAT.
YEAH. IF ONLY ENRICO PALAZZO WERE HERE TO SAVE THE DAY.
YA DON'T NEED NO STINKIN' ENRICO PALAZZO.
'CAUSE HARLEY'S BACK...
10/6

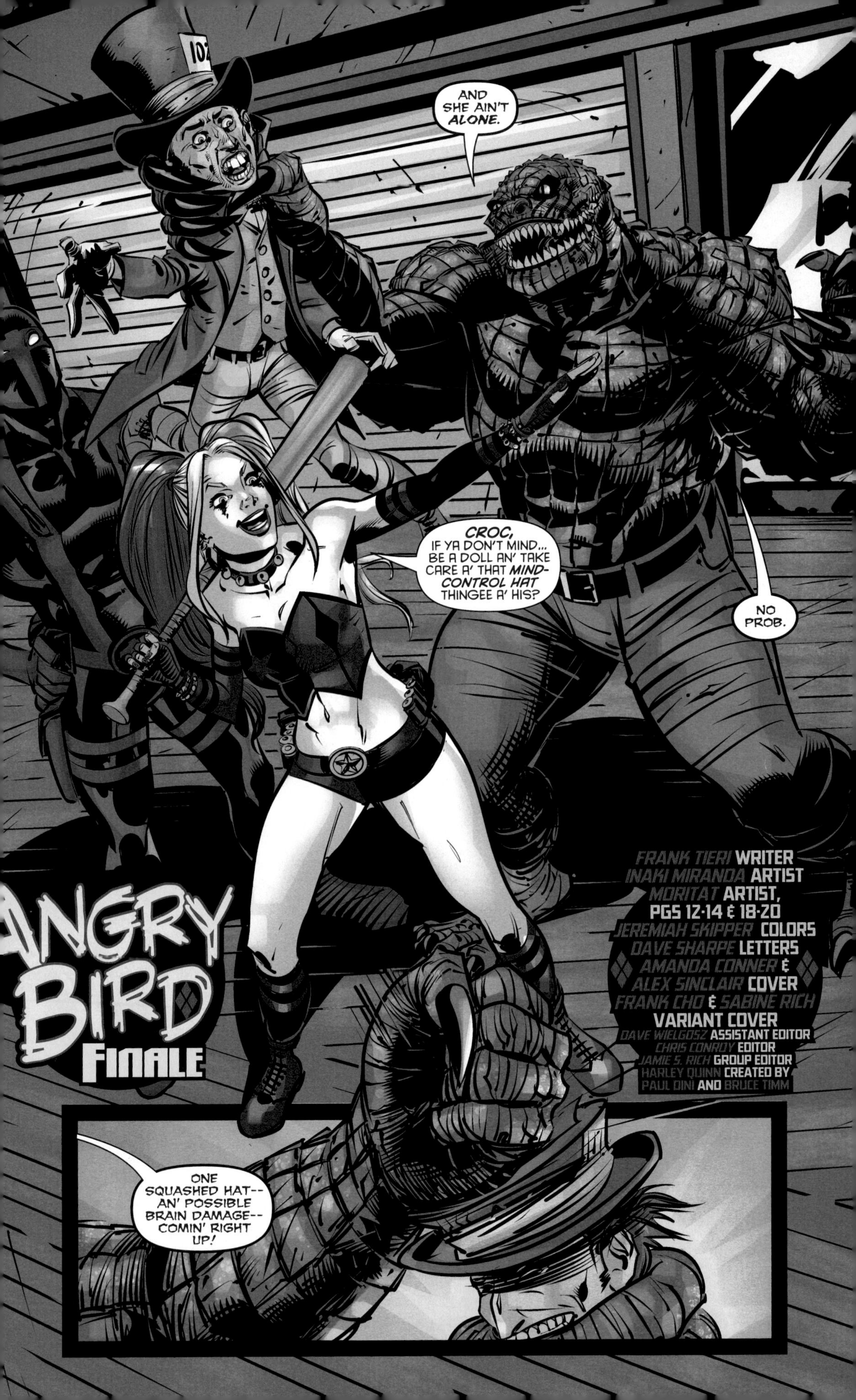
AND SHE AIN'T ALONE.
CROC, IF YA DON'T MIND... BE A DOLL AN' TAKE CARE A' THAT MIND-CONTROL HAT THINGEE A' HIS?
NO PROB.
ANGRY BIRD
FINALE
FRANK TIERI WRITER
INAKI MIRANDA ARTIST
MORITAT ARTIST, PGS 12-14 & 18-20
JEREMIAH SKIPPER COLORS
DAVE SHARPE LETTERS
AMANDA CONNER & ALEX SINCLAIR COVER
FRANK CHO & SABINE RICH VARIANT COVER
DAVE WIELGOSZ ASSISTANT EDITOR
CHRIS CONROY EDITOR
JAMIE S. RICH GROUP EDITOR
HARLEY QUINN CREATED BY PAUL DINI AND BRUCE TIMM
ONE SQUASHED HAT--AN' POSSIBLE BRAIN DAMAGE--COMIN' RIGHT UP!

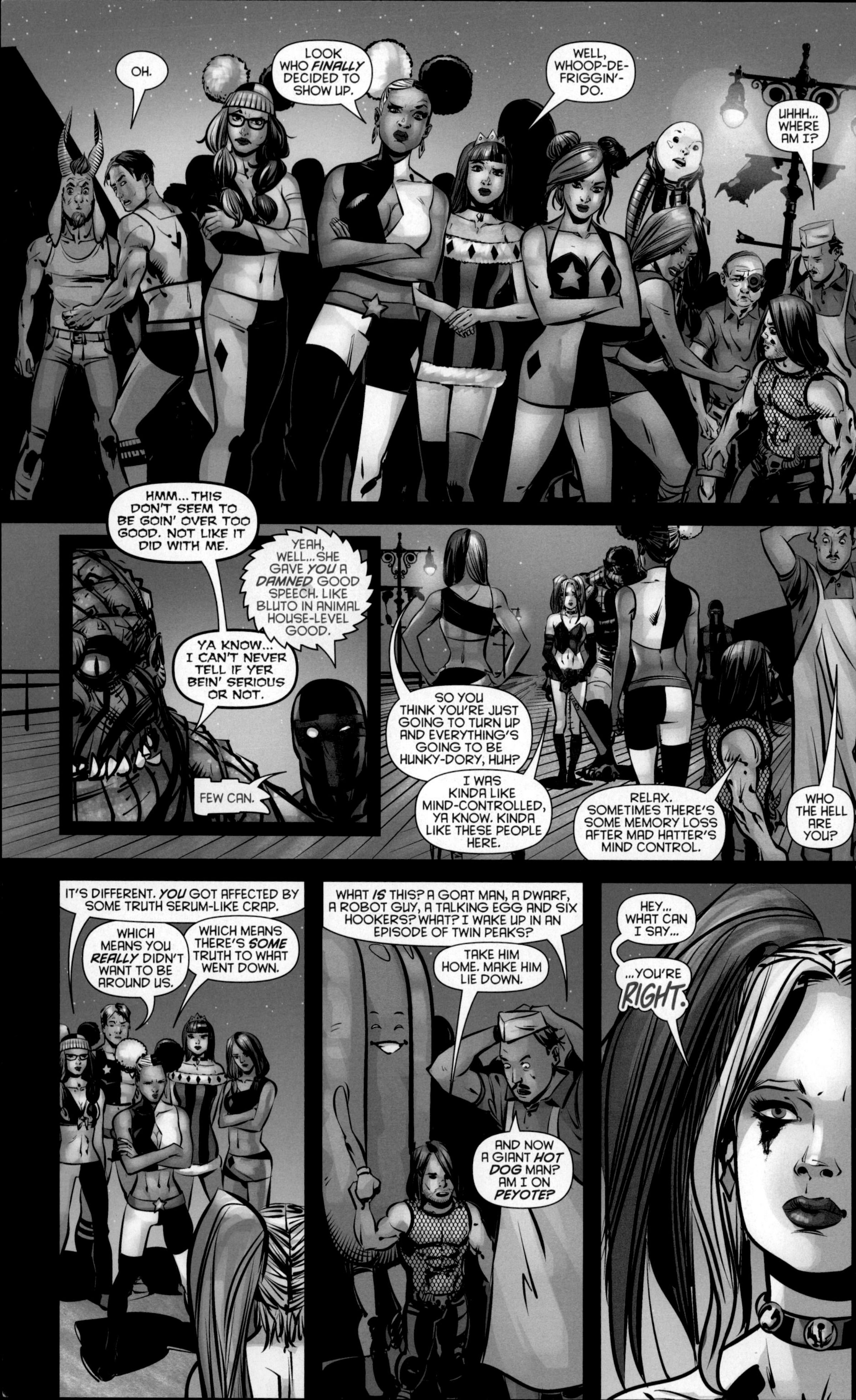
OH.
LOOK WHO FINALLY DECIDED TO SHOW UP.
WELL, WHOOP-DE-FRIGGIN'-DO.
UHHH... WHERE AM I?
HMM... THIS DON'T SEEM TO BE GOIN' OVER TOO GOOD. NOT LIKE IT DID WITH ME.
YEAH, WELL... SHE GAVE YOU A DAMNED GOOD SPEECH. LIKE BLUTO IN ANIMAL HOUSE-LEVEL GOOD.
YA KNOW... I CAN'T NEVER TELL IF YER BEIN' SERIOUS OR NOT.
FEW CAN.
SO YOU THINK YOU'RE JUST GOING TO TURN UP AND EVERYTHING'S GOING TO BE HUNKY-DORY, HUH?
I WAS KINDA LIKE MIND-CONTROLLED, YA KNOW. KINDA LIKE THESE PEOPLE HERE.
RELAX. SOMETIMES THERE'S SOME MEMORY LOSS AFTER MAD HATTER'S MIND CONTROL.
WHO THE HELL ARE YOU?
IT'S DIFFERENT. YOU GOT AFFECTED BY SOME TRUTH SERUM-LIKE CRAP.
WHICH MEANS YOU REALLY DIDN'T WANT TO BE AROUND US.
WHICH MEANS THERE'S SOME TRUTH TO WHAT WENT DOWN.
WHAT IS THIS? A GOAT MAN, A DWARF, A ROBOT GUY, A TALKING EGG AND SIX HOOKERS? WHAT? I WAKE UP IN AN EPISODE OF TWIN PEAKS?
TAKE HIM HOME. MAKE HIM LIE DOWN.
AND NOW A GIANT HOT DOG MAN? AM I ON PEYOTE?
HEY... WHAT CAN I SAY...
...YOU'RE RIGHT.

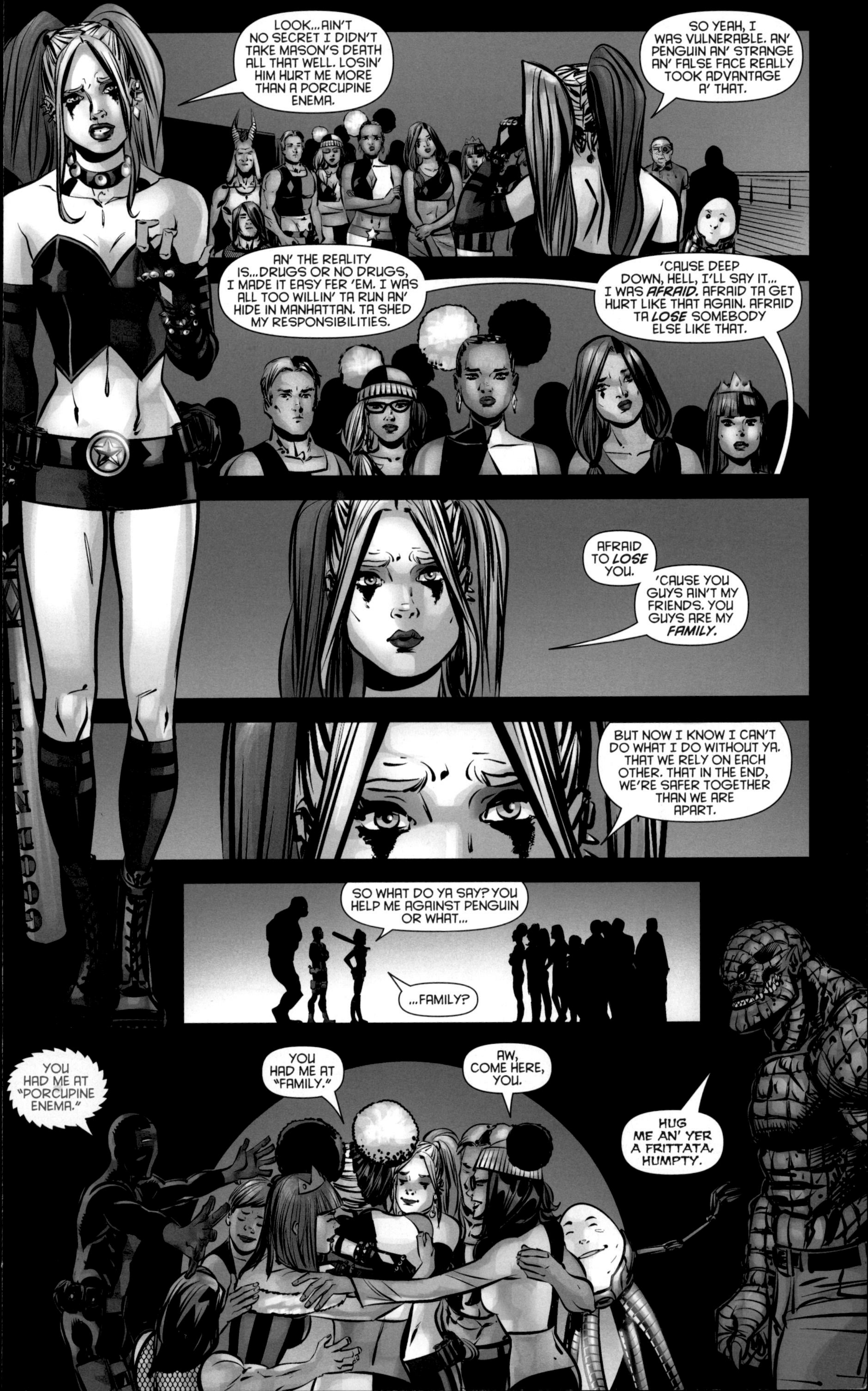
LOOK... AIN'T NO SECRET I DIDN'T TAKE MASON'S DEATH ALL THAT WELL. LOSIN' HIM HURT ME MORE THAN A PORCUPINE ENEMA.
SO YEAH, I WAS VULNERABLE. AN' PENGUIN AN' STRANGE AN' FALSE FACE REALLY TOOK ADVANTAGE A' THAT.
AN' THE REALITY IS... DRUGS OR NO DRUGS, I MADE IT EASY FER 'EM. I WAS ALL TOO WILLIN' TA RUN AN' HIDE IN MANHATTAN. TA SHED MY RESPONSIBILITIES.
'CAUSE DEEP DOWN, HELL, I'LL SAY IT... I WAS AFRAID. AFRAID TA GET HURT LIKE THAT AGAIN. AFRAID TA LOSE SOMEBODY ELSE LIKE THAT.
AFRAID TO LOSE YOU.
'CAUSE YOU GUYS AIN'T MY FRIENDS. YOU GUYS ARE MY FAMILY.
BUT NOW I KNOW I CAN'T DO WHAT I DO WITHOUT YA. THAT WE RELY ON EACH OTHER. THAT IN THE END, WE'RE SAFER TOGETHER THAN WE ARE APART.
SO WHAT DO YA SAY? YOU HELP ME AGAINST PENGUIN OR WHAT...
...FAMILY?
YOU HAD ME AT "PORCUPINE ENEMA."
YOU HAD ME AT "FAMILY."
AW, COME HERE, YOU.
HUG ME AN' YER A FRITTATA, HUMPTY.

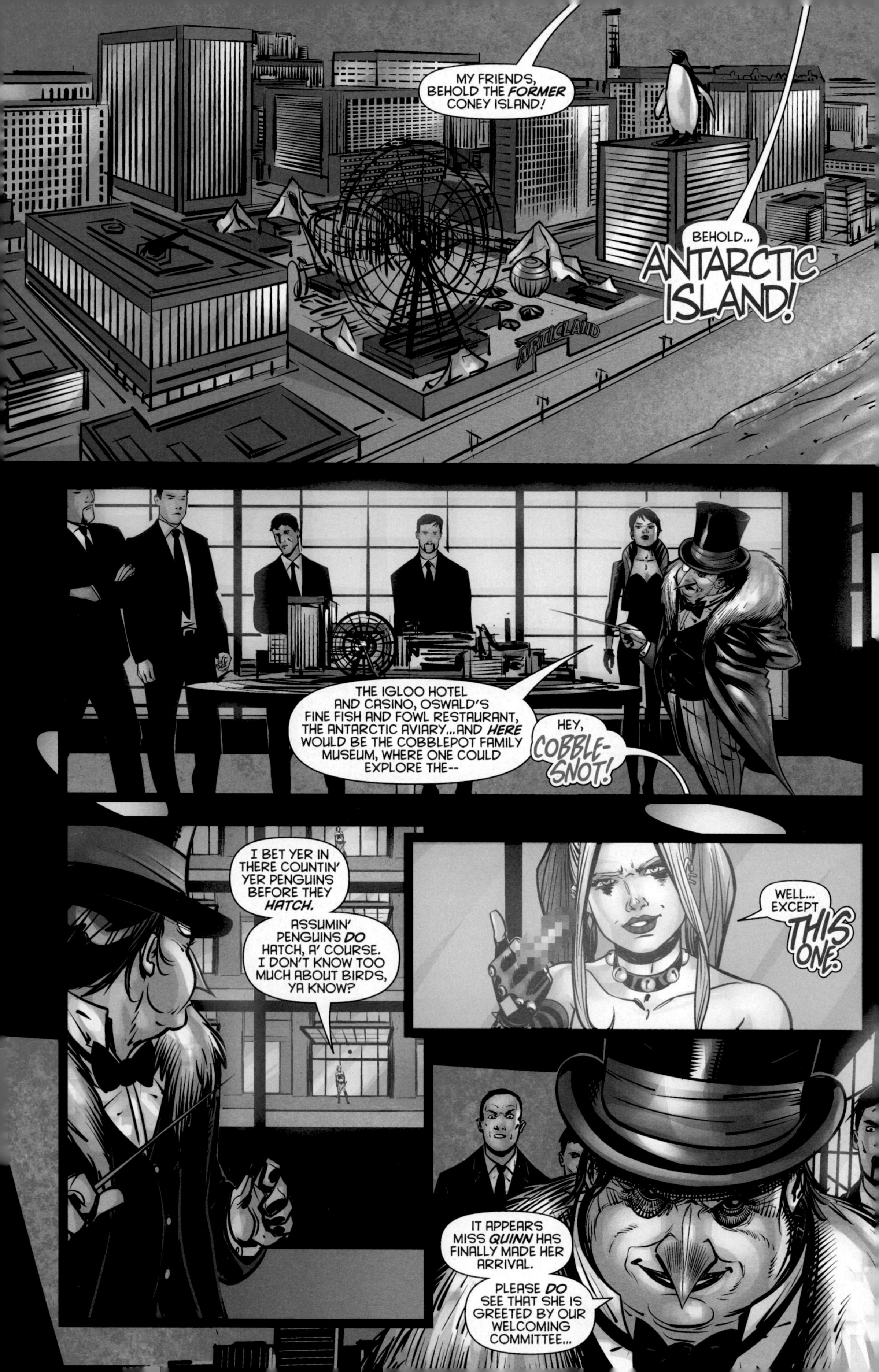
MY FRIENDS, BEHOLD THE FORMER CONEY ISLAND!
BEHOLD... ANTARCTIC ISLAND!
THE IGLOO HOTEL AND CASINO, OSWALD'S FINE FISH AND FOWL RESTAURANT, THE ANTARCTIC AVIARY...AND HERE WOULD BE THE COBBLEPOT FAMILY MUSEUM, WHERE ONE COULD EXPLORE THE--
HEY, COBBLE-SNOT!
I BET YER IN THERE COUNTIN' YER PENGUINS BEFORE THEY HATCH.
ASSUMIN' PENGUINS DO HATCH, A' COURSE. I DON'T KNOW TOO MUCH ABOUT BIRDS, YA KNOW?
WELL... EXCEPT THIS ONE.
IT APPEARS MISS QUINN HAS FINALLY MADE HER ARRIVAL.
PLEASE DO SEE THAT SHE IS GREETED BY OUR WELCOMING COMMITTEE...

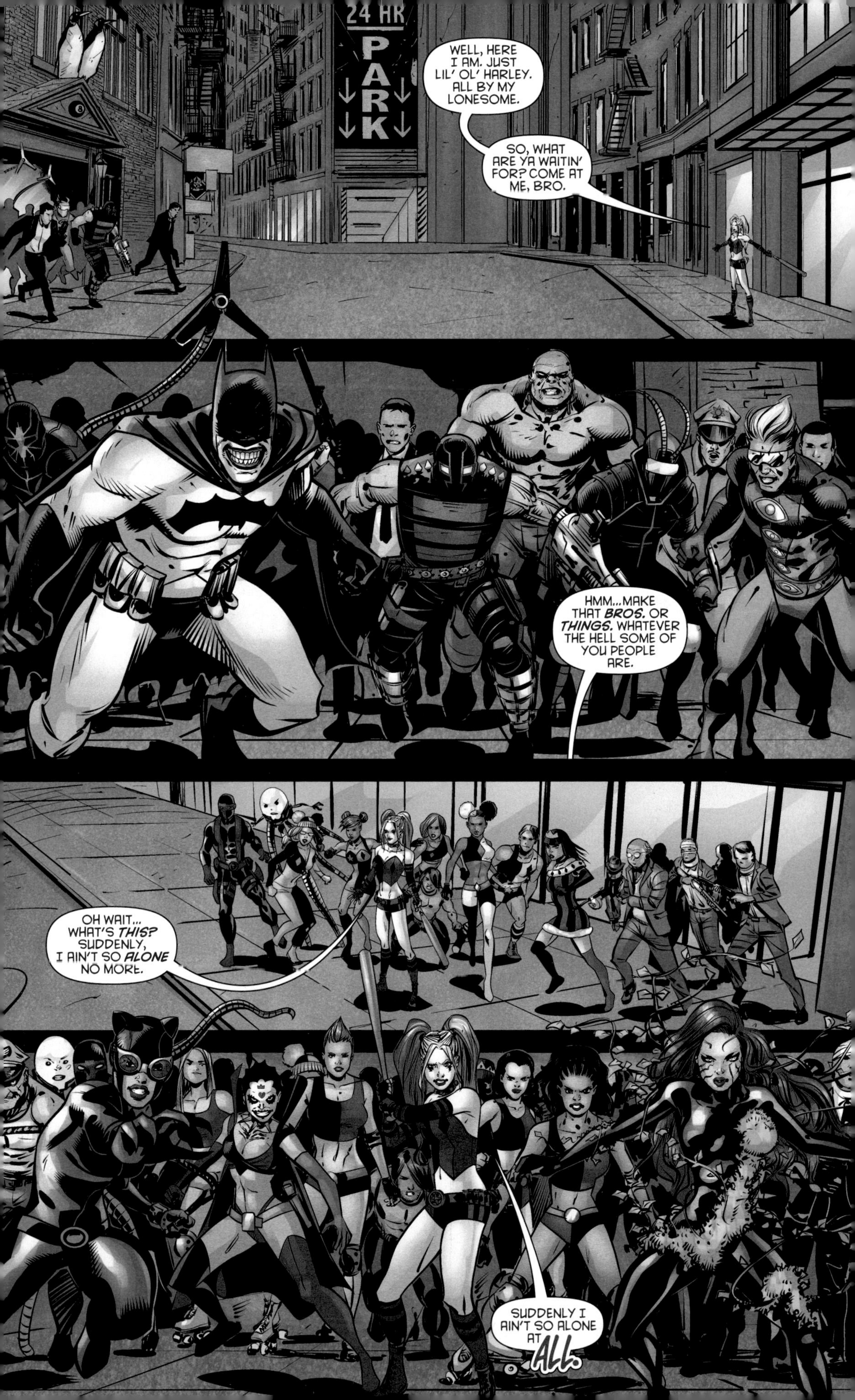
24 HR
PARK
WELL, HERE I AM. JUST LIL' OL' HARLEY. ALL BY MY LONESOME.
SO, WHAT ARE YA WAITIN' FOR? COME AT ME, BRO.
HMM...MAKE THAT *BROS.* OR *THINGS.* WHATEVER THE HELL SOME OF YOU PEOPLE ARE.
OH WAIT... WHAT'S *THIS?* SUDDENLY, I AIN'T SO *ALONE* NO MORE.
SUDDENLY I AIN'T SO ALONE AT ALL.

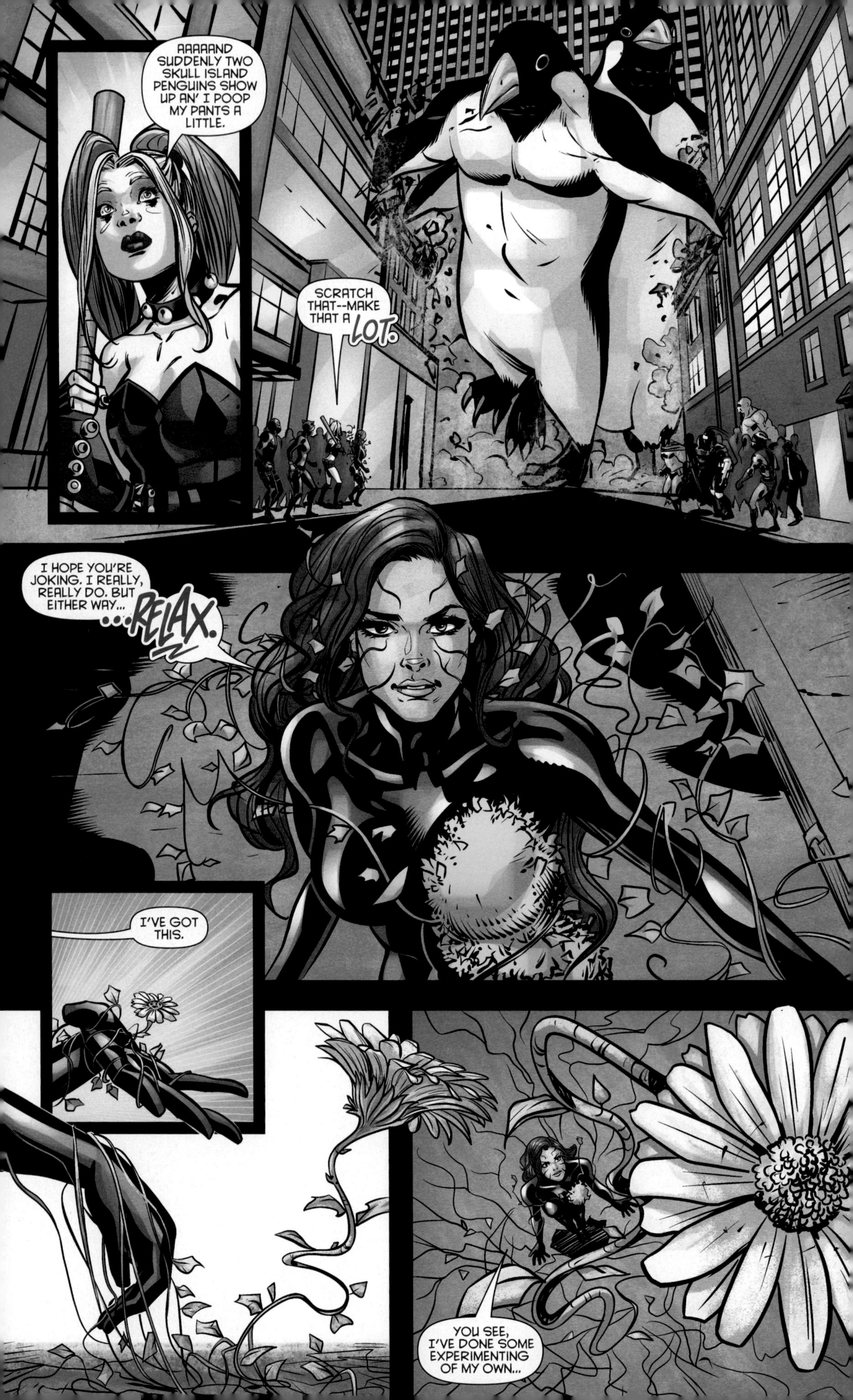
AAAAAND SUDDENLY TWO SKULL ISLAND PENGUINS SHOW UP AN' I POOP MY PANTS A LITTLE.
SCRATCH THAT--MAKE THAT A LOT.
I HOPE YOU'RE JOKING. I REALLY, REALLY DO. BUT EITHER WAY... ...RELAX.
I'VE GOT THIS.
YOU SEE, I'VE DONE SOME EXPERIMENTING OF MY OWN...

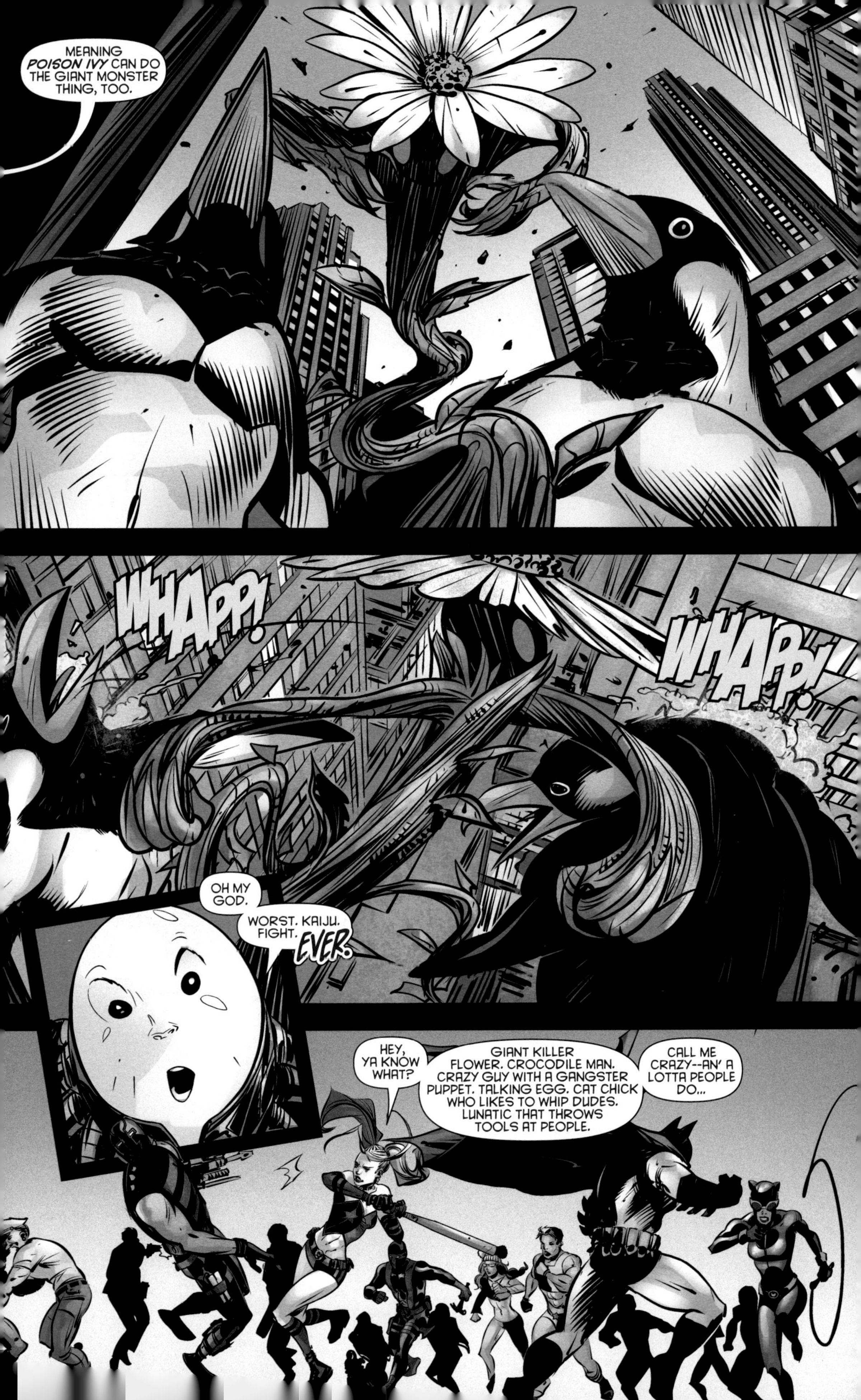
MEANING *POISON IVY* CAN DO THE GIANT MONSTER THING, TOO.
WHAPP!
WHAPP!
OH MY GOD.
WORST. KAIJU. FIGHT. EVER.
HEY, YA KNOW WHAT?
GIANT KILLER FLOWER. CROCODILE MAN. CRAZY GUY WITH A GANGSTER PUPPET. TALKING EGG. CAT CHICK WHO LIKES TO WHIP DUDES. LUNATIC THAT THROWS TOOLS AT PEOPLE.
CALL ME CRAZY--AN' A LOTTA PEOPLE DO...

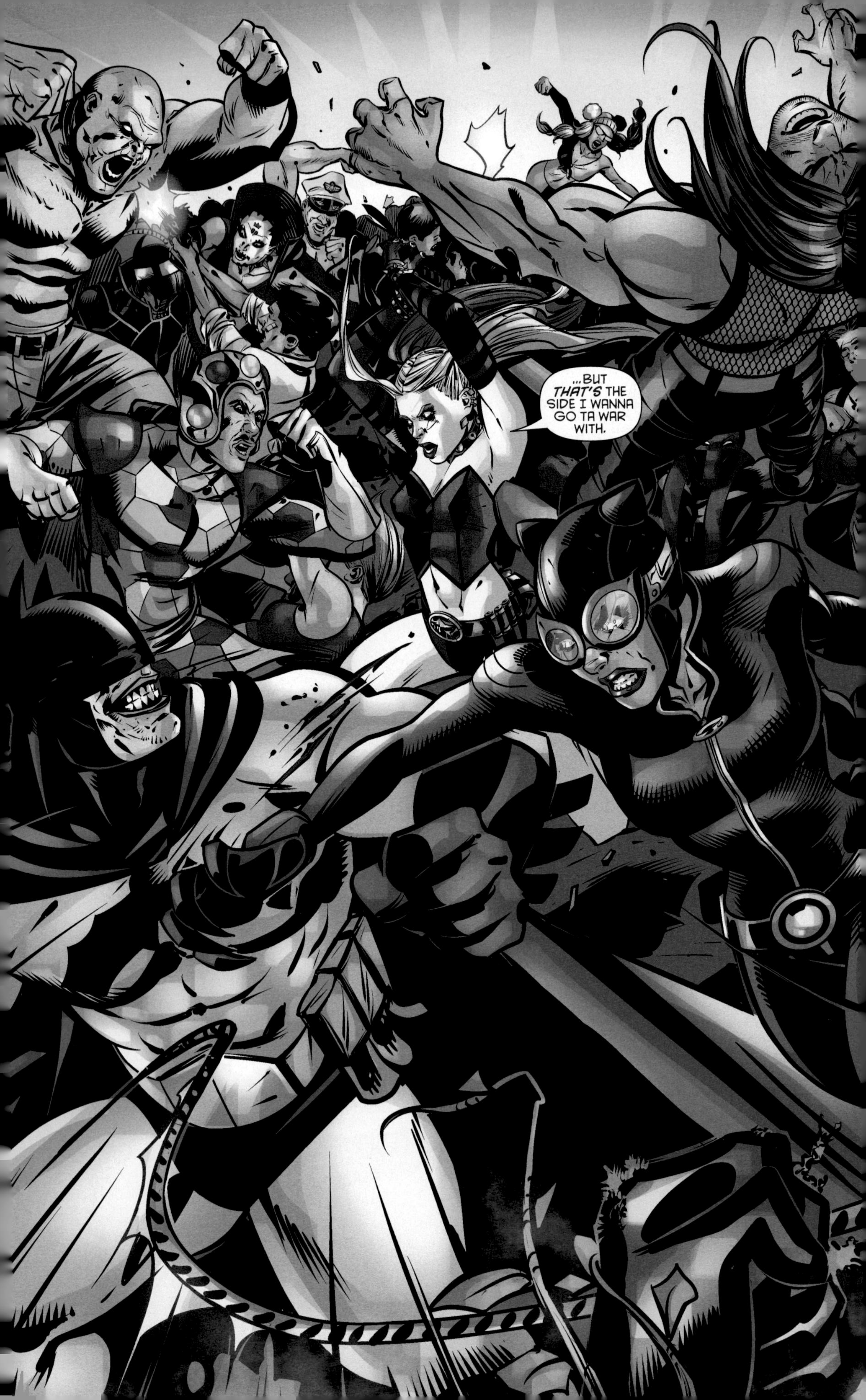
...BUT THAT'S THE SIDE I WANNA GO TA WAR WITH.

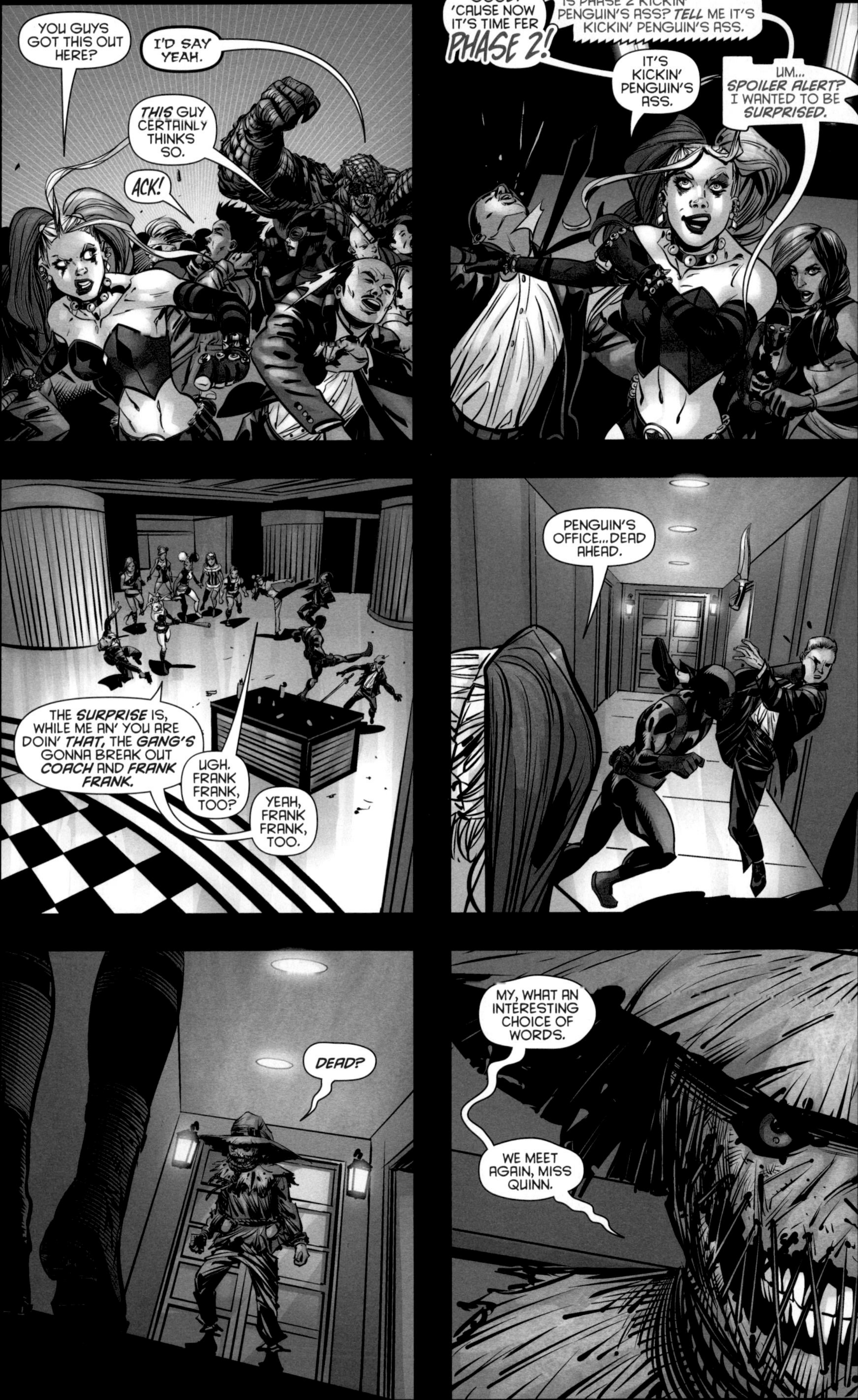

YOU GUYS GOT THIS OUT HERE?
I'D SAY YEAH.
THIS GUY CERTAINLY THINKS SO.
ACK!
GOOD. 'CAUSE NOW IT'S TIME FER PHASE 2!
IS PHASE 2 KICKIN' PENGUIN'S ASS? TELL ME IT'S KICKIN' PENGUIN'S ASS.
IT'S KICKIN' PENGUIN'S ASS.
UM... SPOILER ALERT? I WANTED TO BE SURPRISED.
THE SURPRISE IS, WHILE ME AN' YOU ARE DOIN' THAT, THE GANG'S GONNA BREAK OUT COACH AND FRANK FRANK.
UGH. FRANK FRANK, TOO?
YEAH, FRANK FRANK, TOO.
PENGUIN'S OFFICE...DEAD AHEAD.
DEAD?
MY, WHAT AN INTERESTING CHOICE OF WORDS.
WE MEET AGAIN, MISS QUINN.

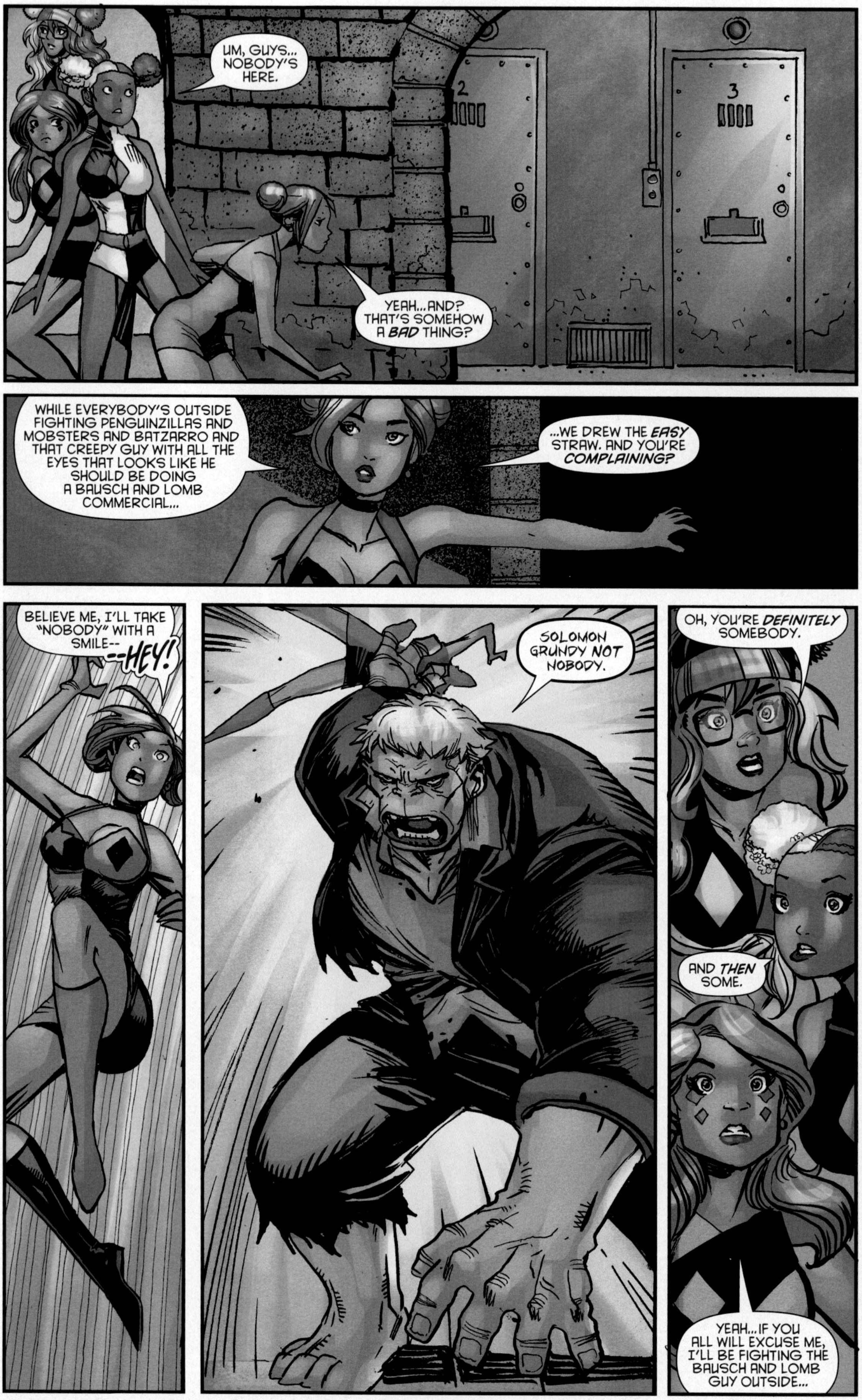
UM, GUYS... NOBODY'S HERE.
YEAH...AND? THAT'S SOMEHOW A BAD THING?
WHILE EVERYBODY'S OUTSIDE FIGHTING PENGUINZILLAS AND MOBSTERS AND BATZARRO AND THAT CREEPY GUY WITH ALL THE EYES THAT LOOKS LIKE HE SHOULD BE DOING A BAUSCH AND LOMB COMMERCIAL...
...WE DREW THE EASY STRAW. AND YOU'RE COMPLAINING?
BELIEVE ME, I'LL TAKE "NOBODY" WITH A SMILE--
--HEY!
SOLOMON GRUNDY NOT NOBODY.
OH, YOU'RE DEFINITELY SOMEBODY.
AND THEN SOME.
YEAH...IF YOU ALL WILL EXCUSE ME, I'LL BE FIGHTING THE BAUSCH AND LOMB GUY OUTSIDE...

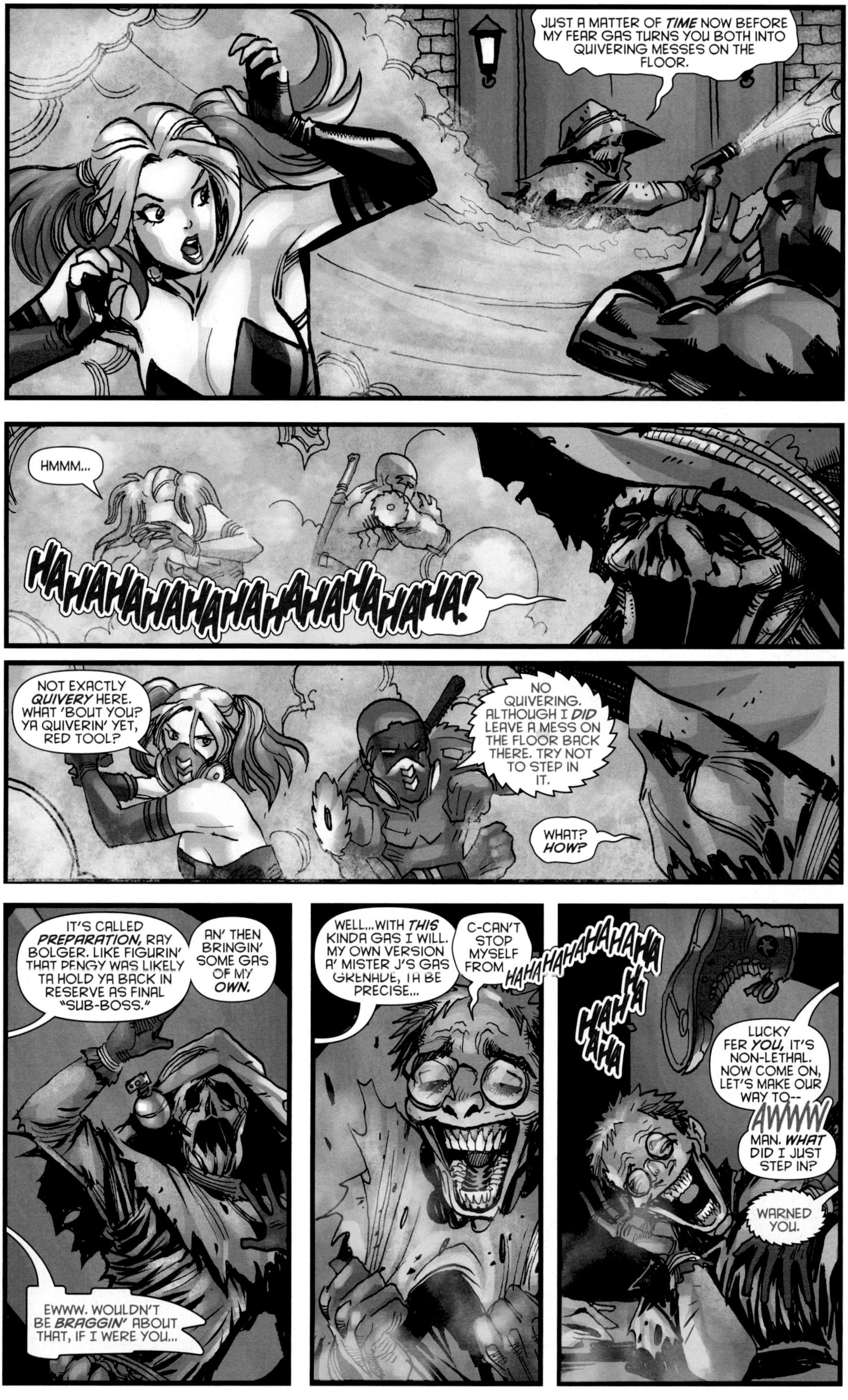
JUST A MATTER OF TIME NOW BEFORE MY FEAR GAS TURNS YOU BOTH INTO QUIVERING MESSES ON THE FLOOR.
HMMM...
HAHAHAHAHAHAHAHAHAHAHAHAHA!
NOT EXACTLY QUIVERY HERE. WHAT 'BOUT YOU? YA QUIVERIN' YET, RED TOOL?
NO QUIVERING. ALTHOUGH I DID LEAVE A MESS ON THE FLOOR BACK THERE. TRY NOT TO STEP IN IT.
WHAT? HOW?
IT'S CALLED PREPARATION, RAY BOLGER. LIKE FIGURIN' THAT PENGY WAS LIKELY TA HOLD YA BACK IN RESERVE AS FINAL "SUB-BOSS."
AN' THEN BRINGIN' SOME GAS OF MY OWN.
EWWW. WOULDN'T BE BRAGGIN' ABOUT THAT, IF I WERE YOU...
WELL...WITH THIS KINDA GAS I WILL. MY OWN VERSION A' MISTER J'S GAS GRENADE, TA BE PRECISE...
C-CAN'T STOP MYSELF FROM
HAHAHAHAHAHAHAHA HA HA HAHA HAHA
LUCKY FER YOU, IT'S NON-LETHAL. NOW COME ON, LET'S MAKE OUR WAY TO--
AWWW
MAN. WHAT DID I JUST STEP IN?
WARNED YOU.

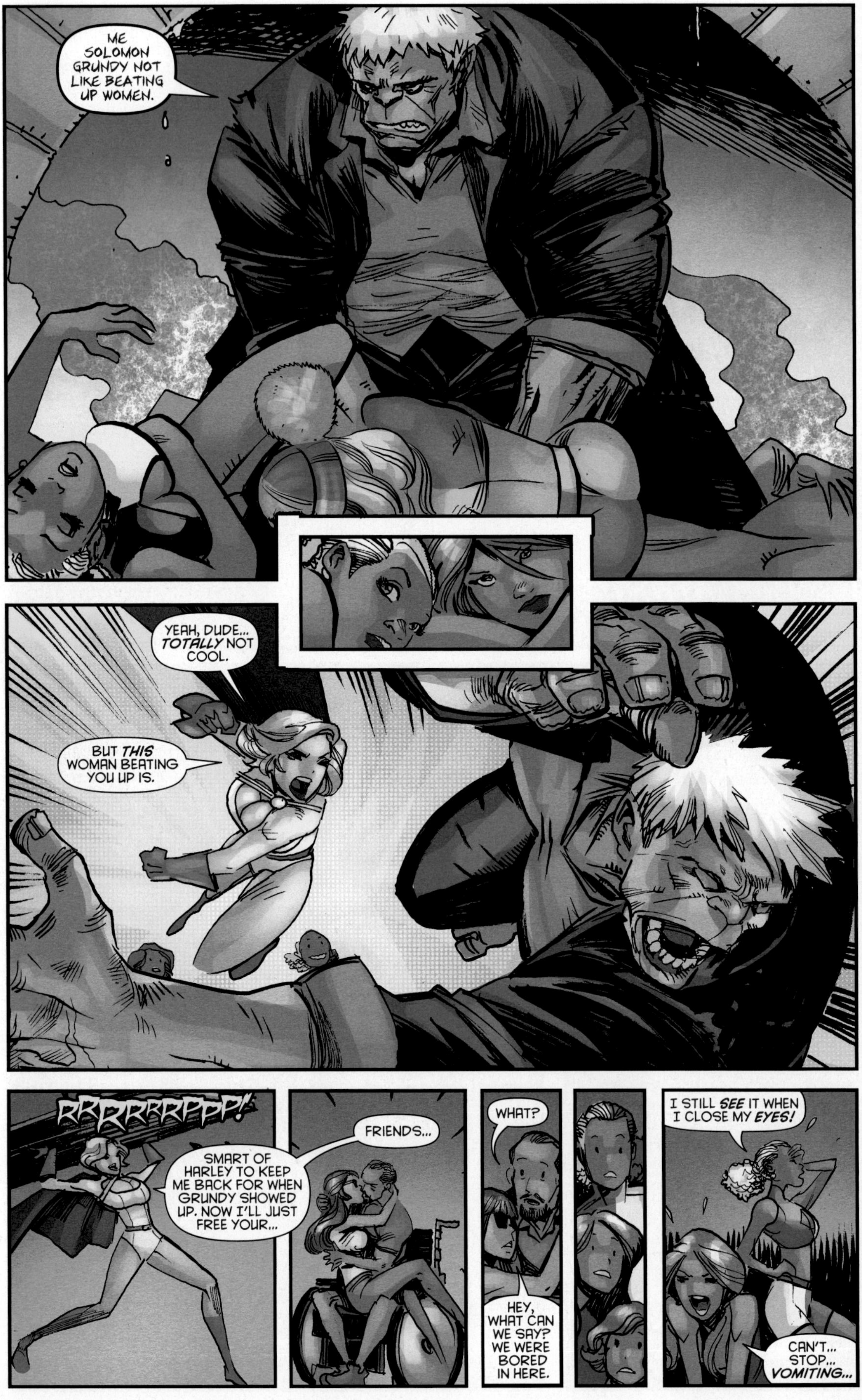
ME SOLOMON GRUNDY NOT LIKE BEATING UP WOMEN.
YEAH, DUDE... TOTALLY NOT COOL.
BUT THIS WOMAN BEATING YOU UP IS.
RRRRRRRPPP!
SMART OF HARLEY TO KEEP ME BACK FOR WHEN GRUNDY SHOWED UP. NOW I'LL JUST FREE YOUR...
FRIENDS...
WHAT?
HEY, WHAT CAN WE SAY? WE WERE BORED IN HERE.
I STILL SEE IT WHEN I CLOSE MY EYES!
CAN'T... STOP... VOMITING...

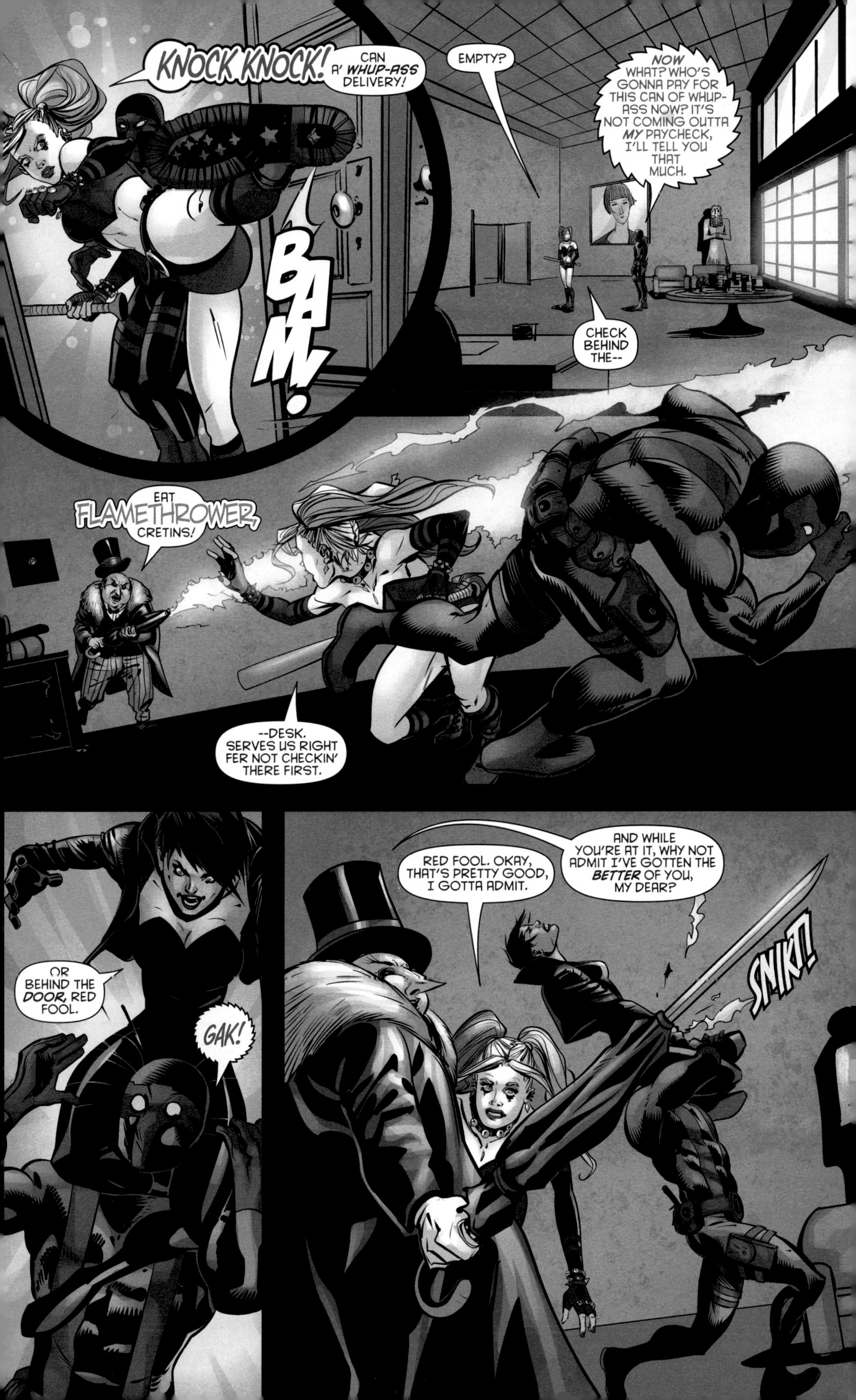
KNOCK KNOCK!
CAN A' WHUP-ASS DELIVERY!
BAM!
EMPTY?
NOW WHAT? WHO'S GONNA PAY FOR THIS CAN OF WHUP-ASS NOW? IT'S NOT COMING OUTTA MY PAYCHECK, I'LL TELL YOU THAT MUCH.
CHECK BEHIND THE--
EAT FLAMETHROWER, CRETINS!
--DESK. SERVES US RIGHT FER NOT CHECKIN' THERE FIRST.
OR BEHIND THE DOOR, RED FOOL.
GAK!
RED FOOL. OKAY, THAT'S PRETTY GOOD, I GOTTA ADMIT.
AND WHILE YOU'RE AT IT, WHY NOT ADMIT I'VE GOTTEN THE BETTER OF YOU, MY DEAR?
SNIKT!

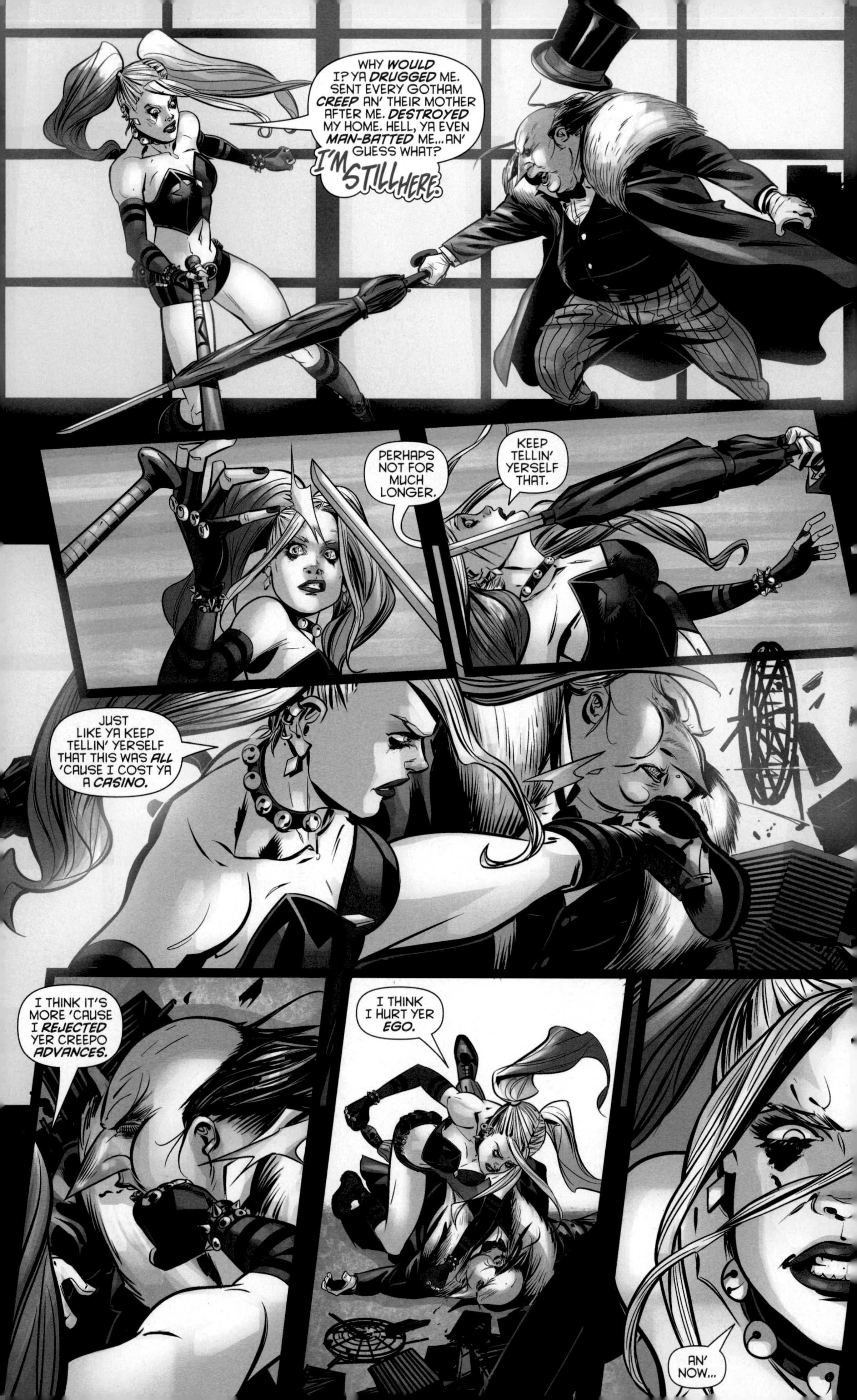
WHY WOULD I? YA DRUGGED ME. SENT EVERY GOTHAM CREEP AN' THEIR MOTHER AFTER ME. DESTROYED MY HOME. HELL, YA EVEN MAN-BATTED ME... AN' GUESS WHAT? I'M STILL HERE.
PERHAPS NOT FOR MUCH LONGER.
KEEP TELLIN' YERSELF THAT.
JUST LIKE YA KEEP TELLIN' YERSELF THAT THIS WAS ALL 'CAUSE I COST YA A CASINO.
I THINK IT'S MORE 'CAUSE I REJECTED YER CREEPO ADVANCES.
I THINK I HURT YER EGO.
AN' NOW...

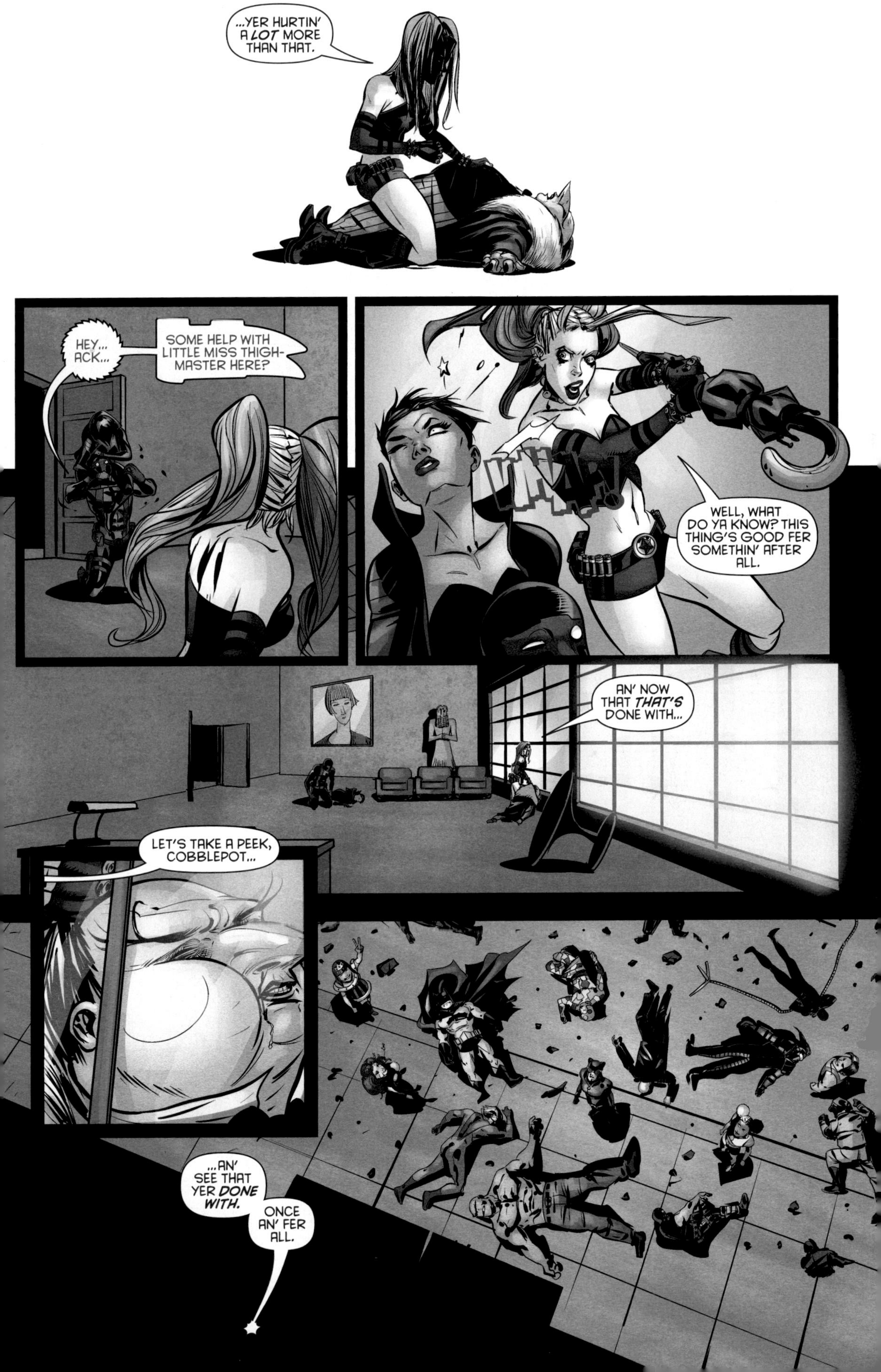
...YER HURTIN' A LOT MORE THAN THAT.
HEY... ACK...
SOME HELP WITH LITTLE MISS THIGH-MASTER HERE?
WELL, WHAT DO YA KNOW? THIS THING'S GOOD FER SOMETHIN' AFTER ALL.
AN' NOW THAT THAT'S DONE WITH...
LET'S TAKE A PEEK, COBBLEPOT...
...AN' SEE THAT YER DONE WITH.
ONCE AN' FER ALL.

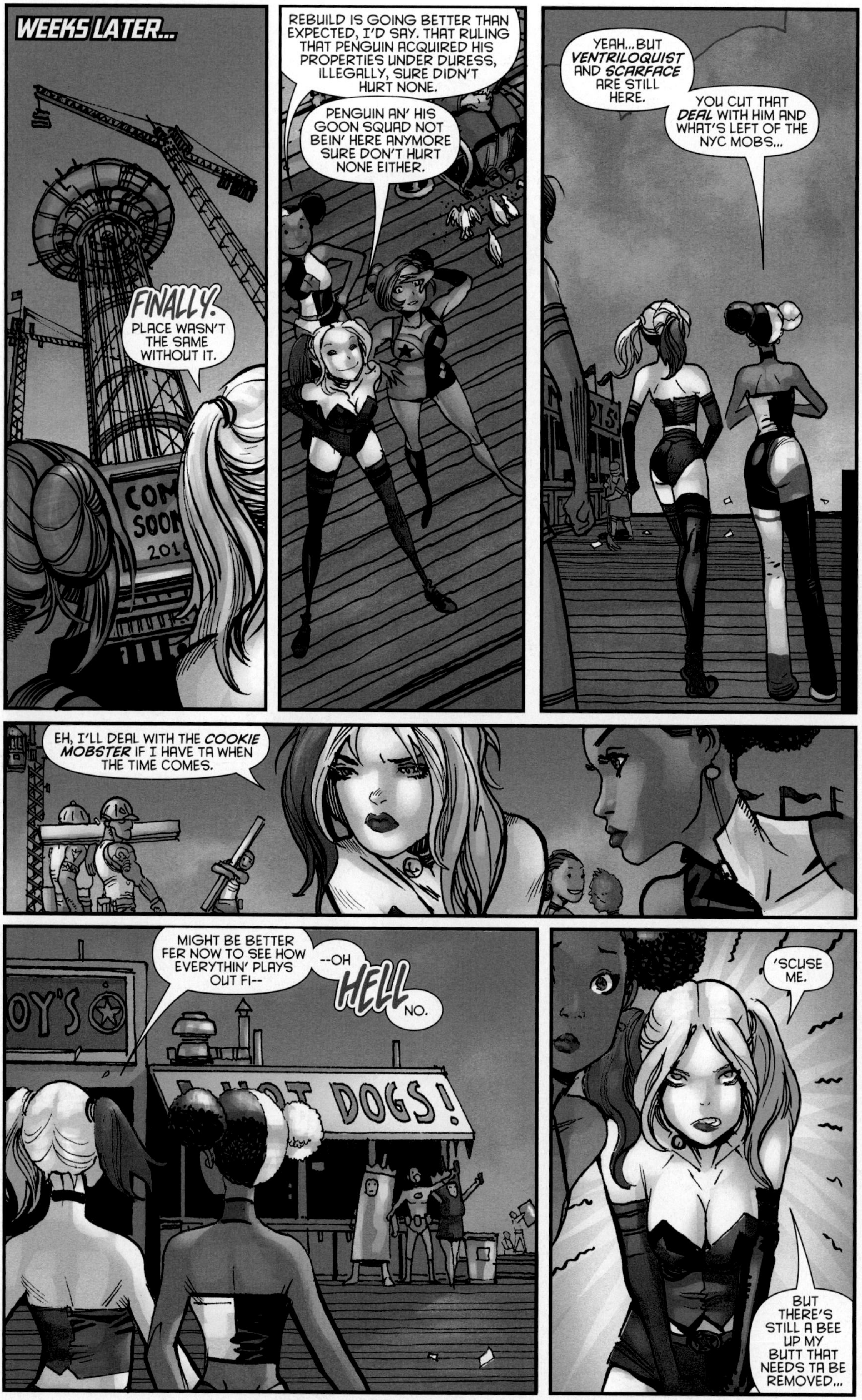
WEEKS LATER...
FINALLY. PLACE WASN'T THE SAME WITHOUT IT.
COM SOON 201
REBUILD IS GOING BETTER THAN EXPECTED, I'D SAY. THAT RULING THAT PENGUIN ACQUIRED HIS PROPERTIES UNDER DURESS, ILLEGALLY, SURE DIDN'T HURT NONE.
PENGUIN AN' HIS GOON SQUAD NOT BEIN' HERE ANYMORE SURE DON'T HURT NONE EITHER.
YEAH...BUT VENTRILOQUIST AND SCARFACE ARE STILL HERE.
YOU CUT THAT DEAL WITH HIM AND WHAT'S LEFT OF THE NYC MOBS...
EH, I'LL DEAL WITH THE COOKIE MOBSTER IF I HAVE TA WHEN THE TIME COMES.
MIGHT BE BETTER FER NOW TO SEE HOW EVERYTHIN' PLAYS OUT FI--
--OH HELL NO.
OY'S
HOT DOGS!
'SCUSE ME.
BUT THERE'S STILL A BEE UP MY BUTT THAT NEEDS TA BE REMOVED...

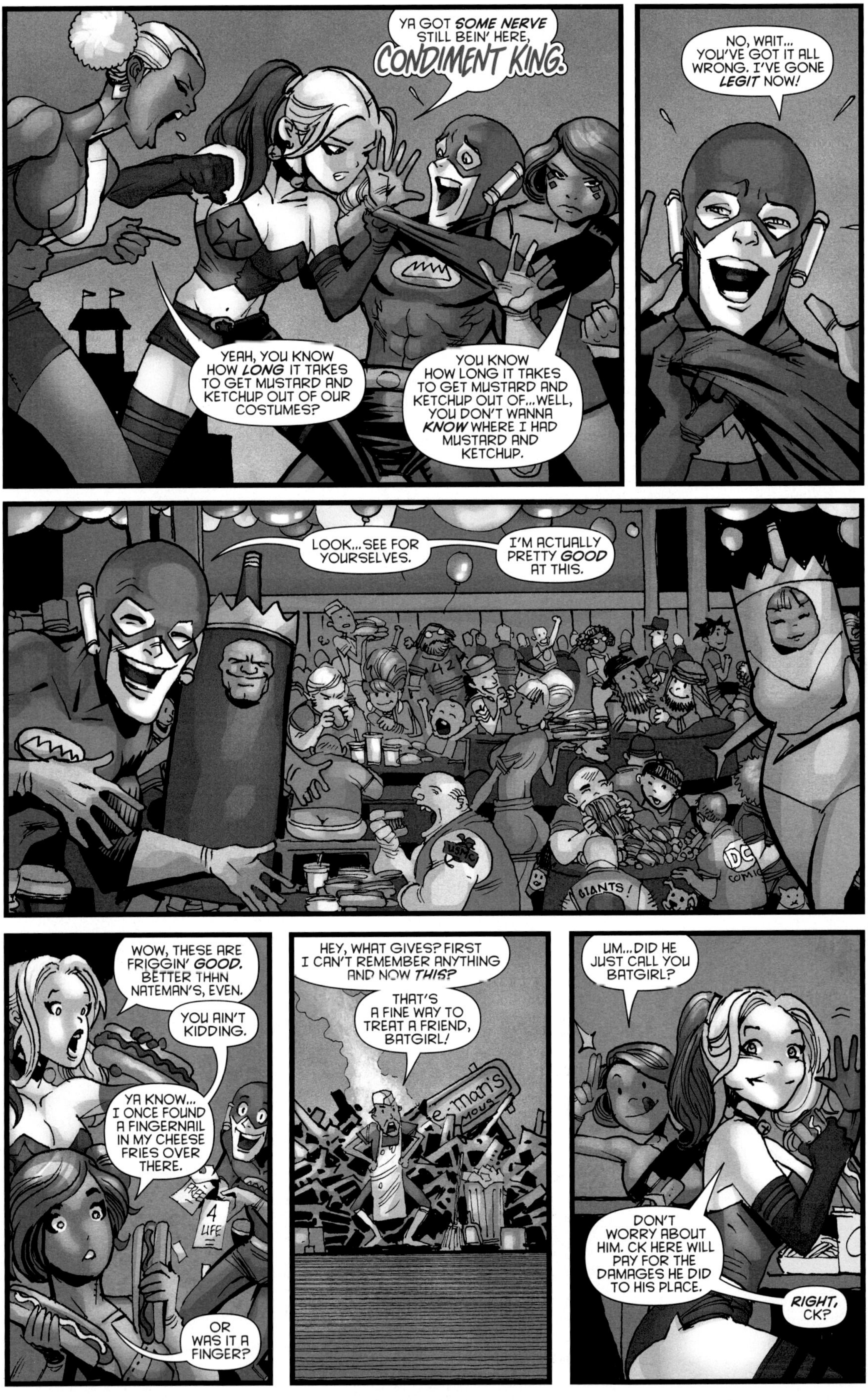
YA GOT **SOME NERVE** STILL BEIN' HERE, CONDIMENT KING.
YEAH, YOU KNOW HOW **LONG** IT TAKES TO GET MUSTARD AND KETCHUP OUT OF OUR COSTUMES?
YOU KNOW HOW LONG IT TAKES TO GET MUSTARD AND KETCHUP OUT OF... WELL, YOU DON'T WANNA **KNOW** WHERE I HAD MUSTARD AND KETCHUP.
NO, WAIT... YOU'VE GOT IT ALL WRONG. I'VE GONE **LEGIT** NOW!
LOOK... SEE FOR YOURSELVES.
I'M ACTUALLY PRETTY **GOOD** AT THIS.
WOW, THESE ARE FRIGGIN' **GOOD.** BETTER THAN NATEMAN'S, EVEN.
YOU AIN'T KIDDING.
YA KNOW... I ONCE FOUND A FINGERNAIL IN MY CHEESE FRIES OVER THERE.
OR WAS IT A FINGER?
HEY, WHAT GIVES? FIRST I CAN'T REMEMBER ANYTHING AND NOW **THIS?**
THAT'S A FINE WAY TO TREAT A FRIEND, BATGIRL!
UM... DID HE JUST CALL YOU BATGIRL?
DON'T WORRY ABOUT HIM. CK HERE WILL PAY FOR THE DAMAGES HE DID TO HIS PLACE.
**RIGHT,** CK?

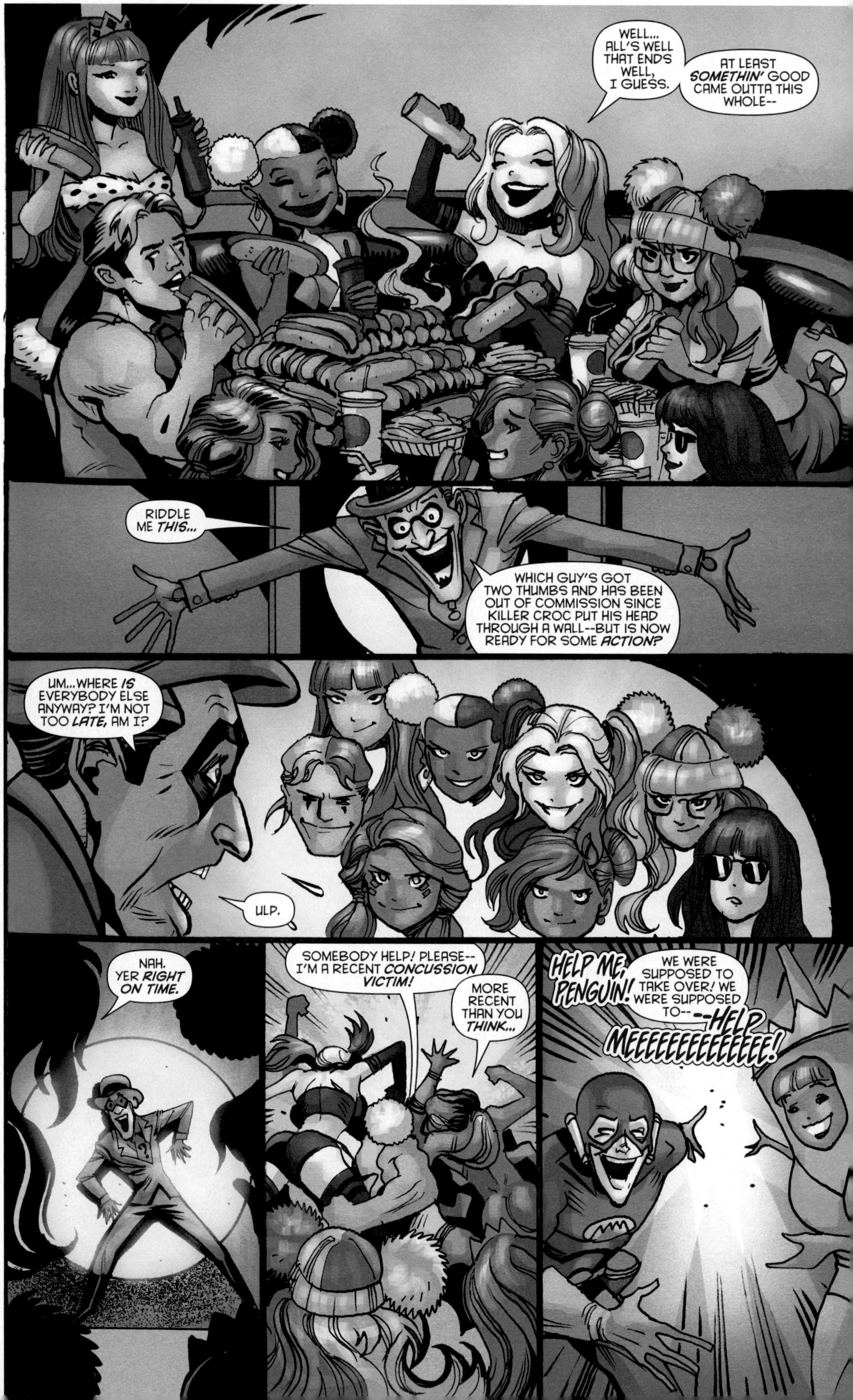
WELL... ALL'S WELL THAT ENDS WELL, I GUESS.
AT LEAST SOMETHIN' GOOD CAME OUTTA THIS WHOLE--
RIDDLE ME THIS...
WHICH GUY'S GOT TWO THUMBS AND HAS BEEN OUT OF COMMISSION SINCE KILLER CROC PUT HIS HEAD THROUGH A WALL--BUT IS NOW READY FOR SOME ACTION?
UM...WHERE IS EVERYBODY ELSE ANYWAY? I'M NOT TOO LATE, AM I?
ULP.
NAH. YER RIGHT ON TIME.
SOMEBODY HELP! PLEASE-- I'M A RECENT CONCUSSION VICTIM!
MORE RECENT THAN YOU THINK...
HELP ME, PENGUIN!
WE WERE SUPPOSED TO TAKE OVER! WE WERE SUPPOSED TO--
--HELP MEEEEEEEEEEEEEE!

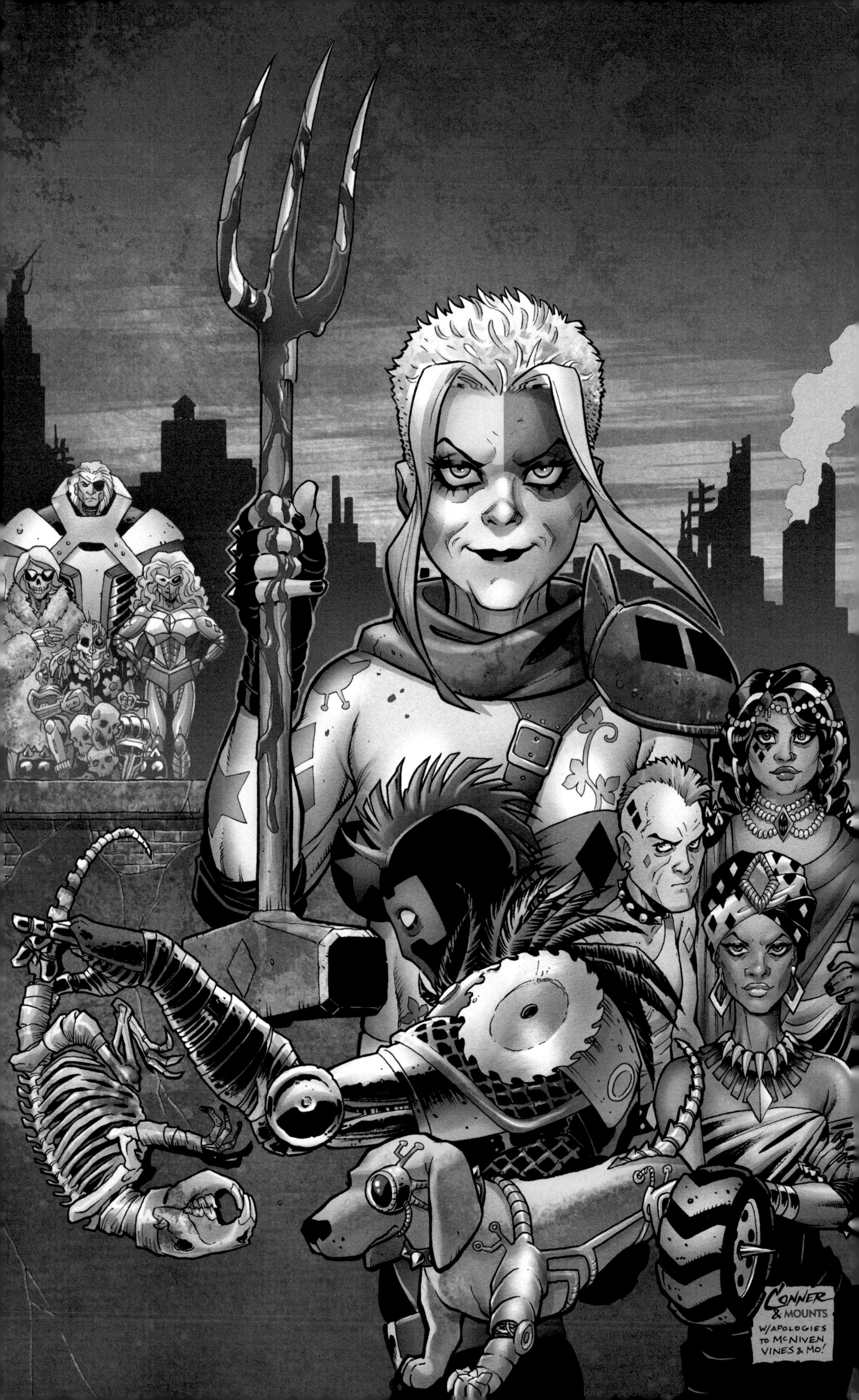
CONNER
& MOUNTS
W/APOLOGIES
TO McNIVEN
VINES & MO!

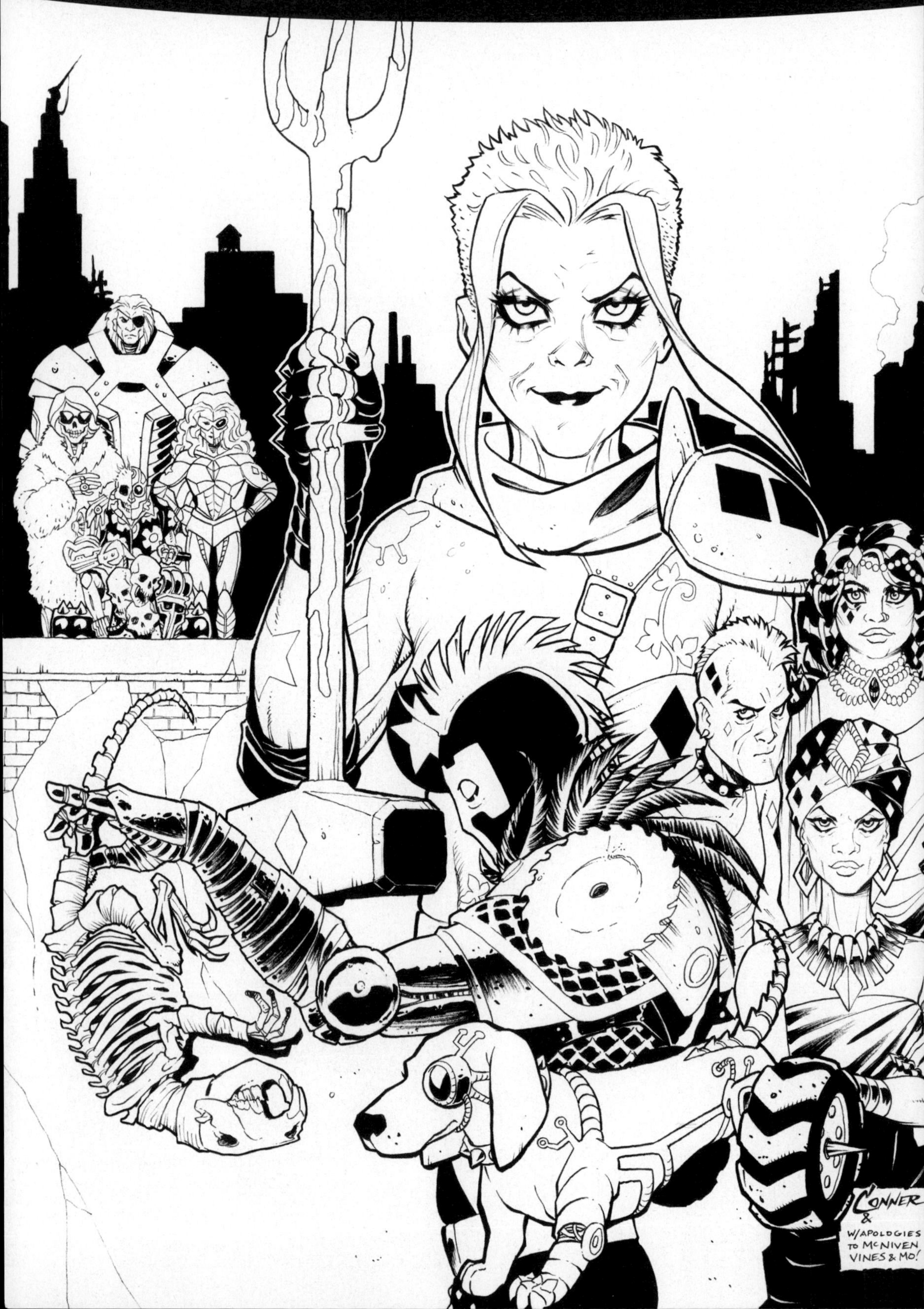
CONNER
&
W/APOLOGIES
TO McNIVEN
VINES & MO!

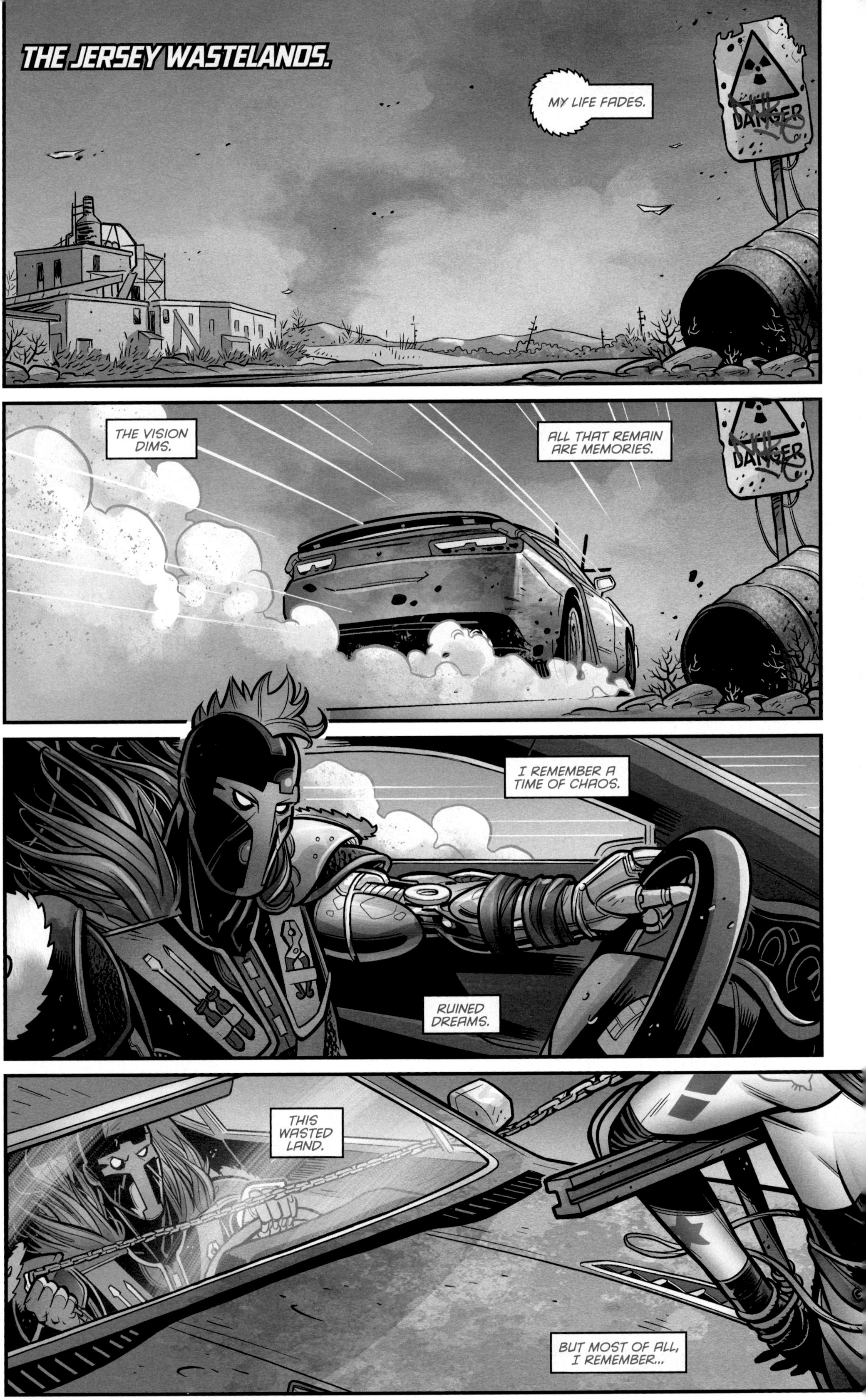
THE JERSEY WASTELANDS.
MY LIFE FADES.
DANGER
THE VISION DIMS.
ALL THAT REMAIN ARE MEMORIES.
DANGER
I REMEMBER A TIME OF CHAOS.
RUINED DREAMS.
THIS WASTED LAND.
BUT MOST OF ALL, I REMEMBER...

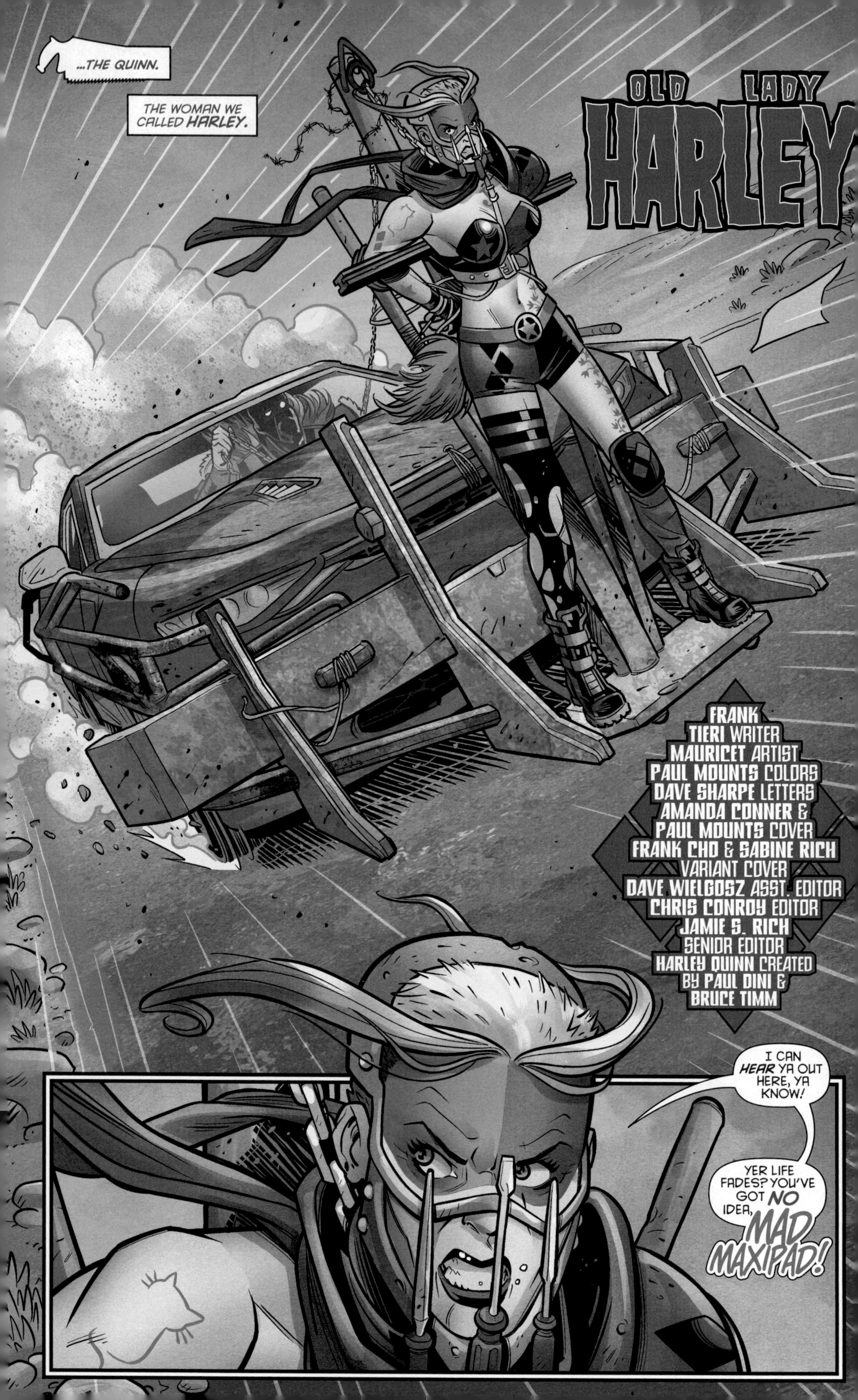
...THE QUINN.
THE WOMAN WE CALLED HARLEY.
OLD LADY HARLEY
FRANK TIERI WRITER
MAURICET ARTIST
PAUL MOUNTS COLORS
DAVE SHARPE LETTERS
AMANDA CONNER & PAUL MOUNTS COVER
FRANK CHO & SABINE RICH VARIANT COVER
DAVE WIELGOSZ ASST. EDITOR
CHRIS CONROY EDITOR
JAMIE S. RICH SENIOR EDITOR
HARLEY QUINN CREATED BY PAUL DINI & BRUCE TIMM
I CAN HEAR YA OUT HERE, YA KNOW!
YER LIFE FADES? YOU'VE GOT NO IDEA, MAD MAXIPAD!

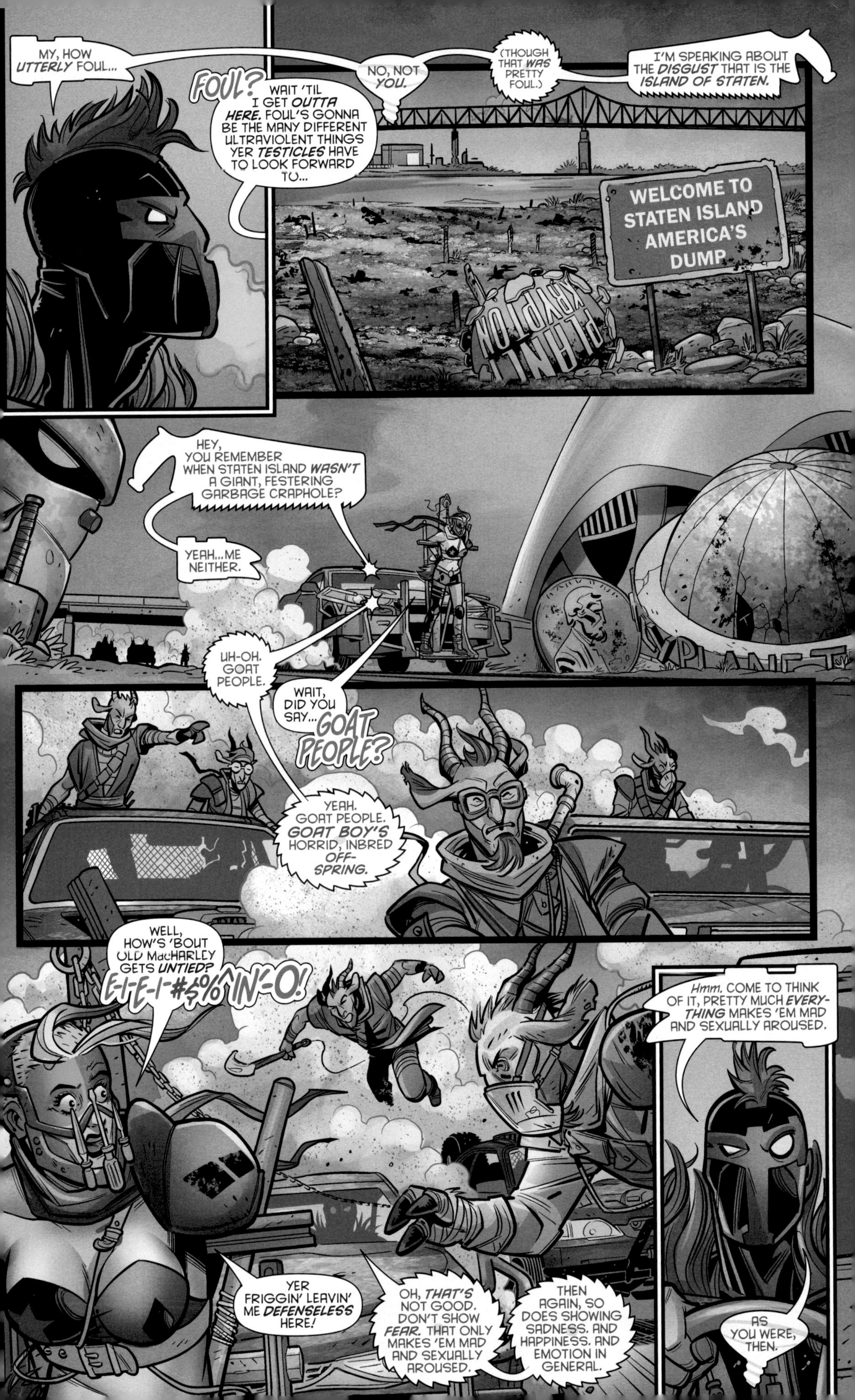

MY, HOW UTTERLY FOUL...
FOUL?
WAIT 'TIL I GET OUTTA HERE. FOUL'S GONNA BE THE MANY DIFFERENT ULTRAVIOLENT THINGS YER TESTICLES HAVE TO LOOK FORWARD TO...
NO, NOT YOU.
(THOUGH THAT WAS PRETTY FOUL.)
I'M SPEAKING ABOUT THE DISGUST THAT IS THE ISLAND OF STATEN.
WELCOME TO STATEN ISLAND AMERICA'S DUMP
PLANET KRYPTON
HEY, YOU REMEMBER WHEN STATEN ISLAND WASN'T A GIANT, FESTERING GARBAGE CRAPHOLE?
YEAH...ME NEITHER.
UH-OH. GOAT PEOPLE.
WAIT, DID YOU SAY...GOAT PEOPLE?
YEAH. GOAT PEOPLE. GOAT BOY'S HORRID, INBRED OFF-SPRING.
WELL, HOW'S 'BOUT OLD MacHARLEY GETS UNTIED?
E-I-E-I-#$%^IN'-O!
Hmm. COME TO THINK OF IT, PRETTY MUCH EVERY-THING MAKES 'EM MAD AND SEXUALLY AROUSED.
YER FRIGGIN' LEAVIN' ME DEFENSELESS HERE!
OH, THAT'S NOT GOOD. DON'T SHOW FEAR. THAT ONLY MAKES 'EM MAD AND SEXUALLY AROUSED.
THEN AGAIN, SO DOES SHOWING SADNESS. AND HAPPINESS. AND EMOTION IN GENERAL.
AS YOU WERE, THEN.

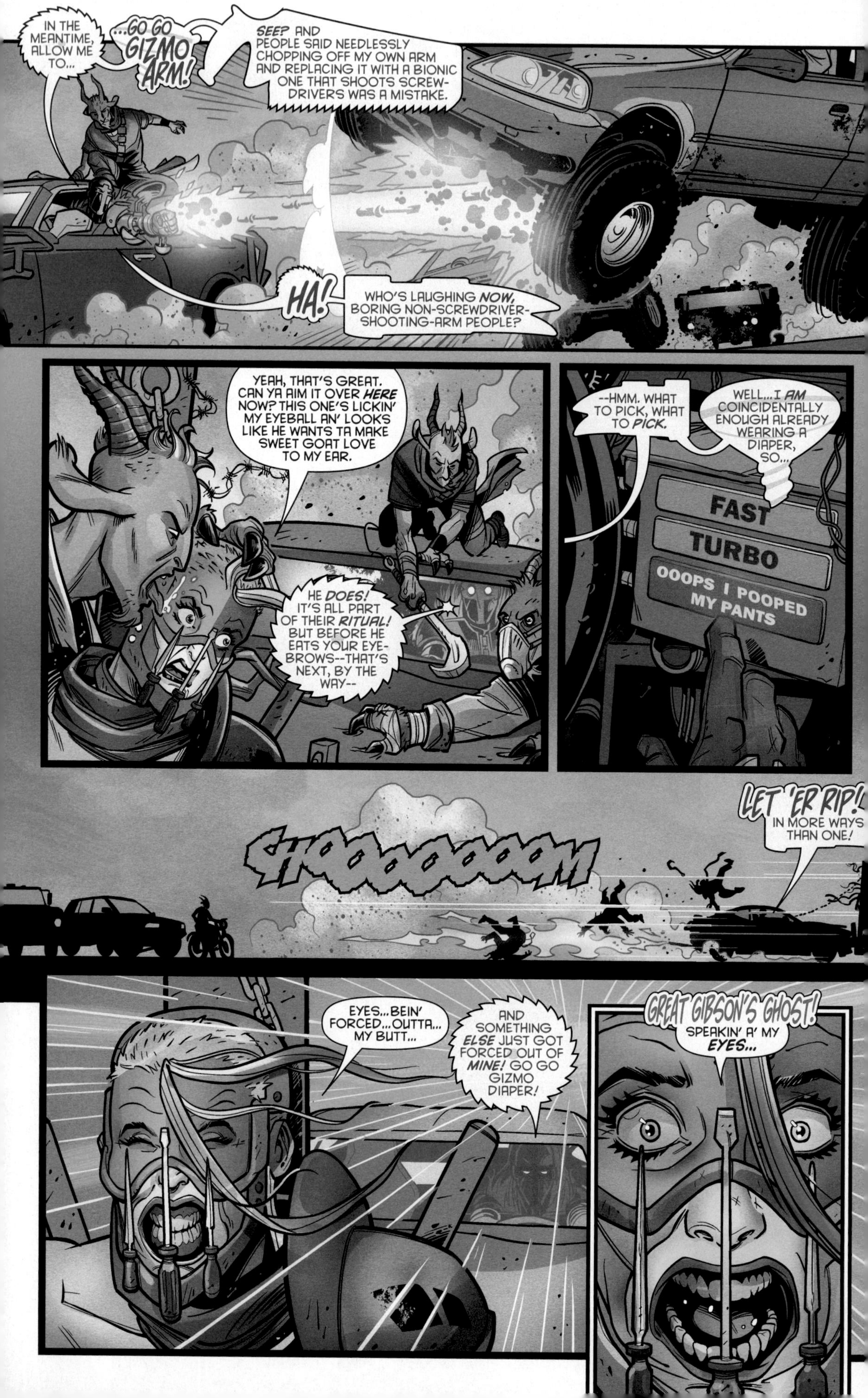
IN THE MEANTIME, ALLOW ME TO...
...GO GO GIZMO ARM!
SEE? AND PEOPLE SAID NEEDLESSLY CHOPPING OFF MY OWN ARM AND REPLACING IT WITH A BIONIC ONE THAT SHOOTS SCREW-DRIVERS WAS A MISTAKE.
HA!
WHO'S LAUGHING NOW, BORING NON-SCREWDRIVER-SHOOTING-ARM PEOPLE?
YEAH, THAT'S GREAT. CAN YA AIM IT OVER HERE NOW? THIS ONE'S LICKIN' MY EYEBALL AN' LOOKS LIKE HE WANTS TA MAKE SWEET GOAT LOVE TO MY EAR.
HE DOES! IT'S ALL PART OF THEIR RITUAL! BUT BEFORE HE EATS YOUR EYE-BROWS--THAT'S NEXT, BY THE WAY--
--HMM. WHAT TO PICK, WHAT TO PICK.
WELL...I AM COINCIDENTALLY ENOUGH ALREADY WEARING A DIAPER, SO...
FAST
TURBO
OOOPS I POOPED MY PANTS
SHOOOOOOOOM
LET 'ER RIP!
IN MORE WAYS THAN ONE!
EYES...BEIN' FORCED...OUTTA... MY BUTT...
AND SOMETHING ELSE JUST GOT FORCED OUT OF MINE! GO GO GIZMO DIAPER!
GREAT GIBSON'S GHOST!
SPEAKIN' A' MY EYES...

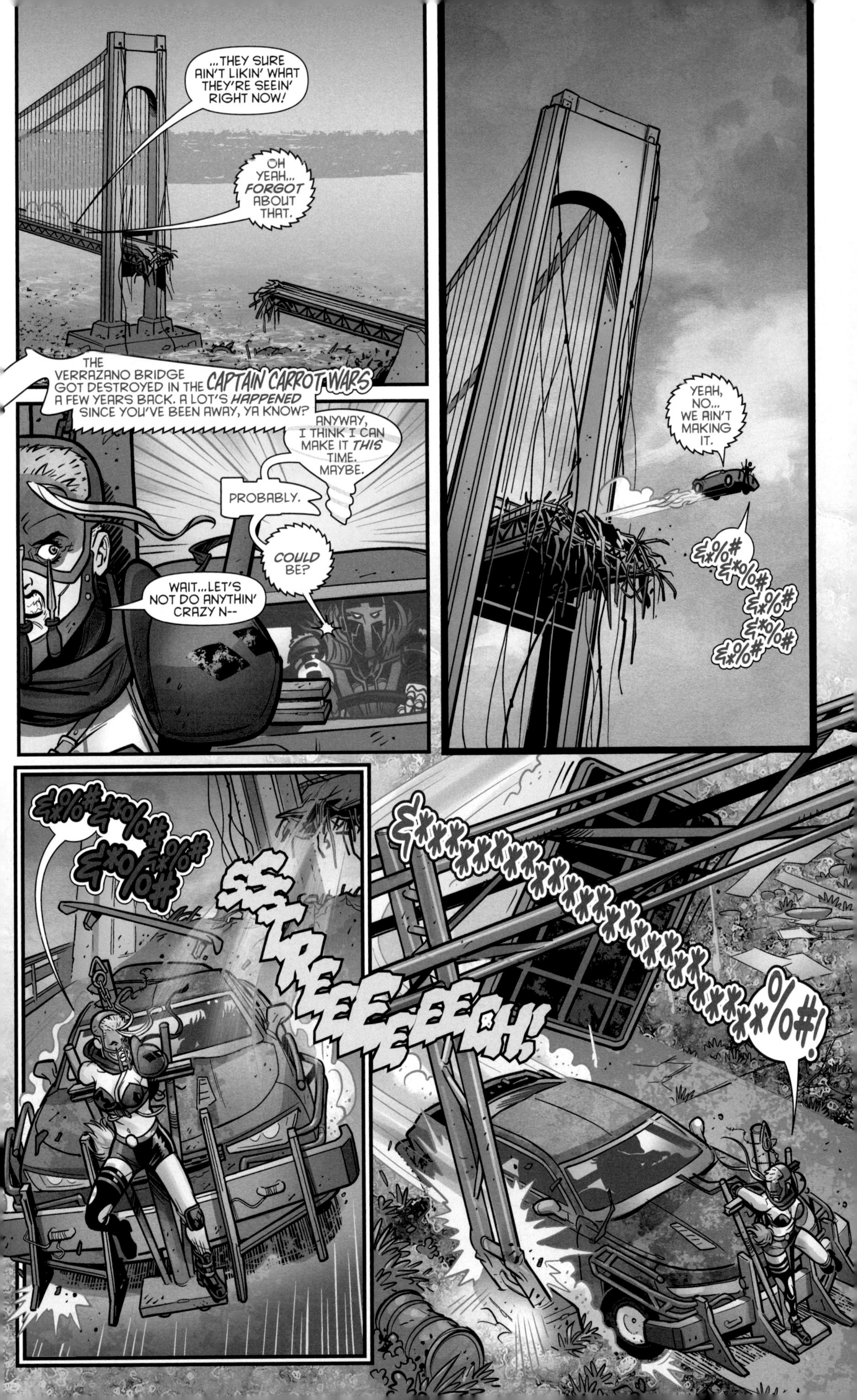

...THEY SURE AIN'T LIKIN' WHAT THEY'RE SEEIN' RIGHT NOW!
OH YEAH... FORGOT ABOUT THAT.
THE VERRAZANO BRIDGE GOT DESTROYED IN THE CAPTAIN CARROT WARS A FEW YEARS BACK. A LOT'S HAPPENED SINCE YOU'VE BEEN AWAY, YA KNOW?
ANYWAY, I THINK I CAN MAKE IT THIS TIME. MAYBE.
PROBABLY.
COULD BE?
WAIT...LET'S NOT DO ANYTHIN' CRAZY N--
YEAH, NO... WE AIN'T MAKING IT.
&*%# &*%# &*%# &*%# &*%#
&*%#&*%# &*%#&*%#
SSSCREEEEEEECH!
&***************************%#!

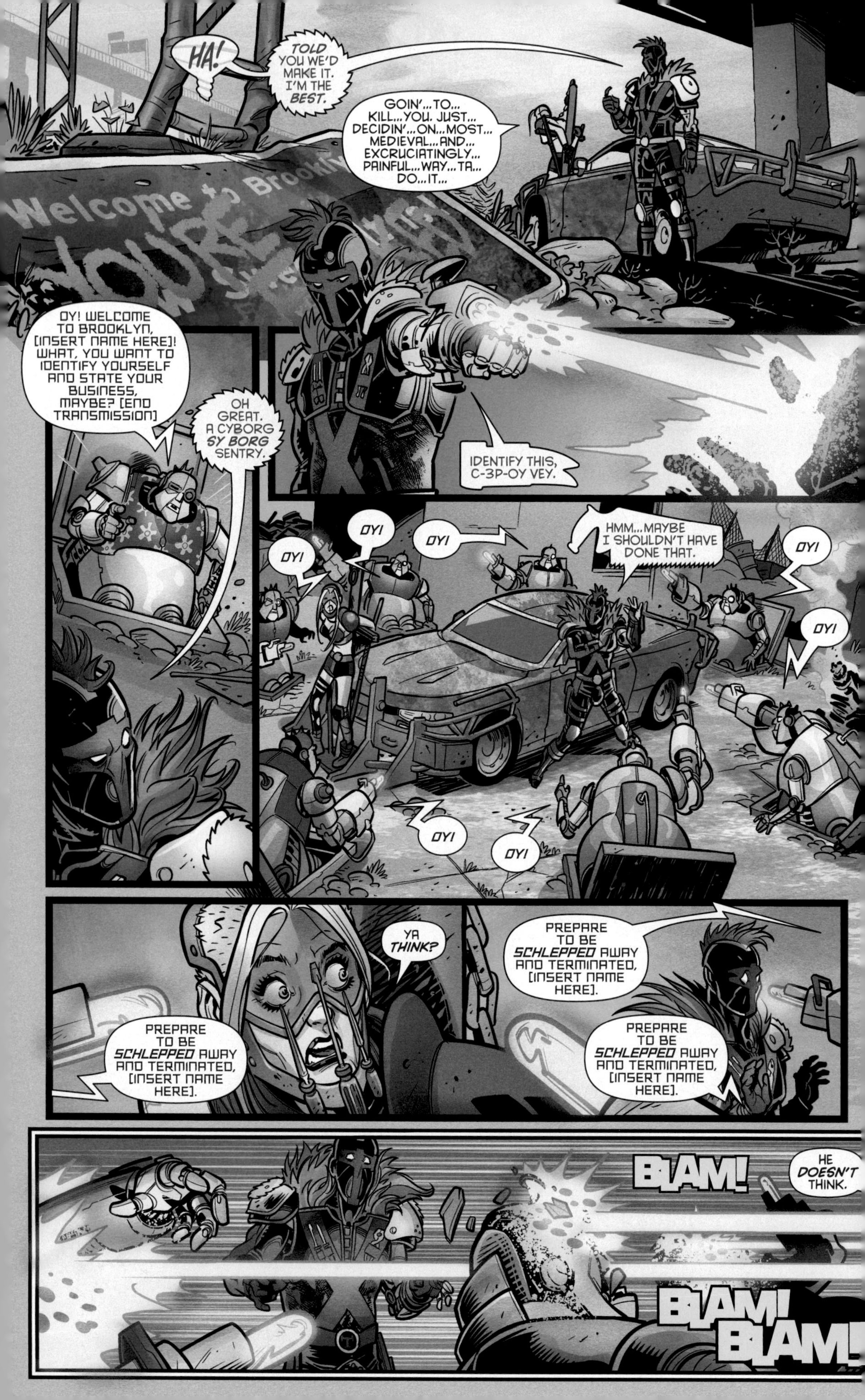
HA!
TOLD YOU WE'D MAKE IT. I'M THE BEST.
GOIN'...TO... KILL...YOU. JUST... DECIDIN'...ON...MOST... MEDIEVAL...AND... EXCRUCIATINGLY... PAINFUL...WAY...TA... DO...IT...
Welcome to Brookly
OY! WELCOME TO BROOKLYN, [INSERT NAME HERE]! WHAT, YOU WANT TO IDENTIFY YOURSELF AND STATE YOUR BUSINESS, MAYBE? [END TRANSMISSION]
OH GREAT. A CYBORG SY BORG SENTRY.
IDENTIFY THIS, C-3P-OY VEY.
OY!
OY!
OY!
HMM...MAYBE I SHOULDN'T HAVE DONE THAT.
OY!
OY!
OY!
OY!
YA THINK?
PREPARE TO BE SCHLEPPED AWAY AND TERMINATED, [INSERT NAME HERE].
PREPARE TO BE SCHLEPPED AWAY AND TERMINATED, [INSERT NAME HERE].
PREPARE TO BE SCHLEPPED AWAY AND TERMINATED, [INSERT NAME HERE].
BLAM!
HE DOESN'T THINK.
BLAM! BLAM!

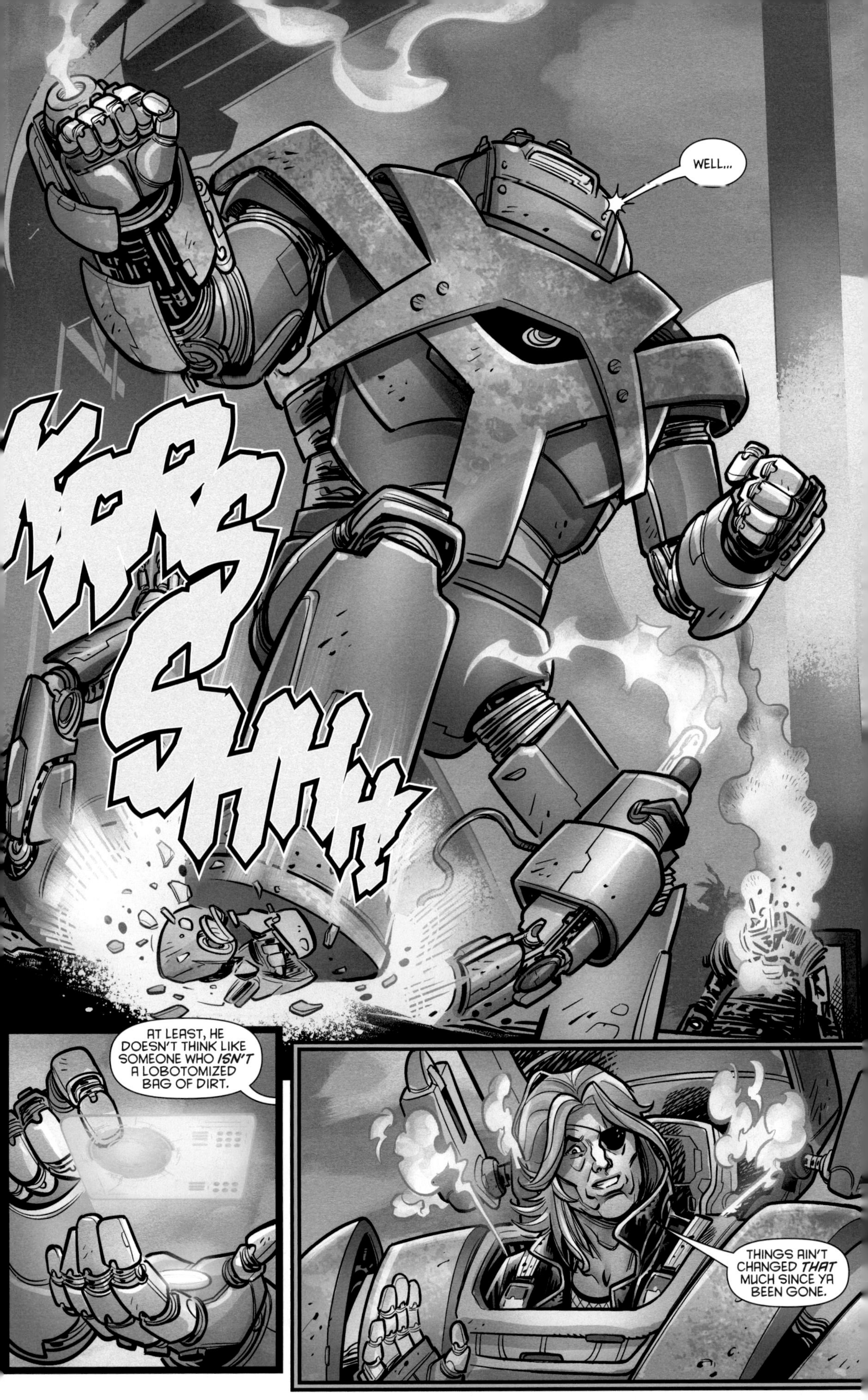
WELL...
AT LEAST, HE DOESN'T THINK LIKE SOMEONE WHO *ISN'T* A LOBOTOMIZED BAG OF DIRT.
THINGS AIN'T CHANGED *THAT* MUCH SINCE YA BEEN GONE.

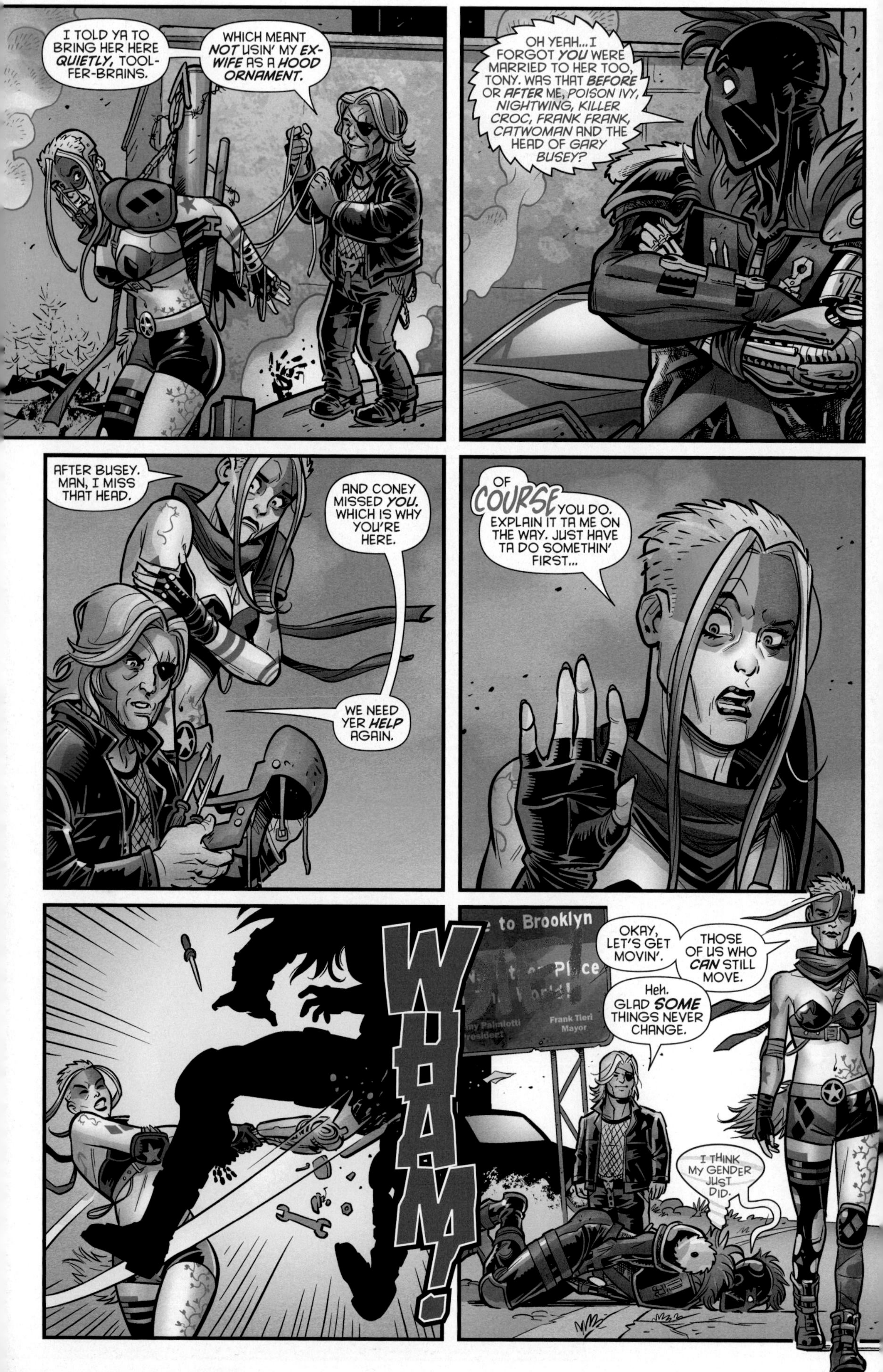
I TOLD YA TO BRING HER HERE QUIETLY, TOOL-FER-BRAINS.
WHICH MEANT NOT USIN' MY EX-WIFE AS A HOOD ORNAMENT.
OH YEAH...I FORGOT YOU WERE MARRIED TO HER TOO, TONY. WAS THAT BEFORE OR AFTER ME, POISON IVY, NIGHTWING, KILLER CROC, FRANK FRANK, CATWOMAN AND THE HEAD OF GARY BUSEY?
AFTER BUSEY. MAN, I MISS THAT HEAD.
AND CONEY MISSED YOU. WHICH IS WHY YOU'RE HERE.
WE NEED YER HELP AGAIN.
OF COURSE YOU DO. EXPLAIN IT TA ME ON THE WAY. JUST HAVE TA DO SOMETHIN' FIRST...
WHAM!
Frank Tieri
Mayor
OKAY, LET'S GET MOVIN'.
THOSE OF US WHO CAN STILL MOVE.
Heh. GLAD SOME THINGS NEVER CHANGE.
I THINK MY GENDER JUST DID.

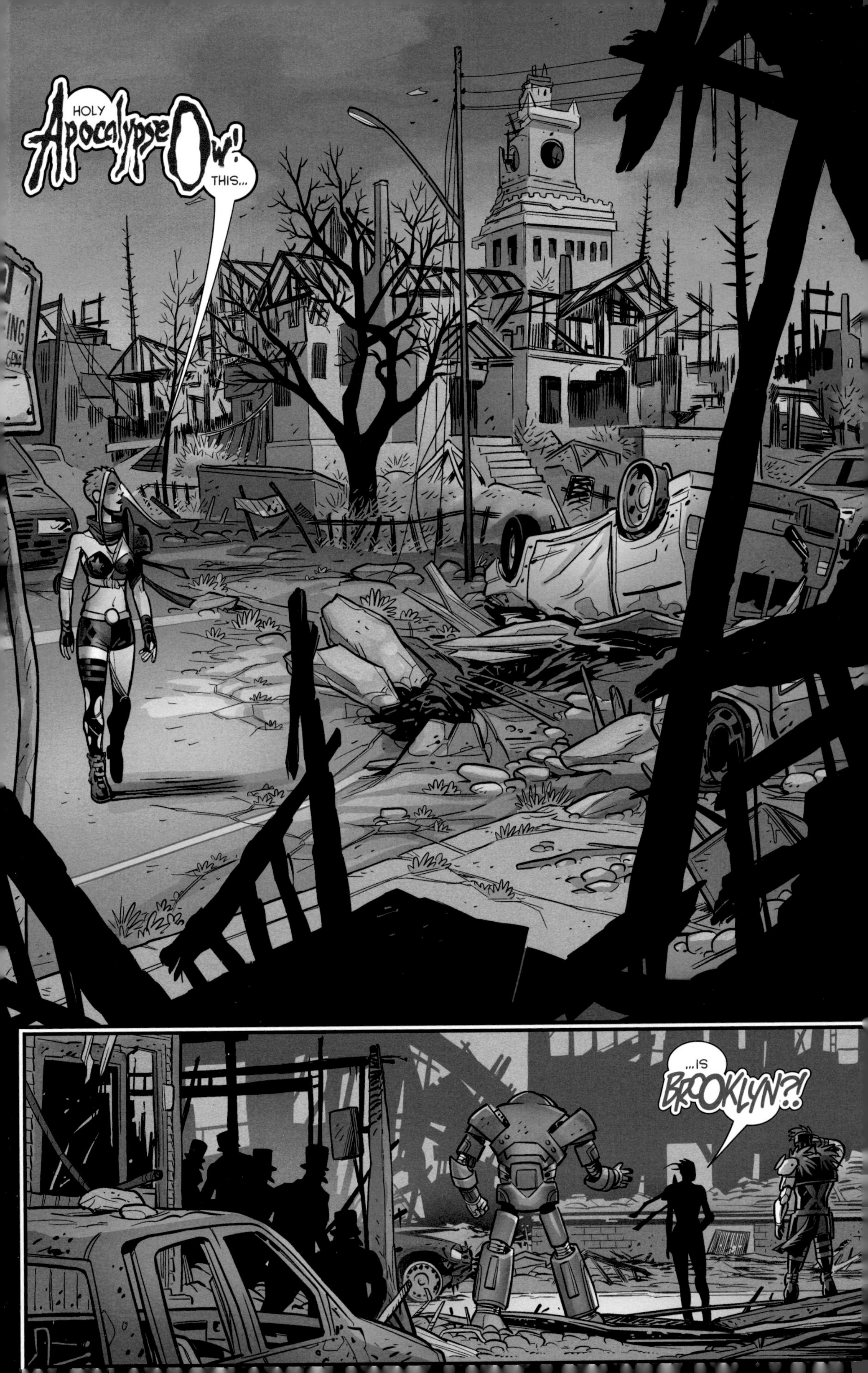
HOLY Apocalypse Ow! THIS...
...IS BROOKLYN?!

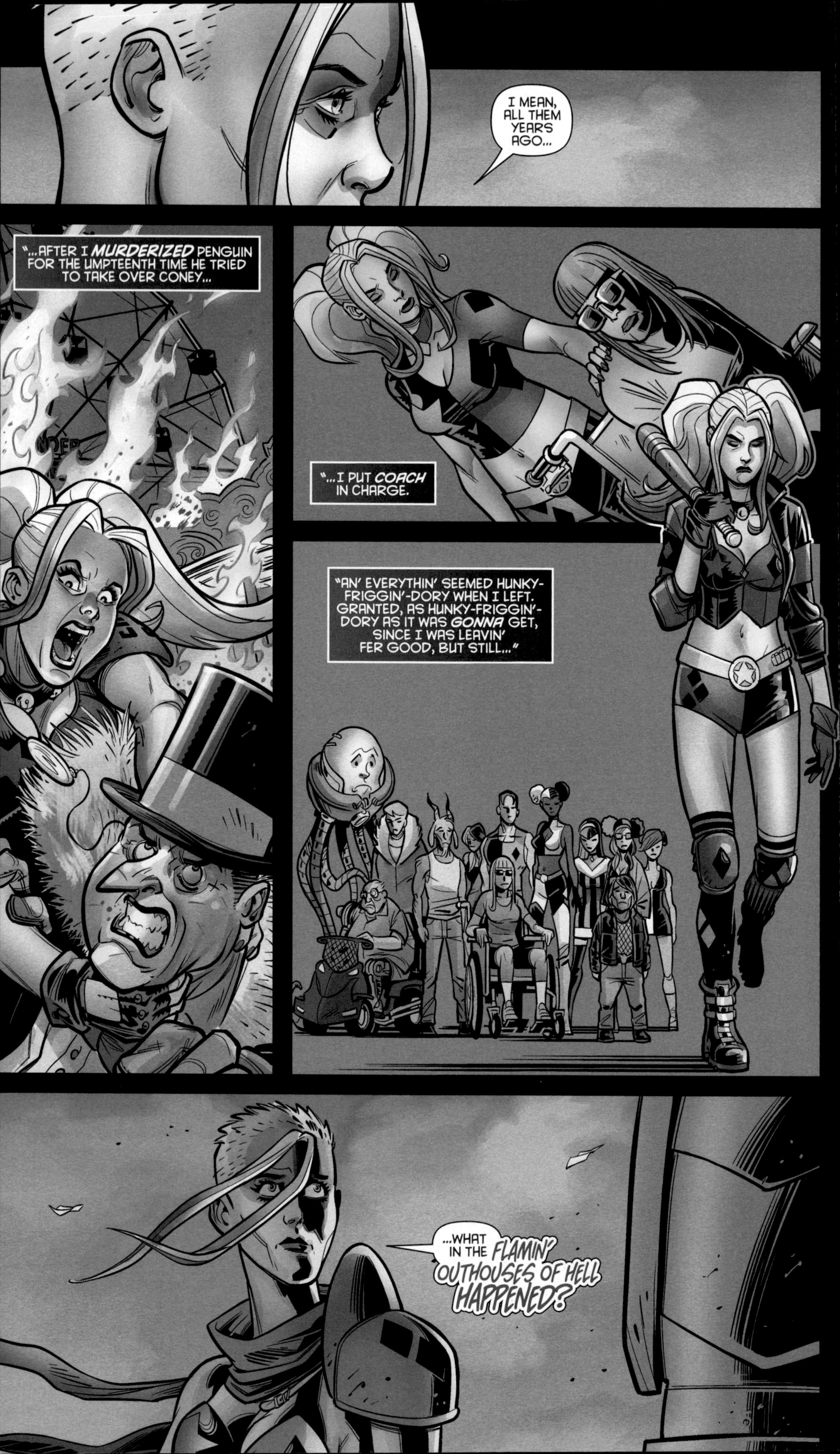
I MEAN, ALL THEM YEARS AGO...
"...AFTER I MURDERIZED PENGUIN FOR THE UMPTEENTH TIME HE TRIED TO TAKE OVER CONEY...
"...I PUT COACH IN CHARGE.
"AN' EVERYTHIN' SEEMED HUNKY-FRIGGIN'-DORY WHEN I LEFT. GRANTED, AS HUNKY-FRIGGIN'-DORY AS IT WAS GONNA GET, SINCE I WAS LEAVIN' FER GOOD, BUT STILL..."
...WHAT IN THE FLAMIN' OUTHOUSES OF HELL HAPPENED?

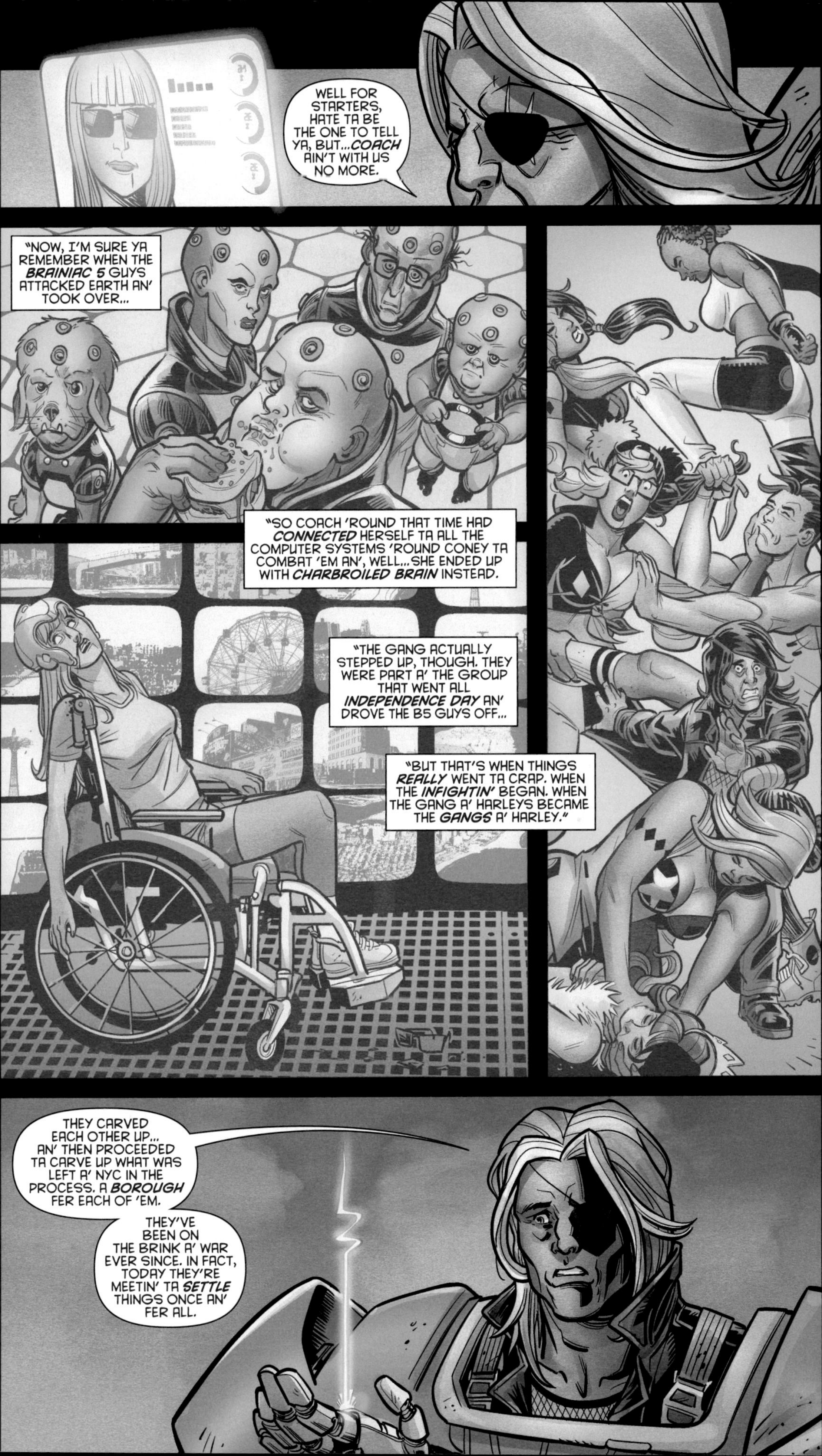

WELL FOR STARTERS, HATE TA BE THE ONE TO TELL YA, BUT...COACH AIN'T WITH US NO MORE.
"NOW, I'M SURE YA REMEMBER WHEN THE BRAINIAC 5 GUYS ATTACKED EARTH AN' TOOK OVER...
"SO COACH 'ROUND THAT TIME HAD CONNECTED HERSELF TA ALL THE COMPUTER SYSTEMS 'ROUND CONEY TA COMBAT 'EM AN', WELL...SHE ENDED UP WITH CHARBROILED BRAIN INSTEAD.
"THE GANG ACTUALLY STEPPED UP, THOUGH. THEY WERE PART A' THE GROUP THAT WENT ALL INDEPENDENCE DAY AN' DROVE THE B5 GUYS OFF...
"BUT THAT'S WHEN THINGS REALLY WENT TA CRAP. WHEN THE INFIGHTIN' BEGAN. WHEN THE GANG A' HARLEYS BECAME THE GANGS A' HARLEY."
THEY CARVED EACH OTHER UP... AN' THEN PROCEEDED TA CARVE UP WHAT WAS LEFT A' NYC IN THE PROCESS. A BOROUGH FER EACH OF 'EM.
THEY'VE BEEN ON THE BRINK A' WAR EVER SINCE. IN FACT, TODAY THEY'RE MEETIN' TA SETTLE THINGS ONCE AN' FER ALL.

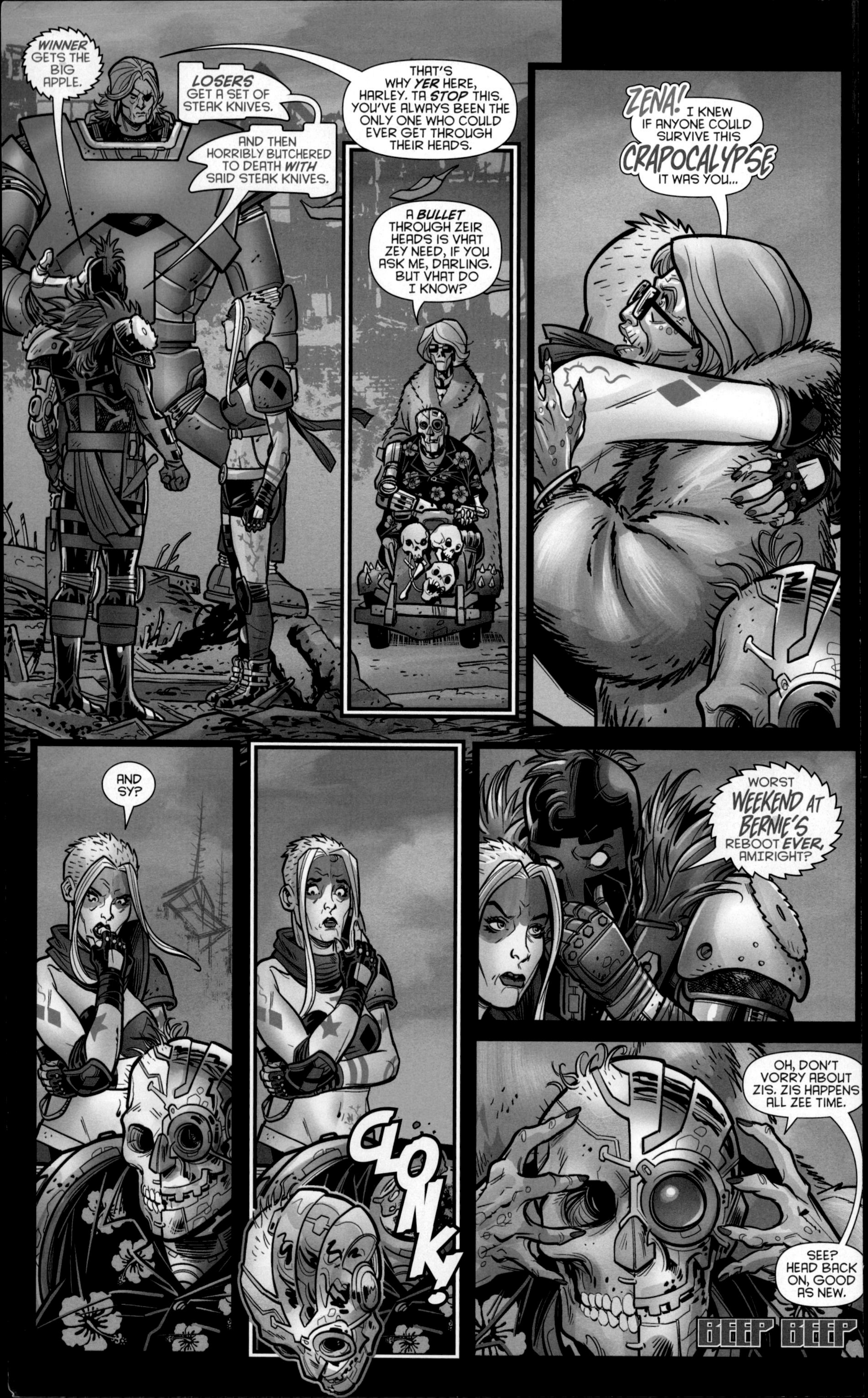
WINNER GETS THE BIG APPLE.
LOSERS GET A SET OF STEAK KNIVES.
AND THEN HORRIBLY BUTCHERED TO DEATH WITH SAID STEAK KNIVES.
THAT'S WHY YER HERE, HARLEY. TA STOP THIS. YOU'VE ALWAYS BEEN THE ONLY ONE WHO COULD EVER GET THROUGH THEIR HEADS.
A BULLET THROUGH ZEIR HEADS IS VHAT ZEY NEED, IF YOU ASK ME, DARLING. BUT VHAT DO I KNOW?
ZENA! I KNEW IF ANYONE COULD SURVIVE THIS CRAPOCALYPSE IT WAS YOU...
AND SY?
CLONK!
WORST WEEKEND AT BERNIE'S REBOOT EVER, AMIRIGHT?
OH, DON'T VORRY ABOUT ZIS. ZIS HAPPENS ALL ZEE TIME.
SEE? HEAD BACK ON, GOOD AS NEW.
BEEP BEEP

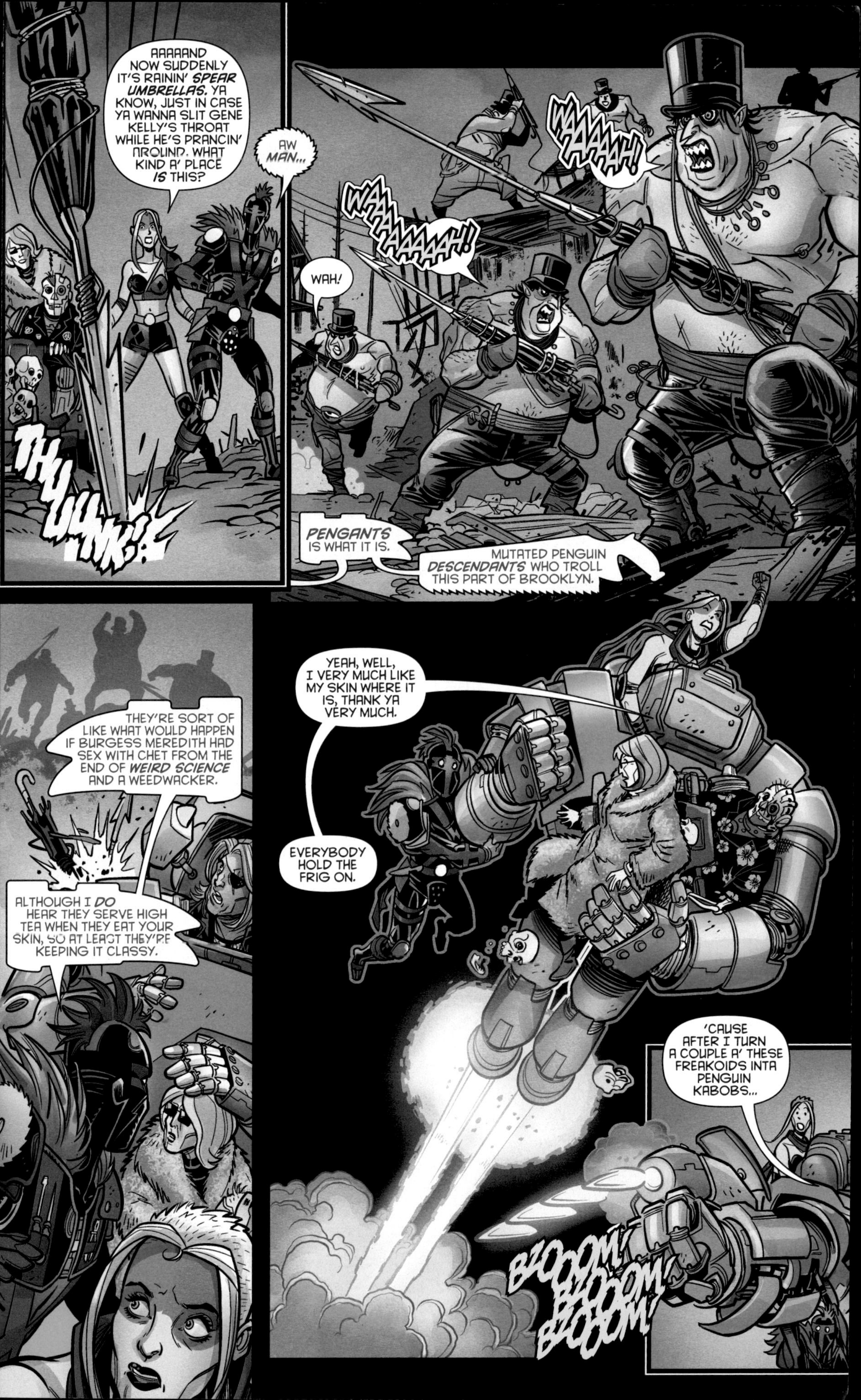
AAAAAND NOW SUDDENLY IT'S RAININ' SPEAR UMBRELLAS. YA KNOW, JUST IN CASE YA WANNA SLIT GENE KELLY'S THROAT WHILE HE'S PRANCIN' AROUND. WHAT KIND A' PLACE IS THIS?
AW MAN...
THUUNK!?!
WAAAAAH!
WAAAAAAAAAH!
WAH!
PENGANTS IS WHAT IT IS.
MUTATED PENGUIN DESCENDANTS WHO TROLL THIS PART OF BROOKLYN.
THEY'RE SORT OF LIKE WHAT WOULD HAPPEN IF BURGESS MEREDITH HAD SEX WITH CHET FROM THE END OF WEIRD SCIENCE AND A WEEDWACKER.
ALTHOUGH I DO HEAR THEY SERVE HIGH TEA WHEN THEY EAT YOUR SKIN, SO AT LEAST THEY'RE KEEPING IT CLASSY.
YEAH, WELL, I VERY MUCH LIKE MY SKIN WHERE IT IS, THANK YA VERY MUCH.
EVERYBODY HOLD THE FRIG ON.
'CAUSE AFTER I TURN A COUPLE A' THESE FREAKOIDS INTA PENGUIN KABOBS...
BZOOOM! BZOOOM! BZOOOM!

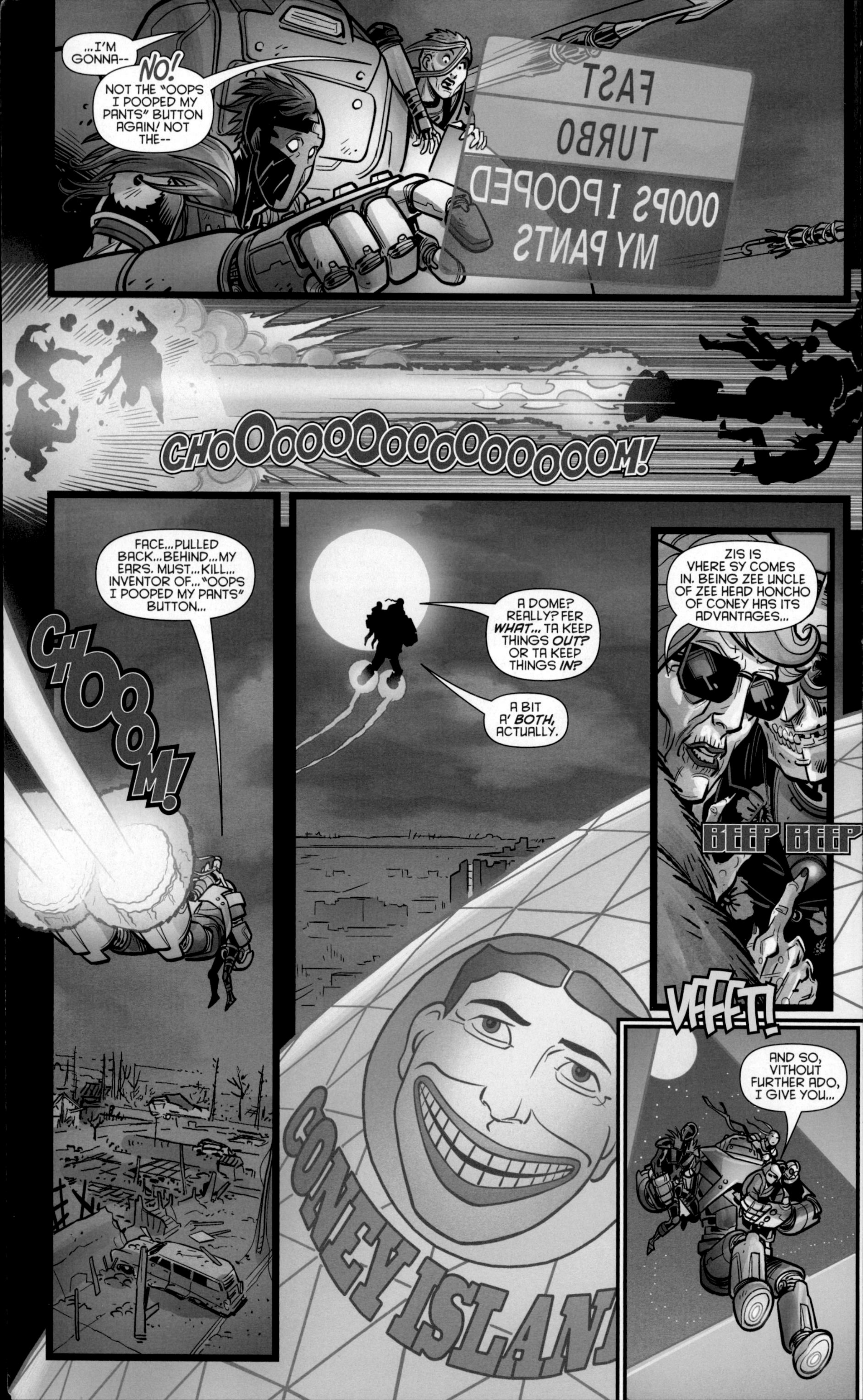
...I'M GONNA--
NO! NOT THE "OOPS I POOPED MY PANTS" BUTTON AGAIN! NOT THE--
FAST
TURBO
OOOPS I POOPED MY PANTS
CHOOOOOOOOOOOOOOOOM!
FACE...PULLED BACK...BEHIND...MY EARS. MUST...KILL... INVENTOR OF..."OOPS I POOPED MY PANTS" BUTTON...
CHOOOOM!
A DOME? REALLY? FER WHAT... TA KEEP THINGS OUT? OR TA KEEP THINGS IN?
A BIT A' BOTH, ACTUALLY.
ZIS IS VHERE SY COMES IN. BEING ZEE UNCLE OF ZEE HEAD HONCHO OF CONEY HAS ITS ADVANTAGES...
BEEP BEEP
VFFFT!
AND SO, VITHOUT FURTHER ADO, I GIVE YOU...
CONEY ISLAN

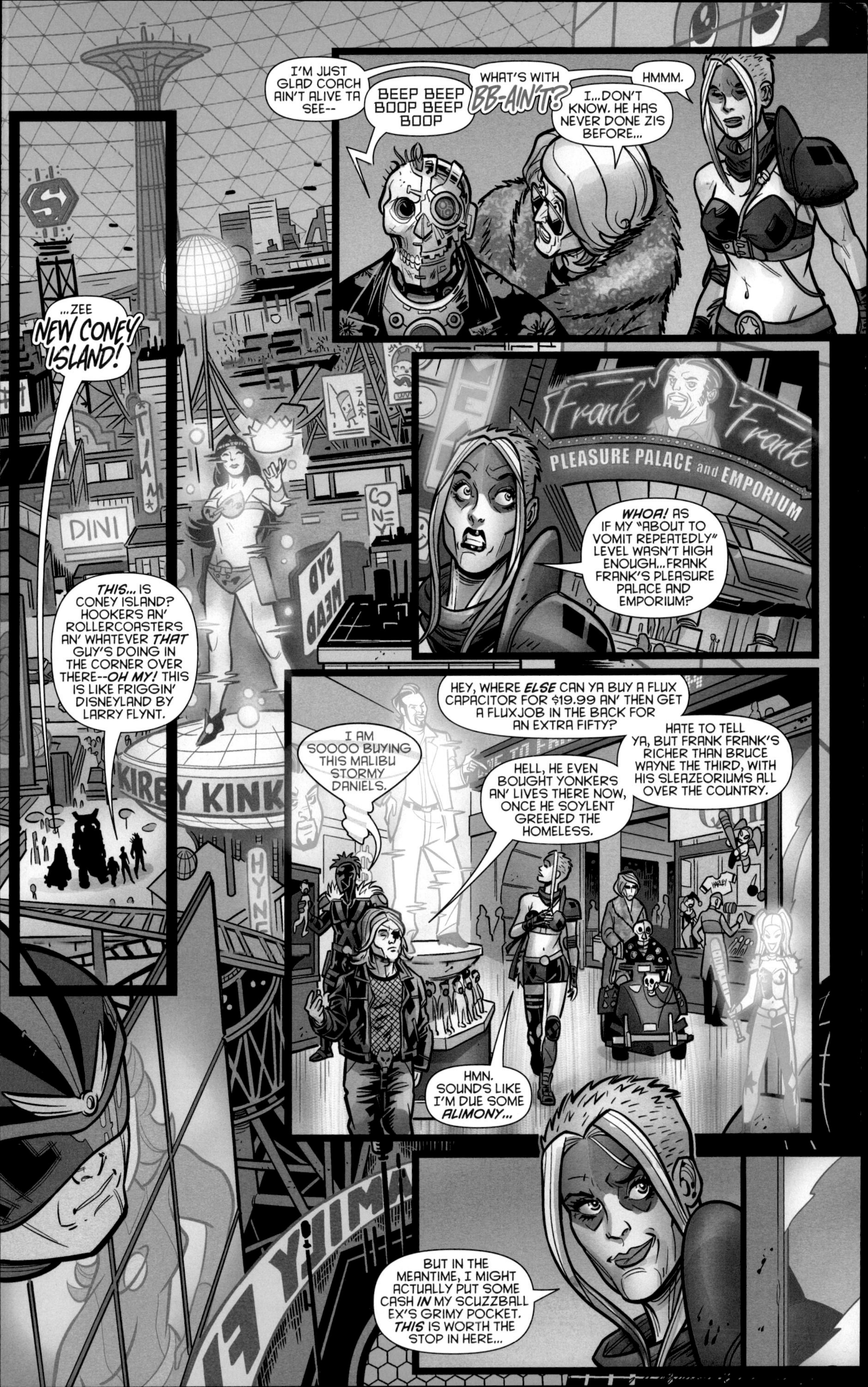

...ZEE
NEW CONEY ISLAND!
THIS... IS CONEY ISLAND? HOOKERS AN' ROLLERCOASTERS AN' WHATEVER THAT GUY'S DOING IN THE CORNER OVER THERE--OH MY! THIS IS LIKE FRIGGIN' DISNEYLAND BY LARRY FLYNT.
I'M JUST GLAD COACH AIN'T ALIVE TA SEE--
BEEP BEEP BOOP BEEP BOOP
WHAT'S WITH BB-AIN'T?
I...DON'T KNOW. HE HAS NEVER DONE ZIS BEFORE...
HMMM.
Frank Frank
PLEASURE PALACE and EMPORIUM
WHOA! AS IF MY "ABOUT TO VOMIT REPEATEDLY" LEVEL WASN'T HIGH ENOUGH...FRANK FRANK'S PLEASURE PALACE AND EMPORIUM?
DINI
CONEY
SYD MEAD
KIRBY KINK
HEY, WHERE ELSE CAN YA BUY A FLUX CAPACITOR FOR $19.99 AN' THEN GET A FLUXJOB IN THE BACK FOR AN EXTRA FIFTY?
I AM SOOOO BUYING THIS MALIBU STORMY DANIELS.
HATE TO TELL YA, BUT FRANK FRANK'S RICHER THAN BRUCE WAYNE THE THIRD, WITH HIS SLEAZEORIUMS ALL OVER THE COUNTRY.
HELL, HE EVEN BOUGHT YONKERS AN' LIVES THERE NOW, ONCE HE SOYLENT GREENED THE HOMELESS.
HMN. SOUNDS LIKE I'M DUE SOME ALIMONY...
BUT IN THE MEANTIME, I MIGHT ACTUALLY PUT SOME CASH IN MY SCUZZBALL EX'S GRIMY POCKET. THIS IS WORTH THE STOP IN HERE...

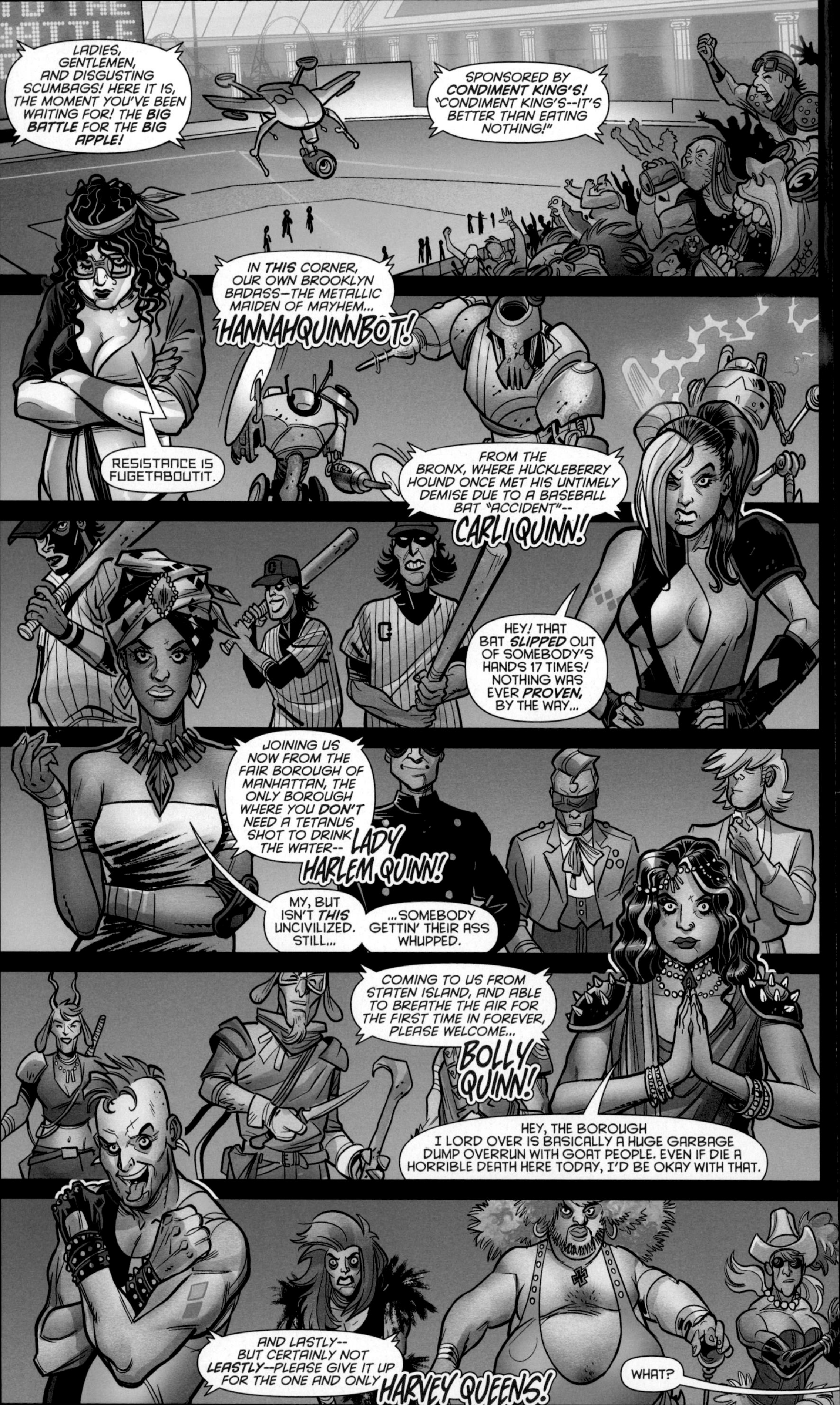

LADIES, GENTLEMEN, AND DISGUSTING SCUMBAGS! HERE IT IS, THE MOMENT YOU'VE BEEN WAITING FOR! THE BIG BATTLE FOR THE BIG APPLE!
SPONSORED BY CONDIMENT KING'S! "CONDIMENT KING'S--IT'S BETTER THAN EATING NOTHING!"
IN THIS CORNER, OUR OWN BROOKLYN BADASS–THE METALLIC MAIDEN OF MAYHEM... HANNAHQUINNBOT!
RESISTANCE IS FUGETABOUTIT.
FROM THE BRONX, WHERE HUCKLEBERRY HOUND ONCE MET HIS UNTIMELY DEMISE DUE TO A BASEBALL BAT "ACCIDENT"-- CARLI QUINN!
HEY! THAT BAT SLIPPED OUT OF SOMEBODY'S HANDS 17 TIMES! NOTHING WAS EVER PROVEN, BY THE WAY...
JOINING US NOW FROM THE FAIR BOROUGH OF MANHATTAN, THE ONLY BOROUGH WHERE YOU DON'T NEED A TETANUS SHOT TO DRINK THE WATER-- LADY HARLEM QUINN!
MY, BUT ISN'T THIS UNCIVILIZED. STILL...
...SOMEBODY GETTIN' THEIR ASS WHUPPED.
COMING TO US FROM STATEN ISLAND, AND ABLE TO BREATHE THE AIR FOR THE FIRST TIME IN FOREVER, PLEASE WELCOME... BOLLY QUINN!
HEY, THE BOROUGH I LORD OVER IS BASICALLY A HUGE GARBAGE DUMP OVERRUN WITH GOAT PEOPLE. EVEN IF DIE A HORRIBLE DEATH HERE TODAY, I'D BE OKAY WITH THAT.
AND LASTLY-- BUT CERTAINLY NOT LEASTLY--PLEASE GIVE IT UP FOR THE ONE AND ONLY HARVEY QUEENS!
WHAT?

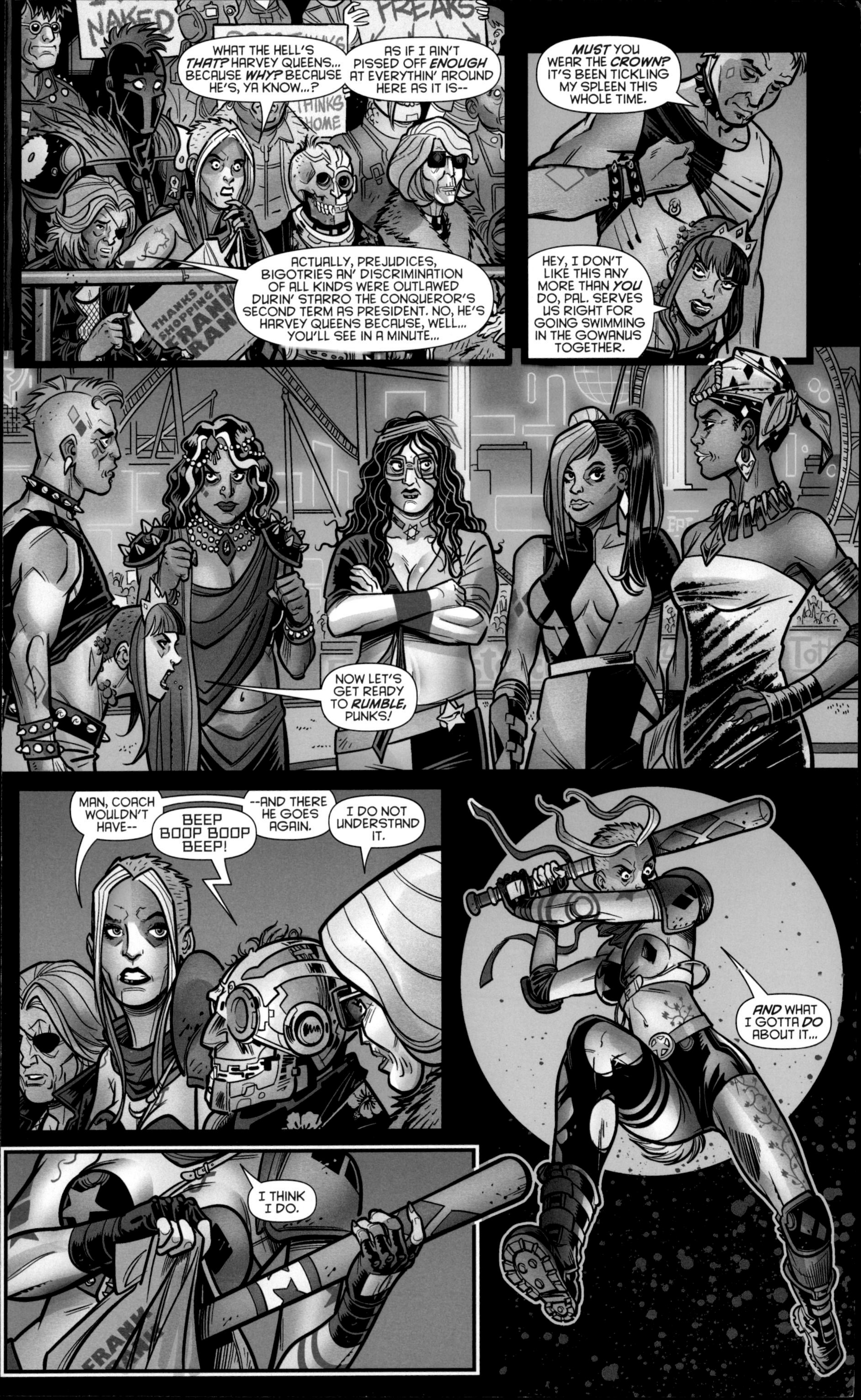
NAKED
FREAKS
WHAT THE HELL'S THAT? HARVEY QUEENS... BECAUSE WHY? BECAUSE HE'S, YA KNOW...?
AS IF I AIN'T PISSED OFF ENOUGH AT EVERYTHIN' AROUND HERE AS IT IS--
THINKS
HOME
ACTUALLY, PREJUDICES, BIGOTRIES AN' DISCRIMINATION OF ALL KINDS WERE OUTLAWED DURIN' STARRO THE CONQUEROR'S SECOND TERM AS PRESIDENT. NO, HE'S HARVEY QUEENS BECAUSE, WELL... YOU'LL SEE IN A MINUTE...
MUST YOU WEAR THE CROWN? IT'S BEEN TICKLING MY SPLEEN THIS WHOLE TIME.
HEY, I DON'T LIKE THIS ANY MORE THAN YOU DO, PAL. SERVES US RIGHT FOR GOING SWIMMING IN THE GOWANUS TOGETHER.
NOW LET'S GET READY TO RUMBLE, PUNKS!
MAN, COACH WOULDN'T HAVE--
BEEP BOOP BOOP BEEP!
--AND THERE HE GOES AGAIN.
I DO NOT UNDERSTAND IT.
AND WHAT I GOTTA DO ABOUT IT...
I THINK I DO.

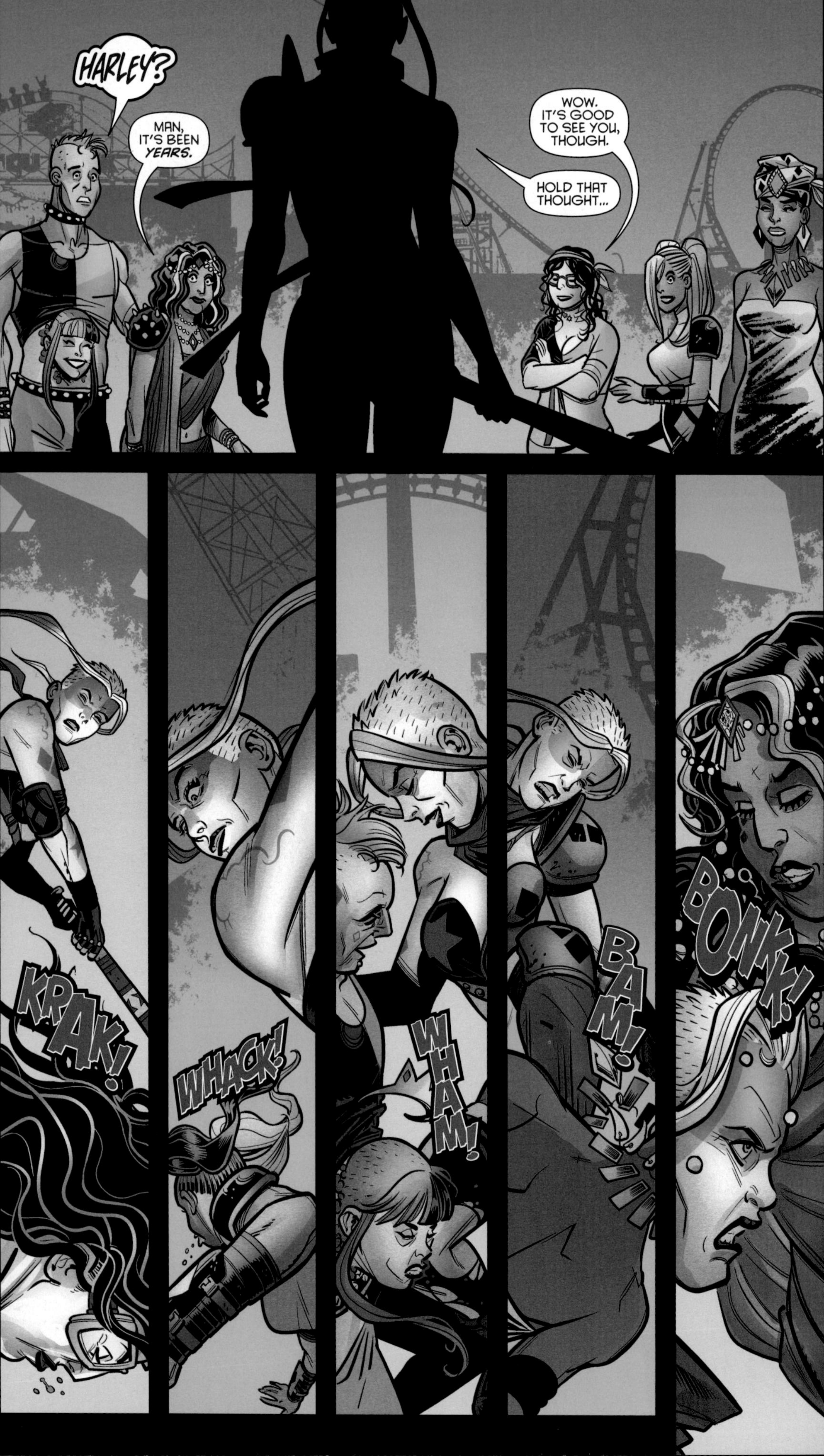
HARLEY?
MAN, IT'S BEEN YEARS.
WOW. IT'S GOOD TO SEE YOU, THOUGH.
HOLD THAT THOUGHT...
KRAK!
WHACK!
WHAM!
BAM!
BONK!

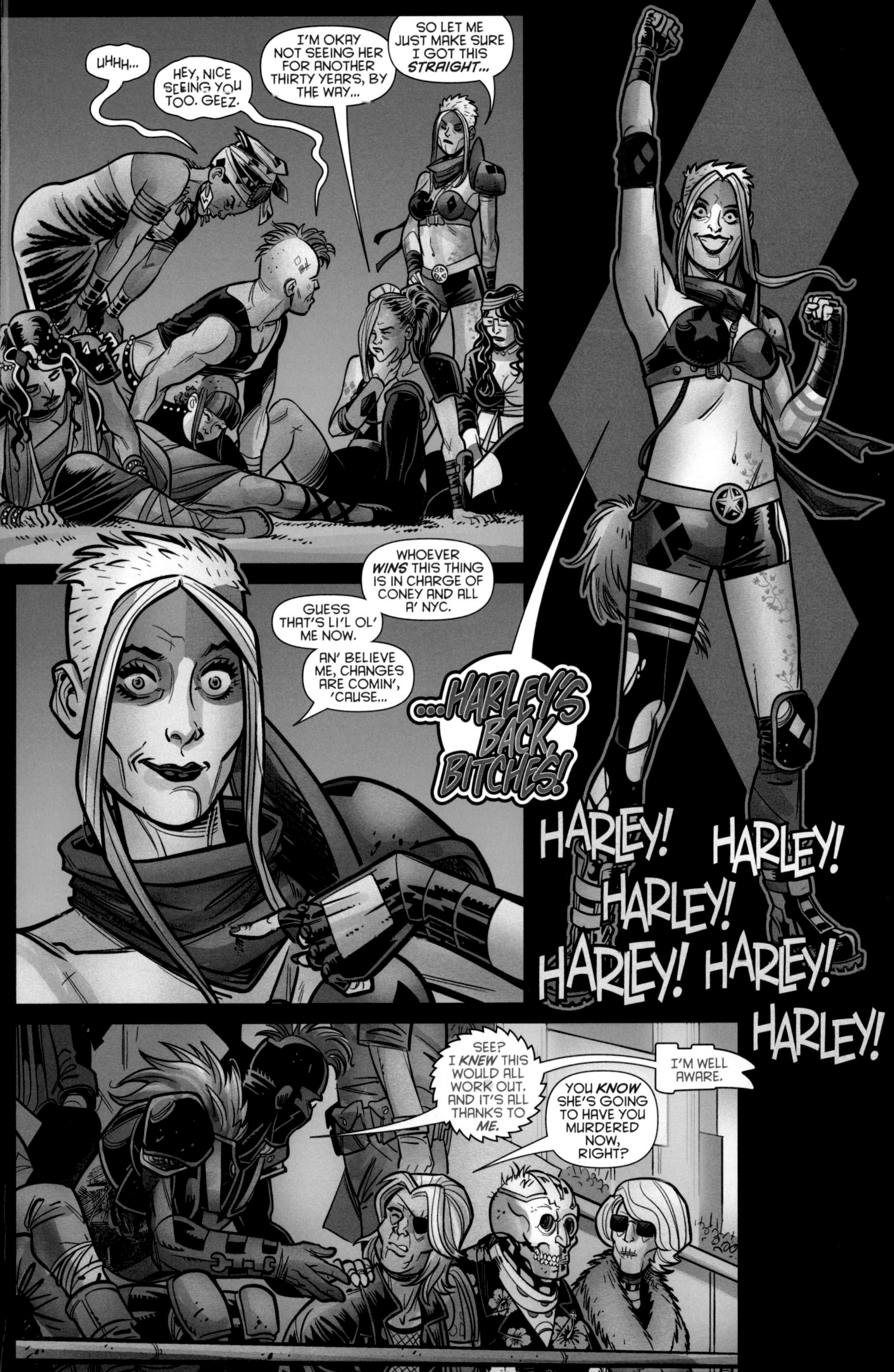
UHHH...
HEY, NICE SEEING YOU TOO. GEEZ.
I'M OKAY NOT SEEING HER FOR ANOTHER THIRTY YEARS, BY THE WAY...
SO LET ME JUST MAKE SURE I GOT THIS STRAIGHT...
WHOEVER WINS THIS THING IS IN CHARGE OF CONEY AND ALL A' NYC.
GUESS THAT'S LI'L OL' ME NOW.
AN' BELIEVE ME, CHANGES ARE COMIN', 'CAUSE...
...HARLEY'S BACK, BITCHES!
HARLEY! HARLEY! HARLEY! HARLEY! HARLEY! HARLEY!
SEE? I KNEW THIS WOULD ALL WORK OUT. AND IT'S ALL THANKS TO ME.
YOU KNOW SHE'S GOING TO HAVE YOU MURDERED NOW, RIGHT?
I'M WELL AWARE.

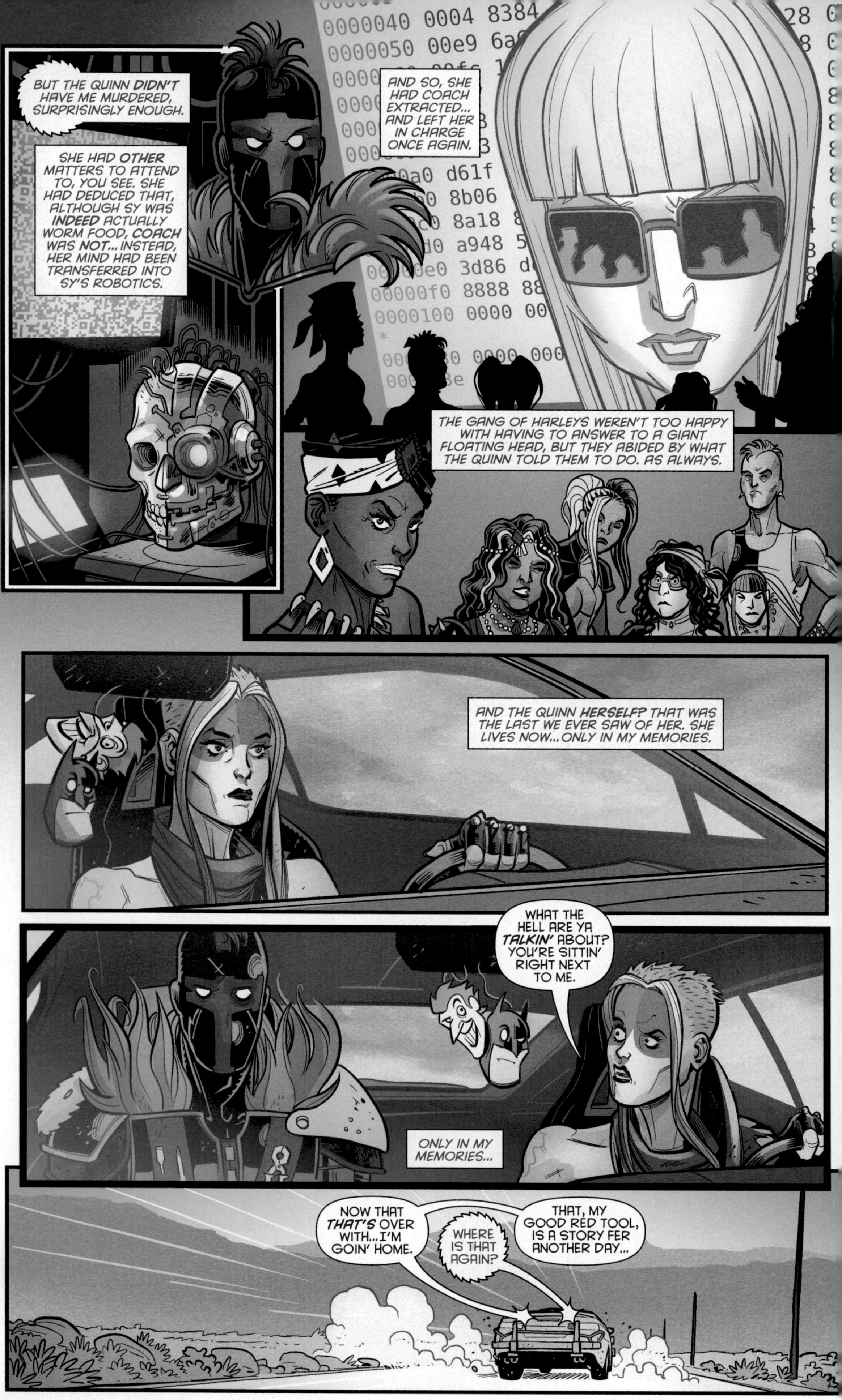
BUT THE QUINN DIDN'T HAVE ME MURDERED, SURPRISINGLY ENOUGH.
SHE HAD OTHER MATTERS TO ATTEND TO, YOU SEE. SHE HAD DEDUCED THAT, ALTHOUGH SY WAS INDEED ACTUALLY WORM FOOD, COACH WAS NOT... INSTEAD, HER MIND HAD BEEN TRANSFERRED INTO SY'S ROBOTICS.
AND SO, SHE HAD COACH EXTRACTED... AND LEFT HER IN CHARGE ONCE AGAIN.
THE GANG OF HARLEYS WEREN'T TOO HAPPY WITH HAVING TO ANSWER TO A GIANT FLOATING HEAD, BUT THEY ABIDED BY WHAT THE QUINN TOLD THEM TO DO. AS ALWAYS.
AND THE QUINN HERSELF? THAT WAS THE LAST WE EVER SAW OF HER. SHE LIVES NOW... ONLY IN MY MEMORIES.
WHAT THE HELL ARE YA TALKIN' ABOUT? YOU'RE SITTIN' RIGHT NEXT TO ME.
ONLY IN MY MEMORIES...
NOW THAT THAT'S OVER WITH... I'M GOIN' HOME.
WHERE IS THAT AGAIN?
THAT, MY GOOD RED TOOL, IS A STORY FER ANOTHER DAY...

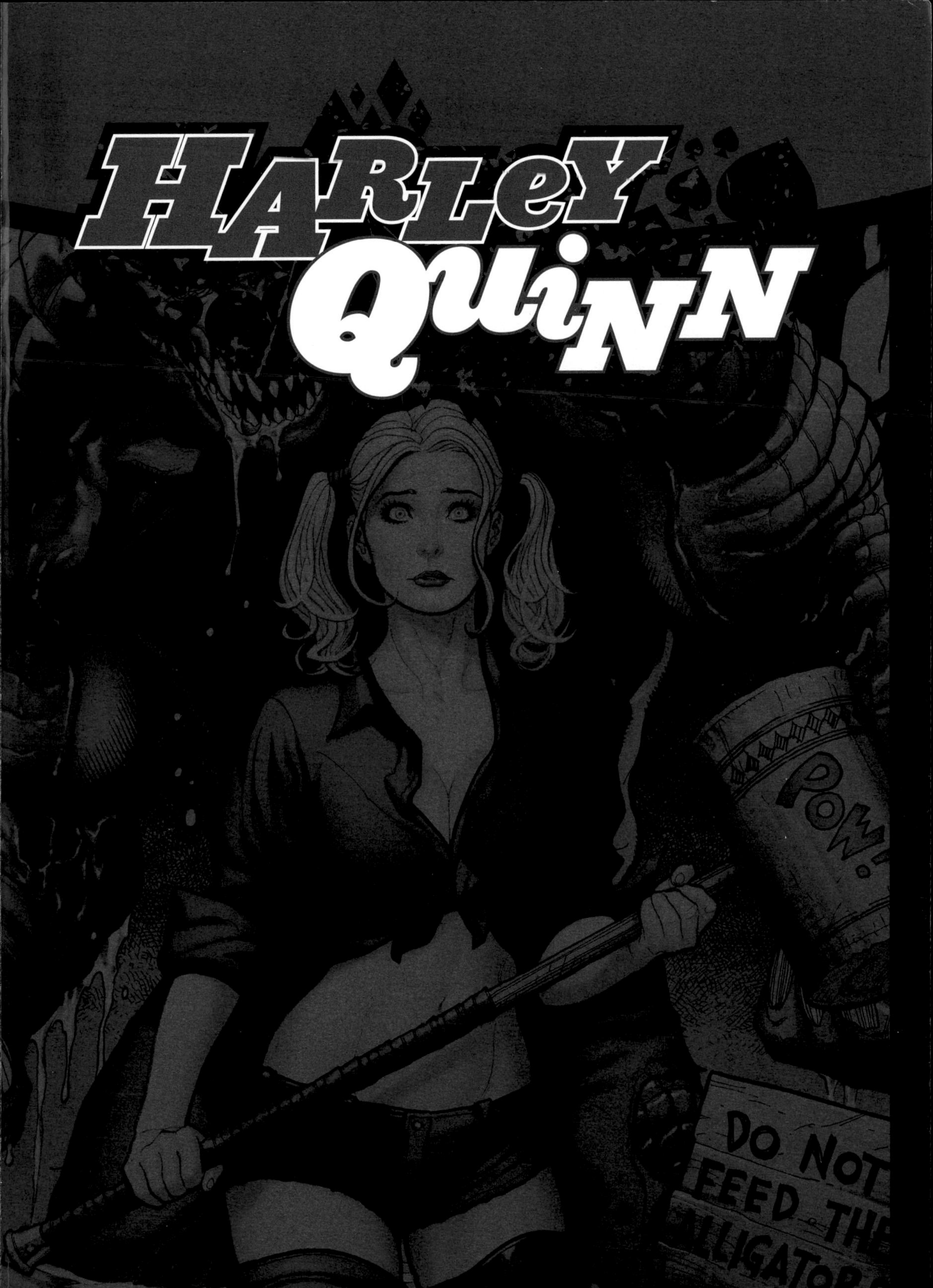

HARLEY
QUINN
POW!
DO NOT
FEED THE
ALLIGATORS


# VARIANT COVER GALLERY

HARLEY QUINN #35 variant cover
by FRANK CHO and SABINE RICH

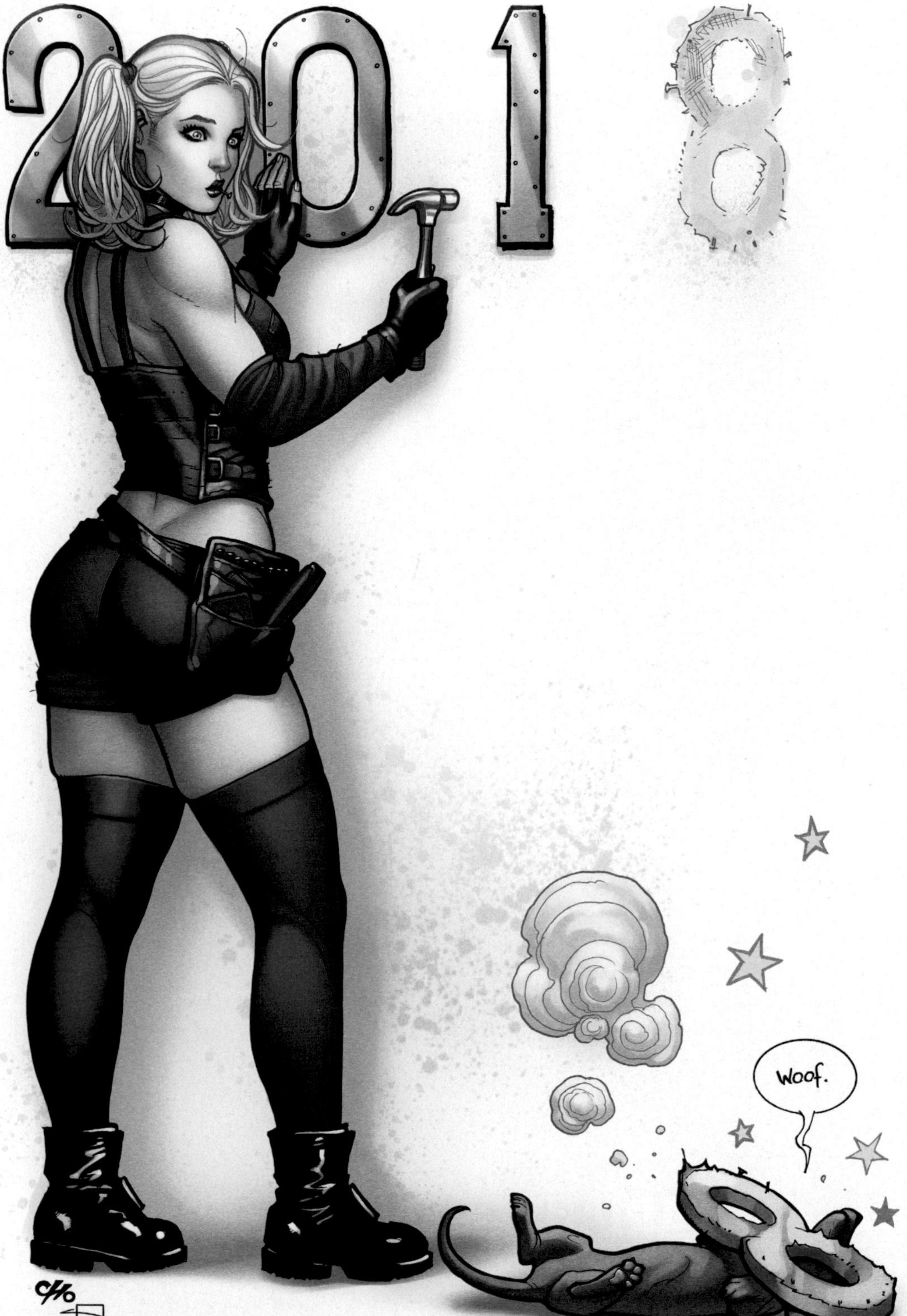

2018
woof.

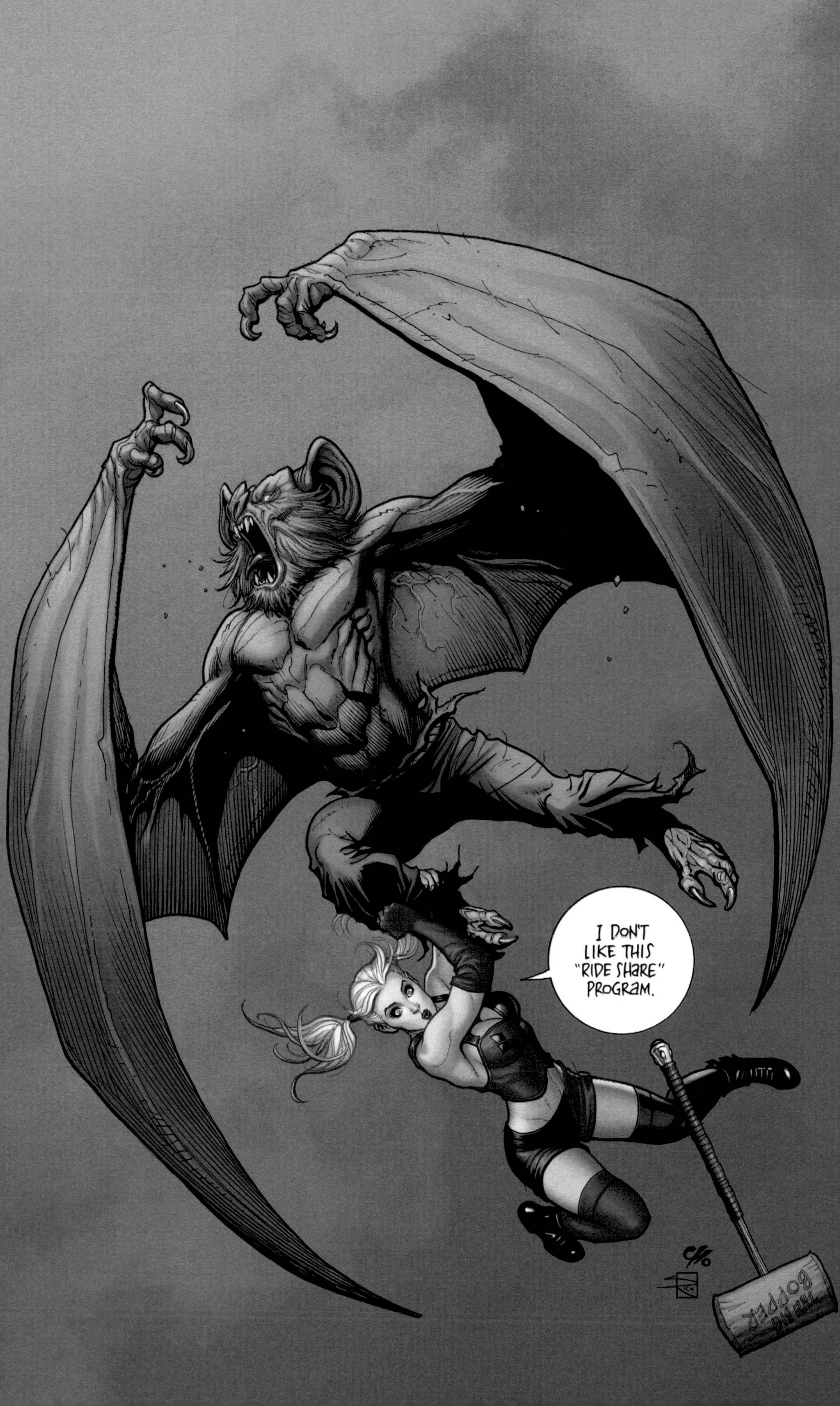
I DON'T LIKE THIS "RIDE SHARE" PROGRAM.
THE BIG BOPPER

HARLEY QUINN #36 variant cover
by FRANK CHO and SABINE RICH

HARLEY QUINN #37 variant cover
by FRANK CHO and SABINE RICH

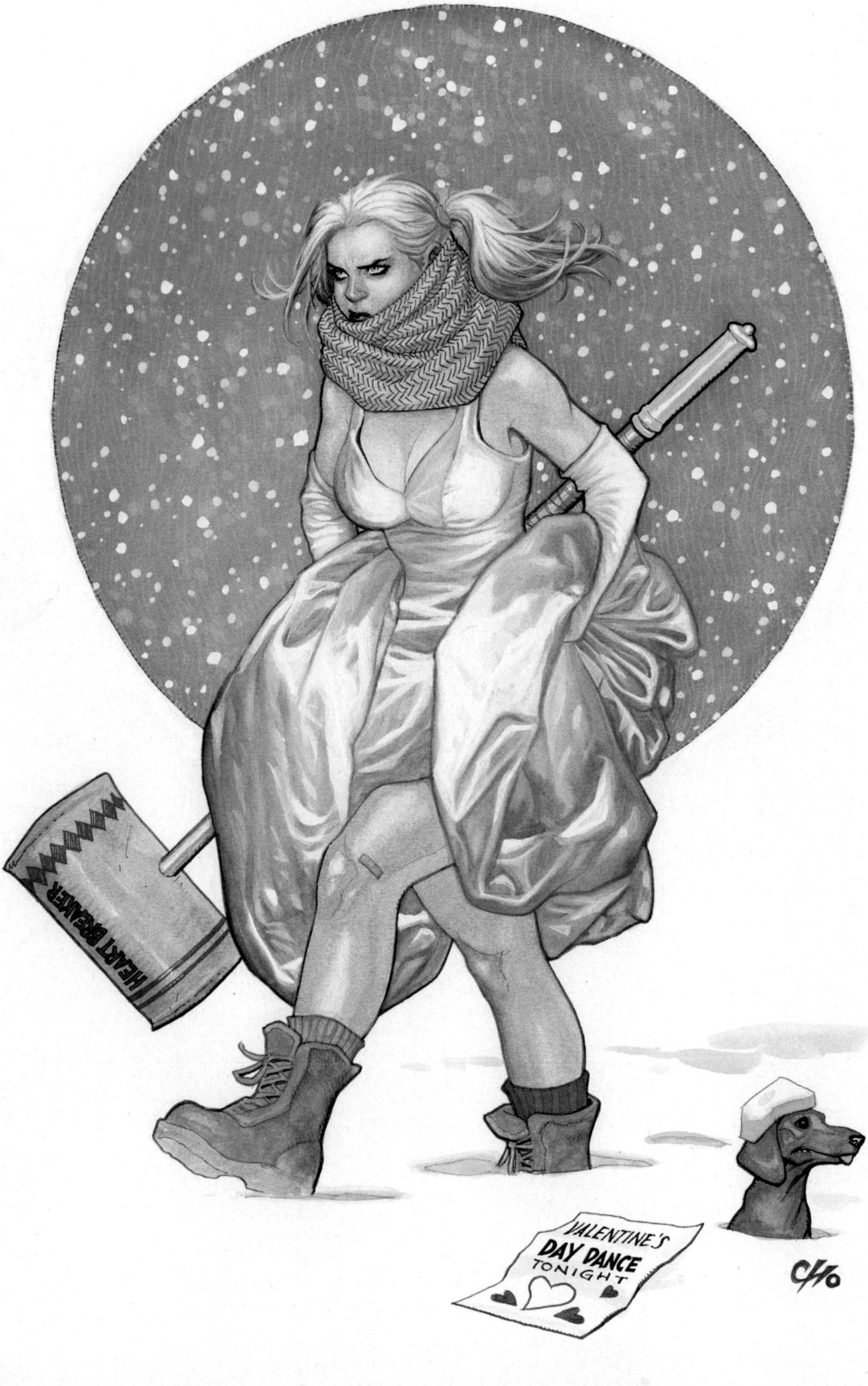
HEART BREAKER
VALENTINE'S
DAY DANCE
TONIGHT
CHO

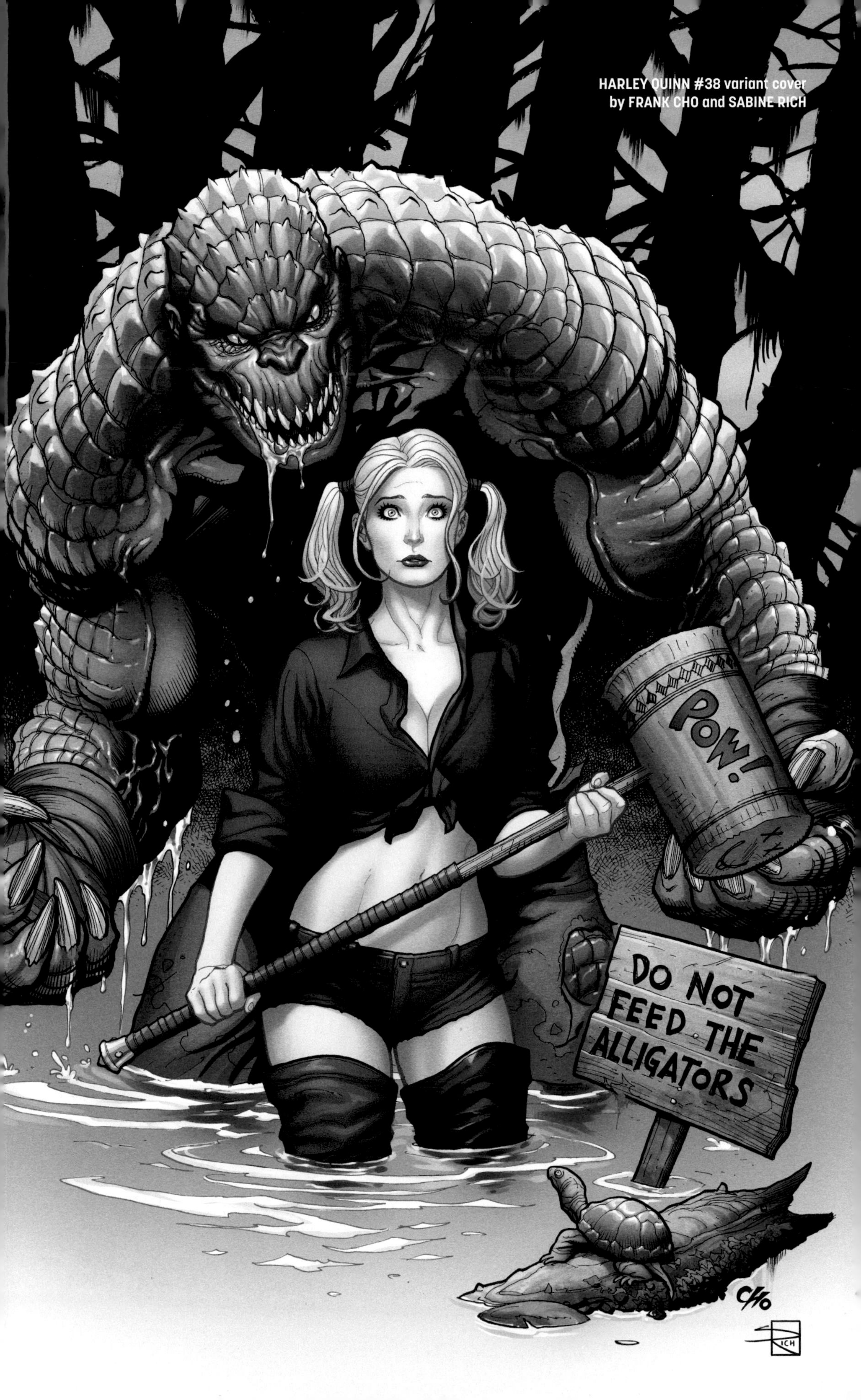
POW!
DO NOT FEED THE ALLIGATORS
CHO

HARLEY QUINN #38 variant cover
by FRANK CHO and SABINE RICH

**HARLEY QUINN #39 variant cover**
**by FRANK CHO and SABINE RICH**

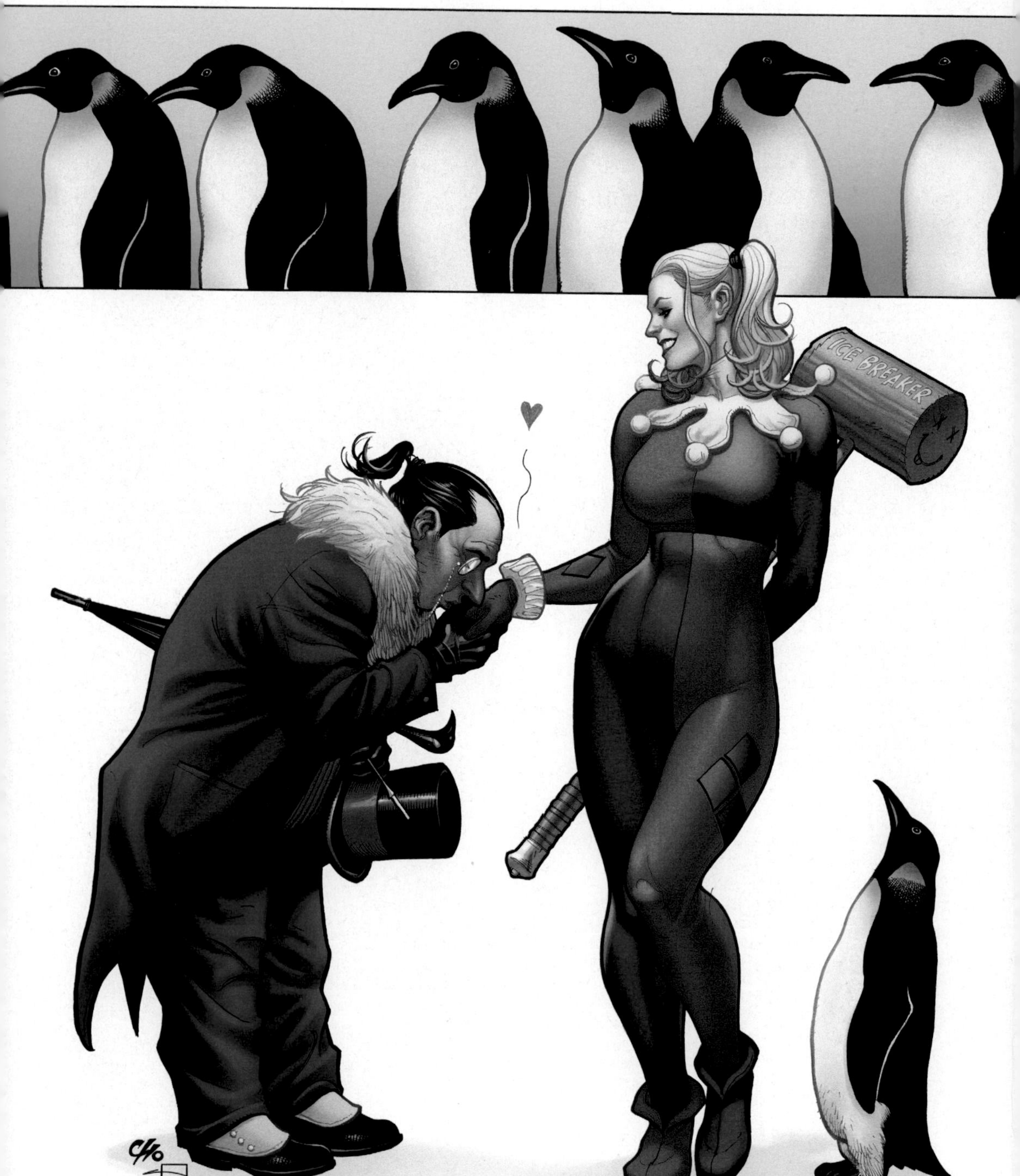
ICE BREAKER

HARLEY QUINN #40 variant cover
by FRANK CHO and SABINE RICH

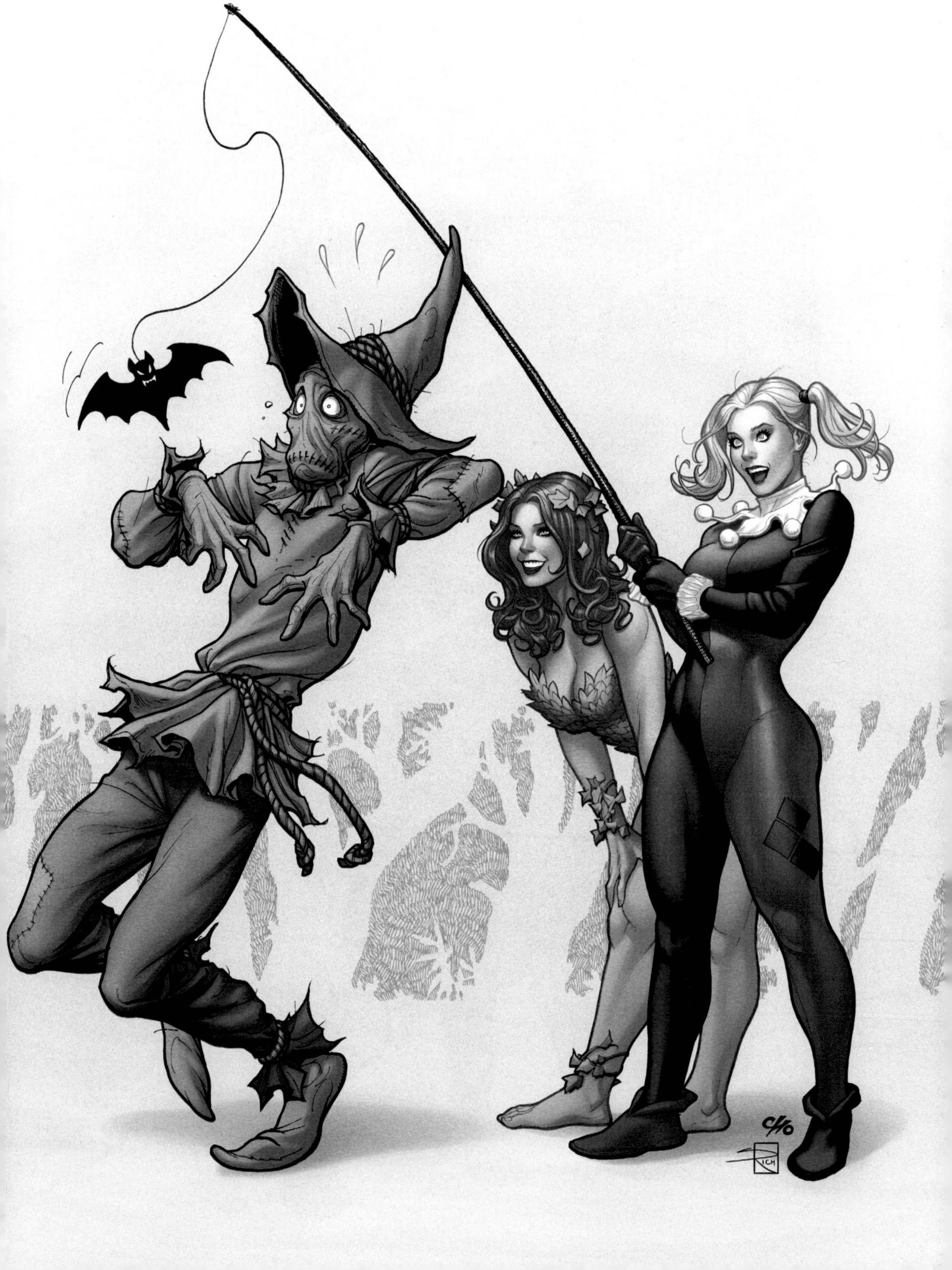
CHO
RICH

**HARLEY QUINN #41 variant cover**
**by FRANK CHO and SABINE RICH**

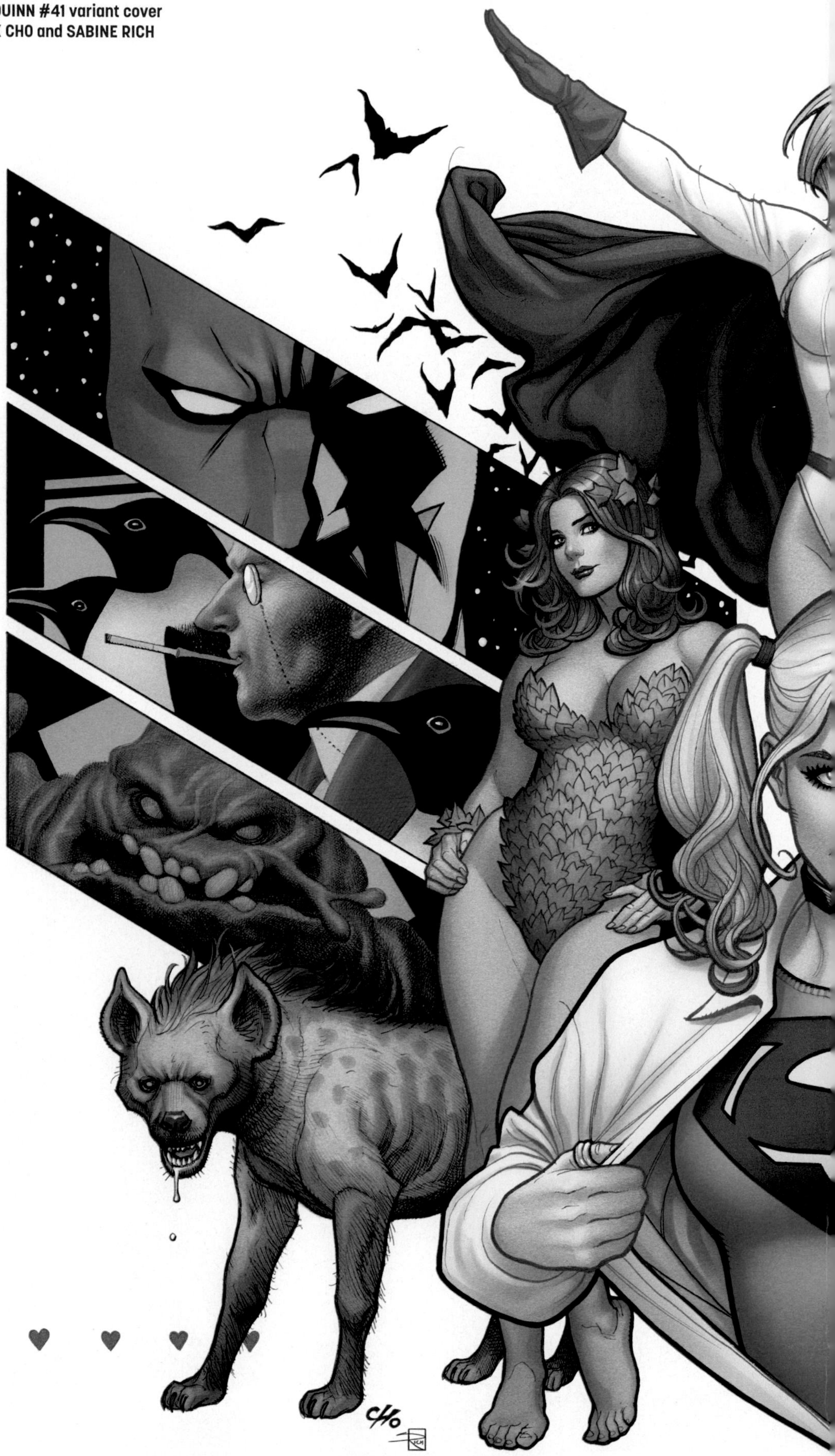
CHO

HARLEY QUINN #42 variant cover
by FRANK CHO and SABINE RICH

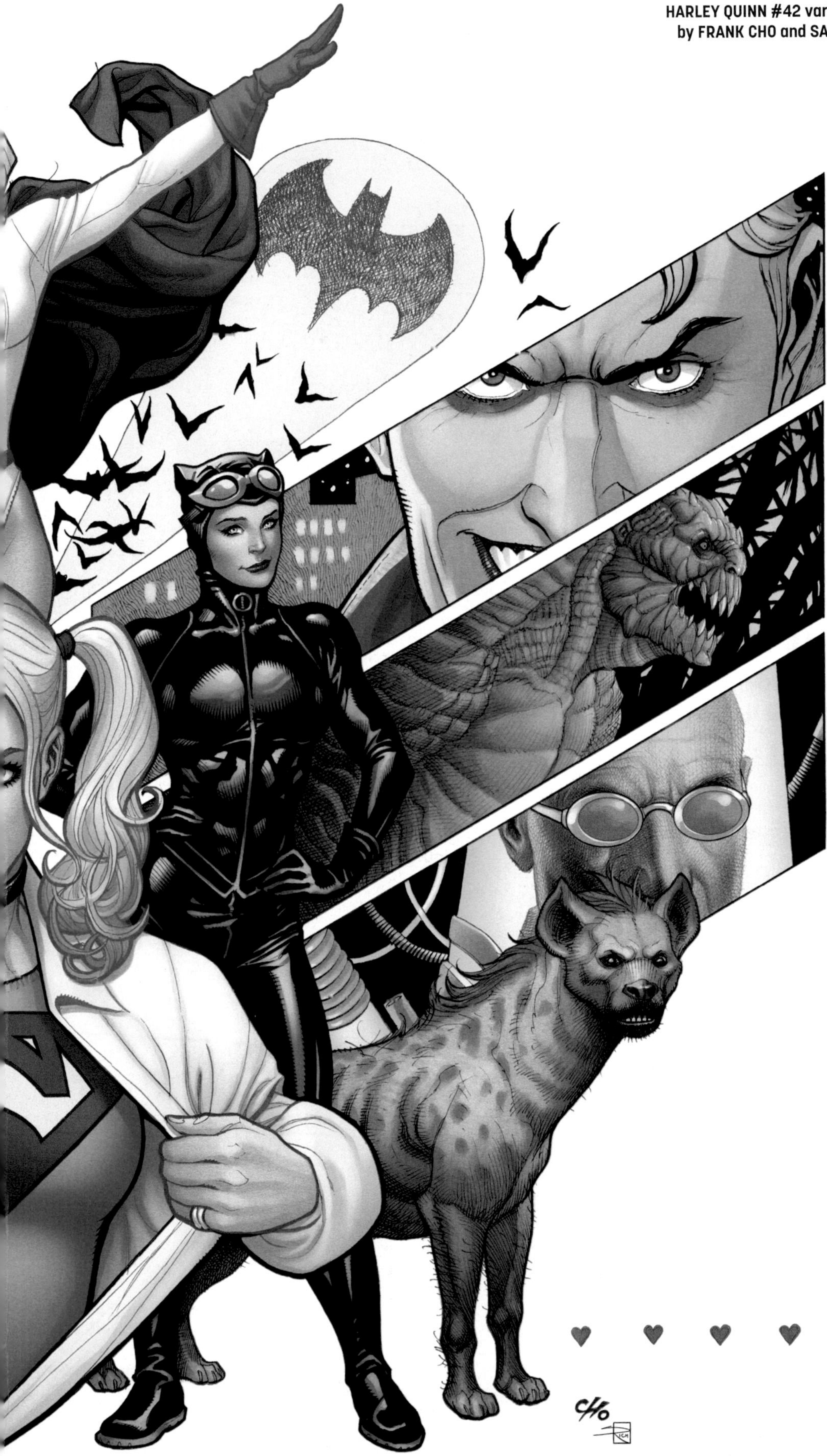
CHO

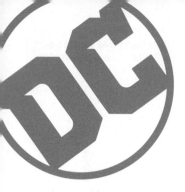

"A smart concept, snappy one-liners and a great twist to match a tag-team of talented artists."
**–NEWSARAMA**

"Every bit as chaotic and unabashedly fun as one would expect."
**–IGN**

# HARLEY QUINN

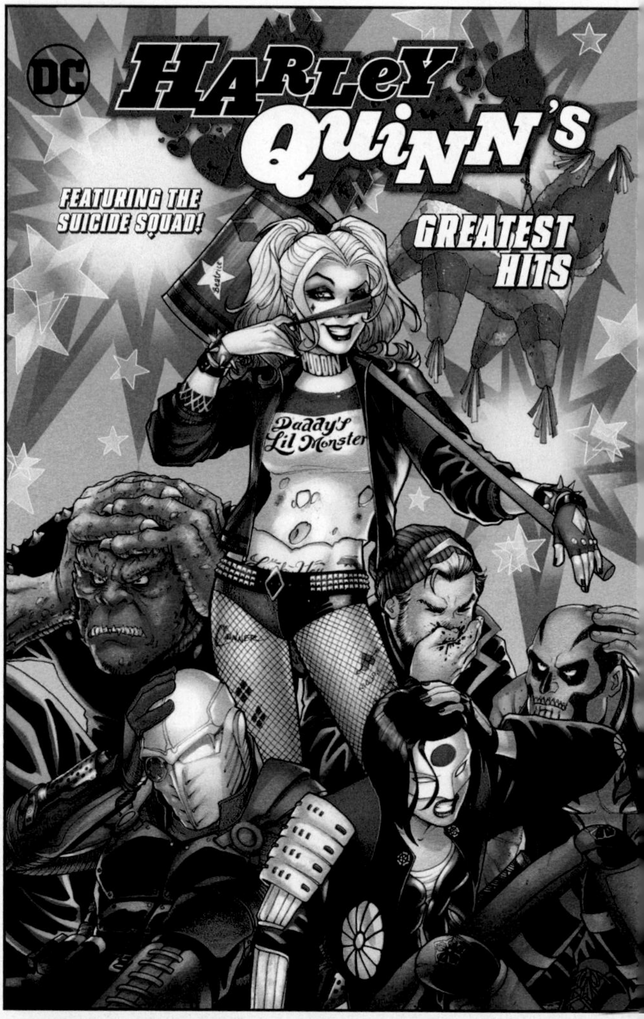

DC
HARLEY QUINN'S
FEATURING THE SUICIDE SQUAD!
GREATEST HITS
Daddy's Lil Monster


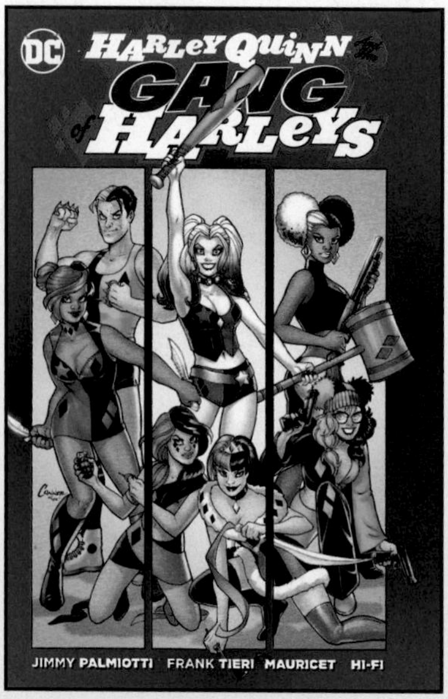

DC
HARLEY QUINN and her GANG of HARLEYS
JIMMY PALMIOTTI FRANK TIERI MAURICET HI-FI


HARLEY QUINN
AND HER GANG OF HARLEYS

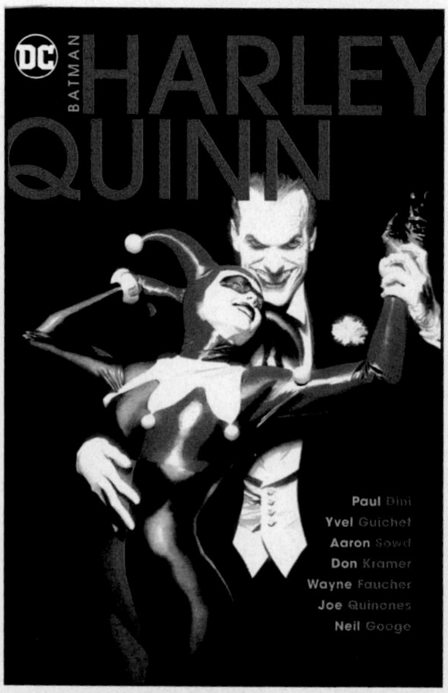

DC
BATMAN
HARLEY QUINN
Paul Dini
Yvel Guichet
Aaron Sowd
Don Kramer
Wayne Faucher
Joe Quinones
Neil Googe


BATMAN HARLEY QUINN

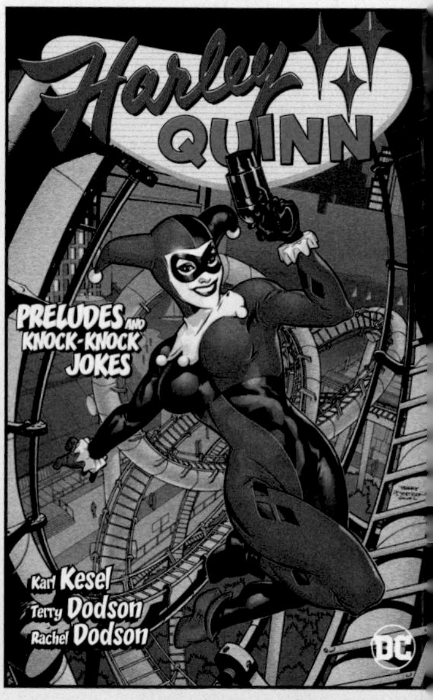

Harley QUINN
PRELUDES AND KNOCK-KNOCK JOKES
Karl Kesel
Terry Dodson
Rachel Dodson
DC


HARLEY QUINN:
PRELUDES AND KNOCK-KNOCK JOKES

Get more DC graphic novels wherever comics and books are sold!

"Chaotic and unabashedly fun."
— **IGN**

# HARLEY QUINN

## VOL. 1: HOT IN THE CITY
### AMANDA CONNER
### with JIMMY PALMIOTTI
### & CHAD HARDIN

**HARLEY QUINN
VOL. 2: POWER OUTAGE**

**HARLEY QUINN
VOL. 3: KISS KISS BANG STAB**

**READ THE ENTIRE EPIC!**

HARLEY QUINN VOL. 4:
A CALL TO ARMS

HARLEY QUINN VOL. 5:
THE JOKER'S LAST LAUGH

"I'm enjoying this a great deal;
it's silly, it's funny, it's irreverent."
— **COMIC BOOK RESOURCES**

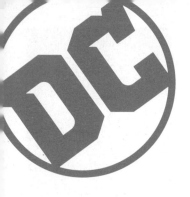

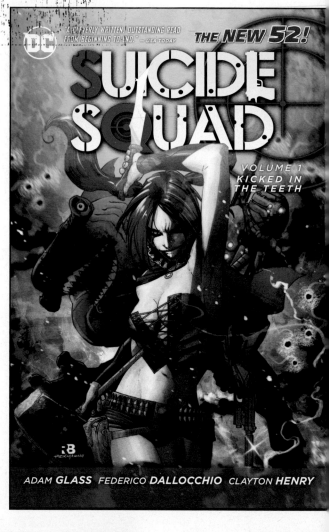

"A pretty irresistible hook..."
**– THE ONION A.V. CLUB**

"A CLEVERLY WRITTEN, OUTSTANDING READ FROM BEGINNING TO END." – USA TODAY
THE NEW 52!
SUICIDE SQUAD
VOLUME 1 KICKED IN THE TEETH
ADAM GLASS FEDERICO DALLOCCHIO CLAYTON HENRY

# SUICIDE SQUAD

## VOL. 1: KICKED IN THE TEETH

ADAM GLASS with
FEDERICO DALLOCCHIO

THE NEW 52!
SUICIDE SQUAD
VOLUME 2 BASILISK RISING
ADAM GLASS FERNANDO DAGNINO

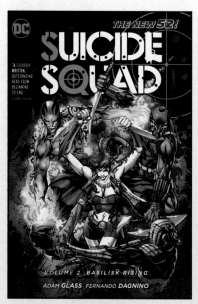

**SUICIDE SQUAD
VOL. 2: BASILISK RISING**

THE NEW 52!
SUICIDE SQUAD
VOLUME 3 DEATH IS FOR SUCKERS
DEADSHOT
ADAM GLASS HENRIK JONSSON SANDU FLOREA

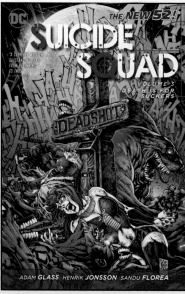

**SUICIDE SQUAD
VOL. 3: DEATH IS FOR SUCKERS**

**READ THE ENTIRE EPIC**

SUICIDE SQUAD VOL.
DISCIPLINE AND PUNIS

SUICIDE SQUAD VOL.
WALLED

"A cleverly written, outstanding read from beginning to end."
**– USA TODAY**

Get more DC graphic novels wherever comics and books are sold!